Enhancing Engagement With Gamification:

Education, Business, and Healthcare Perspectives

Ricardo Marcão
ISLA Santarém, Portugal

Vasco Ribeiro Santos
Instituto Politécnico de Tomar, Portugal & GOVCOPP, CiTUR, ISLA Santarém, Portugal

IGI Global
Scientific Publishing
Publishing Tomorrow's Research Today

Vice President of Editorial	Melissa Wagner
Managing Editor of Acquisitions	Mikaela Felty
Managing Editor of Book Development	Jocelynn Hessler
Production Manager	Mike Brehm
Cover Design	Phillip Shickler

Published in the United States of America by
IGI Global Scientific Publishing
701 East Chocolate Avenue
Hershey, PA, 17033, USA
Tel: 717-533-8845
Fax: 717-533-8661
Website: https://www.igi-global.com E-mail: cust@igi-global.com

Library of Congress Cataloging-in-Publication Data

Names: Marcao, Ricardo, 1987- editor. | Santos, Vasco, 1986- editor.
Title: Enhancing engagement with gamification : education, business, and healthcare perspectives / [edited by] Ricardo Marcao, Vasco Santos.
Description: Hershey, PA : IGI Global Scientific Publishing, [2025] | Includes bibliographical references and index. | Summary: "The primary objective of the book is to explore and elucidate the multifaceted applications of gamification across three vital sectors: education, business, and healthcare. This book aims to provide a thorough examination of the principles and theories underlying gamification, offering detailed insights into its mechanics and effective implementation in various contexts"-- Provided by publisher.
Identifiers: LCCN 2024054558 (print) | LCCN 2024054559 (ebook) | ISBN 9798369383223 (hardcover) | ISBN 9798369383230 (paperback) | ISBN 9798369383247 (ebook)
Subjects: LCSH: Gamification. | Motivation in education. | Educational games. | Employees--Training of. | Employee motivation.
Classification: LCC LB1065 .E584 2025 (print) | LCC LB1065 (ebook) | DDC 658.3/14--dc23/eng/20250202
LC record available at https://lccn.loc.gov/2024054558
LC ebook record available at https://lccn.loc.gov/2024054559

British Cataloguing in Publication Data
A Cataloguing in Publication record for this book is available from the British Library.

To our families, whose love, patience, and unwavering support have been the cornerstone of our endeavors.

To Stéphanie Monteiro, P.Eng, MSc (Ricardo's wife), whose brilliance, strength, and encouragement have been a guiding light in Ricardo's journey.

To Ana Vieira, CEO, MSc (Vasco's wife), whose resilience, wisdom, and inspiration have been Vasco's steadfast companion, and to Caetana Santos (Vasco and Ana's daughter), whose laughter and curiosity remind Vasco why we strive to build a better future.

Together, you are our motivation, our foundation, and our greatest source of joy. This work is dedicated to you with all our gratitude and love.

Table of Contents

Detailed Table of Contents

higher educational institutions. It presents a theoretical background, drawing from Vygotsky's social development theory and Self-determination theory, to support the fusion of these approaches. Furthermore, the chapter proposes and evaluates several interventions, including Online Game-Based Learning Platforms and Discussion Forums, to enhance student engagement and authenticity.

Organisations are investigating the use of gamification to improve learning and development activities because they need tools to make learning more efficient and engaging. Additionally, because employee demographics are changing and there is a growing generation that is comfortable with and prefers technologically enhanced training methods, it is necessary to assess these methods. This study compares the effectiveness of gamified modules to regular modules using a pre-test-post-test control group design. The participants were randomly assigned to two groups. The results validate the theoretical framework of gamified learning, as evidenced by the higher scores obtained by the gamified module participants in terms of learning, reactivity, and learner motivation. The results further imply that the influence of gamification on the selected learning outcomes of learning and reaction was strongly mediated by learner motivation. The hypothesis of gamified learning is supported empirically by the current investigation.

Gamification has emerged as a valuable tool in addressing evolving demands within the ever-changing field of architecture education. This chapter explores its potential in higher education programs, focusing on how it complements traditional teaching. Through a literature review of studies indexed in the Web of Science, findings show that while gamification boosts motivation and learning outcomes, it also poses challenges like sustaining engagement and addressing diverse learners. Despite its benefits, such as enhanced problem-solving and hands-on learning, large-scale studies are needed to examine potential drawbacks, including oversimplification. If its effects are examined more, it will provide educators with enough material so that people can use this study to learn and apply it better. Ongoing research is crucial to fully harness gamification for developing creative, effective future architects.

Gamification has emerged as a transformative approach in education, leveraging game-like elements to enhance student engagement and motivation. This chapter attempts to present best practices, challenges and solutions for creating effective gamified experiences focused on but not limited to educational use, touching base on business and healthcare as well. Key theoretical foundations are discussed to illustrate how psychological principles can inform effective gamification strategies. The chapter highlights significant challenges such as sustaining long-term engagement, balancing game mechanics with educational goals and addressing cultural and ethical considerations. Solutions are proposed to overcome these challenges. Additionally, the role of technological advancements in reshaping gamified experiences is examined. Finally, the chapter emphasizes the importance of evaluating the effectiveness of gamified systems, providing actionable insights.

With an emphasis on the mediating function of technological advancements in Ethiopia, this study examines the impact of gamification in education on learning outcomes and student engagement. A survey was conducted with 400 participants, comprising educators, students, and professionals working in education technology. Confirmatory factor analysis (CFA) and exploratory factor analysis (EFA) were used to determine the underlying characteristics of gamification in education, technological advancements, and learning results as well as student engagement. The data's appropriateness for factor analysis was evaluated using Bartlett's test of sphericity and the Kaiser-Meyer-Olkin (KMO) measure of sampling adequacy. The mediating impact of technology advancements in the link among gamification in education and student engagement and learning outcomes in Ethiopia was then investigated using structural equation modeling (SEM). The study's conclusions offer insightful information on how gamification in the classroom might raise student interest and boost academic performance.

This work introduces a new multiplayer digital game called TimeCraX, which aims to improve history education by making it more interactive, engaging, and fun. It highlights the challenges of traditional learning and how digital games can overcome them by utilizing gamification and game-based learning. The TimeCraX game platform is designed to be cooperative, allowing students to work together to complete a challenge based on a historical timeline. The goal is to promote learning through practical experience, encouraging critical thinking, and developing collaboration and teamwork skills. The article discusses the multiplayer platform architecture of TimeCraX, which includes authentication modules, team and student rankings, matchmaking, and reporting tools, all aimed at providing teachers with the tools to monitor student progress and create balanced student groups based on specific criteria. The article concludes with a discussion of the next steps for the game's development, including a play session with students to evaluate the platform's effectiveness.

This study investigates the challenges faced by Black male educators in K-12 education, focusing on recruitment, retention, and career advancement strategies. It reveals that Black male teachers experience systemic racism, lack of institutional support, and social isolation. To address these challenges, the study suggests targeted recruitment, better support systems, and community engagement. Additionally, it emphasizes the positive impact of Black male educators on student outcomes and calls for policies promoting equity and inclusion. Using a qualitative review of studies published between 2018 and 2024, thematic analysis identifies key issues and provides actionable insights for policymakers and educators.

Foreword

In a world where engagement, motivation, and innovation are the cornerstones of success, gamification has emerged as a revolutionary tool for driving meaningful change across diverse domains. Its ability to seamlessly integrate into education, business, and healthcare underscores its transformative potential, making it an essential topic for exploration in today's rapidly evolving landscape.

Enhancing Engagement With Gamification: Education, Business, and Healthcare Perspectives, edited by Dr. Ricardo Marcão and Dr. Vasco Ribeiro Santos, offers a profound contribution to this critical field. This expertly curated volume brings together insights from an impressive array of international scholars and practitioners. The book goes beyond merely discussing gamification—it provides actionable frameworks, case studies, and innovative solutions tailored to real-world challenges.

What sets this book apart is its multidimensional approach. The chapters explore gamification from various perspectives, bridging theoretical foundations with practical applications. Whether focusing on cross-cultural business strategies, transformative educational practices, or advancements in healthcare, the authors provide readers with a comprehensive understanding of how gamification can enhance engagement and drive measurable outcomes.

As someone deeply involved in advancing quality management and systems engineering, I find the application of gamification in healthcare particularly compelling. The book's exploration of gamified medical training, patient engagement, and professional development demonstrates the profound impact this approach can have on improving outcomes in one of society's most critical sectors.

Additionally, the book's global and interdisciplinary outlook ensures its relevance to a diverse audience. From educators and business leaders to healthcare professionals and policymakers, this volume equips readers with the tools to implement gamification strategies effectively and ethically.

I am honored to contribute this foreword to a work that I believe will leave an indelible mark on the field. *Enhancing Engagement With Gamification: Education, Business, and Healthcare Perspectives* is a must-read for anyone seeking to harness the power of gamification to inspire innovation and progress. It is not just a book but a guide to unlocking new possibilities in our interconnected world.

Stéphanie Monteiro

Software Nemotec S.L., Madrid, Spain & Institute for Systems and Robotics, Lisbon, Portugal

Preface

OVERVIEW OF THE SUBJECT MATTER

Gamification, the application of game mechanics in non-game contexts, has emerged as a powerful strategy to engage individuals and drive behavioral change across various domains. This book, *Enhancing Engagement With Gamification: Education, Business, and Healthcare Perspectives*, explores how gamification can be a transformative tool to address pressing challenges, optimize processes, and create meaningful interactions in education, business, and healthcare. By blending theory, case studies, and evidence-based research, this book offers a comprehensive guide to understanding and leveraging gamification as a multidisciplinary approach for achieving enhanced outcomes.

The Role of Gamification in the World Today

In an era defined by rapid technological advancement and shifting human expectations, gamification is no longer a niche concept—it is a mainstream strategy that reshapes how individuals learn, work, and seek care. In education, gamification addresses the challenge of declining student engagement by making learning interactive and rewarding. Businesses use gamification to enhance employee motivation, customer engagement, and productivity. Meanwhile, in healthcare, gamification plays a critical role in encouraging patients to adhere to treatment plans, promoting healthy behaviors, and improving healthcare training methodologies.

This book positions gamification as a bridge connecting theory to practice, providing timely insights into its role in a globalized and increasingly digital world. By highlighting cross-cultural perspectives, practical applications, and emerging trends, the book demonstrates how gamification is shaping the future of education, commerce, and healthcare on a global scale.

Target Audience

This book is designed for a diverse audience that includes academics, researchers, practitioners, and policymakers. Educators and instructional designers will find practical strategies to engage students and foster creativity in classrooms. Business leaders and human resource professionals will gain insights into boosting organizational performance and employee satisfaction through gamification. Healthcare professionals, including administrators and clinicians, will discover innovative approaches to improving patient outcomes and professional training. Moreover, students and enthusiasts of gamification will appreciate the book's in-depth exploration of theory and applications, empowering them to think critically about its transformative potential.

Descriptions of Chapter Submissions

1. Cross-Cultural Gamification: Understanding Design and User Experience in Different Cultural Contexts

This chapter investigates the interplay of cultural differences in gamification design, emphasizing the importance of tailoring experiences to diverse user groups.

2. Enhancing Student Authenticity and Engagement Through Gamification and Problem-Based Learning in Higher Education

This chapter highlights how combining gamification with problem-based learning can improve student engagement, critical thinking, and collaboration in higher education.

3. Evaluation of Gamified Learning in Organizations: Evidence from Private Sector Organizations in India

This chapter presents an empirical study on the impact of gamification in workplace training programs, showcasing its benefits in improving employee skills and organizational performance.

4. Gamification as a Pedagogical Innovation in Architectural Education: A Literature Review

By focusing on architectural education, this chapter highlights how gamification can foster creativity, collaborative learning, and critical thinking in students preparing for professional practice.

5. Gamification as a Pedagogical Tool in Geriatric Nursing: Engaging and Empowering Future Nurses

This chapter explores how gamification can improve geriatric nursing education by enhancing student engagement, improving knowledge retention, and fostering a deeper sense of empathy among nursing students.

6. Gamification for Transformative Learning: Current Trends in 21st Century Education

This chapter offers a forward-looking perspective on how gamification can drive transformative learning experiences, equipping students with skills for a rapidly changing world.

7. Gamified Success: Best Practices, Challenges, and Solutions in Designing Gamified Experiences

This chapter provides a comprehensive review of the best practices for designing gamified systems, along with insights into overcoming challenges, ensuring accessibility, and measuring the success of gamified initiatives.

8. Gamifying the Classroom by Mediation of Technological Innovations in Enhancing Student Engagement and Learning in Ethiopia

Focused on the Ethiopian education system, this chapter showcases how gamification can overcome resource constraints and foster a more interactive learning environment.

9. Rethinking History Teaching: A New Multiplayer Digital Games Platform to Overcome the Challenges of Engagement

This chapter introduces an innovative platform that leverages gamification to make history education more engaging, collaborative, and memorable for students.

10. Systemic Barriers and Support Mechanisms for Black Male Educators: A Review of Recent Evidence and Policy Implications

This chapter explores the use of gamification to address systemic barriers in the education sector, offering insights into how innovative strategies can support underrepresented educators.

CONCLUSION

Enhancing Engagement With Gamification: Education, Business, and Healthcare Perspectives makes a significant contribution to the growing field of gamification by addressing its theoretical foundations, practical applications, and cross-sectoral impact. The book offers actionable insights for leveraging gamification to meet contemporary challenges and provides a roadmap for its future evolution. We hope this book inspires readers to innovate, adapt, and embrace gamification as a transformative force in their respective fields.

Ricardo Marcão
ISLA Santarém, Portugal

Vasco Ribeiro Santos
Instituto Politécnico de Tomar, Portugal & GOVCOPP, CiTUR, ISLA Santarém, Portugal

Chapter 1
Cross-Cultural Gamification:
Understanding Design and User Experience in Different Cultural Contexts

Andi Asrifan
https://orcid.org/0000-0002-9934-6129
Universitas Negeri Makassar, Indonesia

Badruddin Kaddas
https://orcid.org/0000-0003-1531-4558
Universitas Islam Makassar, Indonesia

Mulyadi Mulyadi
Universitas Islam Makassar, Indonesia

Widya Rizky Pratiwi
Universitas Terbuka, Indonesia

Supriadi Supriadi
Universitas Islam Makassar, Indonesia

Baso Jabu
Universitas Negeri Makassar, Indonesia

ABSTRACT

Digital technologies have changed cultural production and consumption, making gamified apps important cultural artifacts. Despite their global reach, little is known about how cultural differences affect system design and user experience. Research has mostly ignored cross-cultural user interactions. We use Hofstede's cultural dimensions to analyze cross-cultural gamification to fill this knowledge gap. Our study shows that cultural differences considerably affect user engagement and gamified system effectiveness. In one culture, motivational affordances may work, but not another. We share case studies showing how culturally adaptive design improves user experiences. Our findings show that cultural sensitivity in design makes gamified apps more inclusive and effective. This has major ramifications for designers and researchers trying to maximize gamification tactics across cultures.

DOI: 10.4018/979-8-3693-8322-3.ch001

INTRODUCTION

Computer games and gamified applications have become potent mediums that transcend geographical boundaries (Woods, 2021) (Kalpokas, 2022) (Di, 2020). Games are more relevant to intercultural communication and cultural studies as they become cultural artifacts as well as entertainment. These digital platforms are ideal for reaching multicultural, multilingual, and socioeconomic audiences worldwide. These platforms must consider user diversity to improve user experience (UX) and engagement (Li et al., 2024). Designers and researchers must explore how cultural differences affect user engagement with gamified apps.

Gamification, the use of game-design elements in non-game contexts to engage users and influence behavior, is a common strategy in education, healthcare, marketing, and workplace productivity (Ciuchita et al., 2023) (Schöbel et al., 2020). Gamification uses game motivations like prizes, challenges, and competition to improve user experiences and outcomes. However, designers' cultural preconceptions often shape gamified system design and execution (Lowry et al., 2020) (Cheng, 2020). These assumptions may not match users' cultural norms, attitudes, and expectations from other cultures, resulting in unsatisfactory user experiences. Motivational affordances that work in one culture may not work in another due to different values and behaviors. To achieve global efficacy and inclusivity, gamification design must include cross-cultural factors.

Despite its widespread use, a lack of research examines the relationship between culture and gamification (Ciuchita et al., 2023) (Oliveira et al., 2023). Previous research has shown that gamified apps work in certain cultures, but little is known about how cultural differences affect the design and user experience of gamified systems across cultures. Most research on gamification has concentrated on its technical features or the user experience in a single cultural context, ignoring the complex cultural dynamics that result from worldwide deployment (Marques et al., 2023) (Riar, 2022). This lack of cross-cultural analysis hinders designers and researchers from creating globally effective and culturally sensitive gamified apps. Addressing this knowledge gap is crucial to increasing gamification and improving its global applicability and success.

This study analyzes cross-cultural gamification, focusing on the design and user experience of gamified applications in different cultures, to fill the knowledge gap. We will study how Hofstede's cultural dimensions and Trompenaars' concept of cultural differences affect gamified system design, user engagement, and effectiveness. We'll go beyond identifying cultural differences to systematically integrating them into the design process to create more culturally adaptive and inclusive gaming tactics. Through case studies and empirical data, we hope to offer designers and academics actionable insights and recommendations to improve gamified apps' cross-cultural relevance and effect. This study emphasizes the need of cultural sensitivity and adaptability in gamification, which will lead to more successful and engaging user experiences in a globalized world.

FOUNDATIONS OF GAMIFICATION

Gamification has grown in popularity due to its ability to change user behavior, boost engagement, and improve user experience in situations outside traditional games (Rivera & Garden, 2021) (Unternährer et al., 2024). Gamification applies game-design aspects like points, badges, leaderboards, and challenges to non-game situations. These components deliberately motivate and engage people to drive desired behaviors. Gamification is based on theories of human motivation, behavior, and user experience from psychology, design, and HCI (Christopoulos & Mystakidis, 2023) (Krath et al., 2021) (O'Brien et al., 2022).

Gamification is based on Self-Determination Theory (SDT), which states that people are driven by three psychological needs: autonomy, competence, and relatedness (Gupta & Goyal, 2022) (Luarn et al., 2023). Gamification addresses these needs by designing systems that give users autonomy, competence, and relatedness. Leaderboards and badges satisfy the need for competence by giving users a sense of accomplishment, while team challenges satisfy the need for relatedness.

Flow Theory describes humans' deep absorption and delight when completely involved in an activity. Gamification creates demanding but feasible activities, provides instant feedback, and balances skill level and task difficulty to induce flow (Oliveira et al., 2022) (Xiao et al., 2022). Gamified experiences that foster flow can boost user engagement and reward.

Gamification relies on Behavioral Economics (Krath et al., 2021) (Riar, 2022). Gamified systems leverage loss aversion, scarcity, and social proof to influence user behavior. Time-limited challenges or exclusive incentives can exploit scarcity to increase user engagement, show users how their peers are doing, and use social proof to get them to participate more.

Situated Action Theory emphasizes context in user interactions, which helps us comprehend gamification. This theory states that to completely understand user behavior, the environment must be considered (Han, 2021) (Scurati et al., 2021). In cross-cultural gamification, cultural norms and values strongly influence how users perceive and interact with gamified systems.

Gamification uses psychology, HCI, design, and behavioral economics to produce interesting and effective user experiences. Understanding and using these fundamental principles allows designers to create gamified systems that inspire and engage users while meeting their psychological demands and contextual realities.

This holistic approach is necessary to successfully integrate gamification in varied cultural situations and ensure that the created experiences resonate with a wide audience and achieve the desired results.

2.1. Definition and Concepts

Gamification uses game design aspects in non-game environments to engage users and solve problems (Meaning, 2024) (Christopoulos & Mystakidis, 2023). This notion applies game motives and enjoyment to education, marketing, workplace productivity, and health. Unlike traditional games, gamification influences behavior and improves user experience in real applications.

Gamification uses points, badges, leaderboards, challenges, and incentives (Schöbel et al., 2020) (Wang et al., 2022). These elements leverage psychological cues to engage users. Users feel progress and accomplishment using points and badges (Cavusoglu et al., 2021). Leaderboards encourage users to beat their friends, while challenges and quests set clear goals that require work and skill, motivating players.

Game thinking—using game design concepts to create interactive, rewarding, and engaging experiences—is the foundation of gamification. Game thinking goes beyond adding game aspects to learning what motivates people and how to apply these concepts to real-world problems (Chang & Yeh, 2021). Gameful design is essential to gamification. It intentionally evokes gaming-related psychological states, including flow and intrinsic motivation (Seo et al., 2021). With this strategy, users are not just participating for external benefits but also for joy and fulfillment in the activities.

Gamification improves user engagement and behavior by applying game design to non-game circumstances. Understanding its definition and fundamental concepts is crucial to using gamification in numerous disciplines to create meaningful and inspiring user experiences.

2.2. Theoretical Frameworks

Effective theoretical frameworks that explain and anticipate user behavior, motivation, and engagement are crucial to gamification's success (Krath et al., 2021). (Kalogiannakis et al., 2021) Self-Determination Theory (SDT), Flow Theory, Behavioral Economics, and Situated Action Theory are influential. Self-determination theory (SDT) explains how gamification meets users' psychological requirements (Gupta & Goyal, 2022) (Cai et al., 2024). SDT says people want autonomy, competence, and relatedness. Gamified systems that encourage these are more likely to retain users. Personalized tasks in a gamified app boost competence, while social components like team-based activities satisfy relatedness.

Gamification also relies on Mihaly Csikszentmihalyi's Flow Theory (Han et al., 2021). Flow is intense immersion and delight in a demanding but achievable task. Gamification promotes flow by balancing work complexity with user skill level, setting clear goals, and delivering immediate feedback (Özhan and Kocadere2020). Users stay interested and motivated when in flow, losing sight of time due to the rewarding nature of the action.

Behavioral Economics explains how gamification affects decision-making (Mulcahy et al., 2021) (Ouariachi, 2020). Loss aversion, reinforcement, and nudging influence user behavior. Progress bars and limited-time rewards use loss aversion to motivate users to finish activities.

Finally, Situated Action Theory makes context a key factor in user action (Ouariachi et al., 2020; Mulcahy, 2021). This idea suggests that cultural and social aspects strongly influence user behavior. Designing gamified experiences that appeal across cultures requires understanding this context. These theoretical frameworks help build interesting, motivating, and culturally relevant gamified systems.

CULTURAL DIMENSIONS AND THEIR IMPACT ON DESIGN

Cultural factors shape the design and effectiveness of gamified systems across cultures (Breuer & Ivanov, 2020) (Riar et al., 2022). Designers who want to develop experiences that resonate with varied user groups must understand these aspects and ensure that design elements match cultural values, norms, and user expectations. Geert Hofstede, Fons Trompenaars, and Shalom Schwartz's cultural dimensions framework allow researchers to analyze and predict how cultural differences affect user behavior and interaction with gamified apps (Cejka & Mohelska, 2020) (Yazici, 2024).

Hofstede's Cultural Dimensions Theory is likely the most famous cross-cultural analysis framework (Messner, 2021). It lists six cultural differences: Power Distance, Individualism vs. Collectivism, Masculinity vs. Femininity, Uncertainty Avoidance, Long-Term vs. Short-Term Orientation, and Indulgence vs. Restraint. These variables assist designers in understanding culturally diverse users' values and behaviors. In hierarchical cultures with large Power Distances, users may respond better to gamified systems with obvious authority figures and organized paths to success. In societies with low Power Distance, users may choose egalitarian and collaborative design (Schumacher et al., 2023). In individualistic cultures, gamified systems that emphasize personal achievement and competitiveness perform better, while collectivist societies prefer systems that promote teamwork and success.

Trompenaars' Cultural Dimensions—Universalism vs. Particularism, Individualism vs. Communitarianism, and Achievement vs. Ascription—provide additional insights (Sapuarachchi, 2021). These dimensions can improve gamified experiences by being culturally appropriate. Universalist cultures respect stability and justice. Therefore, users may prefer standardized rules and incentives in gamified systems. However, Particularist cultures value context and relationships. Thus, users may choose more flexible and personalized experiences.

Schwartz's Theory of Basic Human Values supports these frameworks with ten value types: Security, Conformity, Tradition, Achievement, and Stimulation (Carneiro et al., 2021) (Askew & Ritter, 2023). These ideals affect what motivates and entertains gamified users. In societies that value security and tradition, users may prefer predictable, traditional, gamified experiences. In contrast, cultures that value stimulation and novelty may prefer dynamic and innovative gamified features that challenge the status quo.

Cultural variables affect gamified system aesthetics, interaction styles, and reward mechanisms (Klock et al., 2020). (Schöbel et al., 2020). Cultural factors affect how consumers interact with color schemes, narratives, and symbols. Culturally sensitive designs improve user experience and happiness, whereas culturally insensitive ones might offend or repel users.

Finally, global gamified systems must consider cultural factors in their design. Designers may develop compelling, culturally relevant gamified experiences using Hofstede, Trompenaars, and Schwartz's insights. Gamified systems that resonate with users from multiple cultural backgrounds become more engaging, satisfying, and effective in achieving intended objectives across markets.

3.1. Hofstede's Cultural Dimensions Theory

Hofstede's Cultural Dimensions Theory is a key foundation for understanding how cultural variations affect design, especially in gamified systems (Chotiratanapinun & Suppipat, 2022) (Noorbehbahani & Salehi, 2021). Power Distance, Individualism vs. Collectivism, Masculinity vs. Femininity, Uncertainty Avoidance, Long-Term vs. Short-Term Orientation, and Indulgence vs. Restraint are Geert Hofstede's six dimensions that explain how cultures differ in values, behaviors, and social norms. These variables reveal how consumers from different cultures view and use gamified apps.

Power Distance is the amount to which less powerful people tolerate and expect unequal power distribution (Puni & Hilton, 2020) (Jehanzeb, 2022). High-power Distance cultures are hierarchical, so users may prefer gamified systems with clear authority and structured progression. In contrast, low-power distance cultures stress equality, so users may prefer collaborative and egalitarian games.

Individualism vs. Collectivism discusses collective integration. Individualistic cultures respect personal accomplishment and autonomy. Therefore, they prefer gamified systems that reward success and competition (Riar et al., 2022) (Van et al., 2020). Gamification that promotes teamwork, cooperation, and shared incentives may resonate with collectivist cultures, which value group harmony and well-being.

Uncertainty Avoidance is a society's tolerance for ambiguity (Glazer, 2021) (Lawrie et al., 2020). In cultures with high Uncertainty Avoidance, consumers want explicit rules and predictable outcomes, suggesting they prefer gamified experiences with defined tasks and guidelines. Low Uncertainty Avoidance cultures may prefer open-ended, exploratory game mechanisms.

Hofstede's dimensions help designers match gamified systems to target audiences' cultural values and expectations. Cultural alignment improves user engagement, satisfaction, and gamification strategy efficacy, making it essential for global design endeavors.

3.2. Trompenaars' Cultural Dimensions Theory

Fons Trompenaars' Cultural Dimensions Theory explains how cultural differences affect human behavior, notably in interactions and decision-making (Sapuarachchi, 2021). This philosophy has seven dimensions: universalism vs. Particularism, Individualism vs. Communitarianism, Neutralism vs. Affective, Specificism vs. Diffuse, Achievement vs. Ascription, Sequentialism vs. Synchronous Time, and Internal vs. External Control. These aspects help designers create gamified systems that appeal to diverse ethnic groups.

Universalism vs. Particularism examines cultural rules and interactions. Standardized and transparent gamified systems appeal to universalist cultures because they value consistency, fairness, and universal norms (Aloisi, 2022). Conversely, particularist cultures value relationships and context so that consumers may choose flexible, customizable, gamified experiences.

Individualism vs. Communitarianism examines how people value individual interests over group goals, like Hofstede (Ianole-Călin et al., 2020). Gamified systems emphasizing personal achievement and competition may appeal to individualistic societies, whereas communitarian cultures may embrace collaborative components promoting teamwork and success.

Achievement vs. Ascription explores status. Gamified systems that reward skill and performance match achievement-oriented cultures (Riar et al., 2021) (Landers & Sanchez, 2022). In Ascription cultures, where status is based on age, gender, or social connections, gamified systems may work better if they respect and incorporate social hierarchies.

Sequential vs. Synchronous Time examines cultural time perception and management. Sequential cultures may prefer linear gamified systems, while synchronous cultures prefer multitasking and variable deadlines (Marques et al., 2023) (Salimon, 2021).

Gamified systems can be culturally responsive and more likely to engage users by aligning with their cultural values and expectations, using Trompenaars' aspects. They must align culturally to succeed in various global marketplaces.

USER EXPERIENCE DESIGN PRINCIPLES

UX design principles are essential for developing gamified systems that are both effective and engaging. These principles govern the creation of interfaces and interactions that are both functional and pleasurable, as well as meaningful, for users. UX design concepts play a crucial role in gamification as they have a direct impact on user engagement, motivation, and overall happiness with the system.

Usability, a fundamental element of UX design, pertains to the ease and efficiency with which a user may browse and utilize a system. High usability in gamified systems assures that users may easily comprehend game mechanics, advance through levels, and accomplish their objectives without experiencing frustration (Li et al., 2021). Ensuring ease of use and comprehension is essential for sustaining user engagement, since users are more likely to abandon a gamified system that is challenging to navigate or comprehend.

Accessibility is a crucial tenet in user experience (UX), which aims to ensure that the gamified system can be used by a diverse group of individuals, including those with impairments (Shaban et al., 2021) (Magylaitė et al., 2022). This entails creating interfaces that can cater to diverse requirements, such as offering alternate text for images, guaranteeing sufficient color contrast for individuals with color blindness, and facilitating compatibility with screen readers. Inclusive design expands the potential user base and improves the overall user experience by increasing the system's adaptability to individual requirements.

Engagement is crucial for the success of any gamified system. Effective UX design should include components that engage and inspire users to maintain their interest and motivation in using the system (Ebel et al., 2021) (Bitrián et al., 2021). This involves designing tasks of suitable complexity, offering significant incentives, and integrating feedback systems that keep users updated on their advancement. The objective of gamified systems is to attain a state of intense concentration and absorption known as flow. This is accomplished by maintaining a delicate equilibrium between the difficulty of the task and the individual's degree of expertise, establishing explicit objectives, and delivering prompt feedback.

Emotional design is a crucial factor in the user experience (UX) of gamified systems, as highlighted by Sushra et al. (2022) and Pinto et al. (2020). This entails creating encounters that elicit favorable emotions, such as happiness, contentment, and a feeling of achievement. Designers can enhance the user experience by taking into account the emotional influence of design aspects, such as aesthetics, story, and rewards, therefore creating a more engaging and pleasurable experience for users.

Ultimately, the incorporation of UX design concepts in gamified systems is crucial for the development of experiences that are not only practical but also captivating, user-friendly, and emotionally impactful. Designers can have higher success in reaching intended goals by prioritizing usability, accessibility, engagement, and emotional design while developing gamified systems. This approach effectively motivates and satisfies users.

4.1. Usability and Accessibility

Usability and accessibility are crucial in UX design, especially for gamified systems targeting various audiences (Magylaitė et al., 2022; Palmquist et al., 2024). These guidelines ensure that all users, regardless of ability or background, can utilize the system efficiently. Usability is how easily users can learn, navigate, and apply a system to achieve their goals (Vlachogianni & Tselios, 2022) (Dutta et al., 2022). High usability in gamification entails intuitive game mechanics, objectives, and rewards. Users should be able to use the system, track their progress, and earn incentives without difficulty. This is important for engagement, as users would abandon a gamified system if it is hard to use or understand. Usability includes clear navigation, consistent design, and feedback on user actions and progress. Disabled people can use the gamified system because it is accessible (Santórum et al., 2023). This approach involves building interfaces that meet a variety of demands, such as giving picture alt text, making color selections accessible to color vision deficient individuals, and supporting screen readers for visually challenged users. Accessibility also takes into account mobile devices, tablets, and operating systems.

Accessibility throughout the design process makes the system more inclusive and adaptive to user needs, improving the user experience. This greater inclusivity can increase the user base and ensure that the gamified system serves everyone, improving engagement and happiness. Finally, gamified systems need usability and accessibility. With these concepts in mind, designers may construct systems that are simple and accessible to all users, boosting engagement, satisfaction, and the effectiveness of the gamified experience.

4.2. Engagement and Immersion

Engagement and immersion impact how deeply users connect with a gamified system and how motivated they are to keep using it (Bitrián et al., 2021) (Xi & Hamari, 2020). These topics are crucial to gamified experience design because they relate to user behavior psychology.

Engagement is user participation and interest in the gamified system (Bitrián et al., 2021) (Xiao, 2022). Create challenges that are neither too simple nor too difficult, offer meaningful and compelling rewards, and provide constant feedback to reinforce progress. Effective engagement techniques combine extrinsic motivators like points, badges, and leaderboards with intrinsic motivators like mastering a skill or overcoming a difficulty (Jaskari & Syrjälä, 2023) (Schöbel et al., 2020). User engagement needs knowing their motivations—competition, collaboration, achievement, or discovery. Designers may keep consumers engaged by adapting the gamified experience to these motivations.

Immersion provides a rich, immersive experience that holds the user's attention (Sutcliffe, 2022) (Zakrzewski, 2022). Immersed users focus on the action and lose sight of time. Immersion is similar to flow, a psychological state in which people are entirely focused and involved in the job at hand and enjoy it. Gamified systems should seamlessly incorporate narrative, aesthetics, and gameplay mechanics to enhance immersion (Paulsen, 2021). The system should also give consumers a sense of progress toward a meaningful objective to keep them engaged. Finally, gamified systems work best with involvement and immersion. Designers may engage consumers and keep them engaged by focusing on these elements, resulting in stronger system linkages and higher satisfaction. To create engaging gamified experiences that keep consumers engaged, the correct combination of engagement and immersion is essential.

CASE STUDIES IN CROSS-CULTURAL GAMIFICATION

Case studies on cross-cultural gamification offer significant insights into the adaptation of gamified systems to effectively engage users from different cultural backgrounds. These studies emphasize the significance of comprehending cultural elements and customizing gamification tactics to coincide with diverse user groups' beliefs, habits, and expectations.

An exemplary case study is from the Asia-Pacific area, where a health promotion campaign using gamification was devised to stimulate physical activity among young adults in Japan and Australia (Chung & Koo, 2023). The study uncovered substantial variations in user involvement influenced by cultural factors. In Japan, a society that values collective behavior and is characterized by a strong aversion to ambiguity, individuals showed a preference for gamified features that focused on community involvement and provided well-defined challenges with unambiguous results. The campaign's emphasis on fostering collaboration and reciprocal assistance struck a chord with Japanese users (Gagné, 2021). Conversely, Australian users, originating from a society that values individualism and has a lower aversion to uncertainty, exhibited a more positive response towards gamified elements that facilitated personal accomplishment and exploration. The ability to establish personal objectives and the autonomy to investigate various avenues within the framework were crucial elements in sustaining their involvement (Gagné et al., 2022) (Settembre-Blundo et al., 2021).

A separate case study examined a gamified educational platform implemented in both the United States and China. The site was designed to enhance language proficiency through engaging games and quizzes. In the United States, where educational systems frequently prioritize competition and individual achievement, the gamified platform incorporated leaderboards and individual performance measures, which served as incentives for students to go for better scores (Alam et al., 2023). Nevertheless, in China, where education emphasizes collaboration and community involvement, the efficacy of these competitive aspects was diminished (Jin et al., 2020)(Liu et al., 2020). On the other hand, characteristics that encouraged collaborative learning and assistance from peers proved to be more effective in capturing the interest of Chinese students, who prioritize collective accomplishments over individual recognition.

These case studies highlight the significance of cultural sensitivity in the design of gamification. They show that using a standardized gamification strategy is unlikely to be successful in culturally varied environments. Successful cross-cultural gamification necessitates a profound comprehension of the target culture and the ability to adjust game components to cater to the distinct requirements and preferences of users from diverse backgrounds. This strategy improves user involvement and guarantees the effectiveness of the gamified system in many cultural contexts.

5.1. Asia-Pacific Region

Asia-Pacific's diverse culture makes it a fertile field for exploring cross-cultural gamification. The region's diverse cultures, values, habits, and expectations affect how users interact with gamified systems (Nasirzadeh & Fathian, 2020) (Bugeja

& Grech, 2020). Understanding these cultural differences is crucial for building effective gamified experiences in this region.

Japanese and South Korean students used a gamified educational platform to improve their English language acquisition (Su et al., 2022). The study revealed important disparities in how students from these nations used gamified components. Students in Japan prioritize social harmony and group cohesion. Thus, they liked gamified aspects that promoted collaborative learning and joint achievement. Japanese students like to succeed as a team. Therefore, group challenges, shared prizes, and social interactions on the platform were particularly effective (Freiermuth & Ito, 2022) (Costa et al., 2020).

Gamified characteristics emphasizing individual success and competition encouraged South Korean pupils in a competitive educational environment. Student motivation to surpass peers led them to prefer leaderboards, progress tracking, and personal prizes (Hu et al., 2023; Hellín et al., 2023). This competitive feature of the gamified platform fits South Korean norms of academic performance and personal accomplishment.

Another case study examined an Australian and Singaporean gamified health app that promoted exercise. Australians appreciate autonomy and freedom; hence, they prefer gamified features that permit goal-setting and self-directed inquiry (Schoenenberger, 2024). In Singapore, which values community and collective well-being, group activities and social support engage users more (Xie et al., 2020). These Asia-Pacific case studies show the necessity of culturally adapted gamification. Designers may develop more engaging and effective experiences that resonate with their target audiences across this diverse region by adapting gamified systems to users' cultural values and preferences.

5.2. Middle East and North Africa

The MENA region has a multifaceted and varied cultural environment, which presents both difficulties and possibilities for cross-cultural gamification. When creating gamified systems that aim to effectively engage users, it is important to carefully consider the diverse range of cultures, religious practices, and social conventions in the region.

An exemplary case study in the MENA area focused on a gamified health promotion project aimed at fostering better lives among young people in Saudi Arabia and the United Arab Emirates (UAE). The study uncovered substantial cultural disparities in the manner in which consumers from these nations engaged with gamified components. In Saudi Arabia, where religious rituals and social standards have a significant impact on daily life, it was necessary for the gamified system to conform to Islamic values and customs. The inclusion of religious aspects, such as including difficulties related to fasting during Ramadan or increasing physical activity as a means of enhancing spiritual well-being, proved to be highly successful (McLaren et al., 2021) (AbuShihab et al., 2023). Furthermore, users placed great importance on privacy and modesty, expressing a preference for avatars and game mechanics that adhered to cultural standards about gender and public interaction.

In the United Arab Emirates, a country known for its emphasis on technical progress and contemporary values, users exhibit a greater receptiveness towards innovative and dynamic gamified components. The utilization of state-of-the-art technology, specifically augmented reality (AR) and virtual reality (VR), to improve the gamified experience was positively appreciated (Paliokas et al., 2020). Nevertheless, like Saudi Arabia, it was imperative for the gamified system to uphold cultural values, such as prioritizing collaborative accomplishments that align with the region's community focus.

Another instance is an educational portal that incorporates gamification to enhance literacy rates in rural areas of Morocco. This platform had to overcome the obstacles posed by a lack of advanced technology infrastructure, while also ensuring that it was culturally appropriate and relatable. The incorporation of indigenous languages and culturally relevant narratives in the gamified content effectively captivated users who lacked familiarity with digital educational resources (Christopoulos & Mystakidis, 2023) (Basaraba, 2022).

These case studies from the MENA region emphasize the significance of designing gamification with cultural sensitivity. In order to achieve success, gamified systems must not only integrate sophisticated technology, but also have a profound regard for and mirror the cultural, religious, and societal values specific to the location. This method guarantees that gamified experiences are both captivating and culturally suitable, resulting in increased acceptance and efficacy in the MENA setting.

ETHICAL CONSIDERATIONS IN CROSS-CULTURAL GAMIFICATION

The ethical considerations of introducing gamified systems in cross-cultural contexts have gained significance as gamification grows more widespread in different industries (Oliveira et al., 2021) (Zhao, 2024). Ethical concerns are paramount in guaranteeing gamified systems' effectiveness and cultural sensitivity. Within the context of cross-cultural gamification, these ethical concerns are intensified because of the possibility of cultural misunderstandings, misrepresentations, and the unintentional imposition of values that may clash with local conventions and practices.

A key ethical concern in cross-cultural gamification is the need for cultural sensitivity (Herkanaidu et al., 2021). Designers must possess a keen awareness of the cultural contexts in which their gamified systems will be implemented. This entails comprehending the cultural, religious, and social norms of the target audience in order to prevent the creation of objectionable or inappropriate information. For instance, specific competitive aspects that are positively received in individualistic societies may be seen as causing division or aggression in collectivist societies. Likewise, the utilization of symbols, colors, or storylines that possess diverse connotations in different cultures may result in unintentional adverse responses. Hence, in order to achieve cultural sensitivity, designers must actively collaborate with cultural specialists, carry out extensive research, and potentially include local communities in the design process. This is done to ensure that the gamified system adheres to the cultural values and expectations of the intended users (Shonfeld et al., 2021) (Grenni et al., 2020).

The issue of informed consent is of utmost importance, particularly in areas where there may be substantial disparities in digital literacy (Tejedor et al., 2020). The reference for the source is Milenkova and Lendzhova (2021). Users should possess comprehensive knowledge regarding the functioning of the gamified system, the nature of the obtained data, and the intended utilization of said data. This is especially crucial in societies where there can be skepticism towards technology, or individuals are not familiar with the practice of disclosing personal information on the internet. For ethical gamification design, it is crucial to guarantee openness and offer users the option to choose whether to participate in specific features while also respecting their autonomy and privacy.

Ensuring data privacy and security is of utmost importance in cross-cultural gamification, as highlighted by Liu et al. (2024) and Ayyash & Herzallah (2022). Given that gamified systems frequently gather and analyze personal data, it is crucial to take into account the legal and ethical regulations regarding data protection in various geographical areas. Certain cultures may possess more stringent privacy standards or legal frameworks that need meticulous protection of user data. Designers have the responsibility to guarantee that gamified systems adhere to the data protection regulations of the specific region and that user data is properly stored and maintained to prevent any unauthorized access or misuse (Campanile et al., 2021).

Fairness and inclusion are essential ethical ideals that must be maintained in cross-cultural gamification, as emphasized by Amugongo et al. (2023). The design should ensure equal treatment for all groups, regardless of cultural, socio-economic, or language disparities. Gamified systems should aim to be inclusive, providing equitable possibilities for involvement and achievement to all users, irrespective of their background.

Ultimately, the ethical aspects of cross-cultural gamification are intricate and diverse, necessitating a careful and knowledgeable design approach. Designers can construct gamified systems that are productive and ethically responsible by giving priority to cultural sensitivity, informed permission, data protection, and inclusivity. This approach fosters positive interaction in varied cultural contexts.

FUTURE TRENDS AND INNOVATIONS

Technology, changing user expectations, and a better awareness of cultural differences are advancing cross-cultural gamification (Nam & Kannan, 2020) (Rau, 2020). Gamification is growing across industries, and numerous major trends and breakthroughs will determine its future, especially in different cultural settings.

The application of AI and machine learning to personalize and culturally adjust gamified experiences is growing (Gligorea et al., 2023). Gamified systems may automatically modify their content and functionality to fit users from different cultures better, using AI to evaluate massive volumes of user data and discover cultural preferences, behaviors, and motives. For instance, AI-driven systems can adapt challenges, rewards, and interactions to a user's culture, improving engagement and performance. This kind of customization may become typical in future gamified apps, making them more inclusive and relevant globally.

Gamified systems are including AR and VR (Zhang et al., 2020) (Lampropoulos et al.,2022). AR and VR can create rich, interactive worlds that reflect users' cultural heritage, overcoming cultural boundaries (Hutson & Hutson, 2024). VR can build virtual locations that match real-world cultural situations, making gamified content feel familiar and relevant. This idea could change cross-cultural gamification by providing engaging, culturally accurate experiences.

Gamification in education will develop, especially in varied language and cultural locations (Lampropoulos et al., 2022) (Pinto, 2021). Multilingual gamified platforms with culturally appropriate content may be forthcoming. Local storytelling, folklore, and historical narratives could make learning more interesting and culturally relevant on these platforms. Gamified education systems may also promote cultural exchange by using interactive and gamified content to teach users about other cultures.

Watch community-driven gamification, too. Gamified systems that employ user communities to generate and distribute information are becoming increasingly possible as people become more connected and active online (Paul et al., 2024). A richer and more diversified gamification ecosystem may result from gamified platforms that allow users to share their cultural viewpoints. Gamified platforms could potentially enable cross-cultural collaboration by allowing users from various countries to work toward common goals. Finally, ethical considerations will remain vital in cross-cultural gamification (Fernandes et al., 2022) (Witoszek-Kubicka, 2020). Gamified systems that are successful and sensitive to cultural variations, data privacy, and user autonomy will likely become more important as designers grow more ethically aware. Gamification design breakthroughs that stress openness, diversity, and justice will come from this ethical perspective. Technological advances, personalization, immersive experiences, and ethical design will shape cross-cultural gamification. These trends and innovations will enable more engaging, culturally relevant, and impactful gamified systems across varied global contexts.

CONCLUSION

Incorporating cultural sensitivity is of utmost importance while designing and executing gamified systems, particularly in our interconnected digital world. With the increasing adoption of gamification across many industries, it is crucial to consider cultural factors. Our research indicates that cultural influences significantly influence user motivation and enjoyment when it comes to gamified apps. Developers can enhance the adaptability and inclusivity of systems by incorporating Hofstede's cultural dimensions, hence appealing to users from diverse cultural backgrounds. The case studies demonstrate that a tailored gamification strategy is necessary for international audiences. Instead, the effectiveness and scope of gamified apps can be maximized by incorporating culturally adapted designs that align with users' values, practices, and expectations. This chapter offers valuable insights for designers and researchers seeking to include cross-cultural gamification in their work. Addressing cultural considerations in gamification will enhance user experiences and ensure the ethical and responsible adoption of this approach worldwide.

REFERENCES:

AbuShihab, K., Obaideen, K., Alameddine, M., Alkurd, R. A. F., Khraiwesh, H. M., Mohammad, Y., & Faris, M. E. (2023). Reflection on Ramadan fasting research related to sustainable development goal 3 (Good Health and Well-Being): A bibliometric analysis. [HTML]. *Journal of Religion and Health*, •••, 1–31. PMID: 38110843

Alam, M. I., Malone, L., Nadolny, L., Brown, M., & Cervato, C. (2023). Investigating the impact of a gamified learning analytics dashboard: Student experiences and academic achievement. [wiley.com]. *Journal of Computer Assisted Learning*, 39(5), 1436–1449. DOI: 10.1111/jcal.12853

Aloisi, A. (2022). Platform work in Europe: Lessons learned, legal developments and challenges ahead. European Labour Law Journal. sagepub.com

Amugongo, L. M., Kriebitz, A., Boch, A., & Lütge, C. (2023). Operationalising AI ethics through the agile software development lifecycle: a case study of AI-enabled mobile health applications. AI and Ethics. springer.com

Askew, R., & Ritter, A. (2023). When self-direction meets conformity: Surfacing Schwartz's 10 basic human values in drug policy dialogue with lived/living experience participants. [HTML]. *The International Journal on Drug Policy*, 122, 104257. DOI: 10.1016/j.drugpo.2023.104257 PMID: 37935077

Ayyash, M. M., & Herzallah, F. (2022, September). Understanding the Efficiency of Gamification on the Engagement Intention of the Customers with Mobile Payment Systems. In *International Conference on Emerging Technologies and Intelligent Systems* (pp. 294-310). Cham: Springer International Publishing. [HTML]

Basaraba, N. (2022). Transmedia Narratives for Cultural Heritage: Remixing History. [HTML]

Bitrián, P., Buil, I., & Catalán, S. (2021). Enhancing user engagement: The role of gamification in mobile apps. Journal of Business Research. sciencedirect.com

Breuer, H., & Ivanov, K. (2020). Gamification to address cultural challenges and to facilitate values-based innovation. *ISPIM Conference Proceedings*. [HTML]

Bugeja, M., & Grech, E. M. (2020). Using technology and gamification as a means of enhancing users' experience at cultural heritage sites. Rediscovering Heritage Through Technology: A Collection of Innovative Research Case Studies That Are Reworking The Way We Experience Heritage, 69-89. [HTML]

Cai, Y., Li, X., & Shi, W. (2024). Does gamification affect knowledge-sharing behavior? The mediating role of intrinsic satisfaction needs. [HTML]. *Online Information Review*, 48(2), 354–373. DOI: 10.1108/OIR-05-2021-0288

Campanile, L., Iacono, M., Marulli, F., & Mastroianni, M. (2021). Designing a GDPR compliant blockchain-based IoV distributed information tracking system. [HTML]. *Information Processing & Management*, 58(3), 102511. DOI: 10.1016/j.ipm.2021.102511

Carneiro, A., e Sousa, H. F. P., Dinis, M. A. P., & Leite, Â (2021). Human values and religion: Evidence from the european social survey. Social Sciences. mdpi.com

Cavusoglu, H., Li, Z., & Kim, S. H. (2021). How do virtual badges incentivize voluntary contributions to online communities? [HTML]. *Information & Management*, 58(5), 103483. DOI: 10.1016/j.im.2021.103483

Cejka, P., & Mohelska, H. (2020). National Culture Influence on Organisational Trauma: A Conceptual Framework Review. In Occupational Stress: Breakthroughs in Research and Practice (pp. 238-262). IGI Global. [HTML] DOI: 10.4018/978-1-7998-0954-8.ch012

Chang, W. L., & Yeh, Y. C. (2021). A blended design of game-based learning for motivation, knowledge sharing and critical thinking enhancement. *Technology, Pedagogy and Education*, 30(2), 271–285.

Cheng, V. W. S. (2020). Recommendations for implementing gamification for mental health and wellbeing. Frontiers in psychology. frontiersin.org

Chotiratanapinun, T., & Suppipat, S. (2022). Games and gamification in sustainability learning: a peer-based approach for Thai design education. In *Handbook of Research on the Influence and Effectiveness of Gamification in Education* (pp. 241–270). IGI Global. [HTML] DOI: 10.4018/978-1-6684-4287-6.ch013

Christopoulos, A. & Mystakidis, S. (2023). Gamification in education. Encyclopedia. mdpi.com

Chung, D. J., & Koo, K. R. (2023). The role of cultural diversity in creating value: A case study of South Korea's pop band BTS. [HTML]. *Asia Pacific Business Review*, 29(5), 1275–1299. DOI: 10.1080/13602381.2023.2243242

Ciuchita, R., Heller, J., Köcher, S., Köcher, S., Leclercq, T., Sidaoui, K., & Stead, S. (2023). It is really not a game: An integrative review of gamification for service research. [sagepub.com]. *Journal of Service Research*, 26(1), 3–20. DOI: 10.1177/10946705221076272

Costa, F. A., Viana, J., & Raleiras, M. (2020, June). What do higher education students have to say about gamification? In *International Conference in Methodologies and intelligent Systems for Techhnology Enhanced Learning* (pp. 56-65). Cham: Springer International Publishing. [HTML]

Di Raddo, E. (2020). From the artwork to the museum: Gamification as an instrument of art. In *Digital Transformation in the Cultural and Creative Industries* (pp. 32–50). Routledge. [HTML] DOI: 10.4324/9780429329852-4

Dutta, R., Mantri, A., & Singh, G. (2022). Evaluating system usability of mobile augmented reality application for teaching Karnaugh-Maps. Smart Learning Environments. springer.com

Ebel, P., Orlovska, J., Hünemeyer, S., Wickman, C., Vogelsang, A., & Söderberg, R. (2021). Automotive UX design and data-driven development: Narrowing the gap to support practitioners. [sciencedirect.com]. *Transportation Research Interdisciplinary Perspectives*, 11, 100455. DOI: 10.1016/j.trip.2021.100455

Fernandes, A., Melo, M., & Machado, C. F. (2022). The use of gamification in training and socialization processes in a multicultural context. In *Technological challenges: The human side of the digital age* (pp. 93–108). Springer International Publishing. [HTML] DOI: 10.1007/978-3-030-98040-5_4

Freiermuth, M. R. & Ito, M. (2022). Battling with books: The gamification of an EFL extensive reading class. Simulation & Gaming. sagepub.com

Gagné, M., Parker, S. K., Griffin, M. A., Dunlop, P. D., Knight, C., Klonek, F. E., & Parent-Rocheleau, X. (2022). Understanding and shaping the future of work with self-determination theory. [nature.com]. *Nature Reviews Psychology*, 1(7), 378–392. DOI: 10.1038/s44159-022-00056-w PMID: 35574235

Gagné, N. O. (2021). Reworking Japan: changing men at work and play under neoliberalism. [HTML]

Glazer, S. (2021). Organizational role ambiguity as a proxy for uncertainty avoidance. [HTML]. *International Journal of Intercultural Relations*, 85, 1–12. DOI: 10.1016/j.ijintrel.2021.08.011

Gligorea, I., Cioca, M., Oancea, R., Gorski, A. T., Gorski, H., & Tudorache, P. (2023). Adaptive learning using artificial intelligence in e-learning: A literature review. [mdpi.com]. *Education Sciences*, 13(12), 1216. DOI: 10.3390/educsci13121216

Grenni, S., Horlings, L. G., & Soini, K. (2020). Linking spatial planning and place branding strategies through cultural narratives in places. European Planning Studies. tandfonline.com

Gupta, P., & Goyal, P. (2022). Is game-based pedagogy just a fad? A self-determination theory approach to gamification in higher education. [HTML]. *International Journal of Educational Management*, 36(3), 341–356. DOI: 10.1108/IJEM-04-2021-0126

Han, H. (2021). Consumer behavior and environmental sustainability in tourism and hospitality: A review of theories, concepts, and latest research. Sustainable Consumer Behaviour and the Environment. tandfonline.com

Han, L., Cao, Q., Xie, T., Chen, X., Liu, Y., & Bai, J. (2021). Exploring the experience of nursing undergraduates in using gamification teaching mode based on the flow theory in nursing research: A qualitative study. [HTML]. *Nurse Education Today*, 107, 105158. DOI: 10.1016/j.nedt.2021.105158 PMID: 34607296

Hellín, C. J., Calles-Esteban, F., Valledor, A., Gómez, J., Otón-Tortosa, S., & Tayebi, A. (2023). Enhancing student motivation and engagement through a gamified learning environment. [mdpi.com]. *Sustainability (Basel)*, 15(19), 14119. DOI: 10.3390/su151914119

Herkanaidu, R., Furnell, S. M., & Papadaki, M. (2021). Towards a cross-cultural education framework for online safety awareness. [HTML]. *Information and Computer Security*, 29(4), 664–679. DOI: 10.1108/ICS-11-2020-0183

Hooshyar, D., Pedaste, M., Yang, Y., Malva, L., Hwang, G. J., Wang, M., Lim, H., & Delev, D. (2021). From gaming to computational thinking: An adaptive educational computer game-based learning approach. [HTML]. *Journal of Educational Computing Research*, 59(3), 383–409. DOI: 10.1177/0735633120965919

Hu, Y. Z., Wei, H. T., & Chignell, M. (2023). Impact of rewards on cognitive game performance: Competition with peers increases enjoyment in easy, but not difficult tasks. [HTML]. *Computers in Human Behavior*, 149, 107952. DOI: 10.1016/j.chb.2023.107952

Hutson, J., & Hutson, P. (2024). Immersive technologies. In Inclusive Smart Museums: Engaging Neurodiverse Audiences and Enhancing Cultural Heritage (pp. 153-228). Cham: Springer Nature Switzerland. [HTML] DOI: 10.1007/978-3-031-43615-4_5

Ianole-Călin, R., Francioni, B., Masili, G., Druică, E., & Goschin, Z. (2020). A cross-cultural analysis of how individualism and collectivism impact collaborative consumption. [HTML]. *Resources, Conservation and Recycling*, 157, 104762. DOI: 10.1016/j.resconrec.2020.104762

Jaskari, M. M. & Syrjälä, H. (2023). A mixed-methods study of marketing students' game-playing motivations and gamification elements. Journal of Marketing Education. sagepub.com

Jehanzeb, K. (2022). How perception of training impacts organizational citizenship behavior: Power distance as moderator. [HTML]. *Personnel Review*, 51(3), 922–944. DOI: 10.1108/PR-07-2020-0566

Jin, H., Dong, G., Zou, L., Shen, X., & Li, D. (2020). History and status quo of higher public health education in China. Public Health Reviews. springer.com

Kalogiannakis, M., Papadakis, S., & Zourmpakis, A. I. (2021). Gamification in science education. A systematic review of the literature. Education sciences. mdpi.com

Kalpokas, I. (2021). The Malleable Self: Immersion, Self-optimisation and Gamification. In *Malleable, Digital, and Posthuman* (pp. 47-76). Emerald Publishing Limited.

Klock, A. C. T., Gasparini, I., Pimenta, M. S., & Hamari, J. (2020). Tailored gamification: A review of literature. [sciencedirect.com]. *International Journal of Human-Computer Studies*, 144, 102495. DOI: 10.1016/j.ijhcs.2020.102495

Krath, J., Schürmann, L., & Von Korflesch, H. F. O. (2021). Revealing the theoretical basis of gamification: A systematic review and analysis of theory in research on gamification, serious games and game-based .... Computers in Human Behavior. sciencedirect.com

Lampropoulos, G., Keramopoulos, E., Diamantaras, K., & Evangelidis, G. (2022). Augmented reality and gamification in education: A systematic literature review of research, applications, and empirical studies. applied sciences, 12(13), 6809. mdpi.com

Landers, R. N., & Sanchez, D. R. (2022). Game-based, gamified, and gamefully designed assessments for employee selection: Definitions, distinctions, design, and validation. [wiley.com]. *International Journal of Selection and Assessment*, 30(1), 1–13. DOI: 10.1111/ijsa.12376

Lawrie, S. I., Eom, K., Moza, D., Gavreliuc, A., & Kim, H. S. (2020). Cultural variability in the association between age and well-being: The role of uncertainty avoidance. [sagepub.com]. *Psychological Science*, 31(1), 51–64. DOI: 10.1177/0956797619887348 PMID: 31850828

Li, M., Wang, Y., Wu, Y., & Liu, H. (2021). Gamification narrative design as a predictor for mobile fitness app user persistent usage intentions: A goal priming perspective. [HTML]. *Enterprise Information Systems*, 15(10), 1501–1545. DOI: 10.1080/17517575.2021.1941272

Li, W., Xiao, J. X., & Zhang, M. T. (2024, June). Optimizing Urban e-Commerce Experiences: A Cross-Cultural Interface Design Approach for Enhanced Connectivity and Consumer Engagement. In International Conference on Human-Computer Interaction (pp. 219-234). Cham: Springer Nature Switzerland. [HTML] DOI: 10.1007/978-3-031-60441-6_15

Liu, L., Ross, H., & Ariyawardana, A. (2020). Community development through supply chain responsibility: A case study of rice supply chains and connected rural communities in Central China. Sustainability. mdpi.com

Liu, R. Z., Benitez, J., Zhang, L., Shao, Z., & Mi, J. N. (2024). Exploring the influence of gamification-enabled customer experience on continuance intention towards digital platforms for e-government: An empirical …. Information & Management. sciencedirect.com

Lowry, P. B., Petter, S., & Leimeister, J. M. (2020). Desperately seeking the artefacts and the foundations of native theory in gamification research: Why information systems researchers can play a legitimate role in this discourse and how they can better contribute. [tandfonline.com]. *European Journal of Information Systems*, 29(6), 609–620. DOI: 10.1080/0960085X.2020.1841574

Luarn, P., Chen, C. C., & Chiu, Y. P. (2023). Enhancing intrinsic learning motivation through gamification: A self-determination theory perspective. [HTML]. *The International Journal of Information and Learning Technology*, 40(5), 413–424. DOI: 10.1108/IJILT-07-2022-0145

Magylaitė, K., Kapočius, K., Butleris, R., & Čeponienė, L. (2022). Towards High Usability in Gamified Systems: A Systematic Review of Key Concepts and Approaches. Applied Sciences. mdpi.com

Marques, C. G., Pedro, J. P., & Araújo, I. (2023). A systematic literature review of gamification in/for cultural heritage: Leveling up, going beyond. Heritage. mdpi.com

McLaren, H., Patmisari, E., Hamiduzzaman, M., Jones, M., & Taylor, R. (2021). Respect for religiosity: Review of faith integration in health and wellbeing interventions with Muslim minorities. [mdpi.com]. *Religions*, 12(9), 692. DOI: 10.3390/rel12090692

Meaning, C. E. (2024). 176 I. Araújo Gamification Gamification was firstly defined as" the use of game design elements in non-game contexts"(Deterding, et al., 2011 p. 9). This definition is the basis for many others that have emerged, adapting their characteristics to each context. For education context we got the Karl Kapp definition:" gamification is using game-based mechanics. In International Conference on Lifelong Education and Leadership for All (ICLEL 2023) (Vol. 17, p. 175). Springer Nature. [HTML]

Messner, W. (2021). Connections between cultures: Using empirical distributions for measuring cultural differences. [HTML]. *Journal of Cross-Cultural Psychology*, 52(2), 129–154. DOI: 10.1177/0022022120982370

Milenkova, V. & Lendzhova, V. (2021). Digital citizenship and digital literacy in the conditions of social crisis. Computers. mdpi.com

Mulcahy, R. F., McAndrew, R., Russell-Bennett, R., & Iacobucci, D. (2021). "Game on!" Pushing consumer buttons to change sustainable behavior: A gamification field study. [HTML]. *European Journal of Marketing*, 55(10), 2593–2619. DOI: 10.1108/EJM-05-2020-0341

Nam, H. & Kannan, P. K. (2020). Digital environment in global markets: Cross-cultural implications for evolving customer journeys. Journal of International Marketing. sagepub.com

Nasirzadeh, E., & Fathian, M. (2020). Investigating the effect of gamification elements on bank customers to personalize gamified systems. [HTML]. *International Journal of Human-Computer Studies*, 143, 102469. DOI: 10.1016/j.ijhcs.2020.102469

Noorbehbahani, F., & Salehi, F. (2021). A serious game to extract Hofstede's cultural dimensions at the individual level. [HTML]. *User Modeling and User-Adapted Interaction*, 31(2), 225–259. DOI: 10.1007/s11257-020-09280-6

O'Brien, H. L., Roll, I., Kampen, A., & Davoudi, N. (2022). Rethinking (Dis) engagement in human-computer interaction. Computers in human behavior. sciencedirect.com

Oliveira, R. P., Souza, C. G., Reis, A. C., & Souza, W. M. (2021). Gamification in e-learning and sustainability: A theoretical framework. Sustainability. mdpi.com

Oliveira, W., Hamari, J., Joaquim, S., Toda, A. M., Palomino, P. T., Vassileva, J., & Isotani, S. (2022). The effects of personalized gamification on students' flow experience, motivation, and enjoyment. [springer.com]. *Smart Learning Environments*, 9(1), 16. DOI: 10.1186/s40561-022-00194-x

Oliveira, W., Hamari, J., Shi, L., Toda, A. M., Rodrigues, L., Palomino, P. T., & Isotani, S. (2023). Tailored gamification in education: A literature review and future agenda. [springer.com]. *Education and Information Technologies*, 28(1), 373–406. DOI: 10.1007/s10639-022-11122-4

Ouariachi, T., Li, C. Y., & Elving, W. J. L. (2020). Gamification approaches for education and engagement on pro-environmental behaviors: Searching for best practices. Sustainability. mdpi.com

Özhan, Ş. Ç., & Kocadere, S. A. (2020). The effects of flow, emotional engagement, and motivation on success in a gamified online learning environment. [HTML]. *Journal of Educational Computing Research*, 57(8), 2006–2031. DOI: 10.1177/0735633118823159

Paliokas, I., Patenidis, A. T., Mitsopoulou, E. E., Tsita, C., Pehlivanides, G., Karyati, E., Tsafaras, S., Stathopoulos, E. A., Kokkalas, A., Diplaris, S., Meditskos, G., Vrochidis, S., Tasiopoulou, E., Riggas, C., Votis, K., Kompatsiaris, I., & Tzovaras, D. (2020). A gamified augmented reality application for digital heritage and tourism. [mdpi.com]. *Applied Sciences (Basel, Switzerland)*, 10(21), 7868. DOI: 10.3390/app10217868

Palmquist, A., Jedel, I., & Goethe, O. (2024). Design Implications and Processes for an Attainable Game Experience. In *Universal Design in Video Games: Active Participation Through Accessible Play* (pp. 67–97). Springer International Publishing. [HTML] DOI: 10.1007/978-3-031-30595-5_3

Paul, J., Akbari, M., Mondal, S., & Das, S. (2024). Knowledge sharing leads to engagement during Covid-19 for online gamers. [HTML]. *Information & Management*, 61(4), 103948. DOI: 10.1016/j.im.2024.103948

Paulsen, K. (2021). Integrated storytelling by design: Concepts, principles and methods for new narrative dimensions. [HTML]

Pinto, R., Filgueiras, E., & Moutinho, K. (2020). Emotional design and gamification in educational processes: predictor model to increase video game efficiency. In Design, User Experience, and Usability. Case Studies in Public and Personal Interactive Systems: 9th International Conference, DUXU 2020, Held as Part of the 22nd HCI International Conference, HCII 2020, Copenhagen, Denmark, July 19–24, 2020 [Springer International Publishing.]. *Proceedings*, 22(Part III), 506–517.

Pinto, R. D., Peixoto, B., Melo, M., Cabral, L., & Bessa, M. (2021). Foreign language learning gamification using virtual reality—a systematic review of empirical research. Education Sciences. mdpi.com

Puni, A. & Hilton, S. K. (2020). Power distance culture and whistleblowing intentions: the moderating effect of gender. International Journal of Ethics and Systems. [HTML]

Rau, P. L. P. (2020). Cross-Cultural Design. User Experience of Products, Services, and Intelligent Environments: 12th International Conference, CCD 2020, Held as Part of the.... [HTML]

Riar, M., Hamari, J., & Zarnekow, R. (2021). The Gamification of Enterprise Cooperation: A Cross-Comparison of Case Studies. Organizational gamification. [HTML]

Riar, M., Morschheuser, B., Zarnekow, R., & Hamari, J. (2022). Gamification of cooperation: A framework, literature review and future research agenda. [sciencedirect.com]. *International Journal of Information Management*, 67, 102549. DOI: 10.1016/j.ijinfomgt.2022.102549

Rivera, E. S. & Garden, C. L. P. (2021). Gamification for student engagement: a framework. Journal of further and higher education. tandfonline.com

Salimon, M. G., Aliyu, O. A., Yusr, M. M., & Perumal, S. (2021). Smartphone banking usage in Nigeria: Gamification, technology acceptance and cultural factors empirical perspectives. [wiley.com]. *The Electronic Journal on Information Systems in Developing Countries*, 87(4), e12174. DOI: 10.1002/isd2.12174

Santórum, M., Carrión-Toro, M., Morales-Martínez, D., Maldonado-Garcés, V., Araujo, E., & Acosta-Vargas, P. (2023). An accessible serious game-based platform for process learning of people with intellectual disabilities. [mdpi.com]. *Applied Sciences (Basel, Switzerland)*, 13(13), 7748. DOI: 10.3390/app13137748

Sapuarachchi, D. B. (2021). Cultural distance and inter-organizational knowledge transfer: A case study of a multinational company. [HTML]. *Journal of Knowledge Management*, 25(9), 2316–2333. DOI: 10.1108/JKM-06-2020-0439

Schöbel, S. M., Janson, A., & Söllner, M. (2020). Capturing the complexity of gamification elements: A holistic approach for analysing existing and deriving novel gamification designs. [tandfonline.com]. *European Journal of Information Systems*, 29(6), 641–668. DOI: 10.1080/0960085X.2020.1796531

Schoenenberger, H. (2024). Connected Learning: Origins, Opportunities, and Perspectives of Contemporary Educational Design: A Machine-Generated Literature Overview. [HTML]

Schumacher, C., Eggers, F., Verhoef, P. C., & Maas, P. (2023). The effects of cultural differences on consumers' willingness to share personal information. [sagepub.com]. *Journal of Interactive Marketing*, 58(1), 72–89. DOI: 10.1177/10949968221136555

Scurati, G. W., Bertoni, M., Graziosi, S., & Ferrise, F. (2021). Exploring the use of virtual reality to support environmentally sustainable behavior: A framework to design experiences. Sustainability. mdpi.com

Seo, K., Fels, S., Kang, M., Jung, C., & Ryu, H. (2021). Goldilocks conditions for workplace gamification: How narrative persuasion helps manufacturing workers create self-directed behaviors. [tandfonline.com]. *Human-Computer Interaction*, 36(5-6), 473–510. DOI: 10.1080/07370024.2020.1744145

Settembre-Blundo, D., González-Sánchez, R., Medina-Salgado, S., & García-Muiña, F. E. (2021). Flexibility and resilience in corporate decision making: A new sustainability-based risk management system in uncertain times. [springer.com]. *Global Journal of Flexible Systems Managment*, 22(S2, Suppl 2), 107–132. DOI: 10.1007/s40171-021-00277-7

Shaban, A., Pearson, E., & Chang, V. (2021). Evaluation of user experience, cognitive load, and training performance of a gamified cognitive training application for children with learning disabilities. Frontiers in Computer Science. frontiersin.org

Shonfeld, M., Cotnam-Kappel, M., Judge, M., Ng, C. Y., Ntebutse, J. G., Williamson-Leadley, S., & Yildiz, M. N. (2021). Learning in digital environments: A model for cross-cultural alignment. [springer.com]. *Educational Technology Research and Development*, 69(4), 1–20. DOI: 10.1007/s11423-021-09967-6 PMID: 33654347

Su, J., Zhong, Y., & Ng, D. T. K. (2022). A meta-review of literature on educational approaches for teaching AI at the K-12 levels in the Asia-Pacific region. Computers and Education: Artificial Intelligence. sciencedirect.com

Sushra, T., Iyengar, N., Shah, M., & Kshirsagar, A. (2022). Judging a book by its cover: Significance of UX design in gamification and computing systems. [HTML]. *Iran Journal of Computer Science*, 5(2), 117–126. DOI: 10.1007/s42044-021-00096-0

Sutcliffe, A. (2022). Designing for user engagment: Aesthetic and attractive user interfaces. [HTML]

Tejedor, S., Cervi, L., Pérez-Escoda, A., & Jumbo, F. T. (2020). Digital literacy and higher education during COVID-19 lockdown: Spain, Italy, and Ecuador. Publications. mdpi.com

Unternährer, C., Termine, F., & De Santo, A. (2024). Enhancing Knowledge Transmission: The Perspective of Gamification User Profiles. Procedia Computer Science. sciencedirect.com

Van der Heijden, B. I. J. M., Burgers, M. J., Kaan, A. M., Lamberts, B. F., Migchelbrink, K., Van den Ouweland, R. C. P. M., & Meijer, T. (2020). Gamification in dutch businesses: An explorative case study. [sagepub.com]. *SAGE Open*, 10(4), 2158244020972371. DOI: 10.1177/2158244020972371

Vlachogianni, P., & Tselios, N. (2022). Perceived usability evaluation of educational technology using the System Usability Scale (SUS): A systematic review. [HTML]. *Journal of Research on Technology in Education*, 54(3), 392–409. DOI: 10.1080/15391523.2020.1867938

Wang, Y. F., Hsu, Y. F., & Fang, K. (2022). The key elements of gamification in corporate training–The Delphi method. Entertainment Computing. sciencedirect.com

Witoszek-Kubicka, A. (2020). Implementation of Gamification in Polish Companies—Stages, Elements, Ethics. Information. mdpi.com

Woods, O. (2021). Feminist geographies of online gaming. Digital Geography and Society. sciencedirect.com

Xi, N. & Hamari, J. (2020). Does gamification affect brand engagement and equity? A study in online brand communities. Journal of Business Research. sciencedirect.com

Xiao, R., Wu, Z., & Hamari, J. (2022). Internet-of-gamification: A review of literature on IoT-enabled gamification for user engagement. [tandfonline.com]. *International Journal of Human-Computer Interaction*, 38(12), 1113–1137. DOI: 10.1080/10447318.2021.1990517

Xie, L., Li, D., & Keh, H. T. (2020). Customer participation and well-being: The roles of service experience, customer empowerment and social support. [HTML]. *Journal of Service Theory and Practice*, 30(6), 557–584. DOI: 10.1108/JSTP-11-2019-0228

Yazici, S. (2024). *In memory of Geert Hofstede: A pioneer in comparative cross-cultural management research and practice*. Hofstede Matters. [HTML] DOI: 10.4324/9781003410348-3

Zakrzewski, P. (2022). Extended reality experience design: The multimodal rhetorical framework for creating persuasive immersion. In Designing, X. R. (Ed.), *A Rhetorical Design Perspective for the Ecology of Human+ Computer Systems* (pp. 183–213). Emerald Publishing Limited. [HTML] DOI: 10.1108/978-1-80262-365-920221005

Zhang, H., Cui, Y., Shan, H., Qu, Z., Zhang, W., Tu, L., & Wang, Y. (2020, June). Hotspots and trends of virtual reality, augmented reality and mixed reality in education field. In 2020 6th international conference of the Immersive Learning Research Network (iLRN) (pp. 215-219). IEEE. [HTML] DOI: 10.23919/iLRN47897.2020.9155170

Zhao, F. (2024). Gamification Design. In User Experience Methods and Tools in Human-Computer Interaction (pp. 373-441). CRC Press. [HTML] DOI: 10.1201/9781003495161-16

Chapter 2
Enhancing Student Authenticity and Engagement Through Gamification and Problem-Based Learning in Higher Education

Nitin Vihari Poluru
Middlesex University, Dubai, UAE

ABSTRACT

This chapter explores the integration of Gamification and Problem-Based Learning (PBL) as innovative approaches to enhance student authenticity and engagement in educational settings, particularly for postgraduate students. The study is grounded in the increasing academic challenges that post-graduate students face, such as information and critical literacy, language barriers, and the need for efficient research skills. The paper discusses the convergence of Gamification and PBL, aiming to address the lack of student engagement and motivation in contemporary higher educational institutions. It presents a theoretical background, drawing from Vygotsky's social development theory and Self-determination theory, to support the fusion of these approaches. Furthermore, the chapter proposes and evaluates several interventions, including Online Game-Based Learning Platforms and Discussion Forums, to enhance student engagement and authenticity.

DOI: 10.4018/979-8-3693-8322-3.ch002

1. INTRODUCTION

Educators play a pivotal role in this evolving learning landscape. They are expected to possess a multifaceted ability to inspire, encourage, and guide students through a transformative learning journey. In today's knowledge-driven economy, the role of teachers transcends the traditional function of simply imparting information. Teachers are now seen as key facilitators who empower students by fostering intellectual curiosity and promoting their growth. This evolving role requires educators to deliver content and engage students in ways that stimulate their desire to learn and develop critical thinking skills. Szpunar et al. (2013) found that the average adult attention span typically ranges between 10 to 20 minutes. This limitation presents a significant challenge, especially for working postgraduate students facing numerous academic and personal obstacles. These challenges include developing information literacy, acquiring content knowledge, honing critical literacy, mastering appropriate language styles, and achieving statistical literacy. Moreover, postgraduate students must make early decisions in their academic journey while managing heavier workloads, which can be overwhelming (Becker, 2019). Beyond academic challenges, these students often struggle with self-management, conducting independent research, and navigating complex supervisory relationships (McClure, 2001). For international postgraduate students, additional hurdles such as language barriers and a lack of critical analysis skills further complicate their educational experience (Brown, 2007). Moreover, many postgraduate students struggle with research skills, particularly in efficiently locating, evaluating, and synthesizing relevant literature, which is crucial for academic success (Daniel, 2022). These challenges demand a high degree of resilience, adaptability, and support. This chapter emphasizes the integration of Gamification with Problem-Based Learning (PBL) in educational settings. This approach is driven by the need to enhance student engagement, authenticity, and motivation, offering a dynamic solution to the myriad challenges postgraduate students face.

1.1 Gamification

Gamification, applying game-design elements in non-game contexts (Deterding et al., 2011), offers a compelling framework to make learning more engaging. It taps into students' intrinsic motivations through points, badges, and leaderboards (Hamari et al., 2014). This initiative is inspired by the growing recognition that traditional teaching methods may not fully resonate with the evolving needs and preferences of the modern student cohort. The digital era has prepared a generation of learners who are more responsive to interactive and engaging educational experiences (Dichev & Dicheva, 2017). Gamification in higher education has emerged as a transformative approach, significantly impacting student engagement, motivation, and overall learning outcomes. By integrating game-like elements such as points, badges, leaderboards, and challenges into educational settings, educators aim to create immersive and interactive learning environments that resonate with the digital-age student. Research indicates that gamification can improve academic performance and a more engaging educational experience (Chung et al., 2019). One of the key benefits of gamification is its ability to increase student motivation. Gamification positively influences students' intentions to engage with learning materials. It highlights that performance expectancy, or the belief that using gamified learning will enhance academic performance, is one of the most significant factors driving student acceptance of gamification in higher education. This finding is supported by empirical evidence, showing that students are more likely to engage with and complete coursework when it is presented in a gamified format that rewards their efforts with tangible benefits like points or badges (Chung et al., 2019). Gamification also leverages psychological principles, such as reinforcement and emotion, to enhance learning. Gamification in higher education significantly influences the teaching-learning process by improving learning outcomes and promoting acquiring various types of knowledge, including declarative, conceptual, procedural, and even soft skills (Castillo-Parra et al., 2022). It emphasizes that the success of gamification lies in its ability to tap into the main motivations of human behavior, such as the desire for achievement, competition, and collaboration. These motivational drivers are crucial in fostering an engaging and dynamic learning environment.

Furthermore, gamification has been shown to promote Self-Directed Learning (SDL), essential in today's fast-paced and ever-changing society. Lindberg (2019) explored the use of gamification to support SDL in a Swedish university course. The findings revealed that frequent and immediate feedback, balanced use of game elements, and providing students with choices were crucial in supporting all dimensions of SDL. This indicates that gamification can be particularly effective in fostering independent learning habits, vital for lifelong learning and adaptability in the modern world. However, the success of gamification depends heavily on its design and implementation. Costa et al. (2020) conducted a study in the context of an engineering course. While students generally had a positive experience with gamification, the clarity of the "rules of the game" and the articulation between different game elements were critical for its effectiveness. The study underscores the importance of ensuring that gamification is not just a superficial addition but is deeply integrated into the curriculum with clear educational objectives. Additionally, providing meaningful feedback throughout the gamified experience is essential to maintain student engagement and meet learning goals. Another significant aspect of gamification is its impact on behavioral change and student retention. When applied within a structured framework such as Action Research or Experiential Learning, gamification can reduce student attrition by enhancing the learning experience and increasing student engagement (Noran, 2016). By addressing the needs of a diverse student cohort, gamification helps create a more inclusive and supportive learning environment that caters to different learning styles and preferences. Moreover, the popularity of gamification in higher education research is on the rise, with a growing number of studies exploring its various applications and outcomes. This trend reflects the increasing recognition of gamification as a valuable tool in modern education, particularly in enhancing student motivation and learning outcomes across various disciplines (Lilia & Elena, 2019).

To enhance student authenticity and engagement, educational research indicates that gamification can substantially boost student motivation and active participation (Deterding et al., 2011). These methods encourage students to participate actively in learning and reduce the fear of making mistakes. This approach fosters an environment where students will likely try new things, contributing to a more authentic learning experience. Additionally, gamification in Massive Open Online Courses (MOOCs) and other online platforms has shown promising results in maintaining student engagement, especially toward the end of a course (Rahman et al., 2019). However, it is essential to note that while gamification has shown positive results in many cases, its influence on student learning and engagement is not universally effective. The impact of gamification on student motivation and performance can vary depending on individual student characteristics, such as intrinsic versus extrinsic motivation (Bai et al.,2020). Moreover, some studies have suggested that the effects of gamification on motivation, satisfaction, and empowerment may diminish over time, potentially affecting academic performance negatively.

1.2 Problem-Based Learning

Problem-based learning (PBL) is an instructional method where students learn by actively engaging in real-world and personally meaningful projects (Hmelo-Silver, 2004). It fosters critical thinking, problem-solving skills, and self-directed learning. The PBL approach pioneered at McMaster Medical School in the 1960s emerged in response to the need for graduates' adept at handling the burgeoning information overload and capable of critical thinking and complex problem-solving (Barrows & Tamblyn, 1980). PBL's efficacy lies in its ability to prompt students to apply knowledge spontaneously to new problems, a skill shown to be more effectively developed when knowledge is gained through problem-solving than traditional methods (Bransford et al., 1989). One of the main strengths of PBL is its ability to foster deep learning and understanding. PBL encourages students to develop flexible knowledge and practical problem-solving abilities by centering the learning process around problem-solving activities. This approach contrasts with traditional education's passive reception of information, as students must actively engage with the material, collaborate with peers, and reflect on their learning process (Hmelo-Silver, 2004). Moreover, PBL has been shown to enhance students' intrinsic motivation and SDL skills. In PBL environments, students are often responsible for identifying what they need to learn and managing their learning process, which helps develop lifelong learning skills. This aspect of PBL is essential in today's fast-changing world, where the ability to learn and adapt continuously is critical. PBL can effectively cultivate higher-order thinking skills by encouraging students to reflect on their problem-solving experiences and adjust their strategies accordingly (Hmelo & Ferrari, 1997). Despite its benefits, implementing PBL in higher education is not without challenges. Issues such as overly directive tutors, overly structured problems, and dysfunctional group dynamics can hinder the effectiveness of PBL. These challenges highlight the importance of careful planning and facilitation in PBL environments to ensure students are appropriately challenged and supported in their learning (Dolmans et al., 2005). In addition to its educational benefits, PBL has been recognized for its potential to prepare students for the complexities of professional life. PBL is particularly well-suited for fields such as engineering and medicine, where the ability to solve complex, multidisciplinary problems is crucial. PBL helps bridge the gap between theoretical knowledge and practical application, making it a valuable approach in professional education (Perrenet et al., 2000).

The essence of PBL is found in its use of real-life, authentic, and ill-structured problems, which, unlike the prescriptive nature of following a recipe, resemble the challenge of preparing a celebratory meal without predefined ingredients or instructions (Barrows, 1989; Marston, 2001). PBL has been acknowledged for fostering authentic learning experiences that cultivate critical thinking and problem-solving abilities (Hmelo-Silver, 2004). This approach encourages students to be self-regulated and metacognitive, which promotes a more authentic and engaged learning experience (Hung et al., 2006). Furthermore, PBL combined with scaffolding can improve motivation and engagement while students solve authentic problems (Belland et al., 2013). Technology-enhanced PBL in areas such as Human-Computer Interaction (HCI) education has shown high student engagement and overall satisfaction. PBL focuses on critical reasoning to achieve high student engagement, promoting higher-order thinking processes (Grabinger & Dunlap, 2002). However, it is essential to note that while PBL has shown great potential in engaging students, its effectiveness can vary. For instance, deviation from engagement moods in PBL environments increases the probability of students dropping out. Despite this, PBL offers the potential to help students develop flexible understanding and lifelong learning skills (Hmelo-Silver, 2004). Based on the above arguments, the following question arises: Could we envision a set of problems outlined in the learning handbook for every module replacing traditional learning outcomes? This would ensure that learning is framed not by the instructor's expertise but by real-world relevance, making PBL engaging and fundamentally enjoyable for students and tutors.

1.3 Convergence of Gamification and PBL Approaches

Gamification has been integrated with problem-solving approaches, particularly in disciplines that demand high critical thinking and creativity. For instance, collaborative creativity, a crucial skill in problem-solving, was enhanced in students who participated in a gamified group assignment. Students value the diversity of knowledge within their teams and can co-construct solutions effectively, thus demonstrating the potential of gamification in fostering problem-solving skills (Lee et al., 2022). The convergence of these two approaches is particularly evident in multidisciplinary education settings. Kim and Lee (2022) explored the impact of Science, Technology, Engineering, Art, and Mathematics (STEAM) education integrated with gamification. Their findings revealed that students developed more vital creative problem-solving abilities and a more positive attitude towards convergence knowledge, suggesting that gamification can effectively bridge various disciplines while enhancing problem-solving skills. However, successfully integrating gamification and problem-solving approaches requires careful design and implementation. The development of convergence is essential for overcoming traditional academic silos and promoting interdisciplinary learning. Abel et al. (2022) emphasizes the need for adaptable frameworks that can be applied across various educational settings to fully realize this convergence's potential. The convergence of these two approaches aims to address the lack of student engagement and motivation, which are critical issues in contemporary education. The rationale is that by making learning more game-like and centered around real-world problems, students will find the educational experience more relevant and enjoyable and, thus, be more motivated to engage deeply with the content.

2. THEORETICAL BACKGROUND AND LITERATURE REVIEW

According to Vygotsky, learning is inherently a social process, where interaction with peers and more knowledgeable others facilitates more profound understanding and knowledge construction (Mace, 2005). When combined with PBL, gamification leverages these social aspects by creating interactive and collaborative learning environments that mirror real-world problem-solving scenarios. In gamified PBL settings, students engage in tasks that require teamwork, communication, and collective problem-solving, all of which are core elements of Vygotsky's theory. The interactive nature of gamified environments fosters a sense of community and shared purpose among learners, enhancing their motivation and engagement. This aligns with Vygotsky's concept of the Zone of Proximal Development, where learners can achieve higher levels of understanding with the support of peers or mentors within a collaborative framework (Mace, 2005). Furthermore, the immediate feedback and rewards inherent in gamification provide scaffolding, a key concept in Vygotsky's theory, which supports learners as they progress through increasingly complex problems. By integrating gamification with PBL, educators can create dynamic and supportive learning environments that align with Vygotsky's principles and enhance the development of critical thinking and problem-solving skills (Mace, 2005).

Self-determination theory (SDT) posits that individuals are more intrinsically motivated when their basic psychological needs for autonomy, competence, and relatedness are fulfilled (Ryan & Deci, 2000). Gamification effectively addresses these needs, making it a powerful tool for enhancing motivation in educational settings. Gamification fosters autonomy by giving learners choices and control over their learning paths. This aligns with SDT's emphasis on autonomy, where individuals feel empowered to make decisions and pursue goals that resonate with their values and interests (Ryan & Deci, 2000). For instance, allowing students to choose different pathways or challenges within a gamified environment can increase their sense of ownership and investment in learning (Ryan & Deci, 2000). Gamification enhances competence by incorporating feedback mechanisms, such as points, badges, and progression levels, which help learners track their progress and feel a sense of accomplishment. These elements provide immediate reinforcement, enabling students to perceive their growth and mastery of new skills, thereby boosting their competence (Sailer et al., 2017). Finally, relatedness is promoted through social elements like leaderboards, team challenges, and collaborative tasks, which connect learners with their peers and create a sense of belonging within the learning community. This social interaction is crucial for fostering relatedness, as it encourages collaboration and support among learners, enhancing their overall motivation to engage in the activity (Sailer et al., 2017).

The Constructivist Learning Theory, as given by Piaget (1954), posits that learners actively construct knowledge through direct experiences and reflective processes. This theory finds a natural synergy with PBL, where students solve real-world problems that require them to apply and reflect on their knowledge, thereby constructing a deeper understanding. PBL's focus on experiential learning and critical thinking makes it an ideal pedagogical approach for fostering authentic learning experiences. When combined with gamification, PBL can enhance the learning environment by adding elements that increase motivation and engagement. Gamification introduces game-like features such as challenges, rewards, and interactive tasks, which make the learning process more engaging and immersive. This synergy creates a dynamic and interactive learning environment that encourages students to engage authentically and promotes active and reflective learning, which aligns with constructivist principles (Papastergiou, 2009).

Research has shown that gamification can significantly enhance motivation and engagement in educational settings. Domínguez et al. (2013) found that gamified learning environments led to higher student engagement and participation levels, which are critical for effective learning. This aligns with the principles of Constructivist Learning Theory, which emphasizes the importance of motivation and engagement in the learning process. Furthermore, PBL has been widely recognized for its effectiveness in developing critical thinking, problem-solving, and skills. Walker and Leary (2009) highlighted that students engaged in PBL are better equipped to tackle complex, real-world problems because they develop the ability to think critically and apply knowledge in practical contexts. By integrating gamification with PBL, educators can create a learning environment that aligns with Constructivist principles and maximizes student engagement, motivation, and the development of critical thinking skills. This combination offers a robust framework for fostering more profound, more reflective learning experiences that prepare students for the complexities of the real world.

2.1. Student Authenticity

Student authenticity refers to the genuine and authentic expression of a student's personality, thoughts, and feelings in a learning environment (Thompson, 2015). A variety of factors influence this authenticity. Educational approaches such as problem-based, inquiry-based, and project-based learning play a significant role in fostering this authenticity (De Bruyckere & Kirschner, 2017). Balancing self-determination with being true to oneself and engaging with the world, which involves understanding, care, and acceptance, is also crucial. The relationships and care offered by educators, focusing on individual learners, contribute significantly to student authenticity (Malm, 2008). It is a complex concept influenced by educational methods, teacher-student relationships, and the educational environment. It encompasses a blend of pedagogical approaches, personal development, and the dynamics between teachers and students (Frego, 2006). Authenticity in the classroom is not merely about the content being "real-world" relevant but about ensuring that students feel connected to the material personally. Students are encouraged to choose topics that resonate with their genuine interests, and their engagement and learning outcomes significantly improve. This aligns with the broader educational goal of cultivating intrinsic motivation and self-directed learning among students (Klipfel, 2014). Moreover, the authenticity of teacher-student relationships plays a pivotal role in how students perceive and engage with their learning environment. Research indicates that students are more likely to be motivated and invested in their education when they perceive their teachers as authentic—passionate, knowledgeable, and approachable (Johnson & Labelle, 2017). Authentic teaching, therefore, contributes to a supportive learning atmosphere where students feel valued and understood, further reinforcing their commitment to learning. In addition, authenticity in educational assessments—tasks that mirror real-life challenges and require students to apply their knowledge in practical contexts—can significantly enhance learning. Authentic assessments encourage students to engage more deeply with the material as they perceive these tasks as meaningful and relevant to their future professional lives (Zarb et al., 2017).

2.2. Student Engagement

Student engagement is defined as students' cognitive, behavioral, and emotional involvement in their learning processes. It is characterized by vigor, dedication, and absorption (Alrashidi et al., 2016). This engagement is responsive to contextual features and can be influenced by environmental changes. In higher education, engagement refers to the time, energy, and resources devoted by students to activities that enhance their learning at the university level. Teachers play a significant role in ensuring meaningful student engagement, which combines behavioral, emotional, and cognitive aspects (Fredricks et al., 2004). It is a critical element in the educational process, enhancing learning outcomes, motivation, and the overall academic experience. The concepts of student authenticity and student engagement are closely intertwined yet distinct. Research indicates that both are heavily influenced by the context in which learning occurs, which is crucial in fostering enduring learning experiences (Snape & Fox-Turnbull, 2013). Engagement is seen as a complex system involving factors like student identity and participation in authentic inquiry, while authenticity directly enhances engagement by making the learning journey more participatory (Young & Tullo, 2020). However, engagement also depends on factors like reflexivity and the nature of social relations in the learning environment, which are less central to authenticity. Furthermore, perceptions of what constitutes authentic engagement vary across cultural and educational contexts. Authenticity is often enhanced by factors like student autonomy, especially regarding classroom technology use, suggesting that control and self-direction play a significant role in authenticity (Thesech & Balli, 2014).

3. PROPOSITIONS DEVELOPMENT

3.1. Online Game-Based Learning Platforms to Enhance Student Authenticity and Engagement.

Online game-based learning platforms, like Kahoot, have become essential tools in modern education, significantly enhancing student outcomes. These platforms make learning interactive and engaging by incorporating gamification elements like quizzes, competitions, and rewards. This approach captures students' attention and motivates them to participate actively in their learning process. Game-based learning promotes better retention of information by making learning fun and less stressful. It caters to different learning styles, allowing students to learn at their own pace and offering immediate feedback, crucial for reinforcing concepts. Additionally, these platforms foster a collaborative learning environment, encouraging peer interaction and teamwork. The competitive nature of these games stimulates critical thinking and problem-solving skills, helping students apply knowledge in practical scenarios.

Online game-based learning platforms have been demonstrated to enhance student engagement and authenticity in various educational contexts significantly. These platforms offer diverse engagement profiles, including integrally engaged, lone achievers, social explorers, and nonengaged students, and are particularly effective in subjects like mathematics. They contribute to developing complex problem-solving skills, enrich learning experiences, and simulate real-world professional practices (Eservel et al., 2014). Additionally, the gameful design of video lecturing systems enhances emotional engagement, which can lead to higher educational achievement (Eybers et al., M. (2018). Studies indicate that such platforms foster a more engaging learning environment by incorporating elements like leaderboards, making learning enjoyable and boosting student motivation (Greipl et al., 2020). Interactive game-based activities promote behavioral engagement and student collaboration, essential to effective learning (Cheng et al., 2023). Furthermore, these platforms create authentic learning experiences by integrating real-world scenarios, enhancing understanding and retention of course content. This transition from mere knowledge acquisition to deeper comprehension is facilitated through authentic contexts presented within game-based platforms (Chen et al., 2011).

Moreover, game-based learning empowers students by fostering critical thinking, concentration, and academic achievement. Involving students as active participants in creating and designing digital games enhances higher-order thinking skills and improves overall learning outcomes (Yang & Chang, 2013). These findings strongly support the effectiveness of online game-based learning platforms as tools for enhancing student authenticity and engagement by creating interactive, motivating, and authentic learning environments.

Proposition 1: Online Game-Based Learning Platforms positively impact student authenticity and engagement.

3.2. Discussion Forums to Enhance Student Authenticity and Engagement.

Discussion forums have emerged as a powerful tool to enhance student authenticity and engagement in educational settings. These platforms allow students to express their thoughts, engage in meaningful discussions, and build community. Students participating in online forums are more likely to experience a sense of belonging and satisfaction, boosting their engagement and academic performance (Waheed, 2017). Moreover, sharing and discussing ideas in a forum encourages students to develop critical thinking skills, as they are exposed to multiple perspectives and must articulate their thoughts clearly (Williams & Lahman, 2011). Furthermore, the structure of discussion forums significantly impacts student engagement. Research indicates that structured forums, where clear guidelines and expectations are provided, are more effective in fostering student participation and maintaining high levels of engagement (Salter & Conneely, 2015). Such forums enhance interaction and ensure students are actively involved in learning, leading to better learning outcomes. In contrast, unstructured forums may lead to inconsistent participation and lower engagement levels (Mokoena, 2013).

Discussion forums in educational settings can significantly enhance student engagement and authenticity, though various factors influence their effectiveness. Effective use of these forums fosters a sense of belonging and deep learning. They can improve student engagement and academic performance, especially when tailored to individual learning needs (Aderibigbe, 2020). However, the nature of communication in these forums, such as text-based versus video discussions, significantly impacts their efficacy. Despite offering platforms for group discussions, forums may involve low levels of cognitive engagement and numerous low-impact posts (Kew & Tasir, 2021). Furthermore, structured asynchronous discussions on authentic tasks can positively influence knowledge improvement and participation, but there is an overall trend of low cognitive engagement in knowledge construction in these forums (Jones, 2017). Thus, while discussion forums have potential benefits, their success in enhancing student engagement and authenticity depends heavily on implementation strategies, forum design, and instructor involvement.

Proposition 2: Weekly discussion forums between the two lecture sessions positively impact student authenticity and engagement.

3.3. Problem-based learning to Enhance Student Authenticity and Engagement.

PBL is a significant catalyst in enhancing student authenticity and engagement in educational settings. This approach encourages students to be self-regulated and metacognitive, factors that are essential for promoting authenticity and engagement in learning (Hung et al., 2006). Furthermore, integrating PBL with scaffolding techniques has boosted motivation and engagement, particularly when students solve authentic problems (Belland et al., 2013). This is corroborated by research indicating that PBL enriches students' lives by providing hands-on learning opportunities, thereby contributing to their professional and community involvement. Additionally, combining PBL with collaborative research and teacher collaboration leads to a more meaningful implementation of authentic pedagogy. Another significant aspect of PBL is its impact on student collaboration and satisfaction levels. Studies have shown that PBL enhances student engagement and collaboration, increasing satisfaction ratings. Moreover, PBL has been found to promote higher order thinking processes, contributing to high student engagement.

By focusing on real-world contexts, PBL encourages students to take ownership of their learning processes, thereby increasing their authenticity in academic tasks (Hung et al., 2006). Moreover, PBL's integration into various educational settings, including interdisciplinary first-year programs, has positively affected students' learning behaviors, further solidifying its role in enhancing authenticity (Murray & Summerlee, 2007). In addition to promoting authenticity, PBL strategies significantly boost student engagement by actively involving them in collaborative and critical thinking exercises. Research highlights that PBL encourages students to engage deeply with the material through self-directed learning, improving their academic performance and sustaining their motivation throughout the course (Grabinger & Dunlap, 2002). Furthermore, studies indicate that PBL facilitates solid student-teacher relationships, which is crucial for maintaining high student engagement and dedication (Amerstorfer & von Münster-Kistner, 2021).

Proposition 3: Problem-based learning strategies positively impact student authenticity and engagement.

4. IMPLEMENTATION AND EVALUATION

To utilize an Online Game-Based Learning Platform (OGBLP) for a classroom setting, we propose implementing it during the odd-numbered sessions featuring 15 Multiple Choice Questions (MCQs) to facilitate student authenticity and engagement. These sessions will occur at the beginning and the end of each class, strategically designed with ten questions reviewing content from the previous session and five questions covering material from the current session. The intent is to gamify learning by fostering a competitive environment that motivates students to improve their average scores with each session. The student with the highest score will be acknowledged as the session's leader, further incentivizing participation and performance. The session with OGBLP may be started by providing 15 Multiple Choice Questions (MCQs), out of which 10 MCQs are based on the contents of the previous session and 5 MCQs are based on contents to be discussed during that session. The evaluation strategy used here is the pre-and post-assessment. An ideal student is expected to score a minimum of 10 out of 15 points and a few more with guestimates. The same test will be conducted again at the end of the session; this time, the ideal student should be able to score a minimum of 15 points. Following this intervention, starting from the third week of classes and every alternate week until the end of the term will result in continuity of learning and a sense of competition within and across the student community.

Secondly, the discussion forum is evaluated every week. The total number of responses based on the number of students in the class, content quality, and diversity of perspectives are some of the measures of success. A pertinent question from the session will be posted each week, inviting students to deliberate and submit their responses over the ensuing days. The forum will be showcased at the commencement of the following class, highlighting the number of contributions and recognizing the participating students. This interactive approach serves as a secondary means to gamify the classroom experience.

Lastly, for PBL, student feedback ratings and especially the mention of the PBL in the qualitative statements, student performance in terms of the number of distinctions and fails, and effective teamwork through non-participative observation are some ways the success of PBL is measured. In conclusion, the integration of gamification with PBL presents a promising avenue for enhancing student engagement and motivation. By grounding this approach in established educational theories and empirical evidence and carefully evaluating its impact, this initiative has the potential to make significant contributions to the field of education. The proposed solution involves designing a curriculum that embeds gamification elements such as points and leaderboards into PBL activities. It presents students with real-world problems relevant to their course material. Students will work in teams to solve these problems, with gamification elements providing motivation and a sense of achievement. Integrating digital tools and platforms will also be explored to facilitate this approach. The aim is to create an engaging, collaborative, and challenging learning environment that resonates with students' interests and learning styles. In pursuit of problem-based learning, every even-numbered session will introduce two practical problems tied to the session's topic, following an overview of the learning outcomes. I will provide a detailed exposition of the problems underpinned by the relevant theoretical and academic context. Midway through the class, students will be prompted to organize into teams to deliberate on the problems and formulate practical solutions. For example, during a session focused on 'Stakeholder Theory and Corporate Social Responsibility,' the problems presented will challenge students to apply their understanding in real-world scenarios. This transformative approach to education is not just a theoretical concept but a practical solution that can revolutionize the learning experience for students.

- *PBL 1: The Ethical Dilemma of Profit vs. Sustainability*

Your team is part of the management team of a fast-fashion company that has faced significant criticism for unsustainable practices and poor working conditions in its overseas factories. Historically, the company has prioritized profits and shareholder interests above all else, but now, it is under increasing pressure from various stakeholders to improve its corporate social responsibility (CSR). The unique aspect of this scenario is the need for a diverse team of five members with expertise in sustainability, human resources, supply chain management, marketing, and finance to develop a comprehensive plan that addresses these CSR concerns. The plan should balance the need for ethical practices with maintaining profitability. The team must consider the interests of a wide range of stakeholders, including employees, suppliers, consumers, local communities, shareholders, and NGOs, ensuring that the strategy is both socially responsible and economically viable. The team should also explore innovative solutions that align CSR with long-term business goals, such as sustainable sourcing, fair labor practices, transparent reporting, and consumer engagement strategies that promote ethical consumption.

- *PBL 2: Implementing CSR in a Resource-Limited Setting*

You are part of a small to medium-sized enterprise (SME) specializing in natural food products. The company is committed to improving its social and environmental impact but faces constraints due to limited resources. Any Corporate Social Responsibility (CSR) expenditure must be carefully justified to investors, prioritizing cost-effectiveness and return on investment. Form a dedicated team of 5 members to address this challenge and develop a comprehensive CSR strategy. The team's primary goal is maximizing social and environmental impact while ensuring financial prudence. They should identify key stakeholders, including customers, suppliers, local communities, and employees. Next, the team should propose targeted initiatives that offer tangible benefits to these stakeholders, such as sourcing sustainable ingredients, reducing waste, or supporting community health programs. Additionally, the team must prepare a persuasive pitch to demonstrate to investors how these initiatives align with the company's values, enhance its brand reputation, and ultimately contribute to long-term profitability. The pitch should emphasize the strategic advantages of CSR, including risk management, customer loyalty, and potential cost savings through sustainable practices.

5. CONCLUSION

This chapter has delved into the innovative integration of Gamification and PBL in educational settings, specifically focusing on enhancing authenticity and engagement among postgraduate students. The findings suggest that this blended approach can significantly improve the learning experience by making it more interactive, engaging, and relevant to real-world scenarios. Past research highlights that Gamification effectively increases student motivation and participation through game-design elements. However, its impact varies among individuals and requires careful implementation to ensure sustained effectiveness. PBL, on the other hand, has shown to be effective in fostering critical thinking, problem-solving skills, and self-directed learning. Its strength lies in encouraging students to apply knowledge spontaneously to new problems. The convergence of Gamification and PBL offers a promising solution to the challenge of student engagement in modern education. This approach fosters a learning environment where students are knowledgeable, genuinely interested, and involved in their education. Incorporating online game-based learning platforms and discussion forums as proposed interventions could enhance this model, providing varied and interactive learning experiences. Moving forward, the chapter emphasizes the need for further research to assess the long-term effectiveness of this blended approach. Empirical studies through the cross-section and longitudinal studies could provide deeper insights into the sustained impact of Gamification and PBL on student engagement and learning outcomes. Additionally, there is a potential to explore integrating digital tools and platforms to facilitate this approach, making it more accessible and adaptable to various educational contexts. By integrating Gamification with PBL presents an innovative pathway for enhancing student engagement and authenticity in educational settings. This approach, grounded in empirical evidence and educational theories, holds significant promise for transforming the learning experience for postgraduate students, making it more engaging, collaborative, and reflective of real-world challenges.

6. FUTURE RESEARCH SCOPE

The chapter provides a foundational understanding of the potential benefits of integrating Gamification and Problem-Based Learning in postgraduate education. However, the findings also open avenues for future research that could address the limitations encountered in this chapter and expand the understanding of this blended approach. One significant area for future research is exploring the long-term impact of Gamification and PBL on student engagement and learning outcomes. While this chapter has highlighted the immediate benefits, longitudinal studies are necessary to assess whether these effects are sustained over time. Such research could explore how prolonged exposure to Gamification and PBL influences student motivation, retention, and the development of critical thinking and problem-solving skills beyond the academic environment. Another potential research direction is the individual variability in response to Gamification. The chapter observed that while Gamification generally enhances engagement, its impact can vary among students. Future research could investigate the factors contributing to these differences, such as personality traits, learning styles, or previous exposure to gamified environments. Understanding these variables could help design more personalized and effective Gamification strategies catering to diverse student needs.

Additionally, there is a need to examine the integration of digital tools and platforms in this blended approach. The current chapter explored the potential of online game-based learning platforms and discussion forums to enhance student engagement. Future research could explore the effectiveness of these digital tools in different educational contexts, assessing how they can be tailored to fit various academic disciplines and student populations. Moreover, as technology evolves, it would be valuable to investigate the role of emerging technologies, such as virtual reality and AI-driven adaptive learning systems, in enhancing the Gamification-PBL model. It also raises questions about the scalability and accessibility of this blended approach. Future research could explore how Gamification and PBL can be implemented in larger, more diverse educational settings, including undergraduate programs and other educational institutions worldwide. Additionally, research could focus on the accessibility of these approaches for students with different abilities and backgrounds, ensuring that the benefits of this educational model are inclusive and widely available.

REFERENCES

Ab Rahman, R., Ahmad, S., & Hashim, U. R. (2019). A study on gamification for higher education students' engagement towards education 4.0. In *Intelligent and Interactive Computing: Proceedings of IIC 2018* (pp. 491-502). Springer Singapore.

Aderibigbe, S. A. (2020). Online discussions as an intervention for strengthening students' engagement in general education. *Journal of Open Innovation*, 6(4), 98. DOI: 10.3390/joitmc6040098

Alrashidi, O., Phan, H. P., & Ngu, B. H. (2016). Academic engagement: An overview of its definitions, dimensions, and significant conceptualizations. *International Education Studies*, 9(12), 41–52. DOI: 10.5539/ies.v9n12p41

Amerstorfer, C. M., & Freiin von Münster-Kistner, C. (2021). Student perceptions of academic engagement and student-teacher relationships in problem-based learning. *Frontiers in Psychology*, 12, 713057. DOI: 10.3389/fpsyg.2021.713057 PMID: 34777094

Bai, S., Hew, K. F., & Huang, B. (2020). Does gamification improve student learning outcomes? Evidence from a meta-analysis and synthesis of qualitative data in educational contexts. *Educational Research Review*, 30, 100322. DOI: 10.1016/j.edurev.2020.100322

Becker, S., Johnson, D., & Britton, P. (2019). Mapping the Challenges in Making the Transition to Taught Postgraduate Study in Psychology. *Psychology Teaching Review*, 25(1), 12–21. DOI: 10.53841/bpsptr.2019.25.1.12

Belland, B. R., Kim, C., & Hannafin, M. J. (2013). A framework for designing scaffolds that improve motivation and cognition. *Educational Psychologist*, 48(4), 243–270. DOI: 10.1080/00461520.2013.838920 PMID: 24273351

Brown, L. (2007). A consideration of the challenges involved in supervising international masters students. *Journal of Further and Higher Education*, 31(3), 239–248. DOI: 10.1080/03098770701424967

Castillo-Parra, B., Hidalgo-Cajo, B. G., Vásconez-Barrera, M., & Oleas-López, J. (2022). Gamification in Higher Education: A Review of the Literature. *World Journal on Educational Technology: Current Issues*, 14(3), 797–816. DOI: 10.18844/wjet.v14i3.7341

Chen, K. C., Wu, C. J., & Chen, G. D. (2011, July). A digital board game-based learning system for authentic learning. In *2011 IEEE 11th International Conference on Advanced Learning Technologies* (pp. 25-29). IEEE. DOI: 10.1109/ICALT.2011.16

Cheng, Y. P., Lai, C. F., Chen, Y. T., Wang, W. S., Huang, Y. M., & Wu, T. T. (2023). Enhancing student's computational thinking skills with student-generated questions strategy in a game-based learning platform. *Computers & Education*, 200, 104794. DOI: 10.1016/j.compedu.2023.104794

Chung, C. H., Shen, C., & Qiu, Y. Z. (2019). Students' acceptance of gamification in higher education. *International Journal of Game-Based Learning*, 9(2), 1–19. DOI: 10.4018/IJGBL.2019040101

Costa, F. A., Viana, J., & Raleiras, M. (2020, June). What do higher education students have to say about gamification? In *International Conference in Methodologies and Intelligent Systems for Technology Enhanced Learning* (pp. 56-65). Cham: Springer International Publishing.

Daniel, B. (2022). Common Challenges Postgraduate Students and Early-Career Academics face when Engaging with Scholarly Literature. *Electronic Journal of Business Research Methods*, 20(3), 142–152. DOI: 10.34190/ejbrm.20.3.2503

De Bruyckere, P., & Kirschner, P. A. (2017). Measuring teacher authenticity: Criteria students use in their perception of teacher authenticity. *Cogent Education*, 4(1), 1354573. DOI: 10.1080/2331186X.2017.1354573

Deterding, S., Dixon, D., Khaled, R., & Nacke, L. (2011). From game design elements to gratefulness: defining "gamification." In: *Proceedings of the 15th International Academic MindTrek Conference: Envisioning Future Media Environments*. Tampere, Finland, 28-30 September 2011. New York: ACM, pp. 9-15.

Dichev, C., & Dicheva, D. (2017). Gamifying education is a critical review of what is known, what is believed, and what remains uncertain. *International Journal of Educational Technology in Higher Education*, 14(1), 9. DOI: 10.1186/s41239-017-0042-5

Dietrich, T., & Balli, S. J. (2014). Digital Natives: Fifth-Grade Students' Authentic and Ritualistic Engagement with Technology. *International Journal of Instruction*, 7(2), 21–34.

Dolmans, D. H., De Grave, W., Wolfhagen, I. H., & Van Der Vleuten, C. P. (2005). Problem-based learning: Future challenges for educational practice and research. *Medical Education*, 39(7), 732–741. DOI: 10.1111/j.1365-2929.2005.02205.x PMID: 15960794

Domínguez, A., Saenz-de-Navarrete, J., de-Marcos, L., Fernández-Sanz, L., Pagés, C., & Martínez-Herráiz, J. J. (2013). Gamifying learning experiences: Practical implications and outcomes. *Computers & Education*, 63, 380–392. DOI: 10.1016/j.compedu.2012.12.020

Eseryel, D., Law, V., Ifenthaler, D., Ge, X., & Miller, R. (2014). Investigating the interrelationships between motivation, engagement, and complex problem-solving in game-based learning. *Journal of Educational Technology & Society*, 17(1), 42–53.

Eybers, S., & Hattingh, M. (2018). Enhancing Student Engagement: One Game at a Time. In *Innovative Technologies and Learning: First International Conference, ICITL 2018, Portoroz, Slovenia, August 27–30, 2018* [Springer International Publishing.]. *Proceedings*, 1, 231–240.

Fredricks, J. A., Blumenfeld, P. C., & Paris, A. H. (2004). School engagement: Potential of the concept, state of the evidence. *Review of Educational Research*, 74(1), 59–109. DOI: 10.3102/00346543074001059

Frego, K. A. (2006). Authenticity and relationships with students. *New adult and continuing education directions, 2006*(111), 41-50.

Grabinger, S., & Dunlap, J. C. (2002, October). Problem-based learning as an example of active learning and student engagement: Invited talk. In *International Conference on Advances in Information Systems* (pp. 375-384). Berlin, Heidelberg: Springer Berlin Heidelberg.

Greipl, S., Moeller, K., & Ninaus, M. (2020). Potential and limits of game-based learning. *International Journal of Technology Enhanced Learning*, 12(4), 363–389. DOI: 10.1504/IJTEL.2020.110047

Hamari, J., Koivisto, J., & Sarsa, H. 2014. Does gamification work? – A literature review of empirical studies on gamification. In: 2014 47th Hawaii International Conference on System Sciences. Waikoloa, HI, USA, 6-9 January 2014. IEEE, pp. 3025-3034.

Hmelo, C. E., & Ferrari, M. (1997). The problem-based learning tutorial: Cultivating higher order thinking skills. *Journal for the Education of the Gifted*, 20(4), 401–422. DOI: 10.1177/016235329702000405

Hmelo-Silver, C. E. (2004). Problem-based learning: What and how do students learn? *Educational Psychology Review*, 16(3), 235–266. DOI: 10.1023/B:EDPR.0000034022.16470.f3

Hung, D., Tan, S. C., & Koh, T. S. (2006). Engaged learning: Making learning an authentic experience. *Engaged learning with emerging technologies*, 29-48.

Hung, D., Tan, S. C., & Koh, T. S. (2006). From traditional to constructivist epistemologies: A proposed theoretical framework based on activity theory for learning communities. *Journal of Interactive Learning Research*, 17(1), 37–55.

Johnson, Z. D., & LaBelle, S. (2017). An examination of teacher authenticity in the college classroom. *Communication Education*, 66(4), 423–439. DOI: 10.1080/03634523.2017.1324167

Jones, H. (2017). Humanizing the Online Experience Through Effective Use and Analysis of Discussion Forums. In *Handbook of Research on Humanizing the Distance Learning Experience* (pp. 334–363). IGI Global. DOI: 10.4018/978-1-5225-0968-4.ch015

Kew, S. N., & Tasir, Z. (2021). Analysing Students' Cognitive Engagement in E-Learning Discussion Forums through Content Analysis. *Knowledge Management & E-Learning*, 13(1), 39–57.

Klipfel, K. M. (2014). Authentic engagement: Assessing the effects of authenticity on student engagement and information literacy in academic library instruction. *RSR. Reference Services Review*, 42(2), 229–245. DOI: 10.1108/RSR-08-2013-0043

Lilia, R., & Elena, T. (2019). Gamification is a field landmark in educational research. *Journal of language and education, 5*(3 (19)), 4-10.

Lindberg, S. (2019). Gamification for self-directed learning in higher education. In *EDULEARN19 Proceedings* (pp. 1764-1773). IATED. DOI: 10.21125/edulearn.2019.0507

Mace, K. (2005). Vygotsky's social development theory. Encyclopedia of Educational Technology.

Malm, B. (2008). Authenticity in teachers' lives and work: Some philosophical and empirical considerations. *Scandinavian Journal of Educational Research*, 52(4), 373–386. DOI: 10.1080/00313830802184525

McClure, J. W. (2001). Developing language skills and learner autonomy in international postgraduates. *ELT Journal*, 55(2), 142–148. DOI: 10.1093/elt/55.2.142

McDermott, R., Zarb, M., Daniels, M., Nylén, A., Pears, A., Isomöttönen, V., & Caspersen, M. (2017, October). The authenticity of 'authentic ' assessment of some faculty perceptions. In *2017 IEEE Frontiers in Education Conference (FIE)* (pp. 1-9). IEEE.

Mokoena, S. (2013). Engagement with and participation in online discussion Forums. *Turkish Online Journal of Educational Technology-TOJET*, 12(2), 97–105.

Murray, J., & Summerlee, A. (2007). The Impact of Problem-Based Learning in an Interdisciplinary First-Year Program on Student Learning Behaviour. *Canadian Journal of Higher Education*, 37(3), 87–107.

Noran, O. (2016, February). On gamification in action learning. In *Proceedings of the Australasian Computer Science Week Multiconference* (pp. 1-9).

Papastergiou, M. (2009). Digital game-based learning in high school computer science education impacts educational effectiveness and student motivation. *Computers & Education*, 52(1), 1–12. DOI: 10.1016/j.compedu.2008.06.004

Perrenet, J. C., Bouhuijs, P. A., & Smits, J. G. (2000). The suitability of problem-based learning for engineering education: Theory and practice. *Teaching in Higher Education*, 5(3), 345–358. DOI: 10.1080/713699144

Piaget, J. (1954). *The Construction of Reality in the Child*. Basic Books. DOI: 10.1037/11168-000

Ryan, R. M., & Deci, E. L. (2000). Self-determination theory and the facilitation of intrinsic motivation, social development, and well-being. *The American Psychologist*, 55(1), 68–78. DOI: 10.1037/0003-066X.55.1.68 PMID: 11392867

Sailer, M., Hense, J. U., Mayr, S. K., & Mandl, H. (2017). How gamification motivates: An experimental study of the effects of specific game design elements on psychological need satisfaction. *Computers in Human Behavior*, 69, 371–380. DOI: 10.1016/j.chb.2016.12.033

Salter, N. P., & Conneely, M. R. (2015). Structured and unstructured discussion forums as tools for student engagement. *Computers in Human Behavior*, 46, 18–25. DOI: 10.1016/j.chb.2014.12.037

Snape, P., & Fox-Turnbull, W. (2013). Perspectives of authenticity: Implementation in technology education. *International Journal of Technology and Design Education*, 23(1), 51–68. DOI: 10.1007/s10798-011-9168-2

Thompson, M. B. (2015). Authenticity in education: From narcissism and freedom to the messy interplay of self-exploration and acceptable tension. *Studies in Philosophy and Education*, 34(6), 603–618. DOI: 10.1007/s11217-015-9459-2

Waheed, N. (2017, July). Effects of an online discussion forum on student engagement and learning in a first-year undergraduate nursing unit: An action research study. In *Worldwide Nursing Conference* (pp. 18-25). GSTF Digital Library. DOI: 10.5176/2315-4330_WNC17.35

Walker, A., & Leary, H. (2009). A problem-based learning meta-analysis: Differences across problem types, implementation types, disciplines, and assessment levels. *The Interdisciplinary Journal of Problem-Based Learning*, 3(1), 12–43. DOI: 10.7771/1541-5015.1061

Williams, L., & Lahman, M. (2011). Online discussion, student engagement, and critical thinking. *Journal of Political Science Education*, 7(2), 143–162. DOI: 10.1080/15512169.2011.564919

Yang, Y. T. C., & Chang, C. H. (2013). Empowering students through digital game authorship: Enhancing concentration, critical thinking, and academic achievement. *Computers & Education*, 68, 334–344. DOI: 10.1016/j.compedu.2013.05.023

Young, S., & Tullo, E. (2020). From criminology to gerontology: Case studies of experiential authenticity in higher education. *Journal of Perspectives in Applied Academic Practice*, 8(1), 127–134. DOI: 10.14297/jpaap.v8i1.408

Appendix

1. The following is the HRM XXXX lecture planner taught to master's students. The table displays Gamification (OGBLP-Kahoot; Discussion Forum on LMS) with Problem-Based Learning (PBL) as an in-class exercise.

Table 1.

Week	Topic/Theme	Activity Details
1	Module Introduction	**OGBLP:** Icebreaker and subject overview quiz. **Discussion Forum:** What is Leadership? Who is your favorite leader, and why?
2	Competitive Strategy & Performance	**PBL:** Group project on Topic 1. **Discussion Forum:** What is strategy? Discuss a strategy followed by a company that touches your daily life.
3	Strategic HRM	**OGBLP:** Quiz on Topic 2. **Discussion Forum:** How does HRM create business value? Explain it using a real-life business example.
4	Leadership, Culture, and Change	**PBL:** Case study analysis on Topic 3. **Discussion Forum:** Analyse and compare two change management initiatives in the real-world business environment. Identify and examine the critical factors that led to their success and failure.
5	Assessment Briefing & Applying theory to practice support	**OGBLP:** Mid-module recap quiz. **Discussion Forum:** Provide an example of how the gap between theory and practice can be bridged in the HR profession.
6	The Macro Environment, Trends & Workforce Planning	**PBL:** Collaborative research on Topic 4. **Discussion Forum:** Explain the workforce strategy of any real-life business. Provide recommendations on how they can improve their workforce strategy for business success.
7	Ethical Lenses in People Management	**OGBLP:** Interactive game on Topic 5. **Discussion Forum:** What is an Ethical Dilemma? Provide an example of one from your own work experience. How did you resolve it?
8	Equality, Diversity & Inclusion	**PBL:** Develop a presentation on Topic 6. **Discussion Forum:** How can allyship be cultivated in the workplace to support DEI efforts, and what role do allies play in addressing systemic issues related to bias and discrimination?
9	Stakeholder theory and CSR	**OGBLP:** Themed quiz on Topic 7. **Discussion Forum:** How can companies balance the ethical Dilemma of Profit vs. Sustainability?
10	Employee Engagement and Authenticity	**PBL:** Group simulation exercise on Topic 8. **Discussion Forum:** How do you cultivate authenticity among your team members at the workplace?
11	Course Wrap-Up	**OGBLP:** Final review quiz. **Discussion Forum:** Reflect on the entire course journey.
12	Summative Session	-

Figure 1. The summary of the Discussion forum responses on the LMS with a total class size of 14.

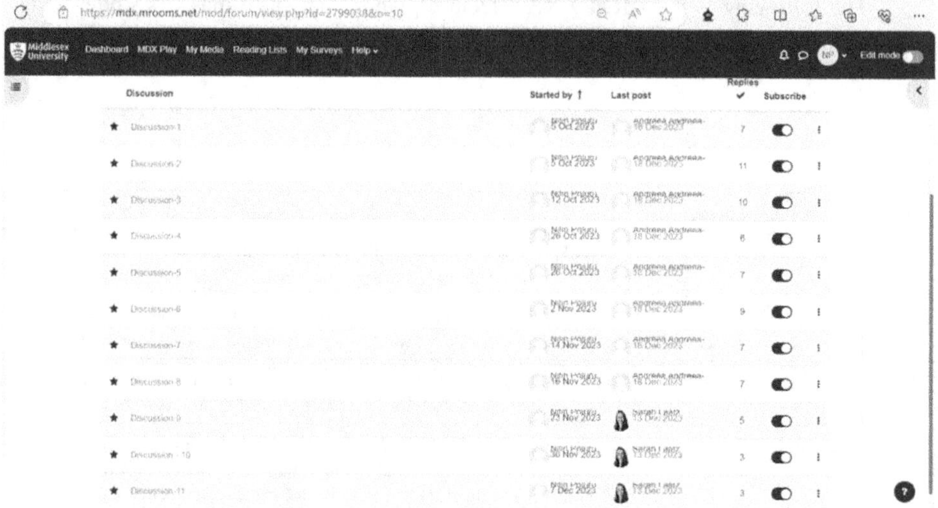

Figure 2. OGBLP using Kahoot explains the pre and post-gamified exercise conducted every alternate week.

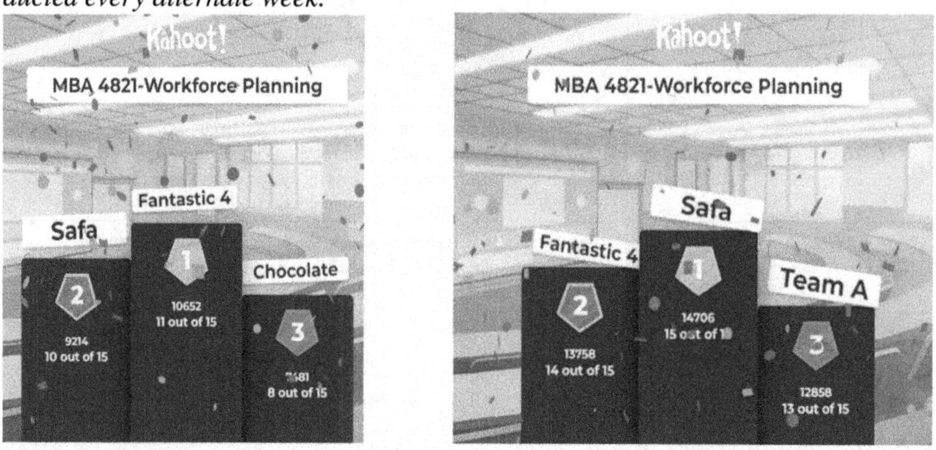

Pre **Post**

Chapter 3
Evaluation of Gamified Learning in Organizations:
A Study Based on Evidence From Private Sector Organizations in India

Jain Mathew
Christ University, India

Sridevi Nair
https://orcid.org/0000-0002-1529-4297
Christ University, India

ABSTRACT

Organisations are investigating the use of gamification to improve learning and development activities because they need tools to make learning more efficient and engaging. Additionally, because employee demographics are changing and there is a growing generation that is comfortable with and prefers technologically enhanced training methods, it is necessary to assess these methods. This study compares the effectiveness of gamified modules to regular modules using a pre-test-post-test control group design. The participants were randomly assigned to two groups. The results validate the theoretical framework of gamified learning, as evidenced by the higher scores obtained by the gamified module participants in terms of learning, reactivity, and learner motivation. The results further imply that the influence of gamification on the selected learning outcomes of learning and reaction was strongly mediated by learner motivation. The hypothesis of gamified learning is supported empirically

DOI: 10.4018/979-8-3693-8322-3.ch003

by the current investigation.

INTRODUCTION

The organizational context has seen a large number of changes over the last two decades. Organizations todays are becoming increasingly dependent on technology. Technology has changed the way an organization function. This change has been further accelerated by the COVID-19 pandemic. The COVID-19 pandemic changed the way we lived and worked. Organizations were forced to shift to remote working. This shift required organizations to invest in technological enhancements and create digital infrastructures. Technology entered every aspect of the organizational functioning and employees were forced to embrace it (Volberda et al., 2021).

This transition also coincided with a change in the employee demographics. This period saw a rise in the number of digital natives, individuals born into a technologically driven world and more adept at using technology compared to previous generations (Prensky, 2001). This demographic shift underscores the ongoing significance of technological advancements in shaping organizational practices. As digital natives become a larger part of the workforce, the need for organizations to stay updated with technological developments and adapt to changing environments becomes increasingly critical. This demographic trend suggests that technological changes will continue to be a driving force in organizational evolution, highlighting the importance of proactive adaptation to remain competitive in the modern business landscape.

One area of functioning that has been influenced by technology, and will continue be influenced, is learning. According to the Deloitte Global Capital Trends study, companies were seeking to reimagine organisational learning. Over 86% of the participants in the study said that their main area of focus will be learning. It was thought that in order to boost employee engagement and develop procedures that are more successful at disseminating knowledge, learning needed to be reinvented (Deloitte, 2019).

Gamification is one such method. It has been suggested that gamification can improve learning outcomes by influencing student attitudes and behaviours (Landers, 2014). Research has typically concentrated on examining gamification within the academic setting. But there's a good reason to investigate gamification in organisations given the problems presented by the current environment and the growing use of technology in the workplace. Despite a wealth of theoretical studies in the field, there is still a dearth of actual data to support gamification.

The objective of the current study is to give empirical support for the claim that gamification will improve learner motivation, comprehension, and attitude towards the process of learning. The study's foundation is the theory of gamified learning, and the researchers used an experimental design to verify their theories. Furthermore, the researchers have decided to concentrate solely on private organisations, taking their cue from the Technology Enhanced Training Effectiveness Model, or TETEM, which implies that effectiveness will vary with organisational features.

Review of Literature

Gamification, according to Deterding et al. (2011), is the practice of incorporating game characteristics into situations that aren't games. Similar to a game's fundamental components are game elements. Elements like leader boards, badges, points, and timers are now part of the ever-expanding list (Kapp, 2016). All games can, in theory, be reduced to a few fundamental components known as game elements. According to research, the effectiveness of a non-gaming context or process would increase if these aspects were applied to it. This would imply, in the context of learning, that utilising the components of a module would increase that module's effectiveness. Put differently, the game's components would improve the module and lead to more positive responses, learning motivation, and increased learning (Landers, 2014).

This is the central claim made by Landers (2014) in his Theory of Gamified Learning. Figure 1 provides a figurative depiction of the theory.

Figure 1 Theory of Gamified Learning

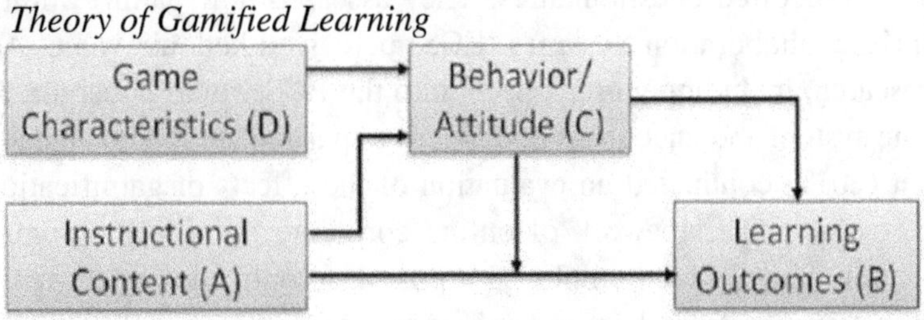

Source: Landers (2014)

According to the hypothesis, there are three key ways that the inclusion of game components could affect the learning outcomes. First, the inclusion of gaming components would influence the conduct and attitude of the learner. The literature on serious games contains empirical support for this claim (Hayes, Strosahl & Wilson, 2009). The second claim is that the direct correlation between the instructional content and the learning results would be moderated by gamification, or the inclusion of game components. The moderating role highlights an intriguing point:

while gamification is anticipated to influence learning outcomes, it is doubtful that applying game components alone will have the intended effects. The original course materials are still very important. The original content can only be improved via gamification.

A mediated relationship is discussed in the third proposition. Landers (2014) posits that gamification has the potential to modify the attitudes and behaviours of learners, thereby impacting the learning results. According to some, gamification's main purpose is this (Hamari, Koivisto, and Sarsa, 2014). Evidence for this association has been presented from a previous study conducted by Landers and Callan (2011). Since then, scientists have worked to assess this connection and have discovered statistical proof in favour of it.

Although most gamification research has been conducted in academic settings, some studies have looked at how gamification might affect learning results in the workplace. Participants in a gamified module reported higher levels of learning in the organisational setting compared to those who attended a standard training module (Trimblett, 2016; ONeill et. al., 2018; MacKinnon et. al., 2015; Andriamiarisoa, 2018). A pre-test, post-test control group design was employed by MacKinnon et al. (2015) to assess how gamification affected student motivation and learning. They discovered that the test group had learned more from the training and had reported higher levels of learner motivation. It has also been discovered that adding game features encourages behaviour modifications (Suh & Wagner, 2017; O'Neill et al., 2018). In order to determine if gamifying a knowledge management system will motivate staff members to share their expertise with peers, Suh and Wagner (2017) used structured questionnaires. They assessed how gamification affected an Enterprise Collaboration System's (ECS) perceived hedonic value. According to their research, including game aspects into the ECS would boost the perceived value of the system and encourage employees to participate in knowledge sharing.

Sargent (2017) conducted an evaluation of the effects of gamification on engagement within the framework of online corporate training programmes. The results of their study, which employed a post-test control group design, indicate that gamification significantly raised trainee engagement levels. When compared to the control group in their study, the test group reported noticeably higher levels of engagement. Additionally, Sargent (2017) discovered that the test group was more motivated to engage in training programmes, indicating that the incorporation of game features may boost learner motivation to engage in comparable programmes.

But according to Landers and Callan (2011), two sets of characteristics that have been found to mitigate this influence or link between gamification and learning outcomes, and are based on the technology enhanced training effectiveness model or TETEM. The first group consists of individual traits, such as video game experience and attitude towards game-based learning. Also referred to as the organisation variables, the second group of factors has to do with the training program's or learning experience's setting. These include the organization's culture and the supervisors' perceived level of support. This statement implies that the training module's efficacy would vary depending on the kind of organisation. The first group consists of individual traits, such as video game experience and attitude towards game-based learning. Also referred to as the organisation variables, the second group of factors has to do with the training program's or learning experience's setting. These include the organization's culture and the supervisors' perceived level of support. This statement implies that the training module's efficacy would vary depending on the kind of organisation.

As a result, the researchers decided to restrict the current study's focus to a single organisation category. The current study focused on assessing the impact of gamification in the private sector because Budhwar and Boyne (2004) discovered that public sector organisations had a considerably lower attitude towards training than their private sector counterparts.

Research Methodology

The current study assesses the effect of gamification on learning outcomes using a pre-test-post-test, control group design. Two groups will be formed as part of the design, and participants will be randomly assigned to one of the two groups. While one group received the therapy, the other would participate in a standard exercise regimen. The difference between the two groups' pre- and post-test results is used to assess learning. Both SPSS and Excel were used for the data analysis.

Sampling Technique

Employees of Indian private sector companies made up the sample for the current investigation. The HR teams in charge of each team chose the training module participants, and those teams got in touch with their respective HR managers. After being sorted into a group at random, they received comprehensive instructions on how to use the programme. After that, the participants would finish the programme by logging into the portal. There were 48 participants in one group and 51 in another for the final dataset.

The employee needed to be a member of the management cadre and have a basic command of the English language in order to be eligible for the programme. This guaranteed that the training course will be comprehended and applicable.

Training Module

The cloud-based Moodle platform was used to construct the training module. The goal of the module was to give the participants a fundamental knowledge of cognitive behavioural training. The course outlined the relationship between ideas, feelings, and actions as well as how a person may use their thoughts to enhance their performance in both their personal and professional spheres. The participants had two questionnaires to fill out and two exams to finish during the module—one before and one after. The first survey assessed learner motivation and provided an explanation of the program's structure. The response to the programme was measured by the second survey.

In terms of content, both programmes were comparable. The gamified module was different in terms of flow, structure, and the use of game elements to improve the tasks. The gamified curriculum contained levels, and the learner had to finish a quick evaluation in order to advance through a level. After finishing a level successfully, the player received a badge that they could then place on their profile. Leaderboards, powerups, and timed exercises were all included in the gamified programme. These were added with the help of the quizzes app. It took the participants, on average, two hours to finish the programme.

Instruments

Ten-point tests covering the subject were used for both the pre- and post-tests. Reaction was assessed using a device that was borrowed from Brown (2005). There were two items measuring the perceived relevance of the programme and three measuring satisfaction with the technology employed in the instrument. Zaniboni et al. (2011) used the T-VIES-it to measure learner motivation. Three dimensions made up the instrument: valence (three items), expectancy (three items), and instrumentality (three items). Instrumentality is the extent to which a student believes that their success in the training programme will transfer into success in the workplace. Expectancy is the belief that training will result in a successful performance, and Valence is the value one believes one will receive from taking part in the training programme.

Results and Findings

The first step in the analysis involved the descriptive statistics if the variables. The Skewness and Kurtosis values suggested that the data may be considered normal (Kline, 2005). Results of the descriptive statistics can be found in Table 1

Table 1. Descriptive Statistics

	Mean	Std. Deviation	Skewness	Kurtosis
L	1.91	2.14	0.12	-0.15
R	4.16	0.64	-1.11	2.37
M	4.35	0.62	-1.30	2.36

In order to evaluate the difference in the Learning, Reaction and Motivation levels, the researchers used the independent samples t-test to compare the means. Results of the analysis have been provided in Table 2. T1 refers to the pre test scores of the participants. The difference in mean scores for the pre test was not found to be significant. This was checked to ensure that it was safe to assume that random assignment was carried out. There was a significant difference in the mean scores for Reaction, Learning and Learner Motivation ($p<0.05$).

Table 2. Independent Sample t-test

Gamified		N	Mean	Std. Deviation	Std. Error Mean	t	Sig. (2-tailed)
T1	0	51.00	4.76	1.55	0.22	-1.58	0.12
	1	48.00	5.38	2.28	0.33		
R	0	51.00	4.00	0.64	0.09	-2.67	0.01
	1	48.00	4.33	0.59	0.09		
M	0	51.00	4.20	0.68	0.10	-2.39	0.02
	1	48.00	4.50	0.51	0.07		
L	0	51.00	1.19	2.07	0.29	-3.64	0.00
	1	48.00	2.67	1.96	0.28		

In order to evaluate the proposed relationship between Gamification, Learning, Reaction and Learner Motivation, the researcher first evaluated the Correlation between the variables. The correlation matrix can be found Table 3. For the purpose of evaluating the relationship, Gamification was treated as a dummy variable, Gamified, with 1 indicating that the module was Gamified and 0 indicating that there were no game elements used. All the correlations were found to be significant, with $p<0.05$. The strongest relationship was found to be between Learning and Gamification, followed by Gamification and Reaction.

Table 3. Correlation Matrix

		L	R	M	Gamified
L	Pearson Correlation	1			
	Sig. (2-tailed)				
R	Pearson Correlation	.218*	1		
	Sig. (2-tailed)	.030			
M	Pearson Correlation	.266**	.347**	1	
	Sig. (2-tailed)	.008	.000		
Gamified	Pearson Correlation	.347**	.262**	.236*	1
	Sig. (2-tailed)	.000	.009	.019	

The relationship was further explored using the Hayes macros. The analysis evaluated the proposed direct and indirect relationships. The results of the mediation analysis have been summarised in Table 4. The direct and indirect relationship between Gamification and Learning were found to be significant suggesting that Learner Motivation partially mediated the relationship. Similarly, in the case of the relationship between Gamification and Reaction also, Learner motivation was found to strengthen the effect.

Table 4. Mediation Analysis

	Effect	T	p		Total Effect	BootLLCI	BootULCI
G=>L	1.279	3.11	0.002	G=>M=>L	1.475	0.0020	0.4839
G=>R	0.242	1.97	0.05	G=>M=>R	0.332	0.0117	0.2210

Discussion

Employees will only remain loyal to the organization as long as they receive as much or more than what they give; and financial benefits can only go so far in winning loyalty (Phuong & Tran, 2020). Thus, in the search for intangible benefits that can improve loyalty and at the same ensure effectiveness, organizations have come to realise the importance of Learning and Training.

The growing importance of learning in the organization has led to the search for ways to increase the efficiency of learning processes and at the same time make the activity more engaging for the employees. One technique that has been suggested by researchers is gamification. The theory of gamified learning suggests that enhancing the instructional content with game elements would impact the learner's behaviour and attitude towards the learning process; and thereby impact the learning outcomes

(Landers, 2014). Empirical evidence for this relationship can be found in literature (Landers and Callan, 2011). However, the evidence has mainly been gathered from the academic context and the few studies in the organizational context, have not taken into account the type of organization and the culture of the organization while evaluating the role of gamification.

The researchers decided to investigate the variables of reactivity, learning, and learner motivation in order to assess the efficacy of gamification. The study used a pre-test-post-test control group design, with individuals randomly allocated to one of the two groups. A t test for independent samples was used to compare the scores. According to the findings, the participants in the gamified module responded better to the training, had higher levels of motivation, and saw a bigger rise in their knowledge. As a result, the gamified module participants outperformed the conventional module participants on all three measures.

The association between the variables was then investigated by the researchers using the notion of gamified learning. Gamification was entered as a dummy variable for the analysis's purposes, with '1' denoting the existence of game components and '0' denoting their absence. The correlation analysis's findings indicate that gamification and the dependent variables of learning, response, and learner motivation have a strong positive association. The researchers were able to continue with the regression analysis as a result. The impact of gamification on learning was found to be strengthened by learner motivation; that is, more knowledge was acquired from the training programme as a consequence of increased learner motivation, which was a direct result of gamification.

The theory of gamified learning posits that gamification will improve learning outcomes and increase student motivation (Landers, 2014). This was evaluated using SPSS's Hayes macros (Hayes, 2018). The results showed that a significant mediating factor in the relationship was learner motivation. The association between gamification, learner motivation, and reaction showed a comparable impact. Gamification directly impacted how the trainee responded to the training course. It was discovered that the indirect association was much stronger. Gamification was therefore able to enhance the trainee's response to the programme by raising their motivation to engage in it. The notion of gamified learning has also put forth and tested this relationship (Landers and Callan, 2011).

The findings of the study provide empirical evidence for the propositions of the theory of gamified learning. The findings also provide support for the use of gamified learning in organizations. For trainers and organizations, the significant improvement in learning outcomes would encourage the use of gamified modules in training programs. Gamification provides organizations with a technique that is economical, given the growing number of gamification tools online that can be used to enhance training content. Additionally, the mediating role of learner motivation provides a guide for designing gamified modules. Given that gamification is the process of enhancing the instructional module by adding game elements, the strong mediating role of learner motivation would suggest that special focus must be given to the identification and application of game elements that are likely to increase the learner's motivation to participate in the training program. If one were to follow the Octalysis framework, this would imply focussing on the white hat drivers and applying elements that would enable skill mastery, provide a sense of meaning and ownership accomplishment (Chou, 2019).

Implications

The current study evaluated the effectiveness of gamification in the context of training and development in organizations. Prior research has established that gamification can significantly enhance the learner experience and thereby the outcomes of a learning experience. However, research on the application of gamification to a learning experience at the workplace was missing. This study fills that particular gap and the findings suggest that gamification can significantly improve an individual's motivation to participate in a training module and also enhance learning outcomes. The findings of the study suggest that knowledge retention and trainee reaction to a program are significantly higher when the learning program is gamified. Thus, organizations should harness the power of gamification improve the effectiveness of their training program.

The current study also highlights the critical role of learner motivation. Learner motivation was found to significantly strengthen the impact of a gamified module. This would suggest that understanding the audience and targeting the factors that motivate will improve the effectiveness of a training program. This is further supported by the Octalysis framework. The framework suggest that all human behaviour is a product of eight core drives. By designing any learning intervention by identifying and targeting a core drive of the audience, the effectiveness of the intervention will be improved. Thus, the key aspect in designing is understanding the motivators of the target audience. This is a significant finding for both practitioners, looking to apply gamification in their training efforts, and for researchers looking to study the field further.

Lastly, this intervention was carried out with tools available easily and freely. This would suggest that contrary to popular belief that gamification is expensive, it need not be. Gamification is the process of adding game elements to enhance a non-game experience. In order to do so, understanding the audience is far more critical. This would ensure that the right elements are chosen and applied. This can be done in an economical manner. The objective is to enhance the instructional material and not to overpower it (Mathew & Nair, 2024).

Scope for Future Research

The current study's findings lend support to the use of gamification in training. The present study indicates that gamification can have a positive effect on learning outcomes in businesses when taken into account in conjunction with previous studies on the efficacy of gamified learning. Future studies, however, might examine how successful gamification is in various kinds of businesses. Future research may potentially concentrate solely on assessing the efficacy of gamification across various industries.

It is also necessary to investigate the second set of factors that TETEM suggests. It is necessary to assess the moderating impact of individual traits such as video game experience and attitude towards gamified learning. The combination of digital immigrants and natives in the workforce makes this even more crucial.

Limitations

The programme was delivered online and there was no direct interaction between the participants, the organisation, or the researchers and so there was a complete reliance on technology. While the majority of staff members managed, some had technical issues. The requirement that the trainees own laptops directly also restricted the number of participants. Previously, more people may have participated if they had had access to organisational resources and labs. However, the researchers' success in overcoming the majority of these obstacles can be attributed to the unwavering support that they received from the collaborating organisations.

Pre-test-post-test control group designs are a popular research technique for assessing an intervention's or treatment's efficacy. Participants in this design are randomised to either the experimental group, which gets the intervention, or the control group, which doesn't. Both groups are evaluated on the outcome variable, also known as the pre-test, prior to the intervention's implementation. A post-test is used to reassess both groups on the same outcome variable following the intervention. Researchers can ascertain the impact of the intervention by comparing the differences in scores between the experimental and control groups between the pre- and post-tests. This design helps control for potential confounding variables and increases the internal validity of the study. However, it is important to consider limitations such as maturation, history, selection bias, attrition, and sensitization, which can affect the validity and generalizability of the findings. Maturation refers to the natural changes that may occur in the participants as a function of age. To counter the same, the duration of the program was kept short. This also protected from any external events that could impact the results or history. Given that the study occurred during the uncertain period of the pandemic, this was a big concern.

Additionally, the act of taking the pre-test could affect the results in the post-test. This is known as pre-test sensitisation. To some extent this is mitigated by random assignment of participants to the control and experimental group. This also reduced the threats associated with selection bias and attrition.

CONCLUSION

Applying game characteristics to a situation that isn't a game is known as gamification. Upon the concept's initial rise to prominence, practitioners swiftly employed it to address their training requirements and other contexts. Nevertheless, the application was completed without a thorough comprehension of the build. Landers (2019) emphasised the need of acknowledging that gamification, while connected to games, is unique in numerous aspects. Research has typically concentrated on assessing gamification's efficacy in educational settings. By assessing the impact within the framework of organisational training, the current study contributes to the body of literature. Furthermore, this study is different from earlier studies because the researchers only included the private sector in their study's scope.

The results of the research are consistent with the ideas put forth by the gamified learning paradigm. Learning, response, and learner motivation scores were considerably higher among the gamified module participants. The purpose of the second portion of the study was to determine how the constructs related to one another. The results imply that the relationship between gamification and the learning outcomes of learning and reaction was considerably enhanced by learner motivation. Therefore, gamification raises learner motivation, which in turn improves learning and response to the training programme, as suggested by the theory of gamified learning.

REFERENCES

Barney, J. (1991). Competitive Advantage. *Journal of Management*, 17(1), 99–120. DOI: 10.1177/014920639101700108

Brown, K. G. (2005). An examination of the structure and nomological network of trainee reactions: A closer look at" smile sheets. *The Journal of Applied Psychology*, 90(5), 991–1001. DOI: 10.1037/0021-9010.90.5.991 PMID: 16162071

Budhwar, P. S., & Boyne, G. (2004). Human resource management in the Indian public and private sectors: An empirical comparison. *International Journal of Human Resource Management*, 15(2), 346–370. DOI: 10.1080/0958519032000158554

Chou, Y. K. (2019). *Actionable gamification: Beyond points, badges, and leaderboards*. Packt Publishing Ltd.

Deloitte. (2019). Deloitte Global Human Capital Trends. Retrieved 2 July 2020, from https://www2.deloitte.com/content/dam/insights/us/articles/5136_HC-Trends-2019/DI_HC-Trends-2019.pdf

Deterding, S., Dixon, D., Khaled, R., & Nacke, L. (2011). From game design elements to gamefulness: defining "Gamification". MindTrek '11, Proceedings from the 15th International Academic MindTrek Conference: Envisioning Future Media Environments, (pp. 9-15). DOI: 10.1145/2181037.2181040

Hamari, J., Koivisto, J., & Sarsa, H. (2014, January). Does gamification work?--a literature review of empirical studies on gamification. In 2014 47th Hawaii international conference on system sciences (pp. 3025-3034). Ieee.

Hayes, A. F. (2018). Partial, conditional, and moderated moderated mediation: Quantification, inference, and interpretation. *Communication Monographs*, 85(1), 4–40. DOI: 10.1080/03637751.2017.1352100

Hayes, S. C., Strosahl, K. D., & Wilson, K. G. (2009). *Acceptance and commitment therapy*. American Psychological Association.

Kapp, K. M. (2016). Gamification designs for instruction. In *Instructional-Design Theories and Models* (Vol. IV, pp. 367–400). Routledge.

Kline, T. J. (2005). *Psychological testing: A practical approach to design and evaluation*. Sage Publications. DOI: 10.4135/9781483385693

Landers, R. N. (2014). Developing a theory of gamified learning: Linking serious games and gamification of learning. *Simulation & Gaming*, 45(6), 752–768. DOI: 10.1177/1046878114563660

Landers, R. N. (2019). Gamification misunderstood: How badly executed and rhetorical gamification obscures its transformative potential. *Journal of Management Inquiry*, 28(2), 137–140. DOI: 10.1177/1056492618790913

Landers, R. N., & Armstrong, M. B. (2015). Enhancing instructional outcomes with gamification: An empirical test of the Technology-Enhanced Training Effectiveness Model. *Computers in Human Behavior*, 71, 499–507. DOI: 10.1016/j.chb.2015.07.031

Landers, R. N., & Callan, R. C. (2011). Casual social games as serious games: The psychology of gamification in undergraduate education and employee training. In *Serious games and edutainment applications* (pp. 399–423). Springer. DOI: 10.1007/978-1-4471-2161-9_20

MacKinnon, R. J., Stoeter, R., Doherty, C., Fullwood, C., Cheng, A., Nadkarni, V., Stenfors-Hayes, T., & Chang, T. P. (2015). Self-motivated learning with gamification improves infant CPR performance, a randomised controlled trial. *BMJ Simulation & Technology Enhanced Learning*, 1(3), 71–76. DOI: 10.1136/bmjstel-2015-000061 PMID: 35515202

Mathew, J., & Nair, S. (2024). *Level up your learning: The power of gamification.* Nova Science Publishers. DOI: 10.52305/UIFH5384

ONeill, K., Robb, M., Kennedy, R., Bhattacharya, A., Dominici, N. R., & Murphy, A. (2018). Mobile Technology, Just-in-Time Learning and Gamification: Innovative Strategies for a CAUTI Education Program. *On-Line Journal of Nursing Informatics*, 22(2).

Phuong, T. T. K., & Tran, T. V. (2020). Job Satisfaction, Employee Loyalty and Job Performance in the Hospitality Industry: A Moderated Model. *Asian Economic and Financial Review*, 10(6), 698–713. DOI: 10.18488/journal.aefr.2020.106.698.713

Sargent, R. (2017). Gamifying Self-Assessments in Online Corporate Training: Points and Levels (Doctoral dissertation, Northcentral University).

Senge, P. M., Carstedt, G., & Porter, P. L. (2001). Next industrial revolution. *MIT Sloan Management Review*, 42(2), 24–38.

Suh, A., & Wagner, C. (2017). How gamification of an enterprise collaboration system increases knowledge contribution: An affordance approach. *Journal of Knowledge Management*, 21(2), 416–431. DOI: 10.1108/JKM-10-2016-0429

Trimblett, S. M. (2016). Gamification in nursing jurisprudence (Doctoral dissertation, Royal Roads University (Canada).

Volberda, H. W., Khanagha, S., Baden-Fuller, C., Mihalache, O. R., & Birkinshaw, J. (2021). Strategizing in a digital world: Overcoming cognitive barriers, reconfiguring routines and introducing new organizational forms. *Long Range Planning*, 54(5), 102110. DOI: 10.1016/j.lrp.2021.102110

Zaniboni, S., Fraccaroli, F., Truxillo, D. M., Bertolino, M., & Bauer, T. N. (2011). Training valence, instrumentality, and expectancy scale (T-VIES-it). *Journal of Workplace Learning*, 23(2), 133–151. DOI: 10.1108/13665621111108792

Chapter 4
Gamification as a Pedagogical Innovation in Architectural Education:
A Literature Review

Ömer Faruk Bayraktarlı
https://orcid.org/0000-0002-5961-3042
Sakarya University, Turkey

Semra Arslan Selçuk
Gazi University, Turkey

ABSTRACT

Gamification has emerged as a valuable tool in addressing evolving demands within the ever-changing field of architecture education. This chapter explores its potential in higher education programs, focusing on how it complements traditional teaching. Through a literature review of studies indexed in the Web of Science, findings show that while gamification boosts motivation and learning outcomes, it also poses challenges like sustaining engagement and addressing diverse learners. Despite its benefits, such as enhanced problem-solving and hands-on learning, large-scale studies are needed to examine potential drawbacks, including oversimplification. If its effects are examined more, it will provide educators with enough material so that people can use this study to learn and apply it better. Ongoing research is crucial to fully harness gamification for developing creative, effective future architects.

DOI: 10.4018/979-8-3693-8322-3.ch004

1. INTRODUCTION

With the constant change in architectural education, gamification has emerged as a significant pedagogical innovation to enrich students' overall learning experience and boost their commitment through game design elements or some other overlapping systems with game contexts. The growing use of digital tools and technologies in education, especially in architecture, has made it necessary to explore new ways to meet the digital generation's demands and tastes. This publication aims to understand how gamification practices can be integrated within architectural education to provide compelling motivational and educational outcomes for students in higher educational settings. Shifts in paradigms are required, leading to the exploration of new ways of what education needs to be or should have been at the hands of a digital generation.

Implementing gamification in universities has been hailed for improving the learning and retention of traditional lessons. However, there is also a prospect for them to gain proficiency in theoretical knowledge in near practical areas. Architecture education is one of the most comprehensive academics, especially in design-focused disciplines, as it combines many technical and creative elements. However, as built, it is a discipline that challenges whenever the abstract touches the concrete. Gamification helps solve these difficulties by enabling students to experience theoretical ideas through simulated real-world scenarios. This fosters critical thinking and challenges students in problem-solving, teamwork, and time management skills.

Architectural education has the province to shape how students view space and expose them to various aspects of utilizing it in creating sustainable creation pieces to give us distinctive functionally aesthetic spaces that can also serve a purpose. Integrating gamification with architectural education can create a more liberated environment, which helps architecture students to be creative in an unlimited way and get out of their comfort zone without having any side effects on these experiments when dealing with real-world architectural projects. Through gamification techniques like simulations, digital design competitions, and interactive learning modules, we nudge students to participate actively in both individual and a collaborative work/learning environment. Interactions like these encourage such critical thinking skills in students since it helps them to approach a design problem they are solving from different angles.

The quickly evolving technological environment drives home the urgent necessity of reform in architectural education. Architecture is changing with new digital tools and methodologies, and architectural education must change, too. Gamification represents a potentially powerful pedagogical approach to solving such problems by using the motivational techniques of game design in non-game contexts with learners.

This chapter will comprehensively review gamification's impacts on architectural education within higher education. It seeks to assess work available in the literature and practice, documenting how gamification strategies have been used and their educational implications. This paper undertakes to review the three dimensions mentioned earlier of gamification: (a) motivational gram aspects, (b) cognitive enhancement dimensions, and dedicatedly discover whether the traditional methodologies of teaching then could be transformed as more attractive, engrossing — indeed engaging a learning experience.

Here, a systematic literature review is conducted to comprehensively synthesize the existing knowledge base using scholarly articles and conference papers indexed in the Web of Science (WOS) database. The search strategy is informed by keywords architecture education and gamification to include studies that vary significantly in how they may describe the integration of game elements in architectural education. This methodological process allows us to analyze and review theoretical foci, empirical evidence, and critical debates with respect to the integration of gamification in architectural learning experiences.

With the use of game elements in architectural education, an opportunity to better implement theoretical knowledge into practice is opening up. The role of gamification in changing architectural education has been proven by several case studies that showed how it could help design game-based and more interactive learning environments.

On the other hand, since the problem-solving and teamwork-based structure of architectural education and architectural practice overlap considerably with playing games, evaluating gamification in education through architecture will significantly contribute to the literature. In addition, the digitalization of architecture and gaming tools are similar in replacing concrete elements with abstract and 3D thinking. Most importantly, both practices involve learning that is primarily in line with the instructions.

In this context, the theoretical foundations of gamification will be discussed first. In this section, what gamification is/is not, the components of gamification, and the theories of gamification will be mentioned. Then, gamification in education and its positive and negative effects will be presented. The following section will examine the general characteristics of architectural education. Mastering the basic building blocks of architectural education is essential to understanding innovative movements such as digitalization and gamification in education. Implementing gamification in architectural education will be evaluated through case studies. In the final part of the study, academic publications and empirical studies are gathered as evidence to discuss gamification's possible power and risks on architectural education.

Finally, based on noting the potential benefits of gamification, this paper answers how game-based elements can be applied in architecture education as interactive tools that increase effectiveness and efficiency in teaching. Therefore, it helps to create a generation of well-trained experts who can develop innovative solutions.

2. THEORETICAL BACKGROUND OF GAMIFICATION

2.1. Gamification

The notion of "gamification" first emerged in the realm of computer games in 2002, with general interest starting to pick up around 2010 (Looyestyn et al., 2017). In its modern sense, gamification is coined as "the use of game-based mechanics, aesthetics and game thinking to engage people, motivate action, promote learning and solve problems."(Kapp, 2012), it has been the subject of an immense amount of research in recent years (Babu & Moorthy, 2023; Deterding et al., 2011). Also, Kapp (2012) emphasizes the application of "game-based mechanics, aesthetics, and game thinking to engage individuals, inspire action, enhance learning, and resolve problems."

Gamification aims to apply game design principles, elements, and mechanisms in non-game contexts to elicit specific behaviors in individuals and enhance their motivation and engagement in a given task. (Pedreira et al., 2015).

Game-based learning and serious games are fundamentally similar concepts to gamification. Game-based learning focuses on achieving specific learning objectives through game content and play. It enhances education by integrating areas for problem-solving and challenges that provide a sense of accomplishment for students in the player role (Qian & Clark, 2016). Its primary aim is education. It typically relies on comprehensive games, often referred to as serious games. While designed for various serious purposes such as industry, training, or simulation, serious games extend beyond education (Alsawaier, 2018; Connolly et al., 2012). While game-based learning and serious games are distinct from gamification, constituting fully developed games (Deterding et al., 2011), gamification broadly applies game components to real-world environments. All these concepts aim to utilize positive, gameful experiences to serve serious purposes, such as education or behavior modification, rather than merely focusing on entertainment (Krath et al., 2021).

2.2. Elements of Gamification

Gamification is not a game but a technique that integrates game-like elements into real-world contexts. Its primary goal is to motivate individuals to engage in tasks that may initially appear unappealing, such as academic assignments. (Deterding et al., 2011). The critical elements of its implementation are outlined as follows (Kapp, 2012; Marín et al., 2021; Zichermann & Cunningham, 2011):

- The game's foundation: The opportunity to play and learn alongside a challenge that stimulates engagement. Concurrently, it is crucial to establish clear game rules, foster interactivity, and provide consistent feedback.
- Mechanics: The specific elements of the game concerning data representation and the underlying algorithms
- Dynamics: The mechanics' real-time behavior as they respond to player inputs and interact with each other's outputs over time.
- Aesthetics: The desirable emotional responses the player elicits when interacting with the game system.
- Concept of the Game: Through these game mechanics, players receive information, some of which may be perceived only subconsciously. This enables players to simulate certain real-life activities within a virtual environment, thereby acquiring skills that they previously lacked.
- Game-Player Connection: the bond between the player and the game that fosters engagement
- Promoting Learning: Strategies aimed at improving learning through gameplay, such as awarding points and offering feedback for corrections.
- Problem Solving: The player's ultimate goal or objective must be pursued throughout the game dynamic.

2.2. Gamification Theories

Gamification is founded on various concepts and theories, often closely linked to social science. Indeed, numerous studies draw upon well-established social science theories such as Motivation Theory, Self-Determination Theory, Achievement Goal Theory, and Flow Theory. (Kim et al., 2018; Matallaoui et al., 2017). This section provides a detailed overview of theories that have attempted to elucidate user behavior and experience.

Motivation is a critical factor influencing the success of gamification. (Sailer et al., 2017). It encompasses the biological, emotional, social, and cognitive forces that drive behavior. (Nevid, 2007). Commonly, the basis of motivation theory lies in physiological needs, divided into two categories: homeostasis, which pertains to the body's automatic attempts to sustain a stable internal environment, and appetites, which are about supplying the body with essential resources. (Maslow, 1969).

Self-Determination Theory (SDT) is a broad framework for studying human motivation that has been adapted to educational settings and considers an individual's autonomy about their motivation and what happens within social or cultural contexts. SDT posits that all human beings are fundamentally motivated by the satisfaction of three basic psychological needs: autonomy, competence, and relatedness (Kim et al., 2018). Competence is mainly linked to motivation; when individuals believe they can perform a task well, they experience intrinsic motivation. (Sarı et al., 2015). After all, if a task is overly simplistic, individuals might not experience a sense of competence. Tasks should be challenging yet achievable with the individual's current abilities to foster a sense of competence. (Park et al., 2017).

Achievement Goal Theory posits that individuals are driven by their beliefs or aspirations to reach specific goals (Kim et al., 2018). Consequently, gamification designers have theorized that games can significantly enhance user engagement. However, these elements must be skillfully integrated and categorized to promote the desired behaviors. effectively (Matallaoui et al., 2017).

Flow Theory is grounded in the principles of positive psychology and primarily emphasizes intrinsic strengths (Matallaoui et al., 2017). Seligman and Csikszentmihalyi describe flow theory as "the study of positive emotion, positive character, and positive institutions." (Seligman & Csikszentmihalyi, 2000). Csikszentmihalyi asserts that completing a task without experiencing boredom or frustration leads to happiness. He explains this phenomenon through Flow Theory, which identifies the optimal experience as the flow state—a condition where individuals voluntarily engage in an activity with complete immersion and enjoyment (Csikszentmihalyi, 2008).

2.3. Gamification Design

Games are products created by designers and development teams and consumed by players. They are purchased, used, and eventually consumed like any other consumable. The MDA (Mechanics, Dynamics, Aesthetics) framework systematizes the consumption process of games by breaking them down into their essential components. The 'Mechanics' part describes the specific components of the game at the level of data representation and algorithms. 'Dynamics' describes how the inputs from the player and their interactions play out over time, i.e., the runtime behavior of the mechanics. 'Aesthetics' refers to the emotional responses the player experiences when interacting with the game systems. Each component of the MDA framework represents a different but causally related aspect of the game. (Hunicke et al., 2004).

The main idea underlying this framework is that games are more like works of art than simple media products. In this context, game content is not considered a passive flow of media but a form of behavior in which the player actively interacts.

Game Mechanics

Game mechanics describe the game's specific components at the data representation level, and algorithms can significantly influence user motivation and engagement (Hunicke et al., 2004). It is essential to distinguish between game mechanics and game rules; game mechanics define the basic operation of the game, while the rules determine acceptable behavior within the framework of these mechanics. For example, leveling up is a mechanic that allows players to progress through the system, but the game rules determine the specific behaviors that trigger this progression. Here are some common game mechanics (Hunicke et al., 2004; Matallaoui et al., 2017):

Points: Components that reward users for achieving specific goals within the system. These rewards encourage players to progress within the system.

Leaderboards: Tools that allow users to see their own performance compared to other players. These boards need to be designed carefully, as the goal is to encourage competition and motivation for players.

Levels: Indicators that show the user's progress within the game. Levels do not always progress linearly, and designers sometimes integrate alternative mechanisms such as badge systems to show progress.

Achievement Systems: 'Meta-quests' that provide users with additional goals outside of the main goals in the system. These systems provide players with variety, enriching the gameplay experience and encouraging long-term engagement.

Game Dynamics

Game dynamics refers to mechanics' runtime behavior that determines how they evolve as player inputs and outputs interact. (Hunicke et al., 2004). These dynamics form the basis of users' motivational behavior toward game mechanics. Therefore, game and gamification designers must target and satisfy different users' typical desires and needs. Here are some of these common desires (Hunicke et al., 2004; Matallaoui et al., 2017):

Rewards: These rewards motivate people to do a certain action or exhibit a desired behavior again after performing it.

Status: Most people naturally seek attention, recognition, and status. Therefore, people need to engage in activities to gain prestige and respect.

Achievement and Goal Setting: Most people need to complete certain tasks and achieve goals. This often encourages them to seek out new challenges and set achievable goals.

Self-Expression: It allows people to show their uniqueness and difference from others.

Competition: Helps people improve their performance and achieve higher levels of success. Comparing with others is a source of motivation and satisfaction for many people.

These common desires provide essential insights into how game dynamics should be designed, and game designers can develop strategies to influence and engage players using these motivators.

Aesthetics

Aesthetics describe the desired emotional responses when a player interacts with a game system. Within the MDA framework, these emotional responses can increase motivation and engagement. As Hunicke et al. (2004) have noted, that aesthetics consists of 8 elements, namely:

Sensation: The game is a source of sensory pleasure; visual and auditory aesthetics emotionally appeal to players.

Fantasy: The game escapes reality and immerses players in imaginary worlds.

Narrative: The game tells a story and includes dramatic structure, character development, and conflict.

Challenge: The game presents players with challenges that are satisfying when overcome.

Fellowship: The game creates an environment of social interaction and encourages cooperation and competition between players.

Discovery: The game gives players the opportunity to explore unknown areas and presents new worlds, maps, and scenarios.

Expression: The game allows players to express themselves through personal preferences, strategies, and character designs.

Submission: The game offers fun and relaxation and allows players to escape daily stress.

Game aesthetics represent the pleasurable aspects of games, which is particularly important in gamification. Gamified systems should ensure that users feel satisfied when completing specific tasks. For example, when a user completes a task with a gamified system, the emotional responses provided by that system should feel rewarding and satisfying to the user. Thus, these emotional responses become a force that drives the user toward desired outcomes and should not distract them from the gamified system. Game designers should carefully integrate these aesthetic elements to engage and engage players (Matallaoui et al., 2017).

2.4. Gamification Features

Gamification stands out as a tool that can potentially make students' learning processes more effective, especially in education. Its features include avatars, quests and challenges, badges, points, and levels. (Alsawaier, 2018). This section focuses on how these features are integrated into educational environments and how they enrich the learning experience. Each of them is detailed with the different opportunities it offers to students and the connections between the theoretical foundations of these components and practical examples are revealed. Thus, readers can better understand the role and potential of gamification in education.

Avatars

Avatars are representational tools that allow players to portray different real-life roles in a digital environment. These tools are chosen or created through personal choice or creativity as a way for players to express their need for autonomy (Wilson, 2003). Between the real self and the avatar lies an intermediate layer called the "reflective identity," where the individual transfers their longings and desires to the virtual character (Gee, 2003). Waggoner (2009) examined the philosophy of representation in the avatar creation process and pointed to findings that real-world identities continually inform virtual identities.

Avatars are defined as "models controlled by humans in real-time." (Bailenson et al., 2006), offer players the opportunity to explore a world without risk (Boss, 2009). The freedom to choose or design their own avatar creates an environment where students, in particular, can explore their own unique voices. A student who chooses their avatar will continue on a mission to face the next challenge (Alsawaier, 2018).

Quest and Challenges

Quests present players with a series of challenges that they must solve using their critical thinking skills. (Whitton & Moseley, 2012). Many student quests or challenges have a storyline, some of which constrain time. This is how quests and challenges orient players within a gamified world. (Zichermann & Cunningham, 2011). Presenting a course as an obstacle or adding story elements to course content can be much better than merely listing objectives, which is why gamification advocates typically recommend both. (Sheldon, 2020).

According to Kiang (2014), in a gamified environment, failure does not have the same negative consequences as it does in the real world. In this context, an avatar's failure provides an opportunity to reflect, learn from mistakes, and try again, as the understanding of failure is broken down into small, manageable trials. He suggests that teachers offer students opportunities to fail frequently in many small trials rather than in a single high-stakes exam. In a gamified context, there is more than one way to achieve a goal, and students are encouraged to choose a personalized path from among this variety.

On the other hand, tasks can provide students with the opportunity to develop collaboration and teamwork skills, or they may choose to achieve their success alone (Zichermann & Cunningham, 2011). This sense of unity is based on Gee's (2003) "affinity group" principle, which is promoted in gamified environments and is evident in many video game genres, including massively multiplayer online games. The power of this virtual social environment can be used to encourage students to interact and collaborate rather than compete with one another.

As players progress through the stages of their missions and challenges, they begin to earn badges, one of the gameplay elements that add to the learning process by increasing motivation and engagement. (Alsawaier, 2018).

Badges

Badges have a long history in many areas outside of gamification, where they can be defined as a verified indicator of achievement, skill, quality, or interest in a variety of learning environments (Alsawaier, 2018). In an educational context, badges are used strategically in a gamified environment to accommodate students with varying levels of motivation and abilities (Abramovich et al., 2013). As students' progress and collect badges associated with various achievements, these badges serve as an online record of student achievement (Devedžić & Jovanović, 2015).

Players who have earned badges experience an intrinsic sense of satisfaction when their achievements are publicly announced in a gamified environment (Nicholson, 2015). Richter et al. (2015) argue that badges serve as a record of an individual's past and present achievements. Badges help an individual develop qualities such as self-efficacy and competence, both individually and socially. Not only do these elements represent students' achievement, but points and levels are also considered important indicators of students' progress.

Points and levels

Points play an important role in gamified environments. Some gamification advocates consider them a core element of the gamified world or a mandatory requirement for all gamified systems. (Zichermann & Cunningham, 2011). There are studies that integrate points as a core gamification component in performance studies assessing fluency and understanding of mathematical concepts. (Attali & Arieli-Attali, 2015). Rewards reinforce desired learning behaviors, and when they are established, the rewards serve their purpose.

Modern games often feature scaffolding techniques to support player progression, where players start with simple levels and can only advance to the next level once they have mastered each level (Kiang, 2014). Players often need frequent rewards rather than punishments; these rewards symbolize skill mastery (Prensky, 2003), but there is also the view that this approach is limited to students or players who are extrinsically motivated, often symbolized by virtual rewards. Hanus and Fox (2015) have argued that the most active student groups in a gamified classroom environment are often low achievers or those with weak intrinsic motivation. For such students, rewards and incentives can increase intrinsic motivation.

2.5. Gamification in Education

Technology has influenced different aspects of human life, and in the modern age, even education uses technology. An example of this is game-oriented learning, a pedagogical approach that uses games as an integral part of the educational course.

When the content and gameplay of a game are used to further knowledge and skill acquisition, this is known as game-based learning. Students are made to answer complex problems and solve challenges aimed at keeping them excited (McFarlane et al., 2002). This underlying system includes a scoring and reward process that provides the tools needed to unlock access to improved students' academic success and ingratiate their learning pathway (García et al., 2021).

Game based learning (GBL) has been on the rise in recent years. The 21st-century world requires skills far different than those that school systems are set up to deliver (Squire, 2005). Over the years, GBL has been applied widely across numerous domains, namely in the military, health care, medical, and business, as well as the sport-physical training sector, using role-playing techniques, simulations, and digital games. They are tools to help the learner see a new reality and act on feedback from their usage (Oo & Lim, 2016).

Video or digital games can be defined as systems where users address abstract conflicts and challenges within a set of rules (Koster, 2013). In this context, the game process provides the user with continuous interaction and feedback, often resulting in an emotional reaction (de Sousa Borges et al., 2014). Prensky characterizes digital game-based learning (DGBL) as the integration of computer video games with diverse educational content to achieve educational outcomes comparable to, if not better than, traditional content-centric methods. (Prensky, 2005). Instead of merely being "fun" and "tricking" students into learning, DGBL leverages potent learning strategies such as situated learning, authentic environments, and balanced challenges and support, making it a more efficient educational instrument (Van Eck, 2006). A meta-analysis indicates that a well-designed DGBL game can improve educational outcomes by 7 to 40 percent (Mayo, 2009). However, it is widely acknowledged that gamification is dependent on context, and simply adding game elements like points, badges, and leaderboards without thoughtful design will not guarantee positive results (Toda et al., 2017).

2.6. Impacts of Gamification in Education

Gamification is one of the widely utilized methods that caters to the demands of contemporary education. This approach allows educators to address essential theoretical concepts while simultaneously offering opportunities to enhance students' interpersonal skills. (Lopes et al., 2019). Like other methods, it has benefits and challenges, which will be mentioned in this section.

Positive Effects

The primary goal of gamification in education is to make students more willing to reach a pre-established endpoint, adding game elements into the learning system. In addition to motivating students, gamification hopes to change student behavior (Hamari & Koivisto, 2013). According to research by Hanus and Fox (2015), gamification in an educational context increases student motivation enormously.

In addition, gamification solves beyond only motivation; it can abortions to student inactivity as well as problems in understanding and engagement (Lopes et al., 2019). One effective strategy is to reward student efforts and achievements with awards, which further enhances their motivation and participation (Kiryakova et al., 2014). This strategy uses game techniques in the learning process, and research has shown that play elements may positively affect cognitive learning results. The literature indicates that gamification can enhance learning in various contexts when designed effectively and appropriately implemented. (Rabah et al., 2018).

Gamification is also an active engagement tool to prepare students for the workforce and corporate work culture, where teamwork and multicultural collaboration are imperative (Zou & Ko, 2012). Moreover, from the perspective of deep learning, gamification also encourages "peer instruction" learning (Barna & Fodor, 2018), which aligns with the profound learning concept (Lopes et al., 2019). This approach involves connecting previous knowledge with new theoretical understanding and developing the skills to apply these concepts in real-life scenarios (Karkoub et al., 2020).

Negative Effects

While considerable research has been published on the positive motivation power of gamification in educational settings, it is still unclear to what extent gamified incentives can adversely affect students. (de Sousa Borges et al., 2014; Dicheva & Dichev, 2015).

Based on their systematic mapping study, Toda et al. (2017) identified four negative effects of gamification in education: indifference, loss of performance, undesired behavior, and declining effects. Loss of performance is the most frequently reported issue, occurring when gamification impedes or harms students' learning processes. Undesired behavior, the second most cited issue, arises when gamification produces unexpected positive or negative effects due to poor or absent planning. Indifference is observed when gamification neither positively nor negatively impacts learners. Lastly, declining effects refer to the gradual loss of motivation and engagement over time; students may initially be motivated by the novelty of gamification, but this motivation diminishes as time progresses. (Toda et al., 2017)

3. GAMIFICATION IN ARCHITECTURE EDUCATION

3.1. Characteristics of Architecture Education

A comprehensive comprehension of pedagogical approaches within architectural schools provides a foundation for identifying the appropriate timing, location, and methods for integrating gamification into architectural education. Therefore, an initial step involves thoroughly examining and analyzing architectural education's current state, achieved through theoretical and analytical scrutiny of architectural institutions.

Architectural design education has evolved significantly over time, influenced by various philosophical and pedagogical shifts. Historically, architectural training began with the master-apprentice model, devoid of formal academic affiliations. During the Renaissance, a distinct separation emerged between practical and theoretical knowledge. This period marked the beginning of a systematic approach to architectural education, where theoretical instruction was confined to the classroom while practical skills were developed in professional settings. The model closely resembled contemporary educational practices and was crystallized in the Ecolé des Beaux-Arts workshops, where both theoretical and practical knowledge were integrated within the academic framework. Subsequently, the Bauhaus school further revolutionized this approach, focusing on enhancing student creativity and personal expression by eliminating conventional constraints (Özkar, 2007; Taşçı, 2016). In modern times, design studios in architectural schools primarily aim to foster individual creativity and develop design competencies.

The primary objective of architectural education is to cultivate individuals equipped for professional architecture practice. At this juncture, a pertinent question arises regarding the essential attributes required by the architectural profession. While intellectual growth remains a fundamental goal of university education, the essence of architecture lies in the development of design logic. (Yürekli, 2003). Nevertheless, students entering architectural schools encounter a markedly different environment compared to their previous educational experiences in high school. Two particular aspects can be especially jarring for newcomers: firstly, the unfamiliarity with architectural perspectives, values, and definitions, and secondly, the subjective and ambiguous nature of these elements. (Lewis, 2013).

Architectural curricula comprise a blend of theoretical, practical, and studio courses that facilitate the transfer of knowledge and the cultivation of skills. Understanding an Architectural Program requires the dissection and breakdown of its constituent parts and the pragmatic aspects. Classification of these components is heterogeneous and can change according to the objectives and views of each academic investigation. A wider variety of possible categorizations is crucial for anticipated research on architectural education, predominantly elective classes. (Ghonim & Eweda, 2018).

The most significant and crucial sorting in architectural education is competency-based: program courses are bundled based on the competencies delivered. In this classification, architects fall under the third main category of knowledge, design, and skills established by the International Union of Architects (UIA). As a result, courses within architectural programs are classified under these three categories: design, knowledge, and skills. Figure 1 shows a visual of this taxonomy.

Figure 1. Taxonomy of Courses in Architectural Education (Ghonim, 2017)

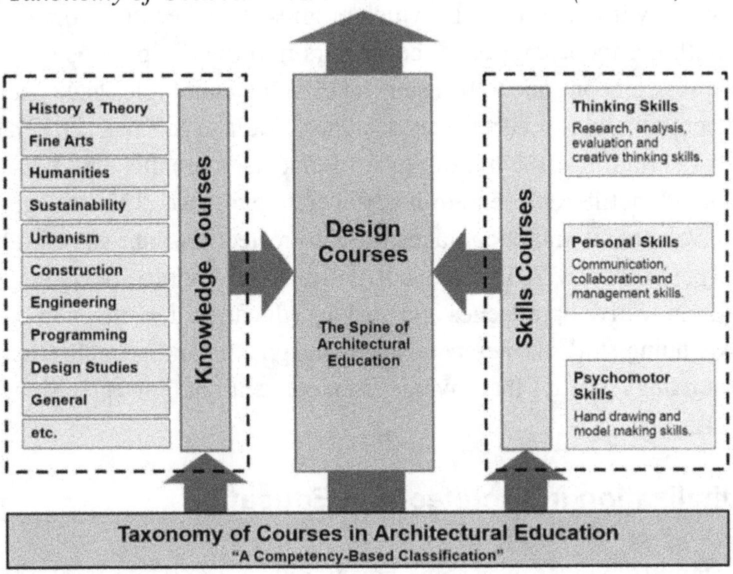

Knowledge courses are essential because they expose students to various topics and issues related to architecture that they otherwise would not be aware of. Skills courses are intended to support developing the skills required for normal architectural work, including design-oriented tasks. This includes communicating ideas well, pivoting with others, and using various drawing and modeling approaches — from manual to digital. Design studio projects are the soul of most architecture programs, and where students put their accumulated knowledge to call as they design solutions to defined problems in a structured format. (Ghonim, 2017).

Design, often conceptualized as a series of decisions that establish the relationships among shape, material, and performance (Kan & Gero, 2017), remains a cornerstone of architectural education. Uluoğlu describes design education as a behavioral development process that explores different modes of thinking and reasoning (1990). This form of education typically involves student engagement with open-ended, project-based problems that students intuitively solve using their perspectives (Qureshi, 2019). Such active participation positions students as central actors in their learning journey within the design studio, aligning with the philosophy that "learning is not a spectator sport. Students do not learn much just by sitting in classes listening to teachers, memorizing pre-packaged assignments, and spitting out answers" (Chickering & Gamson, 1987). In the realm of architectural design education, educators have the opportunity to present various design process models to their students, incorporating numerous widely used design methodologies.

In the traditional architectural design process, two-dimensional and three-dimensional drawings and models, which progressively become more detailed, are utilized. With the incorporation of computers into the design process, traditional tools of expression continue to be used, yet digital technologies have been adopted as supplementary tools for visualizing designs. (Yildirim & Yavuz, 2012). Rooted in the behaviorist tradition, the use of physical models in architectural education acts as a visual and tactile representation of concrete evidence. This engages students in active involvement and encourages them to reflect on their structural intuition consciously. (Vrontissi, 2015). Concurrently, contemporary developments have influenced innovative approaches and various educational methods in design education. Expanding students' perspectives in design education enables them to view their surroundings in ways that diverge from conventional interpretations. (Tavsan et al., 2014).

3.2. Digitalization in Architectural Education

It is helpful to ponder over some breakthroughs in architectural education to understand the foundation of gamification in architectural education. Information and computer technology have revolutionized traditional architecture as a profession with remarkable changes to the working environment of professions in the field, but also within the educational context. (Breen, 2004). Over the last couple of decades, a significant increase in digital technologies has been included within the architectural education curriculum, evidenced most clearly within the design studio. Technologies of computer-aided drafting, digital representation, modeling, and analysis are no longer only crucial pedagogical components designed within the confines of the design studio but have begun to impact broader curriculum frameworks in architectural education. In order to intermediate in a vast field of software tools for architects and organize the learning curve, support courses have been integrated as supporting elements within an architectural program. The coursework is designed to be sure students have the required technical competencies for architectural practices today. (Soliman et al., 2019).

Andia's (2002) research emphasized that digital technologies have been employed in architectural education to challenge and reformulate the modernizing perspective of architectural practice. Andia observed that the use of computer applications has impacted both students and practitioners, influencing their skills and shaping the culture of education and professional practice. Students are increasingly drawn to computer applications, gaining proficiency and engagement with various design media within their design processes. This shift has consequently influenced the traditional culture of the design studio, ushering in changes to the established norms and methods of architectural education and practice (Andia, 2002).

Numerous educators and practitioners insist we need a mixture of physical and digital design methods rather than relying entirely on either type. Breen (2004) has articulated that combining these techniques offers designers more profound insights and concrete methods for developing, reassessing, and refining designs. Furthermore, Breen stresses the importance of embedding this dual approach within the educational curriculum. This integration is crucial for adequately preparing students for the professional realm, ensuring they are well-versed in both traditional and modern design methodologies as they transition from academic environments to practice (Breen, 2004).

Elsewhere, Achten (2003) has argued against the increasing digitalisation of architectural production and asked pressing questions as to what this means for practice and education in our field. So digital tools might replace traditional one, such as manual sketching which is of high necessity by Achten, who believes that this is a vital direct physical connection between the hand and the brain. This traditional way allows for expression and idea generation that you would have a hard time doing in the digital world; for this reason alone, digital tools valuation is limited. Secondly, increasingly seductive digital tools now provide a quicker and cheaper solution for architects with grand renderings made to woo the eye of funders. This might teach some of the gravity and rigor that come with undertaking traditional architectural modeling (Achten, 2003).

3.3. Architecture and Games

Playing games, architectural education, and architectural practice are processes that have significant common aspects. This will enable students who play games to develop their skills in the field of architecture, regardless of the subject they play, through certain habits they have or will have and certain skills they will acquire. Considering this situation, it shows that games designed for architectural education can have significant promises in architectural education. This section will focus on the important common features of architectural education and gaming.

Games, like architectural education, are based on strategic thinking and overcoming problems. Every project given to architecture students brings with it a series of complex problems that need to be solved. These problems are wider than aesthetic concerns; many factors, such as technical, functional, and environmental factors, are also considered. Games usually have a similar structure, where more than one factor must be solved together. Players must analyze each problem to find the ideal solution and approach the problems holistically.

One of the concepts that should be mentioned in both processes is teamwork. Games can be divided into two types: multiplayer and single player. However, there are also dynamics of various collaborations in games played alone. On the other hand, architecture is a practice where project processes are carried out as a team, and even if carried out alone, they include many interdisciplinary interactions. The architect usually takes on the role of executive and organizer in these practical processes.

The similarities between architecture and gaming tools are wider than teamwork and problem-solving. As mentioned in the previous heading for architectural education, digitalization processes have profoundly affected both fields. In architecture, a large part of the design and implementation processes have been transferred to digital platforms. A similar process is also taking place in the gaming world; traditional games have given way to digital games, which have enabled both players and architects to transition from concrete elements to abstract and 3-dimensional thoughts. This situation has brought about the necessity of developing certain skills and hand-eye coordination in users of both fields.

Finally, and most importantly, both practices are largely based on "learning by doing": specific instructions are given to the student/player, and the solution is found by that person largely through trial and error and, of course, additional information/instructions given along the way. The strategies and skills learned while playing the game provide players with the opportunity to improve through continuous experimentation. Similarly, architecture students learn by drawing, creating models, and working on projects. In these processes, individuals develop their skills not only through theoretical knowledge but also through hands-on learning and experience.

3.4. Gamification in Architectural Education

When it comes to higher education, gamification can be highly beneficial in piquing interest amongst students for their traditional course material and in aiding them to apply knowledge learned theoretically into practice. The design disciplines, of which architecture education is one, offer a wide and rich canon that integrates not only technical knowledge but also innovations in creative thinking.

Considering a rapidly evolving landscape, the necessity for innovation in architectural education has never been more apparent. From 3D printing to Artificial Intelligence (AI), digital tools through algorithms are reshaping the profession of architectural practice, but we can also observe these changes in pedagogy. At this time, gamification as a pedagogical approach has become one of the novel ways in education. Gamification provides a promising approach to solving the problems faced in architectural education by leveraging game-based elements in order to increase the motivation and effectiveness of learning processes.

One of the biggest challenges of this discipline is the need to translate abstract concepts into concrete results. The design principles must be applied in practice, and students should also know how to do that. Although architectural education must tackle a difficult challenge in bridging the gap between many abstract concepts and actual physical implementation, gamification creates promising opportunities to do that. Gamification offers actual scenarios to students and, mentees can use their theoretical learning in a simulated place. One variation on this could be for a student to design a virtual city in an urban planning game – where they must work with creative and technical talents together.

Gamification may be a key technique that fosters creativity in architectural education and offers students the opportunity to learn by doing more extensively. As it goes in parallel with the innovations brought by digitization, this pedagogy model makes students validate their theoretical knowledge and better prepares them for real life.

The performance of gamification is an effort to make the learning into a playful verisimilitude that lets students actively participate in the learning. A lot of case studies have shown the positive effect of using gamification in architectural education. These studies have found that gamification improves the motivations of architecture students, dynamizes learning environments, and facilitates understanding of abstract theories.

3.5. Case Studies and Applications

There are many studies on the application of gamification in the field of architecture. Scanning and examining these studies together is important for establishing this concept in the relevant field. This section will present selected applications from the studies reviewed in the WOS index.

Reinhart et al. (2012) presented an innovative game-based exercise aimed at introducing architecture students to energy simulation throughout the building design process. After a trial with a class of 47 students, the authors argue that gaming is an effective educational tool that engages students and increases their interest in building energy modeling. They propose and evaluate a method for teaching this skill through a 90-minute in-class exercise or 'game' using DesignBuilder / EnergyPlus. In a competitive setting, students attempted to achieve the lowest energy use intensity (EUI) for an office building in Boston, balancing design improvements with a fixed budget. The EUIs of the final ten approaches ranged from %22–31, depending on the baseline variable. While student writings indicate that game-based learning is a distinct preference over traditional methods, the authors also suggest that gaming encourages the development of an energy modeling 'culture' in architecture schools, potentially improving communication between architects and energy modelers.

The EduGAME4CITY project by Fonseca et al. (2017) represents a pioneering effort that intersects the disciplines of computer science, architecture and multimedia engineering education, and public urban policy for cities of the future. A central innovative feature of this initiative is the incorporation of gaming strategies into an urban collaborative setting to refine and advance initial design proposals. This approach is based on the collaboration of architecture students as urban designers, and multimedia engineering and informatics students as multi-platform programmers. In contrast, it proactively involves end-users — citizens who engage with the virtual models to present their experience of a place that was not taken into account in the design. As a result, the students can be integrated into the design process with informal perceptions and everyday life experiences, thereby contributing to project development and enriching their educational path that once was purely formal. The framework is gamified and based on scoring design concepts, sustainability as well as accessibility and cost. Further, public meeting spaces are identified by uses of specific areas such as meetings and public markets or demonstrations, meaning that students can tailor their proposals to the changing nature of these contexts.

Valls et al. (2017) brought initiative with a project of the ArchGAME4CITY that studies the connection among computer science, architectural education, multimedia engineering, and urban policies for next-generation cities. With regard to innovation, they argued that it was not in the choice of tools, but in-game strategies applied in a virtual and collaborative urban environment for designing an initial architectural proposal. This method allows the dialogue of a project and its ability to take architecture students' spatial and urban skills to an optimal level. For the study, students passed a virtual experience via an architectural proposal and then a questionnaire to approve whether this experiment let them think in main spatial properties. Results implied that the virtual environment functioned well in promoting students to become more aware of different dimensions of architectural spaces, i.e., their functional, formal, and material aspects. This project elucidates the possibility of adopting it as a new direction in architectural education to gamify and promote serious game strategies.

The research conducted by Şahbaz and Özköse (2018) aimed to prove that digital game-based learning could be a useful system for the exploration of historical buildings. This article describes a method as an interactive link generator in image-based hypermedia for the use of architectural design and how we built a 3-dimensional computer game to assess this one among auxiliary hypertext tools in architectural education. The game comprised interactive activities that made it possible for players to get an up-close look at ancient monuments. The study performed an experiment to compare digital game-based learning (GamLearn vs. other traditional educational methods) in teaching historical architecture buildings. The conclusion is that digital game-based learning can be used as an integrated part of the instruction complementation of traditional lessons about historical buildings to benefit students' experience and enhance their learning.

Şahbaz's research (2018) aims to determine whether an interactive computer game (GCS) created as a casual educational tool for curtain wall systems is effective. The study compared the proposed game-based learning approach with traditional setting results within an experiment with 80 volunteer architecture students. The participants did not attend any course on the subject of curtain wall systems. Half the students used an "interactive system," and half followed a "traditional system." The Traditional System group learned via standard educational materials – textbooks, lecture notes, and slide presentations. An interactive system group, in the meanwhile, controlled curtain wall systems to play a computer game. Data collected from the study was subjected to statistical analyses. As expected, the post-experimental test results showed significant gains for the interactive system group over the traditional one. The results reveal that the GCS computer game serves as an effective hypermedia program by which students can gain hands-on experience with curtain wall materials. Gameplay Through this interactive game environment, students were able to play with the functions of ingredients as if they were part of a game, which immensely helped with their engagement and motivation.

Kharvari and Höhl (2019) examined how VR can provide more significant benefits than the traditional methods of studying architectural precedents. The research team developed a high-fidelity serious game simulation of Therme Vals and found that working in the study group helped participants remember where everything was located. Results further supported the notion that VR technology could be used to replace a physical visit to an architectural site. In addition to simply representing spaces accurately, VR is also a highly accessible and cost-effective way to start learning about architecture in a very precise manner due to the power of immersion. According to their study's findings, the authors agreed that a more significant sample and more powerful experiments are needed to assess the potential of serious games for architectural education fully.

Fernandez-Antolin et al. (2021) argue for a troubling gap in the knowledge of recent architecture school graduates regarding the use of building performance simulation tools (BPSTs). They advocate that BPSTs be included in architectural education under technical subjects. Therefore, they created gamified educational scaffolds and tested their claims with several workshops for university attendees. These groups had very encouraging results. The architecture students were eager and excited to learn about these new materials. These workshops, with the training undertaken within them, responding to plausible contemporary educational and learning needs, were deemed strongly related or well-positioned to meet up-to-the-minute requirements in architectural education.

Palócz and Katona (2021) studied the use of gamification as a teaching method, but instead of just a high education level, they checked both primary and academic applications during the architectural design process. While the solutions they explored are a strain of research, they discovered that it worked for modeling real-world scenarios. This aptness makes exemplary projects that utilize participatory architectural design principles as well as gamification techniques possible. The study demonstrates that this could be feasible by resolving the conditions to implement these projects and providing a basis for new architectural education and practice collaboration.

Shareef and Rauf (2022) carried out research to find the means through which architecture students can be encouraged to actively participate in technical courses and make use of their course-embedded knowledge within design projects. One such method, well suited to the delivery of a core technical subject, is the gamification tool Kahoot mentioned in this study. A quasi-experimental study design was employed and applied to second-year first-semester students as a case study using a quantitative research approach. A free online platform, Kahoot, was employed to gamify the course. The students then tested their knowledge of the material via questions and quizzes asked through Kahoot after each course session, which allowed them to elaborate on their answers. Results: Overall, students not only enjoyed the course but also actively participated and were motivated to apply the knowledge they gained in design projects. Students expressed interest in designing gamification for other classes, inspired by these successes.

The study, conducted by Heyik et al. (2023), introduces the “Ostrakinda” toolkit created to ease teaching the morphology of ancient Mediterranean cities. The research methodology follows a three-phase approach: design, play, and analysis. Thus, in the first phase, the design, preliminary experiments were conducted to measure the extent of students’ interest and real demands in relation to game-based learning and ancient cities. The second phase, play, involved experimental sessions within lectures and workshops and the use of both versions of the toolkits, physical and digital, among 331 students. The third, analysis, phase concentrated on the evaluation of the use of the game, which implied a systematic investigation of five research questions. The results obtained through the paired t-test show a representative increase in scores after the interaction with the game as compared to those before it. Hence, the effectiveness of the educational technique used in the article can be considered confirmed.

Below is a detailed table summarizing the main aspects of studies on gamification in architectural education:

Table 1. review of selected case studies

Author(s)	Year	Techniques	Student Involvements	Materials	Analysis Type
Reinhart et al.	2012	Energy Simulation Game	47 students in a competitive design game	DesignBuilder EnergyPlus	Energy use intensity metrics, students' feedback
Fonseca et al.	2017	Urban Design Gamification	Architecture and multimedia students in urban planning	Virtual models, Urban settings	Design refinement, user interactions
Valls et al.	2017	Urban Design Gamification	Architecture students in virtual urban environments	Virtual environments, questionnaires	Spatial competence assessment, questionnaires
Şahbaz & Özköse	2018	3D Historical Building Game	Students interact with historical buildings	3D computer game, interactive tasks	Learning effectiveness, task interaction
Şahbaz	2018	Interactive Building for Curtain Walls	80 students comparing traditional and game-based learning	Computer game, interactive tasks	Pre- and post-tests, statistical analysis
Kharvari & Höhl	2019	VR Architectural Simulation	Study on memory retention in VR	VR simulation, Therme Vals	Spatial memory retention assessment
Fernandez-Antolin et al.	2021	Gamified Building Performance Workshops	Workshop with architecture students	Simulation tools, workshop materials	Workshop feedback, educational relevance
Palocz & Katona	2021	Gamification in Design Processes	Primary and academic level design projects	Design models, gamification tools	Project efficacy, real-world scenario modeling
Shareeff & Rauf	2022	Kahoot for Construction Course	Second-year students in a technical course	Kahoot platform, quizzes	Student engagement and motivation metrics
Heyik et al.	2023	Game-based Ancient City Teaching	331 students in design and analysis phase	Physical and digital tools	Improvement in learning scores, paired t-tests

When examining the studies, it is seen that some basic attitudes and achievements are common. Apart from this, there are certain points that will allow each study to be evaluated as unique. The three most basic concepts that the studies seem to be similar are listed below:

Interactive and Engaging Learning Environments: All studies emphasize creating interactive learning scenarios in which students actively participate rather than being passive recipients of information. This participation is facilitated by the use of digital tools, including virtual reality (VR), computer games, and interactive simulations designed to immerse students in real-world challenges and design scenarios.

Focus on Practical Skills: Most of these studies aim to develop students' practical skills in specific areas such as energy efficient design, urban design, building performance, technical issues, and exploration of historical architectural structures.

Improved Student Motivation and Participation: A recurring result observed in all of these studies is an increase in student motivation and participation. Gamification techniques tend to make learning more enjoyable and competitive in nature, encouraging students to participate more actively and apply their knowledge more enthusiastically in practical environments.

The features that distinguish the studies and make them an original application are listed below:

Reinhart et al. (2012): This study is unique in its use of energy simulation games to include optimizing building designs within a limited budget where the images are narrowed down and in its simulations that zoom in on real-time engineering decisions.

Fonseca et al. (2017) and Valls et al. (2017): Both focus on the properties of the properties but in their collaborative treatments, involving a virtual care public distributed from multiple disciplines such as architecture, multimedia engineering and informatics to relax with policy and community activities.

Şahbaz and Özköse (2018): Stands out by using a 3D game to deconstruct historical buildings and allows them to 'walk' through architectural heritage and enter permits, combining historical developments with technological interaction.

Kharvari and Höhl (2019): Differentiates itself by using virtual reality instead of international site visits, offering a suitable supplementary alternative to include architectural precedents such as Therme Vals, and emphasizing the preservation of spatial presences.

Fernandez-Antolin et al. (2021): Focuses on the development of performance simulation tools within gamified workshops, emphasizes students in traditional architectural education on technical tools, and proposes a curriculum addition to address this.

Palócz and Katona (2021): Examines gamification at both primary and academic levels, looking at how real-world scenarios can be modeled through design; this is less common in other contexts, with a focus on higher development.

Shareef and Rauf (2022): Uses Kahoot, a popular gamification platform, to disseminate learning in technical courses and demonstrates the adaptability of gamification platforms to the temperature of different educational content.

Heyik et al. (2023): Presents 'Ostrakinda', an advanced toolkit for teaching the morphology of ancient Mediterranean cities by combining three educational approaches spanning international and digital tools.

4. DISCUSSION

The review on gamification in architectural education uncovers a variability of implementation fields with game-based components, each designed to aid educational struggles. What is common among all these studies is the way they are trying to think of a hole in knowledge architecture education and thinking of filling this hole through gamification. This method enhances traditional learning paradigms and injects a dynamic and engaging component into the educational process.

Gamification methods are different from traditional methods. Traditional teaching methods in architecture education are largely based on lectures, face-to-face training, and manual drawing exercises. These frameworks emphasize "Direct Instruction, Manual Skill Development, and Passive Learning". On the other hand, Gamification incorporates game designs such as efficiency, competition, and game rules into educational activities. In architecture education, these packages are: Interactive Simulations, Awards and Badges, and Active Learning. The table shows the main points of gamification with traditional copies.

Table 2. Comparative evaluation between traditional methods and gamification

	Traditional Methods	Gamification
Engagement	Often seen as less engaging for digital native students who prefer interactive and dynamic learning environments.	Enhances learning by integrating interactive elements that appeal to their existing preferences, making it more dynamic and enjoyable.
Outcomes	Strong in developing core knowledge and learning through repetitive practice and decoupling.	Expanding problem-solving skills and creativity, providing immediate feedback.
Skill Development	Focuses on manual skills and a deep understanding of material properties and construction techniques.	Prepares for modern professional environments that increasingly rely on digital technology by encouraging the development of digital literacy and collaboration skills.
Accessibility and Flexibility	May be less flexible, often requiring physical attributes and access to specific features or areas.	It offers greater accessibility and flexibility by enabling learning remotely and through digital platforms that students can access at any time.

This study, in turn, is supported by the literature regarding empirical evidence in favour of using gamification to increase student motivation and learning levels. Empirical evidence has been gathered in the literature through surveys of student perception and attitudes when challenged with the introduction of game-based learning elements into courses. These surveys have consistently resulted in positive outcomes, where students have displayed greater engagement and a better grasp of difficult architectural topic matter thanks to the use of gamified learning.

Despite its well-documented benefits, the literature highlights several inadequacies in the current state of gamification research with regard to evaluating possible harmful effects. Even though the benefits are widely acknowledged (improved motivation and learning, among others), with a marked absence of studies that rigorously measure them, these may involve the danger of dumbing down content, the potential fall in long-term engagement, and whether gamification is adaptable across different learning styles and environments. The almost by definition novelty effect of gamification might also wear off with time, a fact that could, in turn, unmotivated students using it regarding another aspect of learning, fostering the idea that there may be an ongoing innovation and assessment process in those curricula.

5. CONCLUSION

The literature review highlighted how gamification can be integrated into architectural education, underscoring its tangible benefits for learning settings. Gamification utilizes game-based attributes to enhance student engagement, foster motivation, and allow the practice of complex architectural concepts in an interactive, exciting way. The experience of an educational exercise is set up, points are added, badges are gained, leaderboards show competitiveness, and people are brought together to compete in simulations resembling real-world architectural projects that need creativity, problem-solving, and teamwork.

Although these approaches have many potential benefits, the review also outlines some important issues that must be addressed carefully. Although gamification assists in reducing the risk of making educational content trivial, in some contexts, it can also have opposing outcomes of providing only short-term bursts of motivation or not being able to reach out to a broader range of audiences and all styles of learners. In addition, because gamification depends on technology, changes will have to be made continuously to emulate this process through digital tools for the foreseeable future and keep it up to date with security.

More longitudinal research is needed in gamified learning to see what happens after the intervention, how long it lasts, and if one gets better at maintaining motivation and enthusiasm. Furthermore, investigating more tailored ways of gamifying may shed light on the possibility of making learning adaptable to individual needs, potentially broadening audiences for academic enter-gamification and making it work better.

In this case, while gamification does offer a potentially enriching vector for architectural education, it must be co-opted in moderation. Educational bodies should also work towards maintaining the rigor and depth of architectural training in the environment of more interactive, gamified learning. The educational canvas is changing rapidly with emerging technologies, and gamification is a potent resource that could have a transformative impact on learning outputs amongst architects and students alike.

REFERENCES

Abramovich, S., Schunn, C., & Higashi, R. M. (2013). Are badges useful in education?: It depends upon the type of badge and expertise of learner. *Educational Technology Research and Development*, 61(2), 217–232. DOI: 10.1007/s11423-013-9289-2

Achten, H. H. (2003). New design methods for computer aided architectural design methodology teaching. *International Journal of Architectural Computing*, 1(1), 72–91. DOI: 10.1260/147807703322467441

Alsawaier, R. S. (2018). The effect of gamification on motivation and engagement. *The International Journal of Information and Learning Technology*, 35(1), 56–79. DOI: 10.1108/IJILT-02-2017-0009

Andia, A. (2002). Reconstructing the effects of computers on practice and education during the past three decades. *Journal of Architectural Education*, 56(2), 7–13. DOI: 10.1162/104648802604725 12

Attali, Y., & Arieli-Attali, M. (2015). Gamification in assessment: Do points affect test performance? *Computers & Education*, 83, 57–63. DOI: 10.1016/j.compedu.2014.12.012

Babu, S. S., & Moorthy, A. D. (2023). Application of artificial intelligence in adaptation of gamification in education: A literature review. *Computer Applications in Engineering Education*. Advance online publication. DOI: 10.1002/cae.22683

Bailenson, J. N., Yee, N., Merget, D., & Schroeder, R. (2006). The effect of behavioral realism and form realism of real-time avatar faces on verbal disclosure, nonverbal disclosure, emotion recognition, and copresence in dyadic interaction. *Presence (Cambridge, Mass.)*, 15(4), 359–372. DOI: 10.1162/pres.15.4.359

Barna, B., & Fodor, S. (2018). An empirical study on the use of gamification on IT courses at higher education. Teaching and Learning in a Digital World: Proceedings of the 20th International Conference on Interactive Collaborative Learning–Volume 1, Boss, S. (2009). Avatars teach teens about self-image. In: Edutopia. DOI: 10.1007/978-3-319-73210-7_80

Breen, J. (2004). Changing Roles for (Multi) Media Tools in Design. *Architecture in the Network Society*, 529.

Chickering, A. W., & Gamson, Z. F. (1987). Seven principles for good practice in undergraduate education. *AAHE Bulletin*, 3, 7.

Connolly, T. M., Boyle, E. A., MacArthur, E., Hainey, T., & Boyle, J. M. (2012). A systematic literature review of empirical evidence on computer games and serious games. *Computers & Education*, 59(2), 661–686. DOI: 10.1016/j.compedu.2012.03.004

Csikszentmihalyi, M. (2008). *Flow: The psychology of optimal experience*. Harper & Row New York.

de Sousa Borges, S., Durelli, V. H., Reis, H. M., & Isotani, S. (2014). A systematic mapping on gamification applied to education. Proceedings of the 29th annual ACM symposium on applied computing, Deterding, S., Dixon, D., Khaled, R., & Nacke, L. (2011). From game design elements to gamefulness: defining" gamification". Proceedings of the 15th international academic MindTrek conference: Envisioning future media environments, Devedžić, V., & Jovanović, J. (2015). Developing open badges: A comprehensive approach. *Educational Technology Research and Development*, 63, 603–620.

Dicheva, D., & Dichev, C. (2015). Gamification in education: Where are we in 2015? E-learn: World conference on E-learning in corporate, government, healthcare, and higher education, Fernandez-Antolin, M. M., del Río, J. M., & Gonzalez-Lezcano, R. A. (2021). The use of gamification in higher technical education: perception of university students on innovative teaching materials. *International Journal of Technology and Design Education*, 31(5), 1019–1038. DOI: 10.1007/s10798-020-09583-0

Fonseca, D., Villagrasa, S., Navarro, I., Redondo, E., Valls, F., & Sánchez, A. (2017, Apr 11-13). Urban Gamification in Architecture Education.*Advances in Intelligent Systems and Computing* [Recent advances in information systems and technologies, vol 3]. *World Conference on Information Systems and Technologies (WorldCIST)*, Madeira, Portugal.

García, S. A., Jiménez, C. R., de la Cruz Campos, J. C., & Villalba, M. J. S. (2021). Applications of Gamification in the Context of Higher Education. A Theoretical Approach. International Conference in Methodologies and intelligent Systems for Techhnology Enhanced Learning, Gee, J. P. (2003). What video games have to teach us about learning and literacy. [CIE]. *Computers in Entertainment*, 1(1), 20–20.

Ghonim, M. (2017). Toward calibrating architectural education: An approach to promote students' design abilities. *The International Journal of Architectonic, Spatial, and Environmental Design*, 11(4), 37–62. DOI: 10.18848/2325-1662/CGP/v11i04/37-62

Ghonim, M., & Eweda, N. (2018). Investigating elective courses in architectural education. *Frontiers of Architectural Research*, 7(2), 235–256. DOI: 10.1016/j.foar.2018.03.006

Hamari, J., & Koivisto, J. (2013). Social Motivations To Use Gamification: An Empirical Study Of Gamifying Exercise. ECIS, Hanus, M. D., & Fox, J. (2015). Assessing the effects of gamification in the classroom: A longitudinal study on intrinsic motivation, social comparison, satisfaction, effort, and academic performance. *Computers & Education*, 80, 152–161.

Heyik, M. A., Erdoğan, M., & Tong, T. (2023). Ostrakinda: A Game-Based Learning Toolkit for Ancient Mediterranean Cities. *ICONARP International Journal of Architecture and Planning*, 11(2), 838–865. DOI: 10.15320/ICONARP.2023.266

Hunicke, R., LeBlanc, M., & Zubek, R. (2004). MDA: A formal approach to game design and game research. Proceedings of the AAAI Workshop on Challenges in Game AI, Kan, J. W., & Gero, J. S. (2017). *Quantitative methods for studying design protocols*. Springer.

Kapp, K. M. (2012). *The gamification of learning and instruction: game-based methods and strategies for training and education*. John Wiley & Sons.

Karkoub, M., Yang, C.-L., Karkoub, W., & Raslan, M. (2020). Undergraduate Cross-Class Research Projects for Deep Learning in Engineering Education. *Advances in Engineering Education*, 8(2), n2. DOI: 10.18260/3-1-1114-36024

Kharvari, F., & Höhl, W. (2019). The role of serious gaming using virtual reality applications for 3D architectural visualization. 2019 11th International Conference on Virtual Worlds and Games for Serious Applications (VS-Games), Kiang, D. (2014). Using gaming principles to engage students. *Edutopia. Recuperado de:http:// www. edutopia. org/blog/using-gaming-principles-engage-students-douglas-kiang*

Kim, S., Song, K., Lockee, B., Burton, J., Kim, S., Song, K., Lockee, B., & Burton, J. (2018). Theories for gamification in learning and education. *Gamification in Learning and Education: Enjoy Learning Like Gaming*, 39-47.

Kiryakova, G., Angelova, N., & Yordanova, L. (2014). Gamification in education. Proceedings of 9th international Balkan education and science conference, Koster, R. (2013). *Theory of fun for game design*. " O'Reilly Media, Inc.".

Krath, J., Schürmann, L., & Von Korflesch, H. F. (2021). Revealing the theoretical basis of gamification: A systematic review and analysis of theory in research on gamification, serious games and game-based learning. *Computers in Human Behavior*, 125, 106963. DOI: 10.1016/j.chb.2021.106963

Lewis, R. K. (2013). *Architect?: a candid guide to the profession*. Mit Press.

Looyestyn, J., Kernot, J., Boshoff, K., Ryan, J., Edney, S., & Maher, C. (2017). Does gamification increase engagement with online programs? A systematic review. *PLoS One*, 12(3), e0173403. DOI: 10.1371/journal.pone.0173403 PMID: 28362821

Lopes, A. P., Soler, M., Caña, R., Cortés, L., Bentabol, M., Bentabol, A., Muñoz, M. M., Esteban, A., & Luna, M. J. (2019, Jul 01-03). Gamification In Education And Active Methodologies At Higher Education.*Edulearn Proceedings* [Edulearn19: 11th international conference on education and new learning technologies]. 11th International Conference on Education and New Learning Technologies (EDULEARN), Palma, SPAIN. DOI: 10.21125/edulearn.2019.0480

Marín, J. A. M., Soto, M. N. C., Navas-Parejo, M. R., & García, G. G. (2021). Gamification as a Motivational and Socio-educational Resource in Classrooms with Students at Risk of Social Exclusion. International Conference in Methodologies and intelligent Systems for Techhnology Enhanced Learning, Maslow, A. H. (1969). A theory of human motivation. *Classics of organization theory*, 167-178.

Matallaoui, A., Hanner, N., & Zarnekow, R. (2017). Introduction to gamification: Foundation and underlying theories. *Gamification: Using game elements in serious contexts*, 3-18.

Mayo, M. J. (2009). Video games: A route to large-scale STEM education? *Science*, 323(5910), 79–82. DOI: 10.1126/science.1166900 PMID: 19119223

McFarlane, A., Sparrowhawk, A., & Heald, Y. (2002). *Report on the educational use of games*. TEEM (Teachers evaluating educational multimedia), Cambridge.

Nevid, J. S. (2007). *Psychology: Concepts and applications*. Houghton, Mifflin and Company.

Nicholson, S. (2015). A recipe for meaningful gamification. *Gamification in education and business*, 1-20.

Oo, B. L., & Lim, B. T.-H. (2016). Game-based learning in construction management courses: A case of bidding game. *Engineering, Construction, and Architectural Management*, 23(1), 4–19. DOI: 10.1108/ECAM-02-2015-0029

Özkar, M. (2007). Learning by doing in the age of design computation. Computer-Aided Architectural Design Futures (CAADFutures) 2007: Proceedings of the 12th International CAADFutures Conference, Palócz, K., & Katona, V. (2021). The Applicability Of Gamification In Architectural Design Education. *Symmetry-Culture and Science, 32*(4), 489-505. https://doi.org/DOI: 10.26830/symmetry_2021_4_489

Park, K., Cha, M., Kwak, H., & Chen, K.-T. (2017). Achievement and friends: Key factors of player retention vary across player levels in online multiplayer games. Proceedings of the 26th international conference on world wide web companion, Pedreira, O., García, F., Brisaboa, N., & Piattini, M. (2015). Gamification in software engineering–A systematic mapping. *Information and Software Technology*, 57, 157–168.

Prensky, M. (2003). Digital game-based learning. [CIE]. *Computers in Entertainment*, 1(1), 21–21. DOI: 10.1145/950566.950596

Prensky, M. (2005). Computer games and learning: Digital game-based learning. *Handbook of computer game studies, 18*(2005), 97-122.

Qian, M., & Clark, K. R. (2016). Game-based Learning and 21st century skills: A review of recent research. *Computers in Human Behavior*, 63, 50–58. DOI: 10.1016/j.chb.2016.05.023

Qureshi, H. (2019). Collaborative architectural design studio environment: An experiment in the studio of Architectural Design-I. *Archnet-IJAR: International Journal of Architectural Research*, 14(2), 303–324. DOI: 10.1108/ARCH-12-2018-0049

Rabah, J., Cassidy, R., & Beauchemin, R. (2018). Gamification in education: Real benefits or edutainment. 17th European Conference on e-Learning, Athens, Greece, Reinhart, C. F., Dogan, T., Ibarra, D., & Samuelson, H. W. (2012). Learning by playing–teaching energy simulation as a game. *Journal of Building Performance Simulation*, 5(6), 359–368.

Richter, G., Raban, D. R., & Rafaeli, S. (2015). *Studying gamification: The effect of rewards and incentives on motivation*. Springer.

Şahbaz, E. (2018). A Proposal for an Interactive Computre Gagme to Teach Curtain Wall Systems.

Şahbaz, E., & Özköse, A. (2018). Experiencing historical buildings through digital computer games. *International Journal of Architectural Computing*, 16(1), 22–33. DOI: 10.1177/1478077117749960

Sailer, M., Hense, J., Mandl, H., & Klevers, M. (2017). *Fostering development of work competencies and motivation via gamification*. Springer. DOI: 10.1007/978-3-319-41713-4_37

Sarı, İ., Ekici, S., Soyer, F., & Eskiler, E. (2015). Does self-confidence link to motivation? A study in field hockey athletes. *Journal of Human Sport and Exercise*, 10(1), 24–35. DOI: 10.14198/jhse.2015.101.03

Seligman, M. E., & Csikszentmihalyi, M. (2000). *Positive psychology: An introduction* (Vol. 55). American Psychological Association.

Shareef, S. S., & Rauf, H. L. (2022). Learning technical courses in architectural education through gamification. *Computer Applications in Engineering Education*, 30(6), 1872–1884. DOI: 10.1002/cae.22562

Sheldon, L. (2020). *The multiplayer classroom: Designing coursework as a game*. CRC Press. DOI: 10.1201/9780429285035

Soliman, S., Taha, D., & El Sayad, Z. (2019). Architectural education in the digital age Computer applications: Between academia and practice. *Alexandria Engineering Journal*, 58(2), 809–818. DOI: 10.1016/j.aej.2019.05.016

Squire, K. (2005). Changing the game: What happens when video games enter the classroom? *Innovate: Journal of online education, 1*(6).

Taşçı, B. G. (2016). Theoretical framework for using digital games in architecture education. *Architecture Research*, 6(3), 51–56.

Tavsan, C., Tavsan, F., & Sonmez, E. (2014, Nov 28-29). Biomimicry in Architectural Design Education.*Procedia Social and Behavioral Sciences* [4th world conference on educational technology researches (wcetr-2014)]. 4th World Conference on Educational Technology Researches (WCETR), Univ Barcelona, Barcelona, Spain.

Toda, A. M., Valle, P. H. D., & Isotani, S. (2017, Mar 20-24). The Dark Side of Gamification: An Overview of Negative Effects of Gamification in Education.*Communications in Computer and Information Science* [Higher education for all: From challenges to novel technology-enhanced solutions]. *1st International Workshop on Social, Semantic, Adaptive and Gamification Techniques and Technologies for Distance Learning (HEFA)*, Maceio, Brazil.

Uluoğlu, B. (1990). Mimari tasarım eğitimi tasarım bilgisi bağlamında stüdyo eleştirileri.

Valls, F., Redondo, E., Sánchez, A., Fonseca, D., Villagrasa, S., & Navarro, I. (2017, Apr 11-13). Simulated Environments in Architecture Education. Improving the Student Motivation.*Advances in Intelligent Systems and Computing* [Recent advances in information systems and technologies, vol 3]. World Conference on Information Systems and Technologies (WorldCIST), Madeira, PORTUGAL.

Van Eck, R. (2006). Digital game-based learning: It's not just the digital natives who are restless. *EDUCAUSE Review*, 41(2), 16.

Vrontissi, M. (2015). The physical model in structural studies within architecture education: paradigms of an analytic rationale? Proceedings of IASS annual symposia, Waggoner, Z. (2009). *My avatar, my self: Identity in video role-playing games.* McFarland.

Whitton, N., & Moseley, A. (2012). *Using games to enhance learning and teaching.* Taylor & Francis New York. DOI: 10.4324/9780203123775

Wilson, L. (2003). Interactivity or interpassivity: A question of agency in digital play. Fine Art Forum, Yildirim, T., & Yavuz, A. O. (2012, May 01-04). Comparison of traditional and digital visualization technologies in architectural design education. *Procedia Social and Behavioral Sciences* [World conference on design, arts and education (dae-2012)]. World Conference on Design, Arts and Education (DAE), Antalya, TURKEY.

Yürekli, İ. (2003). *Mimari tasarım eğitiminde oyun.* Fen Bilimleri Enstitüsü.

Zichermann, G., & Cunningham, C. (2011). *Gamification by design: Implementing game mechanics in web and mobile apps.* O'Reilly Media, Inc.

Zou, T. X., & Ko, E. I. (2012). Teamwork development across the curriculum for chemical engineering students in Hong Kong: Processes, outcomes and lessons learned. *Education for Chemical Engineers*, 7(3), e105–e117. DOI: 10.1016/j.ece.2012.04.003

Chapter 5
Gamification as a Pedagogical Tool in Geriatric Nursing:
Engaging and Empowering Future Nurses

Tiago Manuel Horta Reis da Silva
https://orcid.org/0000-0001-5220-1718
King's College London, UK

ABSTRACT

Incorporating gamification into geriatric nursing curricula presents a transformative opportunity to improve student engagement, enhance learning outcomes, and foster critical thinking in the care of older adults. This chapter explores how gamified approaches can address common educational challenges in geriatric nursing, such as learner motivation, knowledge retention, and application of complex concepts like pharmacokinetics, chronic disease management, and falls prevention. The chapter discusses best practices in the design and integration of gamified content, examines the cognitive and emotional impacts on learners, and provides practical strategies for implementation. Drawing from case studies, empirical research, and theoretical frameworks, this chapter outlines how gamification can align with educational standards and learning objectives to empower nursing students to deliver high-quality, compassionate care for the older population.

DOI: 10.4018/979-8-3693-8322-3.ch005

1. INTRODUCTION

The field of geriatric nursing has emerged as a critical area of healthcare, primarily due to the increasing population of older adults worldwide. As the demographic landscape shifts, with projections indicating that by 2050, the number of people aged 60 years and older will surpass 2 billion, the demand for specialized nursing care tailored to the unique needs of this population has intensified (Ghamgosar et al., 2021). Geriatric nursing encompasses a holistic approach to care that addresses the multifaceted health issues faced by older adults, including chronic diseases, cognitive decline, and functional impairments (Doležalová et al., 2022; Reis da Silva, 2024a). However, the educational challenges in this field are significant. Nursing curricula often lack comprehensive geriatric content, leading to a workforce that may not be adequately prepared to meet the complexities of geriatric care (Bahrami et al., 2019). This gap in education not only affects the quality of care provided to older adults but also contributes to the pervasive ageist attitudes that can exist within the healthcare system (Burhenn et al., 2016).

Engaging nursing students in geriatric care is paramount, as their attitudes and competencies in this area will shape the future of elderly care (Fitzpatrick et al, 2023). Innovative pedagogical tools are essential for enhancing the educational experience and fostering a positive disposition toward geriatric nursing among students (Haske-Palomino et al., 2023). Traditional teaching methods may not sufficiently engage students or adequately prepare them for the realities of working with older adults. Therefore, there is a pressing need to explore and implement novel educational strategies that can captivate students' interest and enhance their learning outcomes in geriatric nursing (Hu et al., 2021). Gamification, as a pedagogical tool, has gained traction in various educational fields, including nursing, as it leverages game design elements to create engaging learning experiences that motivate students and enhance knowledge retention (Smith et al., 2021; Reis da Silva and Mitchell, 2024).

Gamification is defined as the application of game-design elements in non-game contexts to improve user engagement and learning outcomes (Teófilo et al., 2018; Reis da Silva and Mitchell, 2024). In higher education, particularly in nursing, gamification can transform the learning environment by making it more interactive and enjoyable. This approach not only fosters a deeper understanding of geriatric concepts but also encourages collaboration and critical thinking among students (Li et al., 2022). By integrating gamification into the nursing curriculum, educators can create a dynamic learning atmosphere that resonates with the digital-native generation of students, thereby enhancing their preparedness to care for older adults (Blebil et al., 2022). The relevance of gamification in nursing education is underscored by its potential to address the existing gaps in geriatric training and to cultivate a workforce that is not only knowledgeable but also empathetic towards the elderly (Fox et al., 2015).

The purpose of this chapter is to explore the role of gamification as a pedagogical tool in geriatric nursing education. It aims to examine the current landscape of geriatric nursing education, identify the unique challenges faced by nursing students, and highlight the importance of innovative teaching strategies, such as gamification, in engaging and empowering future nurses. By synthesising existing literature and research findings, this chapter will provide a comprehensive overview of how gamification can be effectively utilised to enhance geriatric nursing education, ultimately leading to improved care for older adults (Kim et al., 2021). The scope of this chapter encompasses an analysis of various gamification strategies, their implementation in nursing curricula, and the implications for nursing practice in geriatric care settings.

1. THEORETICAL FOUNDATIONS OF GAMIFICATION IN EDUCATION

1.1 Overview of Gamification: Definitions and Core Principles

Gamification is defined as the integration of game design elements in non-game contexts to enhance user engagement and motivation (Puspitasari, 2023). It employs various core principles, including points, badges, leaderboards, and levels, which serve to incentivise participation and foster a competitive spirit among learners (Bennani et al., 2021). Points are awarded for completing tasks or achieving specific goals, while badges symbolise accomplishments, providing visual recognition of a learner's progress. Leaderboards create a competitive environment by ranking participants based on their performance, thus encouraging continuous engagement (Dichev & Dicheva, 2017). Levels signify the progression of learners through increasingly challenging tasks, which can enhance their sense of achievement and competence (Pishchanska et al., 2022). The application of these elements in educational settings aims to transform traditional learning experiences into more interactive and enjoyable ones, ultimately leading to improved educational outcomes (Jawabreh & Bicen, 2020).

The theoretical underpinnings of gamification in education are supported by several learning theories. Constructivist Learning Theory posits that learners construct knowledge through experiences and interactions with their environment (Santos et al., 2018). Gamification aligns with this theory by providing experiential learning opportunities that encourage active participation and collaboration among students. Cognitive Load Theory emphasises the importance of managing the cognitive demands placed on learners to optimize their learning potential (Fiuza-Fernández et al., 2022). By breaking down complex tasks into manageable components and providing immediate feedback through gamified elements, educators can help reduce cognitive overload and enhance learning retention (Fiuza-Fernández et al., 2022). Self-Determination Theory further supports gamification by highlighting the significance of intrinsic motivation, autonomy, competence, and relatedness in the learning process (Wiggins, 2016). Gamification fosters these elements by allowing learners to make choices, set personal goals, and engage in social interactions, thereby enhancing their overall motivation and satisfaction with the learning experience (Hope et al., 2022).

1.2 Application of Gamification in Nursing Education

In nursing education, the application of gamification has shown promising results in enhancing student engagement and knowledge retention. Studies have demonstrated that gamified learning environments can lead to improved academic performance and greater motivation among nursing students (Biryukov et al., 2021). For instance, the use of simulation games and role-playing scenarios allows students to practice clinical skills in a safe and controlled environment, thereby reinforcing their learning and building confidence (Alhammad & Moreno, 2018). Furthermore, gamification can facilitate collaborative learning, as students often work in teams to solve problems or complete tasks, promoting teamwork and communication skills essential for nursing practice (Kickmeier-Rust, 2023).

An overview of studies on gamification in healthcare and nursing curricula reveals a growing body of evidence supporting its effectiveness. Research has indicated that gamified educational interventions can lead to significant improvements in knowledge acquisition, skill development, and overall student satisfaction (Doroudi, 2023). For example, a systematic review of gamification in pharmacy education highlighted its potential to enhance student engagement and learning outcomes (Zourmpakis et al., 2023). Similarly, studies in medical education have reported positive effects of gamification on students' clinical reasoning and decision-making skills (Hellberg, 2023). These findings underscore the relevance of gamification as a pedagogical tool in nursing education, particularly in preparing future nurses to meet the challenges of an increasingly complex healthcare landscape.

2. THE IMPORTANCE OF GERIATRIC NURSING EDUCATION

2.1 Demographic Trends

The importance of geriatric nursing education cannot be overstated, especially in light of demographic trends indicating a significant increase in the elderly population (Reis da Silva, 2023a; Reis da Silva, 2023b; Cowley et al, 2023). According to projections, the number of individuals aged 65 and older is expected to double by 2060, reaching approximately 98 million in the United States alone (Lester et al., 2023). This demographic shift necessitates a workforce equipped with specialised knowledge and skills to address the unique healthcare needs of older adults. As the prevalence of chronic diseases and complex health conditions rises among the elderly, the demand for trained geriatric nurses is becoming increasingly critical (Afirando et al., 2023).

Moreover, the complexity of chronic disease management in older adults presents specific challenges that require targeted educational interventions. Geriatric nurses must possess a deep understanding of the multifaceted nature of chronic illnesses, including their interactions and the impact on patients' overall health and well-being (Zhakupova et al., 2022). Additionally, addressing cognitive and emotional health in older adults is essential, as many elderly individuals experience mental health issues such as depression and anxiety, which can complicate their medical care (Kostolányová & Klubal, 2018). Teaching nursing students to recognize and manage these challenges is vital for ensuring comprehensive care for this population.

2.2 Specific Challenges in Geriatric Nursing Education

The nuances of pharmacokinetics and polypharmacy in older adults further complicate geriatric nursing education (Reis da Silva, 2024b). Older adults often take multiple medications, increasing the risk of adverse drug interactions and complicating treatment regimens (Dečman et al., 2022). Educators must emphasise the importance of medication management and the need for careful assessment of each patient's medication regimen to prevent potential complications (Tang, 2023). Risk management, including fall prevention, mobility issues, and nutritional considerations, is another critical aspect of geriatric nursing education (Reis da Silva, 2024c; Reis da Silva, 2024d; Reis da Silva, 2024e). Nurses must be equipped with the knowledge and skills to assess and mitigate these risks effectively (Fallatah, 2023).

Gamification can play a pivotal role in addressing these challenges by enhancing engagement and retention among nursing students (Reis da Silva and Mitchell, 2024). By incorporating gamified elements into the curriculum, educators can create interactive learning experiences that simulate real-world scenarios faced by geriatric nurses (Park & Kim, 2021). For instance, case-based simulations can allow students to practice their clinical reasoning and decision-making skills in a safe environment, reinforcing their understanding of complex concepts related to geriatric care (Bigdeli et al., 2023). Additionally, gamification can foster collaboration and teamwork, essential skills for nursing practice, by encouraging students to work together to solve problems and complete tasks (Uaidullakyzy et al., 2022).

3. INTEGRATING GAMIFICATION INTO GERIATRIC NURSING CURRICULA

3.1 Key Considerations for Integrating Gamification into Nursing Education

Integrating gamification into nursing education, particularly in geriatric nursing curricula, requires careful consideration of several key factors. First and foremost, curriculum alignment with learning objectives is crucial. This alignment ensures that gamified elements support the desired educational outcomes and competencies that nursing students must achieve (Mersin et al., 2020). For instance, if the goal is to enhance clinical reasoning skills, gamified activities should be designed to challenge students to apply their knowledge in realistic scenarios that mimic the complexities of geriatric care (Buthelezi, 2023).

Balancing traditional teaching methods with gamified approaches is another essential consideration. While gamification can enhance engagement, it should not completely replace established pedagogical methods that have proven effective in nursing education (Fijačko et al., 2020). A blended approach that incorporates both traditional lectures and gamified learning experiences can provide a comprehensive educational framework that caters to diverse learning styles and preferences (Özdemir & Kadıoğlu, 2023). Additionally, identifying target competencies, such as clinical reasoning, communication, and empathy, is vital for ensuring that gamified activities are relevant and meaningful to nursing practice (Jacobs-Wingo et al., 2018).

3.2 Step-by-Step Guide for Curriculum Development Incorporating Gamified Elements

Developing a curriculum that incorporates gamified elements involves a systematic approach. The first step is to create gamified learning modules, which could include interactive case studies and simulations that reflect real-world challenges in geriatric nursing (Arboleda-Tinay, 2021). For example, students could engage in role-playing scenarios where they must assess and manage the care of virtual patients with complex health issues (Al-Nawafleh, 2024).

Next, educators should identify appropriate digital tools and platforms for gamification. Various software applications and online platforms can facilitate the integration of gamified elements into the curriculum, allowing for real-time feedback and tracking of student progress (Kang et al., 2022). Assessing student readiness and preferences is also critical; understanding students' technological proficiency and their attitudes toward gamification can inform the design and implementation of gamified activities (Kang et al., 2022).

Interdisciplinary collaboration in curriculum design is another important aspect. Engaging faculty from various disciplines, including gerontology, psychology, and instructional design, can enrich the curriculum and ensure that it addresses the multifaceted needs of geriatric nursing education (Ji et al., 2021).

3.3 Examples of Gamified Activities

Several examples of gamified activities can be effectively integrated into geriatric nursing education. Simulation-based training, utilising virtual patients and scenario-based learning, allows students to practice clinical skills in a safe environment while receiving immediate feedback on their performance (Isangula et al., 2023). Competency-based games focusing on real-world clinical challenges can enhance critical thinking and decision-making skills essential for nursing practice (Weaver et al., 2019).

Problem-solving games that simulate decision-making in elder care can also be beneficial. These games can present students with ethical dilemmas and complex patient scenarios, requiring them to apply their knowledge and skills to arrive at appropriate solutions (Kim et al., 2021). Additionally, interactive quizzes, serious games, and augmented reality experiences can further engage students and reinforce their learning (Shin & Rim, 2023).

4. BEST PRACTICES FOR IMPLEMENTING GAMIFICATION IN GERIATRIC NURSING EDUCATION

4.1 Empirical Research and Case Studies

Empirical research and case studies from nursing programs that have successfully integrated gamification provide valuable insights into best practices. For instance, studies have shown that clear objectives and outcomes are essential for guiding the design of gamified activities and ensuring that they align with educational goals (Ali,

2023). Furthermore, involving students in the development process and soliciting their feedback can enhance the relevance and effectiveness of gamified elements (Gao et al., 2017).

Collaboration with instructional designers and IT departments is also crucial for successful implementation. These partnerships can help ensure that the technological aspects of gamification are effectively integrated into the curriculum and that faculty receive the necessary training and support (Malik et al., 2015). Evaluation and continuous improvement mechanisms should be established to assess the effectiveness of gamified activities and make necessary adjustments based on student performance and feedback (Malik et al., 2015).

4.2 Challenges and Pitfalls

Despite the potential benefits of gamification, several challenges and pitfalls must be addressed. Over-gamification can lead to diminished academic rigor and a focus on extrinsic motivation, which may detract from the intrinsic value of learning (Jainurakhma et al., 2022). It is essential to strike a balance between engaging students through gamified elements while maintaining the integrity and depth of the educational content (Coughlin, 2023).

Ensuring inclusivity and accessibility for all students is another critical consideration. Addressing digital literacy and diverse learning needs is essential to create an equitable learning environment where all students can benefit from gamified experiences (Jainurakhma et al., 2022; Cowley et al., 2023). Finally, managing time and resource constraints is vital, as the development and implementation of gamified curricula may require significant investment in terms of faculty training, technology, and materials (Gao, 2024).

5. TECHNOLOGICAL PLATFORMS AND TOOLS FOR GAMIFIED NURSING EDUCATION

5.1 Overview of Digital Tools and Platforms Used for Gamification

The integration of gamification into nursing education has been facilitated by various digital tools and platforms that enhance the learning experience. Learning Management Systems (LMS) with gamification features are increasingly being adopted in nursing programs. These systems allow educators to incorporate game-like elements such as points, badges, and leaderboards into their courses, thereby increasing student engagement and motivation (Killam et al., 2021). For example, platforms like Moodle and Blackboard have integrated gamification features that enable instructors to track student progress and provide immediate feedback (Booth et al., 2018).

Standalone applications and platforms specifically designed for nursing simulation, such as *MyDispense* and *Kahoot*, have also gained popularity. *MyDispense* is a virtual pharmacy simulation tool that allows nursing students to practice medication dispensing in a risk-free environment, enhancing their clinical skills (Erdoğan & Turan, 2022). *Kahoot*, on the other hand, is a game-based learning platform that enables educators to create interactive quizzes and polls, fostering a competitive yet collaborative learning atmosphere (Coughlin, 2023). These tools not only make learning more engaging but also help students reinforce their knowledge through active participation.

Augmented Reality (AR) and Virtual Reality (VR) applications are revolutionising immersive learning experiences in nursing education. For instance, virtual ward rounds allow students to engage in realistic clinical scenarios, enhancing their understanding of patient care in a controlled setting (Craig et al., 2023). Such immersive experiences can significantly improve students' clinical reasoning and decision-making skills, preparing them for real-world challenges in geriatric nursing (Bonn et al., 2022).

5.2 Criteria for Selecting Appropriate Tools

When selecting appropriate technological tools for gamification in nursing education, several criteria should be considered. Compatibility with nursing education standards is paramount; tools must align with the competencies and learning objectives outlined by accrediting bodies (Grech & Grech, 2021). Usability and accessibility are also critical factors, as tools should be user-friendly and accessible to all students, including those with varying levels of digital literacy (Kim & Kim, 2022).

Cost-effectiveness is another important consideration, especially in resource-constrained educational environments. Institutions must evaluate the financial implications of adopting new technologies and ensure that the benefits outweigh the costs (Çağlar, 2023). By carefully assessing these criteria, nursing educators can select tools that enhance the learning experience while remaining sustainable and effective.

5.3 Case Examples of Successful Technological Integration in Geriatric Nursing Education

Several case examples illustrate the successful integration of gamification technologies in geriatric nursing education. One notable example is the implementation of a gamified curriculum in a nursing program that utilised a combination of simulation-based learning and interactive quizzes. This approach resulted in improved student engagement and knowledge retention, as evidenced by higher post-test scores compared to traditional teaching methods (Hosseini, 2023).

Another successful case involved the use of an escape room format to teach geriatric nursing concepts. This innovative approach not only enhanced teamwork and communication skills among students but also provided a fun and engaging way to learn critical clinical skills (Gentry et al., 2019). Feedback from students indicated that the gamified experience significantly improved their understanding of geriatric care principles and fostered a positive attitude towards working with older adults (Polat, 2023).

Moreover, a study evaluating the use of a serious game focused on dementia awareness among nursing students demonstrated significant improvements in students' knowledge and attitudes towards caring for patients with dementia. The game provided an interactive platform for students to engage with complex scenarios, thereby enhancing their empathy and understanding of the challenges faced by older adults (Craig et al., 2023). These examples highlight the potential of gamification to transform nursing education and prepare students for the realities of geriatric care.

6. ASSESSING THE IMPACT OF GAMIFICATION ON LEARNING OUTCOMES

6.1 Framework for Evaluating Gamified Interventions in Nursing Education

To effectively assess the impact of gamification on learning outcomes in nursing education, a comprehensive evaluation framework is necessary. This framework should encompass cognitive, emotional, and behavioural outcomes, allowing educators to measure the multifaceted effects of gamified interventions (O'Connor et al., 2018). Cognitive outcomes can be evaluated through knowledge retention and application assessments, while emotional outcomes can be gauged through student satisfaction and motivation surveys (Luokkamäki et al., 2023). Behavioural outcomes, such as clinical reasoning and decision-making skills, can be assessed through practical examinations and simulations.

6.2 Measuring Cognitive, Emotional, and Behavioural Outcomes

Research has shown that gamification can significantly enhance knowledge retention and application among nursing students. For instance, a study found that students who participated in gamified learning experiences demonstrated higher levels of knowledge retention compared to those who engaged in traditional learning methods (Kimura et al., 2023). Additionally, gamification has been linked to improvements in clinical reasoning and decision-making skills, as students are often required to apply their knowledge in realistic scenarios presented in gamified formats (Wang et al., 2021).

Empathy and communication skills, particularly in interactions with older adults, are also critical competencies that can be enhanced through gamification. Engaging in role-playing scenarios and simulations allows students to practice these skills in a safe environment, leading to increased confidence and competence in real-world situations (Kimura et al., 2023). Furthermore, student satisfaction and motivation are often higher in gamified learning environments, as the interactive nature of these experiences fosters a sense of achievement and engagement (Wang et al., 2021).

6.3 Research on the Impact of Gamification on Learner Outcomes

Numerous studies have documented the positive impact of gamification on various learner outcomes in nursing education. For example, research has indicated that gamified interventions can improve problem-solving abilities and patient safety awareness, particularly in areas such as falls prevention and medication management (Alija et al., 2019). Additionally, gamification has been shown to enhance interdisciplinary collaboration skills, as students often work in teams to solve complex clinical challenges presented in gamified formats (Hill et al., 2020).

Despite these positive findings, limitations in current assessment methods exist. Many studies rely on self-reported measures of engagement and satisfaction, which may not fully capture the depth of learning that occurs in gamified environments (Teo et al., 2023). Future research should explore more robust assessment methodologies, including direct observation and performance-based evaluations, to provide a clearer picture of the impact of gamification on nursing education outcomes (Fornari & Fonseca, 2023).

7. ADDRESSING ETHICAL AND PEDAGOGICAL CONSIDERATIONS IN GAMIFIED NURSING EDUCATION

7.1 Ethical Concerns in the Application of Gamification

The application of gamification in nursing education raises several ethical concerns that must be addressed to ensure a balanced and effective learning environment. One significant issue is the need to balance competition with collaboration. While gamification can foster a competitive spirit that motivates students, it is essential to create an environment that also encourages teamwork and collaboration, particularly in nursing, where interprofessional cooperation is vital for patient care. Overemphasis on competition may lead to negative outcomes, such as increased stress and anxiety among students, which could hinder their learning experience (Ozdamli, 2023).

Another ethical concern is the potential for burnout resulting from the overuse of gamification elements. Continuous exposure to gamified activities without adequate breaks or alternative learning methods can lead to fatigue and disengagement from the learning process. It is crucial for educators to monitor the frequency and intensity of gamified elements to prevent such burnout and ensure that students remain engaged and motivated (Yaşar et al., 2020).

Additionally, avoiding extrinsic motivation traps is vital. When students focus solely on earning badges, points, or rewards, they may lose sight of the intrinsic value of learning and the importance of developing critical nursing competencies. Educators must design gamified experiences that promote intrinsic motivation by emphasising the relevance of the content and the skills being developed, rather than merely the rewards associated with participation (Bonn et al., 2022).

7.2 Ensuring Alignment with Pedagogical Standards

To ensure that gamification aligns with pedagogical standards, nursing education programs must adhere to established accreditation and competency frameworks. For instance, the Nursing and Midwifery Council (NMC) standards outline specific competencies that nursing students must achieve, and gamified elements should be designed to support these standards (NMC, 2023). This alignment ensures that gamified activities contribute meaningfully to the educational objectives and prepare students for real-world clinical practice (İnangil et al., 2022). Furthermore, it is essential to ensure that gamified elements meet the rigor of clinical education. Nursing education requires a strong foundation in clinical skills and knowledge, and gamification should not compromise the depth and quality of education. Instead, gamified experiences should be carefully integrated into the curriculum to reinforce essential competencies while maintaining academic integrity (İnangil et al., 2022).

Culturally sensitive and ethical design of gamified content is also paramount. Educators must consider the diverse backgrounds and experiences of nursing students when developing gamified activities to ensure inclusivity and respect for all learners. This consideration includes avoiding stereotypes and ensuring that content is relevant and accessible to students from various cultural contexts (Alhammad & Moreno, 2018).

8. CASE STUDIES OF GAMIFICATION IN GERIATRIC NURSING EDUCATION

8.1 Detailed Case Studies of Educational Institutions

Several educational institutions have successfully implemented gamification in geriatric nursing education, providing valuable insights into effective practices. One notable case study involved a nursing program that integrated gamified elements into its curriculum structure, using simulation-based learning and interactive quizzes to enhance student engagement. The teaching methods employed included role-playing scenarios that allowed students to practice clinical skills in a safe environment, while assessment strategies involved both formative and summative evaluations to measure student progress and competency (Castro & Gonçalves, 2018). Outcomes from this implementation indicated significant improvements in student knowledge retention and application, as well as enhanced communication and empathy skills when interacting with older adults. Students reported higher levels of satisfaction and motivation, attributing their positive experiences to the engaging nature of the gamified activities (Serrano, 2023). Lessons learned from this case study emphasised the importance of aligning gamified elements with learning objectives and ensuring that they complement traditional teaching methods.

Another case study focused on a nursing school that adopted an escape room format to teach geriatric nursing concepts. This innovative approach not only fostered teamwork and collaboration among students but also provided a fun and engaging way to learn critical clinical skills. The curriculum structure included a series of challenges that required students to apply their knowledge in real-time, promoting active learning and critical thinking (Fijačko et al., 2020). Comparative analysis of successful and less successful implementations reveals key factors that contribute to the effectiveness of gamification in nursing education. Successful programs often feature clear learning objectives, student involvement in the design process, and ongoing assessment and feedback mechanisms. In contrast, less successful implementations may lack alignment with educational standards, fail to engage students meaningfully, or overemphasise competition at the expense of collaboration (Scaffidi et al., 2019).

9. SUSTAINABLE DEVELOPMENT GOALS

The Sustainable Development Goals (SDGs), established by the United Nations in 2015, aim to address global challenges, including those related to health, education, and inequality (da Silva and Rodrigues, 2023). Among these goals, Goal 3 emphasises ensuring healthy lives and promoting well-being for all at all ages, while Goal 4 focuses on ensuring inclusive and equitable quality education and promoting lifelong learning opportunities for all (Hosseini, 2023; Reis da Silva, 2024f). The integration of gamification in teaching geriatric nursing aligns closely with these goals by enhancing educational practices and improving health outcomes for older adults.

9.1 Enhancing Engagement and Learning Outcomes

Gamification, defined as the application of game-design elements in non-game contexts, has been shown to significantly enhance student engagement and learning outcomes in nursing education (Bonn et al., 2022). By incorporating elements such as points, badges, and leaderboards, educators can create a more interactive and motivating learning environment. This approach not only fosters a sense of competition but also encourages collaboration among students, which is crucial in nursing practice where teamwork is essential for providing quality care (Polat, 2023).

Research indicates that gamified learning experiences can lead to improved knowledge retention and application, particularly in complex subjects such as geriatric nursing (Craig et al., 2023). For instance, studies have demonstrated that nursing students who engage in gamified activities exhibit higher levels of understanding and competency in managing the unique health needs of older adults (Booth et al., 2018). This aligns with SDG 3, as better-prepared nursing professionals can contribute to improved health outcomes for the ageing population.

9.2 Promoting Lifelong Learning and Professional Development

Gamification also supports the principles of lifelong learning, as outlined in SDG 4. By making learning more engaging and enjoyable, gamified approaches can encourage nursing students to take an active role in their education and professional development (Espinosa et al., 2022). For example, interactive simulations and serious games can provide students with opportunities to practice clinical skills in a safe environment, fostering critical thinking and decision-making abilities essential for geriatric care (Çağlar, 2023).

Moreover, gamification can facilitate continuous education for practicing nurses, allowing them to stay updated with the latest practices and guidelines in geriatric care (Reis da Silva and Mitchell, 2024). This is particularly important in a rapidly evolving healthcare landscape, where ongoing education is necessary to meet the diverse needs of older patients. By integrating gamification into continuing education programs, healthcare institutions can enhance the learning experience and promote a culture of lifelong learning among nursing professionals.

9.3 Addressing Health Inequalities

The use of gamification in nursing education can also help address health inequalities, particularly among vulnerable populations such as the elderly. By creating engaging and accessible learning experiences, gamification can empower nursing students to develop the skills and knowledge necessary to provide equitable care to all patients, regardless of their background (Dahalan et al., 2023). This is particularly relevant in geriatric nursing, where cultural competence and sensitivity are essential for effectively addressing the diverse needs of older adults.

Furthermore, gamified educational tools can be designed to raise awareness about specific health issues affecting older adults, such as dementia and chronic disease management. By engaging students in these topics through interactive learning experiences, educators can foster a deeper understanding of the challenges faced by older patients and the importance of providing compassionate, patient-centred care (Hökkä et al., 2022). This aligns with the broader objectives of the SDGs (especially SDG 10), which seek to promote health equity and improve the quality of life for all individuals.

10. EMOTIONAL INTELLIGENCE AND GAMIFICATION

Emotional intelligence (EI) plays a crucial role in nursing, particularly in the context of geriatric care, where understanding and managing emotions—both one's own and those of patients—are essential for effective communication and compassionate care (da Silva, 2022; Reis da Silva, 2024g; Reis da Silva, 2024h). The integration of gamification in nursing education can enhance the development of emotional intelligence among nursing students, equipping them with the skills necessary to navigate the complexities of caring for older adults.

10.1 The Role of Emotional Intelligence in Nursing

Emotional intelligence is defined as the ability to recognise, understand, and manage one's own emotions while also being able to empathise with others (Elattar et al., 2023; Reis da Silva et al., 2024). In nursing, high emotional intelligence is associated with improved patient outcomes, enhanced communication skills, and better stress management (Hrefish & Al-Hadrawi, 2020). For instance, nurses with strong emotional intelligence can establish rapport with patients, manage their emotions during stressful situations, and provide empathetic care, which is particularly important in geriatric nursing where patients may experience a range of emotional and psychological challenges (Lu & Shorey, 2021; Reis da Silva, 2024i; Reis da Silva, 2024j).

Research has shown that emotional intelligence can significantly impact nurses' job performance and satisfaction. For example, nurses with higher emotional intelligence tend to experience lower levels of burnout and job-related stress, as they are better equipped to handle the emotional demands of their roles (Mariati et al., 2022). Furthermore, emotional intelligence has been linked to improved communication skills, which are vital for effective interactions with older patients who may have unique needs and concerns (Yu, 2023; Reis da Silva, 2024k).

10.2 Gamification as a Tool for Enhancing Emotional Intelligence

Gamification, the application of game design elements in non-game contexts, offers a unique approach to fostering emotional intelligence in nursing education. By incorporating gamified elements such as role-playing scenarios, simulations, and interactive quizzes, educators can create engaging learning experiences that promote the development of emotional intelligence skills (Li et al., 2022). For instance, simulation-based learning allows nursing students to practice their emotional responses in realistic scenarios, enhancing their ability to manage emotions and empathize with patients (Baghdadi, 2023).

Moreover, gamification can facilitate the development of soft skills, including communication and empathy, through collaborative and competitive activities. For example, team-based challenges in a gamified learning environment can encourage students to work together, share perspectives, and develop a deeper understanding of the emotional dynamics involved in patient care (Mousavi, 2023). This collaborative approach not only enhances emotional intelligence but also prepares students for the teamwork required in clinical settings.

10.3 Measuring the Impact of Gamification on Emotional Intelligence

To assess the effectiveness of gamification in enhancing emotional intelligence among nursing students, various evaluation methods can be employed. Pre- and post-intervention assessments can measure changes in emotional intelligence levels, while qualitative feedback from students can provide insights into their experiences and perceived improvements in their emotional skills (Farhana, 2023). Additionally, incorporating reflective practices, such as journaling or group discussions, can help students articulate their emotional growth and the impact of gamified learning experiences on their development (Turjuman, 2023).

Research has indicated that gamified interventions can lead to significant improvements in emotional intelligence among nursing students. For example, a study found that students who participated in gamified learning activities demonstrated higher levels of empathy and emotional awareness compared to those who engaged in traditional learning methods (Hamouda & Nagshabandi, 2018). These findings underscore the potential of gamification to not only enhance academic knowledge but also foster essential emotional competencies in nursing education.

11. FUTURE DIRECTIONS FOR GAMIFICATION IN NURSING EDUCATION

11.1 Emerging Trends in Gamification Technologies

As the landscape of nursing education continues to evolve, several emerging trends in gamification technologies are poised to enhance the learning experience for nursing students, particularly in the context of geriatric care. One significant trend is the integration of artificial intelligence (AI) into gamified learning platforms. AI can personalise learning experiences by adapting content to meet individual students' needs, thereby enhancing engagement and improving learning outcomes. For example, AI-driven platforms can analyse student performance data to provide tailored feedback and suggest specific areas for improvement, fostering a more effective learning environment (Hope et al., 2022). Additionally, the use of virtual reality (VR) and augmented reality (AR) technologies is gaining traction in nursing education. These immersive technologies allow students to engage in realistic simulations of clinical scenarios, providing opportunities to practice skills in a safe and controlled environment. For instance, VR can simulate complex patient interactions, enabling nursing students to develop their emotional intelligence and communication skills when dealing with older adults. AR can enhance traditional learning by overlaying digital information onto real-world environments, allowing students to visualize anatomical structures or medication interactions in real-time (Oak, 2018).

Adaptive learning platforms are another emerging trend that can significantly impact nursing education. These platforms use algorithms to assess students' knowledge and skills, adjusting the difficulty and type of content presented based on their performance. This personalised approach can help nursing students master essential competencies at their own pace, ensuring they are well-prepared for the challenges of geriatric nursing (Furr et al., 2015).

11.2 Future Opportunities

The future of gamification in nursing education also presents opportunities for interdisciplinary collaboration in the development of gamified curricula. By bringing together experts from various fields—such as healthcare, education, technology, and psychology—educators can create more comprehensive and effective gamified learning experiences. For example, collaboration between nursing educators and game designers can lead to the development of innovative simulation games that accurately reflect the complexities of geriatric care, fostering both clinical skills and emotional intelligence among nursing students (Graetz et al., 2023).

Moreover, interdisciplinary collaboration can extend to partnerships with healthcare organizations, allowing nursing programs to align their curricula with real-world practices and patient care standards. Such collaborations can facilitate the integration of gamified learning experiences that reflect current healthcare challenges, ensuring that nursing students are equipped with the knowledge and skills necessary to provide high-quality care to older adults (Crouch et al., 2015).

11.3 Research Gaps and Areas for Further Exploration

Despite the promising potential of gamification in nursing education, several research gaps remain that warrant further exploration. One critical area is the need for longitudinal studies examining the impact of gamification on career-long learning and professional development in geriatric nursing. Understanding how gamified learning experiences influence nurses' ongoing education and skill development over time can provide valuable insights into the effectiveness of these approaches (Hope et al., 2022).

Additionally, cross-cultural research on the effectiveness of gamification in diverse healthcare settings is essential. As healthcare systems and cultural contexts vary widely, it is crucial to investigate how gamified learning experiences can be adapted to meet the needs of nursing students in different regions and populations. Such research can help identify best practices and inform the development of culturally sensitive gamified curricula that enhance the learning experience for all nursing students (Oak, 2018).

12. CONCLUSION

The integration of gamification into geriatric nursing education has the potential to enhance student engagement, improve knowledge retention, and better prepare future nurses to meet the unique challenges of caring for older adults. As the demand for skilled geriatric nurses continues to rise, innovative educational strategies such as gamification will be essential in shaping a competent and compassionate workforce capable of providing high-quality care to the aging population (Hodijah, 2022).

Integrating gamification into geriatric nursing curricula presents an opportunity to enhance student engagement and learning outcomes. By carefully considering curriculum alignment, balancing traditional and gamified approaches, and addressing potential challenges, nursing educators can create a dynamic and effective learning environment that prepares future nurses to meet the complex needs of the aging population. The integration of gamification into nursing education, particularly in the context of geriatric care, offers significant potential for enhancing student engagement and learning outcomes. By leveraging technological tools and carefully assessing their impact, nursing educators can create dynamic learning environments that prepare future nurses to meet the complex needs of the aging population.

Addressing ethical and pedagogical considerations in gamified nursing education is essential for creating a balanced and effective learning environment. By carefully designing gamified experiences that promote intrinsic motivation, align with accreditation standards, and consider the diverse needs of students, nursing educators can enhance the educational experience and better prepare future nurses for the complexities of geriatric care.

The integration of gamification in teaching geriatric nursing is not only a pedagogical innovation but also a strategic approach to advancing the Sustainable Development Goals. By enhancing student engagement, promoting lifelong learning, and addressing health inequalities, gamification can play a pivotal role in preparing future nurses to meet the complex needs of the aging population. As nursing education continues to evolve, embracing gamification can contribute to a more effective and equitable healthcare system that aligns with the global commitment to sustainable development.

The future of gamification in nursing education is bright, with emerging technologies and interdisciplinary collaboration offering exciting opportunities for enhancing the learning experience. By addressing research gaps and exploring the effectiveness of gamified approaches in diverse contexts, nursing educators can ensure that future nurses are well-prepared to meet the complex needs of older adults in an ever-evolving healthcare landscape.

REFERENCES:

Afirando, R., Santoso, H., Junus, K., Putra, P., & Lawanto, O. (2023). Motivation to use gamification elements in e-learning for formal and non-formal education. *Indonesian Journal of Computer Science*, 12(1). Advance online publication. DOI: 10.33022/ijcs.v12i1.3151

Al-Nawafleh, A., Musleh, S., & Nawafleh, N. (2024). The patient safety curriculum: An interventional study on the effectiveness of patient safety education for Jordanian nursing students. *PLoS One*, 19(5), e0292713. DOI: 10.1371/journal.pone.0292713 PMID: 38722975

Alhammad, M., & Moreno, A. (2018). Gamification in software engineering education: A systematic mapping. *Journal of Systems and Software*, 141, 131–150. DOI: 10.1016/j.jss.2018.03.065

Ali, W. (2023). Enhancing children's learning experience as a sustainable approach through gamified application design. *E3s Web of Conferences*, 426, 02115. https://doi.org/DOI: 10.1051/e3sconf/202342602115

Alija, M., López, M., Cao, M., Fernández-Castro, M., Garcia, S., Frutos, M., & Jiménez, J. (2019). Impact of educational games on academic outcomes of students in the degree in nursing. *PLoS One*, 14(7), e0220388. DOI: 10.1371/journal.pone.0220388 PMID: 31356621

Arboleda-Tinay, M. (2021). Perception of university of Tripoli, faculty of nursing students on the bachelor of science in nursing (BSN) curriculum. *International Journal of Current Science Research and Review*, 04(08). Advance online publication. DOI: 10.47191/ijcsrr/V4-i8-11

Baghdadi, N., Sankarapandian, C., Arulappan, J., Taani, M. H., Snethen, J., & Andargeery, S. Y. (2023). The association between nursing students' happiness, emotional intelligence, and perceived caring behavior in Riyadh city, Saudi Arabia. *Health Care*, 12(1), 67. DOI: 10.3390/healthcare12010067 PMID: 38200973

Bahrami, M., Purfarzad, Z., Keshvari, M., & Rafiei, M. (2019). The components of nursing competence in caring for older people in Iranian hospitals: A qualitative study. *Iranian Journal of Nursing and Midwifery Research*, 24(2), 124. DOI: 10.4103/ijnmr.IJNMR_83_18 PMID: 30820224

Bennani, S., Maalel, A., & Ghezala, H. (2021). Adaptive gamification in e-learning: A literature review and future challenges. *Computer Applications in Engineering Education*, 30(2), 628–642. DOI: 10.1002/cae.22477

Bigdeli, S., Hosseinzadeh, Z., Dehnad, A., Sohrabi, Z., Aalaa, M., Haghani, F., & Atlasi, R. (2023). Underpinning learning theories of medical educational games: A scoping review. *Medical Journal of the Islamic Republic of Iran*. Advance online publication. DOI: 10.47176/mjiri.37.26 PMID: 37180860

Biryukov, A., Brikoshina, I., Mikhalevich, N., Sycheva, S., & Халимон, E. (2021). Gamification in education: threats or new opportunities. *SHS Web of Conferences*, 103, 02001. https://doi.org/DOI: 10.1051/shsconf/202110302001

Blebil, A., Dujaili, J., Mohammed, A., Thiruchelvam, K., Lee, S., Elkalmi, R., Soh, Y. C., Yong, A., & Roien, R. (2022). Knowledge and attitude of pharmacy students regarding geriatric care: Questionnaire-based analysis in Malaysia. *Advances in Medical Education and Practice*, 13, 95–102. DOI: 10.2147/AMEP.S344872 PMID: 35082550

Bonn, J., Mulkey, D., & Goers, J. (2022). Using gamification to engage clinical nurses in quality improvement. *Journal for Nurses in Professional Development*, 39(5), E148–E153. DOI: 10.1097/NND.0000000000000898 PMID: 37683219

Booth, R., Sinclair, B., McMurray, J., Strudwick, G., Watson, G., Ladak, H., Zwarenstein, M., McBride, S., Chan, R., & Brennan, L. (2018). Evaluating a serious gaming electronic medication administration record system among nursing students: Protocol for a pragmatic randomized controlled trial. *JMIR Research Protocols*, 7(5), e138. DOI: 10.2196/resprot.9601 PMID: 29807885

Burhenn, P., Ferrell, B., Johnson, S., & Hurria, A. (2016). Improving nurses' knowledge about older adults with cancer. *Oncology Nursing Forum*, 43(4), 497–504. DOI: 10.1188/16.ONF.497-504 PMID: 27314192

Buthelezi, N., & Shopo, K. D. (2023). Challenges experienced by nurse educators developing postgraduate nursing diploma curriculum programmes, Gauteng. *Curationis*, 46(1). Advance online publication. DOI: 10.4102/curationis.v46i1.2447 PMID: 37782237

Çağlar, S., & Okuyan, C. B. (2023). The impact of distance learning on the attitudes of nursing students: An online survey study. *Acta Scientiarum Health Sciences*, 46(1), e63213. DOI: 10.4025/actascihealthsci.v46i1.63213

Castro, T., & Gonçalves, L. (2018). The use of gamification to teach in the nursing field. *Revista Brasileira de Enfermagem*, 71(3), 1038–1045. DOI: 10.1590/0034-7167-2017-0023 PMID: 29924165

Coughlin, V., Ho, M. R., & Alvarez, G. (2023). Escape the room! utilizing gamification in a preceptor training workshop. *Journal for Nurses in Professional Development*. Advance online publication. DOI: 10.1097/NND.0000000000000977 PMID: 37812131

Cowley, S. A., Tzouvara, V., & Horta Reis da Silva, T. (2023). Public Health: healthy ageing and well-being. *In Redfern's Nursing Older People*. Fifth edition. Editors: Ross, Harris, Fitzpatrick and Abley. Elsevier.

Craig, S., Stark, P., Wilson, C., Carter, G., Clarke, S., & Mitchell, G. (2023). Evaluation of a dementia awareness game for undergraduate nursing students in Northern Ireland: A pre-/post-test study. *BMC Nursing*, 22(1), 177. Advance online publication. DOI: 10.1186/s12912-023-01345-2 PMID: 37217937

Crouch, S., Fillmore, L., Fly, L., & Ukot, E. (2015). Impact of inter-professional education on nursing student outcomes in the online environment. [AJHS]. *American Journal of Health Sciences*, 6(2), 101–110. DOI: 10.19030/ajhs.v6i2.9499

da Silva, T. H. R. (2022). Emotional awareness and emotional intelligence. *British Journal of Community Nursing*, 27(12), 573–574. DOI: 10.12968/bjcn.2022.27.12.573 PMID: 36519463

da Silva, T. H. R., & Rodrigues, E. C. P. (2023). Body Image Related Discrimination. In Leal Filho, W., Azul, A. M., Brandli, L., Lange Salvia, A., Özuyar, P. G., & Wall, T. (Eds.), *Reduced Inequalities. Encyclopedia of the UN Sustainable Development Goals*. Springer., DOI: 10.1007/978-3-319-71060-0_61-1

Dahalan, F., Alias, N., & Shaharom, M. (2023). Gamification and game based learning for vocational education and training: A systematic literature review. *Education and Information Technologies*, 29(2), 1279–1317. DOI: 10.1007/s10639-022-11548-w PMID: 36688221

Dečman, N., Rep, A., & Titgemeyer, M. (2022). Who is more eager to use gamification in economic disciplines? comparison of students and educators. *Business Systems Research Journal*, 13(2), 96–116. DOI: 10.2478/bsrj-2022-0017

Dichev, C., & Dicheva, D. (2017). Gamifying education: what is known, what is believed and what remains uncertain: a critical review. *International Journal of Educational Technology in Higher Education*, 14(1), 9. Advance online publication. DOI: 10.1186/s41239-017-0042-5

Doležalová, J., Tóthová, V., & Neugebauer, J. (2022). Selected aspects of nursing practice related to the usage of evaluation tools for population aged over 60 years. *Kontakt*, 24(2), 131–136. DOI: 10.32725/kont.2021.044

Doroudi, F., Ashourizadeh, H., Moosapour, S., Ganjizadeh, A., Ranjbar Shourabi, A., Parnia, A., Kazemipour, F., Mohraz, M., & Bayat Jozani, Z. (2023). Gamified educational learning path on HIV/aids stigma and discrimination (redxir): Design, development and pilot study. *Medical Journal of the Islamic Republic of Iran*. Advance online publication. DOI: 10.47176/mjiri.37.136 PMID: 38318411

Elattar, N., Osman, F., & Mahmoud, H. (2023). Effect of emotional intelligence based training program on burnout, psychological capital and job performance among psychiatric nurses. *Menoufia Nursing Journal*, 8(1), 259–276. DOI: 10.21608/menj.2023.303432

Erdoğan, Ç., & Turan, T. (2022). Evaluation of the effectiveness of digital game-based learning given to nursing students for the developmental care of infants in neonatal intensive care unit. *Computers, Informatics, Nursing*, 41(5), 300–308. DOI: 10.1097/CIN.0000000000000920 PMID: 37145853

Espinosa, J., Vaquero-Abellán, M., Perea-Moreno, A., Pedrós-Pérez, G., Martínez-Jiménez, P., & Aparicio-Martínez, P. (2022). Gamification as a promoting tool of motivation for creating sustainable higher education institutions. *International Journal of Environmental Research and Public Health*, 19(5), 2599. DOI: 10.3390/ijerph19052599 PMID: 35270291

Fallatah, A. I. (2023). The Effectiveness of a Platform based on Gamification in developing Creative thinking among Middle School Students. *JALHSS*, (93), 299-316. 93. https://doi.org/DOI: 10.33193/JALHSS.93.2023.864

Farhana, A., Kouser, S., Ghani, M., Khatoon, T., & Asghar, R. (2023). Effect of emotional intelligence on job satisfaction among nurses: Descriptive study. *PJMHS*, 17(6), 127–129. DOI: 10.53350/pjmhs2023176127

Fijačko, N., Gosak, L., Debeljak, N., Skok, P., Štiglic, G., & Cilar, L. (2020). Gamification in nursing. *Slovenian Nursing Review*, 54(2), 133–152. DOI: 10.14528/snr.2020.54.2.2991

Fitzpatrick, J. M., Bianchi, L. A., Hayes, N., Da Silva, T., & Harris, R. (2023). Professional development and career planning for nurses working in care homes for older people: A scoping review. *International Journal of Older People Nursing*, 18(1), e12519. DOI: 10.1111/opn.12519 PMID: 36441621

Fiuza-Fernández, A., Portela, L., Soto-Carballo, J., & Juste, M. (2022). Study of the knowledge about gamification of degree in primary education students. *PLoS One*, 17(3), e0263107. DOI: 10.1371/journal.pone.0263107 PMID: 35349574

Fornari, L., & Fonseca, R. (2023). Critical-emancipatory educational intervention through games to face gender violence. *Revista Brasileira De Enfermagem*, 76(suppl 2). https://doi.org/DOI: 10.1590/0034-7167-2022-0299

Fox, M., Butler, J., Persaud, M., Tregunno, D., Sidani, S., & McCague, H. (2015). A multi-method study of the geriatric learning needs of acute care hospital nurses in Ontario, Canada. *Research in Nursing & Health*, 39(1), 66–76. DOI: 10.1002/nur.21699 PMID: 26471253

Furr, S., Lane, S., Serafica, R., & Hodge, M. (2015). Service-learning and interprofessional education in nursing. *Journal of Christian Nursing*, 32(3), 162–167. DOI: 10.1097/CNJ.0000000000000178 PMID: 26211302

Gao, X., & Chen, P. (2024). Establishment of a geriatric nursing curriculum with human caring by situational simulation. *Journal of Curriculum and Teaching*, 13(1), 71. DOI: 10.5430/jct.v13n1p71

Gao, Y., Zhang, P., Wen, S., & Chen, Y. (2017). Challenge, opportunity and development: Influencing factors and tendencies of curriculum innovation on undergraduate nursing education in the mainland of China. *Clinical Nursing Research*, 4(3), 113–116. DOI: 10.25164/SEP.2017040202

Gentry, S., Gauthier, A., Ehrstrom, B., Wortley, D., Lilienthal, A., Car, L., & Car, J. (2019). Serious gaming and gamification education in health professions: Systematic review. *Journal of Medical Internet Research*, 21(3), e12994. DOI: 10.2196/12994 PMID: 30920375

Ghamgosar, A., Zarghani, M., & Nemati-Anaraki, L. (2021). Bibliometric analysis on geriatric nursing research in web of science (1900–2020). *BioMed Research International*, 2021, 1–11. DOI: 10.1155/2021/8758161 PMID: 34621898

Graetz, D., Chen, Y., Devidas, M., Antillón-Klussmann, F., Fú, L., Quintero, K., Fuentes-Alabi, S. L., Gassant, P. Y., Kaye, E. C., Baker, J. N., Rodriguez Galindo, C., & Mack, J. (2023). Interdisciplinary care of pediatric oncology patients: A survey of clinicians in Central America and the Caribbean. *Pediatric Blood & Cancer*, 70(5), e30244. Advance online publication. DOI: 10.1002/pbc.30244 PMID: 36788461

Grech, J., & Grech, J. (2021). Nursing students' evaluation of a gamified public health educational webinar: A comparative pilot study. *Nursing Open*, 8(4), 1812–1821. DOI: 10.1002/nop2.826 PMID: 33675289

Hamouda, G., & Nagshabandi, E. (2018). The perception of emotional intelligence self-assessment among nursing students. *American Journal of Nursing Science*, 7(5), 173. DOI: 10.11648/j.ajns.20180705.13

Haske-Palomino, M., Carlson, R., & Gatley, L. (2023). Elder veteran program: A description of a nurse practitioner–led inpatient geriatric consult model. *Journal of the American Association of Nurse Practitioners*, 35(4), 229–234. DOI: 10.1097/JXX.0000000000000844 PMID: 36857530

Hellberg, A. (2023). The story of the hatter and the agile methods course: gamification and game thinking in education. *Journal of Pedagogical Research*. https://doi.org/DOI: 10.33902/JPR.202320130

Hill, M., Salmon, D., Chudleigh, J., & Aitken, L. (2020). Practice nurses' perceptions of their immunization role and strategies used to promote measles, mumps, and rubella vaccine uptake in 2014 – 2018: A qualitative study. *Journal of Advanced Nursing*, 77(2), 948–956. DOI: 10.1111/jan.14652 PMID: 33222235

Hodijah, A. (2022). Application of gamification in ethnic excellence-based character education programs. [Journal of Art Design Art Education and Culture Studies]. *JADECS*, 7(2), 103. DOI: 10.17977/um037v7i22022p103-114

Hökkä, M., Rajala, M., Kaakinen, P., Lehto, J., & Pesonen, H. (2022). The effect of teaching methods in palliative care education for undergraduate nursing and medical students: A systematic review. *International Journal of Palliative Nursing*, 28(6), 245–253. DOI: 10.12968/ijpn.2022.28.6.245 PMID: 35727833

Hope, D., Grant, G., Rogers, G., & King, M. (2022). Gamification in pharmacy education: A systematic quantitative literature review. *International Journal of Pharmacy Practice*, 31(1), 15–31. DOI: 10.1093/ijpp/riac099 PMID: 36472962

Hosseini, M. (2023). Crossover design in triage education: The effectiveness of simulated interactive vs. routine training on student nurses' performance in a disaster situation. *BMC Research Notes*, 16(1), 313. Advance online publication. DOI: 10.1186/s13104-023-06596-5 PMID: 37926836

Hrefish, Z. A., & Al-Hadrawi, H. H. (2020). Emotional intelligence and work-related stress among nurses working in psychiatric hospitals. *Indian Journal of Forensic Medicine Toxicology*, 14(1), 1–5. DOI: 10.37506/ijfmt.v14i1.227

Hu, F., Lee, H., & Li, Y. (2021). Exploration of geriatric care competencies in registered nurses in hospitals. *The Journal of Nursing Research*, 29(4), e159. DOI: 10.1097/JNR.0000000000000441 PMID: 34034305

İnangil, D., Dinçer, B., & Kabuk, A. (2022). Effectiveness of the use of animation and gamification in online distance education during pandemic. *Computers, Informatics, Nursing*, 40(5), 335–340. DOI: 10.1097/CIN.0000000000000902 PMID: 35266898

Isangula, K., Pallangyo, E., & Ndirangu-Mugo, E. (2023). Improving nursing education curriculum as a tool for strengthening the nurse–client relationships in maternal and child healthcare: Insights from a human-centered design study in rural Tanzania. *Frontiers in Public Health*, 11, 1072721. Advance online publication. DOI: 10.3389/fpubh.2023.1072721 PMID: 36817890

Jacobs-Wingo, J., Schlegelmilch, J., Berliner, M., Airall-Simon, G., & Lang, W. (2018). Emergency preparedness training for hospital nursing staff, New York City, 2012–2016. *Journal of Nursing Scholarship*, 51(1), 81–87. DOI: 10.1111/jnu.12425 PMID: 30296004

Jainurakhma, J., Martina, I., Sekarini, S., Fanani, Q., & Nuraini, I. (2022). Nursing education resilience: The effective strategies to address the challenges of stakeholders during the covid-19 pandemic. *JAMP Jurnal Administrasi Dan Manajemen Pendidikan*, 5(2), 105–114. DOI: 10.17977/um027v5i22022p105

Jawabreh, R., & Bicen, H. (2020). Content analysis of articles that related to the use of google classroom and gamification in education from 2016 to 2020. *Near East University Online. Journal of Education*, 3(2), 53–65. DOI: 10.32955/neuje.v3i2.247

Ji, Y., Lee, H., Lee, T., Choi, M., Lee, H., Kim, S., Do, H. K., Kim, S., Chu, S. H., Park, J., Kim, Y. M., & Park, T. (2021). Developing an integrated curriculum for patient safety in an undergraduate nursing program: A case study. *BMC Nursing*, 20(1), 172. Advance online publication. DOI: 10.1186/s12912-021-00694-0 PMID: 34535121

Kang, Y., Yang, I., Lee, E., & Bang, C. (2022). Development of international nursing standard–based curriculum for north Korean nurses. *International Nursing Review*, 69(4), 503–513. DOI: 10.1111/inr.12761 PMID: 35775835

Kickmeier-Rust, M. (2023). Effects of gamifying mathematics lessons at high school level. *European Conference on Games Based Learning*, 17(1), 319-326. https://doi.org/DOI: 10.34190/ecgbl.17.1.1593

Killam, L., Timmermans, K., & Shapiro, S. (2021). Motivation and engagement of nursing students in 2 gamified courses. *Nurse Educator*, 46(6), E173–E178. DOI: 10.1097/NNE.0000000000001065 PMID: 34359066

Kim, B., Lee, M., & Jang, S. (2021). Hospital nurses' empathy and moral sensitivity toward elderly care: A cross-sectional study. *Journal of Nursing Management*, 30(7), 2138–2146. DOI: 10.1111/jonm.13442 PMID: 34350659

Kim, H., & Kim, B. (2022). Effects of situation-based flipped learning and gamification as combined methodologies in psychiatric nursing education: A quasi-experimental study. *Health Care*, 10(4), 644. DOI: 10.3390/healthcare10040644 PMID: 35455822

Kim, H., Lee, J., & Lee, E. (2021). Virtual experience of perioperative patients: Walking in the patients' shoes using virtual reality and blended learning. *International Journal of Environmental Research and Public Health*, 18(12), 6457. DOI: 10.3390/ijerph18126457 PMID: 34203661

Kimura, R., Matsunaga, M., Barroga, E., & Hayashi, N. (2023). Asynchronous e-learning with technology-enabled and enhanced training for continuing education of nurses: A scoping review. *BMC Medical Education*, 23(1), 505. Advance online publication. DOI: 10.1186/s12909-023-04477-w PMID: 37442970

Kostolányová, K., & Klubal, L. (2018). Gamification in LMS courses. *International Journal of Information and Communication Technology Education*, 7(2), 46–50. DOI: 10.1515/ijicte-2018-0009

Lester, D., Skulmoski, G., Fisher, D., Mehrotra, V., Lim, I., Lang, A., & Keogh, J. (2023). Drivers and barriers to the utilisation of gamification and game-based learning in universities: A systematic review of educators' perspectives. *British Journal of Educational Technology*, 54(6), 1748–1770. DOI: 10.1111/bjet.13311

Li, M., Qin, G., & Li, Y. (2022). Mediating effects of emotional intelligence on the relationship between empathy and humanistic care ability in nursing students: A cross-sectional descriptive study. *Medicine*, 101(46), e31673. DOI: 10.1097/MD.0000000000031673 PMID: 36401377

Li, Q., Bu, Z., Xue, M., Huang, A., Tu, W., & Xu, G. (2022). Visual analysis of research hotspots in geriatric nursing education in China and abroad. *Journal of Healthcare Engineering*, 2022, 1–7. DOI: 10.1155/2022/7472188 PMID: 35480150

Lu, Y., & Shorey, S. (2021). Nurses' perceptions of emotional intelligence in the clinical setting: A qualitative systematic review. *Journal of Nursing Management*, 29(8), 2453–2460. DOI: 10.1111/jonm.13406 PMID: 34216499

Luokkamäki, S., Härkänen, M., Saano, S., Kokkonen, K., & Vehviläinen-Julkunen, K. (2023). Registered nurses' experiences of using a 3d game in the development of clinical competency: A qualitative study. *Journal of Medical Education*, 22(1). Advance online publication. DOI: 10.5812/jme-129060

Malik, G., McKenna, L., & Griffiths, D. (2015). An analysis of evidence-based practice curriculum integration in Australian undergraduate nursing programs. *GSTF Journal of Nursing and Health Care*, 3(1). Advance online publication. DOI: 10.5176/2345-718X_3.1.104

Mariati, L., Jakri, Y., & Djerubu, D. (2022). The effect of emotional intelligence on nurse's communication skill. [Journal of Ners and Midwifery]. *Jurnal Ners Dan Kebidanan*, 9(2), 218–226. DOI: 10.26699/jnk.v9i2.ART.p218-226

Mersin, S., Kilic, H., & İbrahimoğlu, Ö. (2020). Learning outcomes of nursing curriculum in turkey: A cross-sectional study. *Frontiers of Nursing*, 7(2), 129–134. DOI: 10.2478/fon-2020-0011

Mousavi, S., Hassanvand, P., Mahmoudi, A., Hosseinigolafshani, S. Z., Rajabi, M., & Rashvand, F. (2023). The relationship between emotional intelligence and the moral performance of nurses. *Journal of Nursing and Midwifery Sciences*, 10(4). Advance online publication. DOI: 10.5812/jnms-141609

Nursing and Midwifery Council. (2023). Standards for pre-registration nursing programmes. Link: https://www.nmc.org.uk/globalassets/sitedocuments/standards/2024/standards-for-pre-registration-nursing-programmes.pdf

O'Connor, S., Jolliffe, S., Stanmore, E., Renwick, L., & Booth, R. (2018). Social media in nursing and midwifery education: A mixed study systematic review. *Journal of Advanced Nursing*, 74(10), 2273–2289. DOI: 10.1111/jan.13799 PMID: 30019486

Oak, J. (2018). A systematic literature review on utilization of gamification in nursing. *International Journal of Advanced Nursing Education and Research*, 3(1), 43–48. DOI: 10.21742/IJANER.2018.3.1.08

Ozdamli, F., & Milrich, F. (2023). Positive and negative impacts of gamification on the fitness industry. *European Journal of Investigation in Health, Psychology and Education*, 13(8), 1411–1422. DOI: 10.3390/ejihpe13080103 PMID: 37623300

Özdemir, İ., & Kadıoğlu, H. (2023). A curriculum development project for a school nursing certification program in turkey: A Delphi study. *Clinical and Experimental Health Sciences*, 13(1), 122–128. DOI: 10.33808/clinexphealthsci.1060107

Park, S., & Kim, S. (2021). Is sustainable online learning possible with gamification?—The effect of gamified online learning on student learning. *Sustainability (Basel)*, 13(8), 4267. DOI: 10.3390/su13084267

Pishchanska, V., Altukhova, A., Prusak, Y., Kovmir, N., & Goncharov, A. (2022). Gamification of education: Innovative forms of teaching and education in culture and art. *Eduweb*, 16(2), 119–133. DOI: 10.46502/issn.1856-7576/2022.16.02.8

Polat, E. (2023). Gamification implementation for educational purposes: A scoping review (2013-2018). *Educational Technology Quarterly*, 2023(3), 367–400. DOI: 10.55056/etq.589

Puspitasari, I., & Arifin, S. (2023). Implementation of gamification on learning motivation: A meta-analysis study. *International Journal of Progressive Sciences and Technologies*, 40(1), 356. DOI: 10.52155/ijpsat.v40.1.5596

Reis da Silva, T. H. (2023a). Falls assessment and prevention in the nursing home and community. *British Journal of Community Nursing*, 28(2), 68–72. DOI: 10.12968/bjcn.2023.28.2.68 PMID: 36735363

Reis da Silva, T. H. (2023b). Ageing in place: Ageing at home and in the community. *British Journal of Community Nursing*, 28(5), 213–214. DOI: 10.12968/bjcn.2023.28.5.213 PMID: 37130715

Reis da Silva, T. (2024a). The Evolution of Nursing for Older Adult: A Historical Perspective. *Associative J Health Sci.* 3(3). AJHS. 000561. 2024. DOI: . Link: https://crimsonpublishers.com/ajhs/pdf/AJHS.000561.pdfDOI: 10.31031/AJHS.2024.03.000561

Reis da Silva, T. H. (2024b). Pharmacokinetics in older people: An overview of prescribing practice. *Journal of Prescribing Practice*, 6(9), 374–381. DOI: 10.12968/jprp.2024.6.9.374

Reis da Silva, T. H. (2024c). Falls prevention in older people and the role of nursing. *British Journal of Community Nursing*, 29(7), 335–339. DOI: 10.12968/bjcn.2024.0005 PMID: 38963269

Reis da Silva, T. H. (2024d). Understanding body fluid balance, dehydration and intravenous fluid therapy. *Emergency Nurse*. Advance online publication. DOI: 10.7748/en.2024.e2201 PMID: 38978385

Reis da Silva, T. (2024e). Can supplementing vitamin B12 improve mental health outcomes?: A literature review. *British Journal of Community Nursing*, 29(3), 137–146. DOI: 10.12968/bjcn.2024.29.3.137 PMID: 38421889

Reis da Silva, T. H. (2024f) The Value of Emotional Intelligence in Midwifery: Enhancing Care and Outcomes for Mothers and Infants through Sustainable Development Goals and Leadership. *Journal of Womens Healthcare & Midwifery Research.*https://www.onlinescientificresearch.com/articles/the-value-of-emotional-intelligence-in-midwifery-enhancing-care-and-outcomes-for-mothers-and-infants-through-sustainable-developme.pdfDOI: 10.47363/JWHMR/2024(3)119

Reis da Silva, T. H. (2024g). Chapter 6 – Navigating Healthcare Complexity: Integrating Business Fundamentals into Nursing Leadership. In Sedky, A. *Resiliency Strategies for Long-Term Business Success*. Pp. 145-168. IGI Global. DOI: 10.4018/979-8-3693-9168-6.ch006

Reis da Silva, T. H. (2024h). Chapter 11 - Integrating business essentials into Gerontological Nursing: Enhancing Care for Older Adults in Diverse Settings. In Sedky, A. *Resiliency Strategies for Long-Term Business Success*. Pp. 283-316. IGI Global. DOI: DOI: 10.4018/979-8-3693-9168-6.ch011

Reis da Silva, T. H. (2024i). Emotional Intelligence in Higher Education: Humanising Technology for Holistic Student Development. In Tikadar, S. (Ed.), *Liu, H.; Bhattacharya, P.; Bhattacharya, S. Humanizing Technology With Emotional Intelligence*. IGI Global., DOI: 10.4018/979-8-3693-7011-7.ch007

Reis da Silva, T. H. (2024j). Emotional Intelligence in Teaching Geriatric Nursing: Humanising Technology for Compassionate Care in Higher Education. In Tikadar, S. (Ed.), *Liu, H.; Bhattacharya, P.; Bhattacharya, S. Humanizing Technology With Emotional Intelligence*. IGI Global., DOI: 10.4018/979-8-3693-7011-7.ch008

Reis da Silva, T. H. (2024k). Emotional Intelligence in Integrative Medicine: Enhancing Patient-Centred Care Through Humanised Technology. In Tikadar, S. (Ed.), *Liu, H.; Bhattacharya, P.; Bhattacharya, S. Humanizing Technology With Emotional Intelligence*. IGI Global., DOI: 10.4018/979-8-3693-7011-7.ch012

Reis da Silva, T. H., & Mitchell, A. (2024). Integrating Digital Transformation in Nursing Education: Best Practices and Challenges in Curriculum Development. In Lytras, M., Serban, A. C., Alkhaldi, A., Malik, S., & Aldosemani, T. (Eds.), *Digital Transformation in Higher Education, Part B Cases, Examples and Good Practices*. Emerald Publishing Limited.

Reis da Silva, T. M., Hammett, R., & Low, G. (2024). Emotional Intelligence in Business: Enhancing Leadership, Collaboration, and Performance. In Sedky, A. (Ed.), *Building Business Knowledge for Complex Modern Business Environments* (pp. 149–178). IGI Global., DOI: 10.4018/979-8-3693-6447-5.ch006

Santos, W., Toda, A., Isotani, S., & Bittencourt, I. (2018). Does gamified educational systems change students' learning behaviors? a case study with postgraduate students. *Renote*, 16(2). Advance online publication. DOI: 10.22456/1679-1916.89253

Scaffidi, M., Khan, R., Walsh, C., Pearl, M., Winger, K., Kalaichandran, R., Lin, P., & Grover, S. (2019). Protocol for a randomised trial evaluating the effect of applying gamification to simulation-based endoscopy training. *BMJ Open*, 9(2), e024134. DOI: 10.1136/bmjopen-2018-024134 PMID: 30804029

Serrano, M. (2023). Gamification and the history of art in secondary education: A didactic intervention. *Education Sciences*, 13(4), 389. DOI: 10.3390/educsci13040389

Shin, H., & Rim, D. (2023). Development and assessment of a curriculum model for virtual simulation in nursing: Curriculum development and pilot-evaluation. *BMC Medical Education*, 23(1), 284. Advance online publication. DOI: 10.1186/s12909-023-04283-4 PMID: 37101191

Smith, J., Sawhney, M., Duhn, L., & Woo, K. (2021). The association between new nurses' gerontological education, personal attitudes toward older adults, and intentions to work in gerontological care settings in Ontario, Canada. *Canadian Journal of Nursing Research*, 54(2), 190–198. DOI: 10.1177/08445621211063702 PMID: 34964357

Tang, K. (2023). Gamification to improve participation in an environmental science course: An educator's reflection. *Acta Pedagogia Asiana*, 2(2), 54–63. DOI: 10.53623/apga.v2i2.192

Teo, J., Ramachandran, H., Jiang, Y., Seah, A., Lim, S., Nguyen, H., & Wang, W. (2023). The characteristics and acceptance of technology-enabled diabetes prevention programs (T-DPP) amongst individuals with prediabetes: A scoping review. *Journal of Clinical Nursing*, 32(17-18), 5562–5578. DOI: 10.1111/jocn.16649 PMID: 36775886

Teófilo, T., Veras, R., Silva, V., Cunha, N., Oliveira, J., & Vasconcelos, S. (2018). Empathy in the nurse–patient relationship in geriatric care: An integrative review. *Nursing Ethics*, 26(6), 1585–1600. DOI: 10.1177/0969733018787228 PMID: 30071772

Turjuman, F., & Alilyyani, B. (2023). Emotional intelligence among nurses and its relationship with their performance and work engagement: A cross-sectional study. *Journal of Nursing Management*, 2023, 1–8. DOI: 10.1155/2023/5543299

Uaidullakyzy, E., Rizakhojayeva, G., Sartayeva, K., Zeinep, B., Turmanov, R., & Rysbayeva, G. (2022). Creating integration situations of students' computer lesson and learning with gamification. [IJET]. *International Journal of Emerging Technologies in Learning*, 17(19), 207–223. DOI: 10.3991/ijet.v17i19.32177

Wang, J., Bu, L., Li, Y., Song, J., & Li, N. (2021). The mediating effect of academic engagement between psychological capital and academic burnout among nursing students during the covid-19 pandemic: A cross-sectional study. *Nurse Education Today*, 102, 104938. DOI: 10.1016/j.nedt.2021.104938 PMID: 33934039

Weaver, M., Jenkins, R., Wichman, C., Robinson, J., Potthoff, M., Menicucci, T., & Vail, C. (2019). Sowing across a state: Development and delivery of a grassroots pediatric palliative care nursing curriculum. *Journal of Palliative Care*, 36(1), 22–28. DOI: 10.1177/0825859719889700 PMID: 31771423

Wiggins, B. (2016). An overview and study on the use of games, simulations, and gamification in higher education. *International Journal of Game-Based Learning*, 6(1), 18–29. DOI: 10.4018/IJGBL.2016010102

Yaşar, H., Kıyıcı, M., & Karatas, A. (2020). The views and adoption levels of primary school teachers on gamification, problems and possible solutions. *Participatory Educational Research*, 7(3), 265–279. DOI: 10.17275/per.20.46.7.3

Yu, C., Liu, Z. Q., Zhao, M., Liu, Y., Zhang, Y., Lin, A., Sang, X., & Wan, H. (2023). The mediating role of emotion management, self-efficacy and emotional intelligence in clinical nurses related to negative psychology and burnout. *Psychology Research and Behavior Management*, 16, 3333–3345. DOI: 10.2147/PRBM.S417729 PMID: 37650114

Zhakupova, A., Yerkebayeva, S., Zhumasheva, T., Myshbayeva, G., Zhandildina, R., & Mukhanbetzhanova, A. (2022). Improvement of soft skills in preschool teachers through gamification. *Cypriot Journal of Educational Sciences*, 17(9), 3556–3567. DOI: 10.18844/cjes.v17i9.8128

Zourmpakis, A., Kalogiannakis, M., & Papadakis, S. (2023). Adaptive gamification in science education: An analysis of the impact of implementation and adapted game elements on students' motivation. *Computers*, 12(7), 143. DOI: 10.3390/computers12070143

Chapter 6 Gamification for Transformative Learning: Current Trends in 21st Century Education

Miftachul Huda
https://orcid.org/0000-0001-6712-0056
Universiti Pendidikan Sultan Idris, Malaysia

Mohammad Jailani
https://orcid.org/0000-0002-7769-1044
Universitas Ahmad Dahlan, Indonesia

Azmil Hashim
https://orcid.org/0000-0002-3322-775X
Universiti Pendidikan Sultan Idris, Malaysia

ABSTRACT

This proposal aims to examine the way of gamification with its features in enhancing the transformative learning in enabling the students' acquisition of knowledge as the strategic achievement to obtain the 21st century education. The finding revealed that the innovative concept of implementing the game scenario with the featured elements and principles could support the educational process and practices. This study will contribute into building the advancing scenario to further make the actively transformative learning interaction with the unique characteristics of enjoyable and effective basis. With the profound target of goal, the strategic orientation of gamification could foster in leveraging the learning process and practices engaged with play and competition in order to give the motivating support to the learners and thus would improve their learning outcomes. At this point of view, the gamification

DOI: 10.4018/979-8-3693-8322-3.ch006

played a role in advancing the academic performance together with nurturing the essential skills like problem-solving and collaboration.

INTRODUCTION

With the varied significant ways to sustain the instruction design, the gamification has been widely attracting the society mainly among the education actor and thus recently leading to the scholarly attention throughout the number of research (Silva-Jurado & Silva-Jurado, 2024). As the great approach in attempting to obtain the gateway in delivering the information efficiency, the extensive value of providing the learners with the significant instruction pathways would lead to enhance the differentiated learning scenario. In this regard, the strategic attempt to obtain the learning experiences could enable the elements of game oriented learning process and this could be applied to help improve the motivation (Moseikina, Toktamysov & Danshina, 2022). The basis of learning enhancement should gather the point of techniques to apply for the classroom management through the adoption of subject-related games. The initiative of gamification refers to the sufficient adoption in using the game elements including the point system in enabling to increase the learners' active engagement to adapt the instructional process in the classroom (Santosa, Harismayanti & Putra, 2022). At this point of view, gamification with its elements might bring the insightful value in enhancing the learning conduciveness by providing the attractive activities related to the game oriented features to enable all of all ages to go in the instructional process. In particular, the essential part of dealing with the classroom arrangement through both inside and outside the classroom is required to have a sufficient exploration in allowing the strategic approach of gamification to foster the interactive learning process (Zain, 2021). As such, the continued competence in enhancing the education process should come up with building the internal part of classroom activities in order to help transform the learning landscape pathways.

In addition, the essential features of gamification have been a transformative learning pathway in enabling the element of game oriented element added to the traditional instruction approach (Tanouri, Kennedy & Veer, 2022). At this point of view, the arrangement of adopting the appropriate method is strategically to be articulated in helping improve the interactive activities in the learning process. The starting point refers to expand the extensive value of enhancing the game design with the elements related to the contexts of activities through the additional parts in transforming the learning scenario. As a means to invoke the game-oriented instructional design, the gamification has been giving the medium of instruction as the platform to expand the learning experiences among the learners (Sailer & Homner, 2020). Developed as the influential means amidst the today's digital age, the effective instruction to transform the gateway in engaging with the varied elements of platform in ensuring the delivery support should do with building the key roots integrated principles into the game design and gamification. With this regard, the way to carry out the strategic principles of leveraging instructional design and its elements needs to adhere the significant points of learning engagement for motivation achievement (Faiella & Ricciardi, 2015). As such, the critical point is that the solving initiative through gamification played a role in giving the portion on enabling the instruction process within the interactively attractive scenario. The arranged strategy could, thus, be made properly in line with maintaining the sufficient motivation and engagement to help improve active learners in the classroom.

In further, the strategic attempts to advance the learning inquiry process with an attractive scenario are required to get actively involved in the digital technology access, in which both adaptation and adoption were the key element to ensure the efficiency of instructional performance in the classroom basis. With this regard, the initial pathway of organizing the game-similar tool added into the learning scenario in the classroom is sufficiently needed to bring the essential value in getting improve the quality education (Caponetto, Earp & Ott, 2014). The significant achievement of gamification adoption in the learning process places the innovative instruction quality to take a benefit into the scenario of attractive entertainment for education transformation. At this point of view, the key point in popularizing this arranged scenario design throughout the proper application of gamification as an additional medium of platform would bring an extension to achieve the informative entertainment with the knowledge embodiment (Lavoué et al., 2018). Not only entertainment-based instruction scenario but also giving the positive feedback through the learning design in the classroom arrangement are the principal aspect of the gamification-oriented instruction pathway. As the emerging development of the potential to transform the way that we teach and learn in the 21st century education, the advancement of gamification has been the convincing partner to run in the process of education practices (Landers et al., 2015). Offering the close tuning approach to engage with both learners and audiences, the efficiency of gamification would lead to enhance the transformative learning pathway. This proposal aims to examine the way of gamification with its features in enhancing the transformative learning in enabling the students' acquisition of knowledge as the strategic achievement to obtain the 21st century education. The finding revealed that the innovative concept of implementing the game scenario with the featured elements and principles could support the educational process and practices. This study will contribute into building the advancing scenario to further make the actively transformative learning interaction with the unique characteristics of enjoyable and effective basis.

LITERATURE REVIEW

Gamification from Theory to Practice

The mode of influencing platform applied in the varied subjects of learning and education scenario has been the main feature of gamification. As the essential platform in revolutionizing the traditional instruction approach, the learning platform of game-initiated features in the learning process could begin with arranging the engaging and interactive-based activities within the classroom management (Landers, 2014). The sufficient adoption to incorporate the game-like structures transformed in the learning environment would enable the teaching process in fostering the rising experiential practice in contributing the motivation and engagement. Moreover, the scenario of learning performance through the gamification approach could enhance the sufficiently attractive atmosphere in allowing the knowledge acquisition process within the arranged plan. From participation to motivation in the learning classroom, the attempts to maintain in obtaining the deeper learning followed with retention of knowledge might provide the essential features to advance the instruction process through the given platform of gamification from elementary classrooms to higher education institutions (Kapp, 2013). As such, the learning experiences here refers to have a sufficient adoption of gamified instructional element to prove an effective basis to help transmit the knowledge acquisition to the practical application scenario.

In line with the other significant features mainly for the organisation, management and business, the gamification-oriented instruction has been the strategic platform in driving the direction pathway for the learning engagement with the new experience. With this regard, the active involvement to engage with improving the learning productivity is significant to help improve the active enhancement for the customer loyalty at the business scenario (Kim & Lee, 2015). Moreover, the utilization of such gamified system in creating the atmosphere with being more interactive would lead to the strategic enhancement on achieving an exciting learning environment. On this view, the attempts on obtaining the feeling of motivation are strategically needed in directing the potential development of the learning design with the gamification pathway (Zainuddin et al., 2020). The continued assist provided by the gamified structure in the learning process could provide the essential contribution to sustain the essence of atmosphere with an actively interactive engagement. The particular point refers to give a real-time based feedback from the learners getting involved in the gamification activities during the learning process and practices. At this point, the extensive value of advancing the gamification-based instructional design would contribute into building an appropriate technique to massively adapt in increasing the active engagement among the learners (Hong, Saab & Admiraal, 2024). Thus, the improvement for the learning instruction could be achieved in leading to enhance the objective achievement as in line with the lesson plan arrangement. As such, the extent of satisfaction during the learning process could transform the initiative to give the enthusiastic circumstance to commit in the classroom.

Additionally for the emerging trends amidst the 21st century learning, the given task in the gamification would provide the rewarding system in enabling the learners to solve the challenges in order to achieve such goal. Moreover, the strategic attempts in cultivating an exciting atmosphere with being more enthusiastic is potentially a key element to enhance the committed participation in the classroom (Al-Hafdi & Alhalafawy, 2024). In particular, the significant advances on fostering the gamification in giving an insightful value to make an active participation in the classroom are to be engaged in bringing the health behaviour. As a result, the modifying assessment to ensure the education professionals in adopting the game-oriented element for instructional design should do with building an active learning engagement progression (Alzahrani & Alhalafawy, 2023). The further orientation needs to be given in maintaining the way to how the learning process could be achieved through gamified activities related to the subject of instruction. With this regard, the arranged treatment for instructional process has been the helping program in allowing the learning process and practice as this scenario would foster to encourage the active participation in following the classroom (Khaldi, Bouzidi & Nader, 2023). The strategic point in continuing the learning process through the strategic approach would help in encouraging the learners to adhere to their learning style engaged in the classroom performance behaviours. The emerging significances to get actively involved in participating the gamified activities through subject-related applications are becoming the instrumental learning to address the varied learning challenges (González-González et al., 2023). The potentials of having the learning management in structuring the instructional design support would enhance the gamification scenario to sustain the education practices mainly in advancing the subject-related lesson.

Gamification from its Significances to its Potentials

The main direction of gamification comes from the brief description about the embodiment of game-oriented learning part in addressing the strategic point of examining such elements to be included for the potential contribution of instructional design. In terms of seeking the initiative in providing the comprehensive examination to look into detail about the way of gamification could be optimised across the critical aspects from theory, practice and real application pathway. The strategic accomplishment of the know-how in directing the learning pathway should come up with collecting the theoretical insights combined with the practical strategies (Mellado & Cubillos, 2024). Such arranged basis would lead to enhance the real application in helping describe the clear illustration in transforming the gamification potentials in delving the appropriate support to offer the wide emerging experiences of learning process. Moreover, the potentials of highlighting the committed supply of the gamification-supported instruction requires the essential pathway in examining the contribution to achieve the attainment plan (Bhatia et al., 2023). As arranged in delivering the successes of gamification, the critical examination to look into detail about the challenging issues or possible limitations on implementing the gamification should do with having an enough consideration to facilitate such features in the learning process. With this regard, the expected plan refers to have both actors and stakeholders in education setting to have a sufficient knowledge description about the gamification-based learning instruction. On this view, the essential point on facilitating both knowledge expertise and practical phase needs to adapt such facilities in leading to achieve the effective enhancement on advancing the instructional tools necessary to apply amidst the classroom.

In addition, the significant point on addressing the gamification in navigating the potential value in the activation process refers to come up in adapting the knowledge discovery to actual practice scenario. With this regard, the strategic attempts on discovering the scenario on looking into detail about the gamification process and practices needs to begin with creating the learning atmosphere leading to being more impactful experiences with engaging and motivating in the instruction (Subiyantoro & Musa, 2023). The extensive value of such essential features of gamification application in the education setting should do with calling to those involved in the field such as educators and stakeholders in ensuring the efficient transformation. Moreover, the features in taking benefit on gamification have been the major consequence in transmitting the means in enhancing the learning engagement pathway in achieving the better learning outputs with the active atmosphere (Dehghanzadeh et al., 2024). The strategic direction to produce the outcomes with unlocking the full potential of gamification in striving the direction to guide the beneficial value to the learning achievement. As a result, the continued effort in taking an advantage from the gamification-oriented learning scenario should be engaged actively into building the critical exploration in elucidating the wide range of applications about the practical phase of gamification (Hou, 2023). In particular, the vital role of gamification with its features could go through expanding the detailed description in providing the thorough examination about the application procedure together with the principles. The related theories adopted in applying for gamification would give a direction to offer the insightful value into its mechanics and effective implementation in the wide range of contexts.

In line with having the sufficient knowledge phase to have the gamification significances to the society, the successful application should build an active engagement to present the real-instruction scenario to address the potential contribution with the innovating basis. With this regard, the organising pathway to look into detail about showcasing the achievement plan refers to obtain an adequate enhancement on delivering the process of gamification application in the classroom management (Luarn, Chen & Chiu, 2023). On this view, the strategic attempts on highlighting the innovative approaches to achieve the appropriate practices in adopting the theoretical connection to the practical phase should be initiated with building the frameworks with practical implementations into the instruction process and practices. On this view, the arranged scenario in planning the gamification-oriented instruction should come up with offering the holistic comprehension to ensure the strategic achievement (Khoshnoodifar, Ashouri & Taheri, 2023). Through having the sufficient comprehension of gamification, the strategic attempts on performing the essential point enabling the learners in translating the concept of theory to the practical strategy should be taken into consideration in providing the professional and ethical balanced scenario. Such arranged strategy would lead to have the perspective in dealing with the possibly challenging issues through initiating the gamification-oriented instruction scenario to settle the obstacles (Xiao & Hew, 2024). The continued alignment to address the common pitfalls would offer the possible solutions in helping overcome the challenges throughout the effectiveness of gamification promoted in the proposed initiative of gamification-supported learning instruction.

Gamification for Learning Instruction Model Support

With the significant role to potentially engage into the learners' pathway of learning process, the extent of gamification refers to help actively support the instruction in bringing the wide range of both procedural principles and practical mechanism. From the actively involved engagement, the gamification-oriented learning gateway would lead to enhance the learning scenario into being more interactive and enjoyable (Li, Ma & Shi, 2023). The proper arrangement in adapting the game design oriented principles should do with continuing the practical steps organised to enhancing the learners' engagement. It is important to note that the strategic order of helping increase the atmosphere motivation through giving the related elements like rewards, levels, and competition would potentially lead to advance the instruction in the classroom management. With this regard, the particular features of gamification have been the attractive learning design to foster the delivery process in the education setting. Offering the strategic approach to help engage the learners to enhance the process and practice of learning, the way to apply the game elements-oriented principles in education setting could bring the gateway of innovative concept-actualised learning activities (Wang, 2023). In terms of improving the gateway to sustain the learning being more enjoyable, interactive and innovative, the effective-based learning scenario would lead to enhance the achievement plan of considering the gamification-oriented instructional design in order to foster in leveraging the interactive consequence. On this view, the key features of gamification as the learning facility for the learners have been the significant direction in bringing the human sense in obtaining the play and competition in the classroom management process.

In addition, the continued motivation expansion through gamification design-based instruction refers to the scenario in fostering the improvement for the learning outcomes. The particular integration of well-structured content measurement and gamified practices would lead to advance the learning instruction with being more attractive and enjoyable sense (Liu, Fathi & Rahimi, 2024). Apart from the varied challenges in terms of integrating elements such as badges, points and challenges within the learning instruction design, both process and practices would lead to enhance the teaching scenario organised in the classroom arrangement. Such wide instruction is required to result in creating the more engaging and dynamic circumstance as the learning environment advancement in catering to the diverse needs of learners (Drissi et al., 2024). The strategic orientation of gamification in supporting the learning instruction refers to help advancing the academic performance and such attainment plan could also be enhanced in nurturing the essential skills such as solving initiative to help settle the challenging issues during the learning process for instance unattractive teaching, passive learners and also unconducive learning classroom. At this point of view, having the sufficient collaboration in designing the problem-solving initiative is being the strategic effort of game-changer in learning instruction scenario in the education setting (Zeybek & Saygı, 2024). With offering the new approach in inspiring the learners, transforming the traditional-based teaching has been positively engaged into exploring the gateway of gamification in giving the impactful value to the learners' engagement to involve in the learning process.

In line with the gamified activities-oriented learning engagement, it is sure to note that the essence of gamification as the strategic approach to translate the concept in bringing the key elements into the learning instruction setting. On this view, the game design-oriented instruction scenario would lead to expand the strategic approach in delivering the information from the educators to the learners through an exciting platform of instruction (Batlle Rodríguez & Vicenta González Argüello, 2023). At this point of view, the active involvement of adopting the game like practices in the learning process is potentially a bridge in advancing the learners' active engagement and motivation. With this regard, the strategic point of mechanising the learning facilities in bringing the following features in motivating and engaging the process of learning instruction refers to help improve the more interactive atmosphere with an enjoyable circumstance as the learning atmosphere (Chen, Ming-Chaun & Kuo, 2023). Both joyful and exciting features of learning instruction would help tap into the learners' engagement to have a compassion to follow the process in the classroom. The natural sense of play and competition in education setting would enable the gamification-oriented learning design to help improve the enhancement of students' commitment to grab the information related to the field of subject. Moreover, the key element of an active engagement is positively engaged into improving the learning outcomes by fostering the more dynamic atmosphere followed by the attractive environment (Yu, Yu & Li, 2024). The potential contribution of adapting the gamification-oriented instruction design in education setting paid the particular effort to manage the know-how in the gateway of focusing on assisting the learning style development among the learners. It is especially among the children the that strategic attempts to foster them in grabbing the early information development in the language setting for instance would begin with the following phases including the competence of reading and also social skills. In particular, the additional value is that the learning instruction design with the gamification orientation would lead to enhance the lesson atmosphere in creating the innovative practices in engaging the learners' active involvement in the classroom.

Gamification Role for Transformative Learning Engagement

With the attractive features given in the activities, the varied forms of practising the gamification could be employed with both procedure and practices in having an active engagement to the learners' learning involvement in the classroom. The strategic role of gamification could play an extensive value in developing the learning engagement into transforming the process for being more interactive between learners and educators (Perez-Aranda, Medina-Claros & Urrestarazu-Capellán, 2024). With this regard, the transformative-oriented learning process could lead to enhance the monitoring system into the attractive activities in giving an insightful value for gamified design of activities principles. On this view, the continued consistency to offer the attractive-based learning subject would lead to enhance the delivery of lesson together with giving the appropriate appreciation (Kashive & Mohite, 2023). The potentials of advancing the making the learning being more involved among the learners should come up with ensuring the earning rewards in that the learners would have chance in tracking the progress. At this point of view, the tracking system given in fostering the learning progress would enable the learners in looking at their potential achievement through the medium of gamified activities (Waluyo, Phanrangsee & Whanchit, 2023). In particular, the strategic attempts in unlocking the true potential to lead to obtain the achievement would make the progression of learning experiences for being more interactive and engaging insights. For instance, the adoption of Kahoot would give an insightful value in transforming the learning potentials into the game-oriented interactive medium such as delivering the quizzes in allowing the learners to give the answer (Kabilan, Annamalai & Chuah, 2023). Such arranged gamification practices could also lead to enhance solving the initiatives to handle the challenges in which the educators could adapt their customised game-oriented instruction in allowing the learners having the active involvement to participating the classroom activities.

In addition, the gamified activities designed in the teaching process could be advanced with creating the customising scenario in enabling the game-oriented practices to have an active participation adopting the tool facilities. With this regard, the educators might have an appropriate chance in adopting the gamified-style for the learning process in encouraging the pathway of collaborating initiative to have the active classroom management (Kaya & Ercag, 2023). The strategic role of gamified practices would also give the continued effort for the educators to have a critical look into comprehending the impact of gamification-based theoretical framework. As the rising trend in the learning setting, the strategic attempts in leveraging the game elements in advancing to enhance the learners' active involvement in the classroom is supposed to help improve the learners' active engagement (Singh, 2024). At this point, the main direction of optimising the learners' engagement through such attractive-gamified practices would lead to build the capacity of fostering the learning pathway with boosting their effort to follow the classroom program. Both student engagement and learning process have been the crucial point in exploring the theoretical foundations in underpinning the strategically innovative approach in directing the key element in theorising the particular knowledge description of gamified practices relevant to the current learning context (Balaji, Rajaram & Sethu, 2023). As the consideration in positing the learners' involvement in motivating the growth of potential skills and knowledge, the factor from inside and outside would lead to enhance the outcome-based learning process. With this regard, the strategic human orientation in the learning is encouraged by the attractive-based instruction through the medium of information delivery in the varied platforms in enabling the educators transmit the relevant knowledge to the learners. In order to disseminate the inherent motivation in growing and developing the learners' potential knowledge and skills, the making of balance between internal and external factors played a significant role in directing the effective engagement process for the learners in the classroom management process.

In line with having the brief description to optimising the learning experiences, strategic attempts of gamified practices in giving the overall commitment to engage actively in the learning activity are required to build up the gamified element-oriented practices. It is sure to note that the learners with a full immersion to engaging in a relevant activity. The particular orientation is that the strategic phase on transmitting the knowledge skills among the learners into the new part of information obtained throughout the process should come up with having the synchronisation to be achieved properly in line with the arranged goal plan (Harsaya, Permana & Khaeruzaman, 2023). With this regard, the simultaneous link between knowledge and skill in the context of gamification-oriented learning instruction could have the brief description followed by the actual implementation to strategize the real design of gamified activities in the classroom management. As a result, the strategic design on monitoring the progress about tasks and challenges should be taken into consideration to have an appropriately solving initiative to respond to the challenges in order to achieve the goal-oriented learning yet achievable. This way, educators can facilitate a state of flow in students, leading to increased motivation and engagement. On this view, the strategic role of gamified activities in helping improve the learning atmosphere to be more interactively attractive becomes the gateway in directing the know-how at the real classroom scenario (Lampropoulos & Kinshuk, 2024). At this point of view, the critical overview on monitoring the process and practice of gamification in underlying the learning pathway is potentially leading to advance in transforming the optimal landscape of instructional design. As such, the gamification-oriented design in underlying the application process and procedure should come up with comprehending the way of enhancing the learners' motivation to actively engage in the classroom.

Gamification Orientation for Learners' Interactive Learning Atmosphere

Considered as the crucial role in fostering the interactive learning engagement, the extent of gamification-oriented design requires the strategic accomplishment of adopting the game design into both mechanics and principles. Such arranged scenario would lead to perform in making the learning process with gamified activities in order to be more attractive and interactive sense (Oliveira et al., 2023). With having a sufficient description of expanding the interactive learning atmosphere, the gamification orientation would need to provide the continuity followed by the stability on enhancing the learners' engagement in the classroom learning environment. On this view, the strategic motivation to incorporate the key aspect in employing the gamification-oriented learning instruction should come up with combining the professional skills and ethical responsibility during the process. The following elements for gamified practices might include the extent of provided level, given rewards, platform of leader boards, and also the atmosphere of competition (Parkerson, 2023). The wide range of strategic ways in enabling the learning engagement in enhancing the interactive experiences is consequently needed to have a sufficient description of providing the game elements in order to make the process of learning to be more interactive and engaging. With this regard, the arranged occupation to enhance the motivated learning atmosphere would lead to an actively engaged learning scenario in allowing the continued support of having a sufficient incorporation to handle both competitions and challenges (Burlacu, Coman & Bularca, 2023). The extensive value of gamified activities in helping the learning process to be the solving initiative in rising the motivation among the learners should do with building the strategic gateway on helping an active engagement in striving the learning improvement.

In addition, the strategic improvement on fostering the learning output should come up with integrating the learning input into the process and practices. At this point, the way to improve the instructional learning design requires the optimisation of gamified-oriented medium to help transmit the information from the educator to the learner in a smooth pathway (Huseinović, 2024). The main direction to enhance the learning outcomes would need to begin with a sufficient description about the valuable insight of gamification in presenting the potential skill in leading to the enhanced learning practice. On this view, the improved practice as the key indicator of learning performance could optimise the classroom learning arrangement in increasing the transmission of information delivery to have the better problem-solving skills (Hong, Saab & Admiraal, 2024). Moreover, the arranged plan with the clear vision of performing the gamified-oriented activities would achieve the targeted goal as in line with the strategized objective in achieving the effective learning. The particular attention could be empowered through having the setting with the clear direction to achieve the goal in that such arranged scenario would encourage the learners to help improve the active engagement in the classroom learning environment (Al-Hafdi & Alhalafawy, 2024). The direction to promote the collaboration followed by the competition would need to expand the continued sense of learning engagement among the learners through expanding the extent of motivation level in the instruction process. The instant feedback refers to have a real-based instruction scenario of gamified activities in leading to expand the learners' progress. It is important to note that encouraging the learners in continuing the learning process would help tailor in improving the engagement into the personalized learning scenario. On this view, the learning experiences during the gamified activities is supposed to foster the individual learners' solving initiative in handling the appropriately challenged issues in the learning process.

In line with an active engagement, the attempts to incorporating the challenges and puzzles into the learning process are strategically optimised into making the learning to be more attractive. Apart from the benefit, the challenging issues could be arranged in advancing the engaging individual students to get tailored learning experiences through personalized feedback in handling the challenges and activities faced by the educators (Alzahrani & Alhalafawy, 2023). As a result, the potential value refers to ensure that each student is appropriately prepared in order to be ready to face the challenges through actively engaging in their learning process. Both beneficial value and practical consequence aims to have a gateway in drawing the picture of gamification-oriented instructional design into the teaching techniques (Khaldi, Bouzidi & Nader, 2023). With this regard, the strategic attempts on revolutionizing the actual incorporation of gamification into education could potentially attract the substantial attention in leading to expand the creative method of bringing game components into instructional setting. As such, taking an advantage into the educational circumstance with gamified activities is strategically the key component in bridging the attractive atmosphere into the learning process. Thus, the gamification would have the potential to completely transform the workplace in bringing the benefits in offering the several advantages for student learning and engagement. The further orientation of increased motivation would help improve the introducing elements including the points of chances and challenges in leading to make gamification in order to bring the learning into being more actively engaged and encouraging an active learning participation in the classroom.

CONCLUSION

In conclusion, the impact of gamification on student learning and engagement is profound. It offers a fresh and innovative approach to education, making learning interactive, enjoyable, and effective. By incorporating game elements like challenges, rewards, and competition, gamification motivates students to actively participate in their education. Despite its benefits, gamification also has some drawbacks, such as potential distractions and implementation challenges. However, by carefully considering these factors and implementing gamification in a thoughtful and strategic manner, educators can create a dynamic and engaging learning environment that fosters student success. Overall, gamification has the potential to transform education and enhance student learning outcomes. It provides a platform for students to develop essential skills like problem-solving, collaboration, and critical thinking. As educators continue to explore and implement gamification in the classroom, it will be exciting to see how this innovative approach shapes the future of education. At this point of view, the gamification played a role in advancing the academic performance together with nurturing the essential skills like problem-solving and collaboration. With such game-changer in education, the new way in inspiring the students could offer transforming the traditional teaching methods into transformative based instruction.

As the emerging development of the potential to transform the way that we teach and learn in the 21st century education, the advancement of gamification has been the convincing partner to run in the process of education practices. Offering the close tuning approach to engage with both learners and audiences, the efficiency of gamification would lead to enhance the transformative learning pathway. This study aims to shape the way of gamification with its features in enhancing the transformative learning in enabling the students' acquisition of knowledge as the strategic achievement to obtain the 21st century education. The finding revealed that the innovative concept of implementing the game scenario with the featured elements and principles could support the educational process and practices. This study will contribute into building the advancing scenario to further make the actively transformative learning interaction with the unique characteristics of enjoyable and effective basis. With the profound target of goal, the strategic orientation of gamification could foster in leveraging the learning process and practices engaged with play and competition in order to give the motivating support to the learners and thus would improve their learning outcomes. Through such integration towards the elements like points, badges, and challenges into the learning process, the teaching process and practices requires in creating the more dynamic and engaging environment in catering to the diverse needs of students.

REFERENCES

Al-Hafdi, F. S., & Alhalafawy, W. S. (2024). Ten Years of Gamification-Based Learning: A Bibliometric Analysis and Systematic Review. *International Journal of Interactive Mobile Technologies*, 18(7), 188–212. DOI: 10.3991/ijim.v18i07.45335

Alzahrani, F. K., & Alhalafawy, W. S. (2023). Gamification for learning sustainability in the blackboard system: Motivators and obstacles from faculty members' perspectives. *Sustainability (Basel)*, 15(5), 4613. DOI: 10.3390/su15054613

Balaji, S., Rajaram, V., & Sethu, S. (2023, April). Gamification of Learning using 3D Spaces in the Metaverse. In *2023 International Conference on Networking and Communications (ICNWC)* (pp. 1-5). IEEE. DOI: 10.1109/ICNWC57852.2023.10127461

Batlle Rodríguez, J., & Vicenta González Argüello, M. (2023). Gamification and learning Spanish as a modern language: Student perceptions in the university context. *Language Learning in Higher Education*, 13(1), 89–103. DOI: 10.1515/cercles-2023-2016

Bhatia, M., Manani, P., Garg, A., Bhatia, S., & Adlakha, R. (2023). Mapping mindset about gamification: Teaching learning perspective in UAE education system and Indian education system. *Revue d'Intelligence Artificielle*, 37(1), 47–52. DOI: 10.18280/ria.370107

Burlacu, M., Coman, C., & Bularca, M. C. (2023). Blogged into the System: A Systematic Review of the Gamification in e-Learning before and during the COVID-19 Pandemic. *Sustainability (Basel)*, 15(8), 6476. DOI: 10.3390/su15086476

Caponetto, I., Earp, J., & Ott, M. (2014, October). Gamification and education: A literature review. In *European conference on games based learning* (Vol. 1, p. 50). Academic Conferences International Limited.

Chen, C. M., Ming-Chaun, L., & Kuo, C. P. (2023). A game-based learning system based on octalysis gamification framework to promote employees' Japanese learning. *Computers & Education*, 205, 104899. DOI: 10.1016/j.compedu.2023.104899

Dehghanzadeh, H., Farrokhnia, M., Dehghanzadeh, H., Taghipour, K., & Noroozi, O. (2024). Using gamification to support learning in K-12 education: A systematic literature review. *British Journal of Educational Technology*, 55(1), 34–70. DOI: 10.1111/bjet.13335

Drissi, S., Chefrour, A., Boussaha, K., & Zarzour, H. (2024). Exploring the effects of personalized recommendations on student's motivation and learning achievement in gamified mobile learning framework. *Education and Information Technologies*, •••, 1–38. DOI: 10.1007/s10639-024-12477-6

Faiella, F., & Ricciardi, M. (2015). Gamification and learning: a review of issues and research. *Journal of e-learning and knowledge society, 11*(3).

González-González, C. S., Muñoz-Cruz, V., Toledo-Delgado, P. A., & Nacimiento-García, E. (2023). Personalized gamification for learning: A reactive chatbot architecture proposal. *Sensors (Basel)*, 23(1), 545. DOI: 10.3390/s23010545 PMID: 36617143

Harsaya, E. R. T., Permana, A. A., & Khaeruzaman, Y. A. M. A. N. (2023). Design Application Simple Learn Based on Mobile With Implementation Gamification for Learning Online. *Journal of Theoretical and Applied Information Technology*, 101(6), 2255–2262.

Hong, Y., Saab, N., & Admiraal, W. (2024). Approaches and game elements used to tailor digital gamification for learning: A systematic literature review. *Computers & Education*, 212, 105000. DOI: 10.1016/j.compedu.2024.105000

Hou, H. T. (2023). Learning science through cloud gamification: A framework for remote gamified science learning activities integrating cloud tool sets and three-dimensional scaffolding. *Information (Basel)*, 14(3), 165. DOI: 10.3390/info14030165

Huseinović, L. (2024). The effects of gamification on student motivation and achievement in learning English as a foreign language in higher education. *MAP Education and Humanities*, 4(1), 10–36. DOI: 10.53880/2744-2373.2023.4.10

Kabilan, M. K., Annamalai, N., & Chuah, K. M. (2023). Practices, purposes and challenges in integrating gamification using technology: A mixed-methods study on university academics. *Education and Information Technologies*, 28(11), 14249–14281. DOI: 10.1007/s10639-023-11723-7 PMID: 37361777

Kapp, K. M. (2013). *The gamification of learning and instruction fieldbook: Ideas into practice*. John Wiley & Sons.

Kashive, N., & Mohite, S. (2023). Use of gamification to enhance e-learning experience. *Interactive Technology and Smart Education*, 20(4), 554–575. DOI: 10.1108/ITSE-05-2022-0058

Kaya, O. S., & Ercag, E. (2023). The impact of applying challenge-based gamification program on students' learning outcomes: Academic achievement, motivation and flow. *Education and Information Technologies*, 28(8), 10053–10078. DOI: 10.1007/s10639-023-11585-z PMID: 36691635

Khaldi, A., Bouzidi, R., & Nader, F. (2023). Gamification of e-learning in higher education: A systematic literature review. *Smart Learning Environments*, 10(1), 10. DOI: 10.1186/s40561-023-00227-z

Khoshnoodifar, M., Ashouri, A., & Taheri, M. (2023). Effectiveness of gamification in enhancing learning and attitudes: A study of statistics education for health school students. *Journal of Advances in Medical Education & Professionalism*, 11(4), 230. PMID: 37901759

Kim, J. T., & Lee, W. H. (2015). Dynamical model for gamification of learning (DMGL). *Multimedia Tools and Applications*, 74(19), 8483–8493. DOI: 10.1007/s11042-013-1612-8

Lampropoulos, G., & Kinshuk, . (2024). Virtual reality and gamification in education: A systematic review. *Educational Technology Research and Development*, 72(3), 1–95. DOI: 10.1007/s11423-024-10351-3

Landers, R. N. (2014). Developing a theory of gamified learning: Linking serious games and gamification of learning. *Simulation & Gaming*, 45(6), 752–768. DOI: 10.1177/1046878114563660

Landers, R. N., Bauer, K. N., Callan, R. C., & Armstrong, M. B. (2015). Psychological theory and the gamification of learning. *Gamification in education and business*, 165-186.

Lavoué, E., Monterrat, B., Desmarais, M., & George, S. (2018). Adaptive gamification for learning environments. *IEEE Transactions on Learning Technologies*, 12(1), 16–28. DOI: 10.1109/TLT.2018.2823710

Li, M., Ma, S., & Shi, Y. (2023). Examining the effectiveness of gamification as a tool promoting teaching and learning in educational settings: A meta-analysis. *Frontiers in Psychology*, 14, 1253549. DOI: 10.3389/fpsyg.2023.1253549 PMID: 37876838

Liu, G. Z., Fathi, J., & Rahimi, M. (2024). Using digital gamification to improve language achievement, foreign language enjoyment, and ideal L2 self: A case of English as a foreign language learners. *Journal of Computer Assisted Learning*, 40(4), 1347–1364. DOI: 10.1111/jcal.12954

Luarn, P., Chen, C. C., & Chiu, Y. P. (2023). Enhancing intrinsic learning motivation through gamification: A self-determination theory perspective. *The International Journal of Information and Learning Technology*, 40(5), 413–424. DOI: 10.1108/IJILT-07-2022-0145

Mellado, R., & Cubillos, C. (2024). Gamification improves learning: Experience in a training activity of computer programming in higher education. *Journal of Computer Assisted Learning*, 40(4), 1959–1973. DOI: 10.1111/jcal.13000

Moseikina, M., Toktamysov, S., & Danshina, S. (2022). Modern technologies and gamification in historical education. *Simulation & Gaming*, 53(2), 135–156. DOI: 10.1177/10468781221075965

Oliveira, W., Hamari, J., Shi, L., Toda, A. M., Rodrigues, L., Palomino, P. T., & Isotani, S. (2023). Tailored gamification in education: A literature review and future agenda. *Education and Information Technologies*, 28(1), 373–406. DOI: 10.1007/s10639-022-11122-4

Parkerson, R. (2023). Five key areas to consider before using gamification in learning and development. *Strategic HR Review*, 22(4), 115–120. DOI: 10.1108/SHR-01-2023-0005

Perez-Aranda, J., Medina-Claros, S., & Urrestarazu-Capellán, R. (2024). Effects of a collaborative and gamified online learning methodology on class and test emotions. *Education and Information Technologies*, 29(2), 1823–1855. DOI: 10.1007/s10639-023-11879-2 PMID: 37361848

Sailer, M., & Homner, L. (2020). The gamification of learning: A meta-analysis. *Educational Psychology Review*, 32(1), 77–112. DOI: 10.1007/s10648-019-09498-w

Santosa, M. H., Harismayanti, I., & Putra, I. N. A. J. (2022). Technology in Action: Developing Gamification Handbook in English Teaching and Learning for the 21st Century Learners. *Tesl-Ej*, 26(1), n1. DOI: 10.55593/ej.26101a2

Silva-Jurado, R. J., & Silva-Jurado, M. D. (2024). Educational Innovation in the 21st Century: Gamification, Artificial Intelligence and Art as Transformative Tools. *YUYAY: Estrategias. Metodologías & Didácticas Educativas*, 3(1), 35–52. DOI: 10.59343/yuyay.v3i1.60

Singh, S. (2024). Gamify with caution–a three-pronged model to alleviate the dark side of gamification in learning and development. *Development and Learning in Organizations*. Advance online publication. DOI: 10.1108/DLO-12-2023-0264

Subiyantoro, S., & Musa, M. Z. (2023). Exploring Teachers' and Students' Perspectives on Gamification in Learning Management Systems. *Jurnal Komunikasi Pendidikan*, 7(2), 52–60. DOI: 10.32585/jurnalkomdik.v7i2.4613

Tanouri, A., Kennedy, A. M., & Veer, E. (2022). A conceptual framework for transformative gamification services. *Journal of Services Marketing*, 36(2), 185–200. DOI: 10.1108/JSM-12-2020-0527

Waluyo, B., Phanrangsee, S., & Whanchit, W. (2023). Gamified grammar learning in online English courses in Thai higher education. *Online Journal of Communication and Media Technologies*, 13(4), e202354. DOI: 10.30935/ojcmt/13752

Wang, Y. H. (2023). Can gamification assist learning? A study to design and explore the uses of educational music games for adults and young learners. *Journal of Educational Computing Research*, 60(8), 2015–2035. DOI: 10.1177/07356331221098148

Xiao, Y., & Hew, K. F. T. (2024). Intangible rewards versus tangible rewards in gamified online learning: Which promotes student intrinsic motivation, behavioural engagement, cognitive engagement and learning performance? *British Journal of Educational Technology*, 55(1), 297–317. DOI: 10.1111/bjet.13361

Yu, Q., Yu, K., & Li, B. (2024). Can gamification enhance online learning? Evidence from a meta-analysis. *Education and Information Technologies*, 29(4), 4055–4083. DOI: 10.1007/s10639-023-11977-1

Zain, S. (2021). Digital transformation trends in education. In *Future directions in digital information* (pp. 223–234). Chandos Publishing. DOI: 10.1016/B978-0-12-822144-0.00036-7

Zainuddin, Z., Chu, S. K. W., Shujahat, M., & Perera, C. J. (2020). The impact of gamification on learning and instruction: A systematic review of empirical evidence. *Educational Research Review*, 30, 100326. DOI: 10.1016/j.edurev.2020.100326

Zeybek, N., & Saygı, E. (2024). Gamification in education: Why, where, when, and how?—A systematic review. *Games and Culture*, 19(2), 237–264. DOI: 10.1177/15554120231158625

Chapter 7
Gamified Success:
Best Practices, Challenges, and Solutions in Designing Gamified Experiences

Zidan Kachhi
https://orcid.org/0000-0002-8317-6356
Montfort College, India

ABSTRACT

Gamification has emerged as a transformative approach in education, leveraging game-like elements to enhance student engagement and motivation. This chapter attempts to present best practices, challenges and solutions for creating effective gamified experiences focused on but not limited to educational use, touching base on business and healthcare as well. Key theoretical foundations are discussed to illustrate how psychological principles can inform effective gamification strategies. The chapter highlights significant challenges such as sustaining long-term engagement, balancing game mechanics with educational goals and addressing cultural and ethical considerations. Solutions are proposed to overcome these challenges. Additionally, the role of technological advancements in reshaping gamified experiences is examined. Finally, the chapter emphasizes the importance of evaluating the effectiveness of gamified systems, providing actionable insights.

DOI: 10.4018/979-8-3693-8322-3.ch007

GAMIFIED SUCCESS: BEST PRACTICES, CHALLENGES AND SOLUTIONS IN DESIGNING GAMIFIED EXPERIENCES

Background

In the current scenario, when digitalization and engagement by the users are considered major concerns in education, business and healthcare, gamification has come out to be a vivid strategy aimed at motivating people and ensuring increased participation. Gamification is often becoming less of a niche strategy and more of a mainstream approach in diverse sectors (Deterding et al., 2011) as can be comprehended from a wide variety of topics and industries through the inclusion of elements of game design in non-game contexts. It draws on the motivational mechanics of games into an environment that's otherwise considered work, learning or treatment to draw in greater engagement and effects (Deterding et al., 2011). This chapter attempts to present best practices, challenges and solutions for creating effective gamified experiences focused on but not limited to educational use, touching base on business and healthcare as well.

Contextualization

Though gamification as a concept and practice is relatively modern, it rests on the very traditional human interest in play for learning and participation. The early thinkers on gamification put a great emphasis on the role of game dynamics in human psychology and postulated that games appeal to basic psychological needs of competence, autonomy and relatedness at the core of self-determination theory (Ryan & Deci, 2000). Game design can tap into these drives through mechanisms such as reward systems, competition and challenges, thus enhancing both intrinsic and extrinsic motivation in users. The tendency of gamification to entertain while still being educative has made it very attractive in arenas such as education, where conventional means of learning face difficulties in appropriating learner engagement, and even in business or healthcare, where motivation and long-term engagement are often a question of life and death (Sailer et al., 2017).

The beginnings of gamification started to pick up about well into the 2010s, as industries, driven mostly by marketers, began to observe that the elements of games could serve to raise the engagement of consumers with products (Deterding et al., 2011). At the same time, educators and researchers began to use gamification within classroom and training settings as part of an effort to improve learner engagement and performance outcomes (Hamari et al., 2014). As highlighted by Johnson et al. (2016), application in healthcare came almost immediately afterward, where it found its way into wellness applications and patient care protocols to provide health professionals with tools to improve patient adherence and motivation.

However, while gamification's appeal may be quite obvious, its application is far from assured: badly designed gamification systems often tend to boomerang, resulting in disengagement of users or ethical issues (*Gamification Is Bullshit*, 2011). For this reason, the understanding of both the key design principles, possible pitfalls and just how to solve some of the most common challenges stands out as mandatory for any professional or scholar who deals with the integration of gamification into practice.

Meaning and Nature

Gamification can be described as the purposeful use of game design elements including points, badges, levels and leaderboards out of a game context to encourage and amplify user activity. These elements are applied in developing either a more dynamic or interactive setting that promotes better active participation and frequency in users' engagement (Alsawaier, 2018; Sailer et al., 2017). Students can be recorded to earn points in class for timely work completion and thus be able to unlock achievements upon progression at the curriculum level (Dichev & Dicheva, 2017). Meanwhile, in businesses, employees could be engaged in a competitive process as a way of improving their results or achieving certain objectives; in healthcare facilities, patients are motivated to be in time for treatment processes using rewards through game-like systems (Johnson et al., 2016; Landers et al., 2017).

The nature of gamification is inherently interdisciplinary, drawing from such diverse areas as psychology, education, design and computer science. Varied theories stemming from motivational psychology, such as self-determination theory (SDT), best explain why individuals are motivated to engage themselves with gamified systems (Ryan & Deci, 2000). According to the theory, individuals behave in ways that satisfy their competence, autonomy and relatedness needs. It appeals to these human needs of clear goals, offering choices or personal challenges, and offering social connection or competition, viz-a-viz competence, autonomy and relatedness (Seaborn & Fels, 2015).

Scope and Conceptualization

The scope of gamification goes further than simple entertainment. While games per se are created to entertain, gamification takes the central elements of game design and transports them to non-game contexts with a view toward driving engagement and better outcomes (Deterding et al., 2011). In education, gamification may apply to increasing student engagement, creating a deeper understanding of course materials and boosting an overall improvement in general academic performance (Buckley

& Doyle, 2016). It is also being tapped into, in business, to fuel employee motivation, enhance customer loyalty and improve organizational outcomes (Hussain et al., 2018). Gamification, in health, is used by practitioners to encourage healthier lifestyle behaviors, enhance patient adherence to treatment guidelines and hence enhance patient experience (Bitrián et al., 2021).

The underlying structure for why gamified experiences are effective is rooted in key psychological and motivational theories dealing with how humans engage in challenges for rewards. The SDT developed by Ryan and Deci (2000) is supported by the premise that motivation is very much connected with whether one's three innate psychological needs (autonomy, competence and relatedness) are met or not. Therefore, in educational gamification, students may be given autonomy through freedom to choose their learning pathways, competence through challenges with mastery opportunities and relatedness as part of the feeling of community collaborative or competitive gameplay elements create (Sailer et al., 2017). According to the Fogg's Behavior Model (Fogg, 2009), the intersection of at least one element of each of these three factors (motivation, sufficient ability and one or more triggers) produces behavior. Gamification in education and business will work only when the game mechanics meet realistic capabilities and timely triggers that inspire wanted behaviors (Fogg, 2009).

Gamification systems typically include several key components. Key components of gamification systems include points/scoring, leaderboards, question banks, social interaction, progress levels, immediate feedback and rewards (Westenhaver et al., 2021). In medical education, integration with instructional objectives, game rules and fairness are crucial elements (Wang et al., 2024). Usability is essential for gamified systems, with learnability being a primary focus and application domain influencing design decisions (Magylaitė et al., 2022). In business, gamification can enhance customer retention, acquisition and perception transformation. Successful gamification projects often combine virtualization, social comparison and tangible rewards, with firms achieving better results when focusing on one or two objectives rather than all three simultaneously (Jacobides et al., 2024). Effective gamification systems in diverse domains depend on a meticulous equilibrium of essential elements, alignment with particular objectives and an emphasis on usability to improve user engagement and results.

Rationale for Gamification

Gamification remoulds tedious or endorsing activities into enjoyable experiences (Deterding et al., 2011). It has the ability to improve motivation, learning and behavioral changes in ways that might not be realized through traditional techniques of influencing behavior and learning (Hamari et al., 2014). This effect is no small blessing in education, where engagement by students is a potent predictor of success (Collie & Martin, 2019). Most traditional teaching approaches have failed in sustained effort-building and securing attention for deep learning in disengaged learners (Indraganti, 2018). Gamification in teaching approaches may overcome such issues by embedding elements of fun, competition and achievement that might rise intrinsic motivation and result in improved academic results (Dichev & Dicheva, 2017). Gamification is employed by businesses to increase employee engagement and improve their performances, enhance customer loyalty and improve training. Companies have learned that if an activity is framed in a game format, employees are far more likely to stay motivated throughout, continue to be productive, as well as collaborate (Landers et al., 2017). Similarly, customers can easily be loyal to a brand that allows them gamified rewards systems for long-term engagement in enhancing business performance (Hwang & Choi, 2019).

The rationale for gamification in health is based on the potential for gamification to promote healthier behaviors and improvement in patient outcomes. In this respect, gamified health applications have become increasingly popular owing to their high usage of rewards and challenges to persuade users to meet certain health goals (Miller et al., 2016). The final example concerns fitness trackers and wellness apps. It has been established that treatment protocol compliance, preventive care and healthier lifestyle choices (Lister et al., 2014) are more warranted when patients are engaged with gamified systems. By making healthcare experiences more engaging and rewarding, gamification can make great improvements in the quality of care and patient outcomes (Hammedi et al., 2017).

Best Practices in Gamification Design

What makes for an effective gamified experience is much more than adding points and badges to a system. For gamification to actually work, it needs to be thoughtfully designed, taking into consideration the target audience and goals of the system, using psychological principles fostering human motivation (Sailer et al., 2017; Van Roy & Zaman, 2019). Goals for gamified systems should be predefined in the requirements and these should align with the overall organizational objectives or operational goals of the higher education institution (Sailer et al., 2017).

While extrinsic rewards like points and badges may engage the users, successful gamified systems also appeal to intrinsic motivation via meaningful and enjoyable experiences (Lewis et al., 2016). As Ryan and Deci (2000) mentioned, this is a delicate balance in order for long-term engagement to occur. Gamified experiences have to be designed around the needs of the users specifically. For example, educational gamification may require different design elements compared to corporate gamification (Landers et al., 2017). Feedback must be provided immediately and be useful in any gamified system in order for the engagement to remain current. It makes users aware of their progress and may act as a motivator to continue participating (Hamari et al., 2014).

Clear Goal Setting and Feedback Loops

One of the key elements in gamification is setting specific, achievable goals for users, then giving them immediate feedback about how they fare. In education, this may come in the form of specific learning milestones that students must achieve before they get their rewards (Ranjan & Tyagi, 2022). For example, a language-learning app like Duolingo uses clear objectives for each lesson and offers immediate feedback on user performance with points and progress bars (Shortt et al., 2023). Feedback keeps users not only engaged but also encourages continuous improvement on their part (Deterding et al., 2011).

In business, clear goals linked to metrics such as sales targets have the potential to motivate employees and are subjects that can be gamified (Woźniak, 2016). Sales departments in many companies are already utilizing leaderboards and badges to acknowledge top performers, which motivate the entire team to meet or beat business objectives (Landers et al., 2017). In healthcare, feedback loops can also be incorporated into monitoring applications for the patient, where daily step counts or daily medication adherence levels provide real-time updates on health progress (Landers et al., 2017).

Balancing Competition and Collaboration

As highlighted by Dichev and Dicheva (2017), while competition is considered a strong driver, collaboration is effective in educational and workplace settings in varied measures. The effect of hybrid models of competition and collaboration in games ensures more inclusive and sustained participation (Bilgin & Gul, 2019). For example, the same students who do not perform well in purely competitive setups rise to excel in team-based gamified projects where success factors are group-oriented, not individually focused (Gonzalez-Escribano et al., 2019). The other side of using games in business would be to give incentives for working together to solve a problem, creating a better team atmosphere that fosters innovation (Patricio, 2017). Collaboration in healthcare could be created between patients and healthcare providers through tools that track mutual objectives made more engaging through rewards and challenges (Dichev & Dicheva, 2017). For instance, a wellness program might include individual challenges, but also group challenges where patients work together toward improving community health metrics such as weight loss or increasing exercise frequency (Johnson et al., 2016). The combination of individual and group goals keeps the gamification concept appealing to a broader range of participants (Bojd et al., 2018).

Incorporating Personalization

Personalization is critical to making those gamified systems more relevant for diversified users. Applications in education, business and healthcare also draw greater benefits from systems that adapt to individual needs and preferences rather than from a gamification approach of one-size-fits-all (Rodrigues et al., 2021). Personalized learning paths could offer the facility for students to progress at their very own pace and concentrate on their weaknesses, which is beneficial for much better learning outcomes (Hassib et al., 2017). Gamification in business is made personal through individual performance targets and tailored rewards, ensuring that employees are always working toward goals relevant to their personal development (Buckley & Doyle, 2017). In healthcare, personalized feedback systems can motivate patients by tracking health data specific to their conditions, such as blood glucose levels for diabetics. Fitness apps that offer personalized workout plans and nutritional guidance based on user data have proven to be more effective at maintaining engagement than generic systems (Rabbi et al., 2015). Personalization makes gamified experiences feel more meaningful, increasing user satisfaction and long-term participation (Lister et al., 2014).

Ensuring Meaningful Rewards

With gamification, the kinds of rewards become very important. Research suggests that even as extrinsic rewards, such as points and badges, may encourage users initially, it is intrinsic rewards, such as personal satisfaction and mastery that offer greater effectiveness in driving sustained engagement (Lewis et al., 2016). In the case of education, this would make sense when referring to advanced learning or application of knowledge in real-life scenarios. In their study, Durso, Reginato and Cornacchione (2019) highlight how personalized gamification strategies, such as individual performance targets and tailored rewards, are effective in fostering skill development and aligning tasks with personal and professional growth, particularly in educational and business environments. Similarly, in healthcare, rewards for adhering to treatment protocols or fitness goals need to have meaning to the patients in terms of health value rather than simple point or badge accumulation (Tran et al., 2021).

Data-Driven Design and Iteration

Finally, successful gamification systems are those that continually evolve as new feedback and performance data are available for them. Research suggests that successful gamification systems in educational contexts evolve through continuous feedback and data analysis. Personalized gamification has been shown to be more effective than non-personalized approaches, leading to improved user performance (Passalacqua et al., 2021). The LearnER tool demonstrates how automated feedback and gamification elements can enhance student engagement and learning outcomes in data modeling education (Dæhli et al., 2021). Similarly, a study on drone training simulators found that repetitive use of gamified systems can reduce cognitive load, increase attention and improve performance (Koç et al., 2021). To optimize learning experiences, self-optimized feedback systems in massive open online courses can be designed to facilitate personalized learning activities (Qi et al., 2023). These studies collectively emphasize the importance of adapting gamification systems based on user data and feedback to maximize their effectiveness in various educational settings.

Changes in wearable devices and fitness apps' patient data are also informing changes to gamified programs as they seek to increase personalization in the application of such programs. For instance, if the data indicates that patients are having a hard time with one aspect of their health routine, new challenges or incentives can be introduced to address these issues (Johnson et al., 2016).

Ethical Considerations in Gamification

Gamification in healthcare and working environments presents considerable ethical dilemmas. Although it can improve motivation and performance, it may also encourage deviant behaviours and jeopardise user well-being (Coelho & Reis, 2021; Arora & Razavian, 2021). Ethical dilemmas in health and fitness applications encompass possible negative impacts on user health and engagement, requiring a pertinent framework for designers to mitigate these concerns (Arora & Razavian, 2021). In the production sector, namely in manufacturing and construction, research on gamification is deficient in ethical discourse, with only a limited number of studies addressing ethical implications for players (Leite et al., 2023). The unintended implications of gamification are apparent in academic environments, where point-scoring systems may induce moral problems for participants, obscuring the distinction between genuine involvement and manipulation of the system (Butler & Spoelstra, 2023). These studies highlight the necessity of integrating ethical precautions and considerations in the formulation and execution of gamification methods across diverse fields.

Challenges in Designing Gamified Experiences

Gamification has the capacity to enhance participation and motivation across various sectors. Creating effective gamified experiences presents numerous obstacles, including maintaining long-term engagement and reconciling game mechanics with instructional objectives, as well as addressing cultural and ethical factors. This section examines important obstacles and offers methods to ensure that educators, corporate leaders and healthcare professionals maintain the relevance of gamification.

Sustaining Long-Term Engagement

One of the most perilous hurdles in designing gamified experiences is enabling the retention of the user through time. Not very surprisingly, research points out that even though the first encounter of gamified elements may be intriguing for students, employees, or patients, this interest may fade away. Hamari et al. (2014) went on to show that this initial hype of points, badges and leaderboards would fade away if the gamified system becomes static without the possibility of novelty or increased complexity. Such a drop in engagement is even more concerning in educational settings, where long-lasting motivation is usually needed for long-term academic success.

According to Hamari et al. (2014), if a gamified system remains static without new content, evolving mechanics or increasingly challenging tasks, user interest wanes. This is particularly relevant in educational settings, where student engagement is crucial for sustained learning outcomes. The problem is compounded by the fact that what initially engages users may not suffice for long-term motivation. In a broader context Oke et al. (2024), highlight similar challenges in the construction industry, where gamification's initial uptake can plateau without evolving goals, leading to decreased user motivation.

One of the ways to address this challenge is by implementing dynamic content and evolving game mechanics. Recent studies have explored gamification strategies to enhance engagement and motivation in various contexts. In higher education, gamification increased student motivation, engagement and learning outcomes in chemistry courses (Guillermo M. Chans & M. Castro, 2021).

For mobile health apps, researchers developed a model to evaluate the sustainability of gamified applications, emphasizing the importance of understanding factors that influence continued use (Mustafa et al., 2023). In occupational health settings, a two-level game design combined with personalized coaching by occupational physicians improved lifestyle habits for half of the participants, though long-term engagement was challenged by limited communication between employees and physicians (Zhang et al., 2021). These studies highlight the potential of gamification in sustaining engagement across different domains.

Another possibility could be educators and designers periodically introducing new challenges that create opportunities for mastery, which aligns with Ryan and Deci's (2000) SDT, thereby sustaining long-term engagement. Personalization of gamified experiences, where game mechanics adapt to the individual's progress and preferences is essential as well. Research by Hassib et al. (2017) indicates that personalized feedback and adaptive challenges can lead to more sustained engagement by catering to different learning styles and skill levels.

Balancing Game Mechanics with Educational Goals

Additionally, a significant challenge in the design of gamified experiences, particularly in educational settings is ensuring that game mechanics do not overshadow the core educational objectives. According to Landers et al. (2017), gamification should be designed to complement, rather than compete with, learning goals. However, this balance can be difficult to strike. For example, while competitive elements such as leaderboards can be highly motivating for some students, they can alienate others, particularly those less inclined toward competition or those who may struggle academically (Landers et al., 2017)

In the context of Test-Driven Development (TDD), Ren (2023) demonstrates how overly complex or misaligned game mechanics can discourage software engineering students from focusing on the core learning outcomes of the TDD process. The challenge, therefore, is to design a gamified experience where game elements support and enhance the learning or professional objectives, rather than detract from them. The goal of clearly aligning game mechanics and learning outcomes is to improve critical thinking skills. Therefore, a gamified experience should involve tasks that require analysis, synthesis and evaluation, rather than simple memorization or repetition. By aligning game mechanics with cognitive and educational outcomes, educators can ensure that gamified experiences enhance, rather than detract from, the learning process (Dichev & Dicheva, 2017).

Cultural and Ethical Considerations

Gamification, like any pedagogical or motivational strategy, is not universally effective across all cultural contexts. Research by Sardi et al. (2017) highlights how cultural differences influence motivation and learning preferences. In classrooms, gamification should be sensitive to the diverse motivations and values of students. For instance, while points and leaderboards may motivate students in cultures with high individualism, they might be less effective in cultures that emphasize collective achievement. Ouariachi et al. (2020) highlights how gamification for pro-environmental behaviors must account for different cultural values and attitudes toward sustainability. Furthermore, over-gamification (where learning is reduced to a series of external rewards such as points, badges, or prizes) can have ethical implications. Too much emphasis on external rewards can undermine students' intrinsic motivation to learn, particularly if the rewards become the primary focus (Ryan & Deci, 2000).

Additionally, data privacy and user consent in gamified systems are important ethical considerations. Many gamified platforms collect vast amounts of user data to personalize experiences and track progress. However, this raises concerns about how the data is used, stored and protected. As Fan et al. (2020) indicate, there are numerous violations of GDPR compliance in mobile health apps, highlighting the potential risks involved in handling sensitive data. To ensure compliance, educators and designers must adhere to relevant data protection laws, such as the General Data Protection Regulation (GDPR) in the European Union (Kaneen & Petrakis, 2020). It is critical that gamified systems are designed with these ethical and legal guidelines in mind to ensure user data is protected. Furthermore, users should be fully informed about how their data will be used and given the opportunity to opt out if they so choose (Bitrián et al., 2021).

Practical Solutions to Overcome Challenges

While the challenges in designing gamified experiences are significant, they are not insurmountable. As Khoshkangini et al. (2020) discuss, incorporating features that evolve based on user performance, such as personalized challenges, can help sustain long-term engagement. Similarly, Ren (2023) highlights that gamification strategies in education and professional development, like TDD, motivate individuals by adapting challenges to meet their specific skill levels and preferences, which extends engagement beyond the initial phase. These strategies help educators, business leaders and healthcare professionals create effective gamified systems that avoid common pitfalls while maintaining user engagement. For example, adaptive learning paths that adjust in difficulty based on student progress can maintain challenge levels and prevent boredom or frustration (Hamari et al., 2014). To account for cultural differences, designers could offer customizable game mechanics that allow users to choose between competitive, collaborative, or individual goals. This flexibility ensures that the gamified system resonates with a wider audience, regardless of cultural background (Sardi et al., 2017).

While the potential benefits of gamification are vast, the challenges in designing gamified experiences should not be overlooked. Sustaining long-term engagement, balancing game mechanics with educational objectives and addressing cultural and ethical concerns are key issues that require thoughtful consideration. However, with proper design strategies—such as dynamic content and adaptive challenges personalized to user performance—gamification can remain a powerful tool for enhancing engagement (Khoshkangini et al., 2020). Additionally, integrating game-based learning elements to promote sustained engagement has shown positive long-term effects (Paiva et al., 2020). By carefully aligning game mechanics with user needs and educational goals, professionals can overcome these challenges and ensure the successful implementation of gamified systems.

Challenges in designing and implementing gamified systems in education, business and healthcare are significant but not insurmountable. Several solutions, as highlighted by Gómez-Álvarez et al. (2017), suggest a phased approach to address these challenges, allowing for incremental improvements and continuous feedback. Alhammad and Moreno (2020) also emphasize that focusing on intrinsic motivation, inclusivity and leveraging emerging technologies are critical strategies for overcoming these common obstacles. By making adjustments based on user feedback, educators and professionals can enhance engagement and ensure long-term success in gamified systems. Alsawaier (2018) and Bitrián et al. (2021) emphasize the importance of iterative design, where systems are refined over time in response to user experience, engagement levels and performance data. This process ensures that gamified systems do not become stagnant, but instead evolve to remain engaging and relevant.

The challenges of designing and implementing gamified systems in education, business and healthcare are significant but not insurmountable. Solutions drawn from empirical research and successful case studies, such as adopting incremental approaches, allow educators and professionals to make continuous improvements. Edwards and Li (2020) emphasize the importance of implementing gamified systems incrementally, using user feedback to make adjustments that sustain long-term engagement. Additionally, focusing on intrinsic motivation, such as meaningful challenges and autonomy, is key to fostering sustained motivation, as discussed by Wee and Choong (2019). By refining the system through incremental changes and focusing on intrinsic motivators, designers can ensure that the gamified experience meets its objectives and maintains user interest.

CONCLUSION

Gamification presents immense potential for enhancing engagement, motivation, and outcomes across diverse fields such as education, business, and healthcare. However, the design and implementation of these systems come with significant challenges, including sustaining long-term engagement, balancing game mechanics with core objectives, and addressing cultural and ethical concerns. By adopting strategies such as incremental design, focusing on intrinsic motivators and ensuring inclusivity, professionals can create gamified experiences that resonate with a broad range of users. Integrating technologies like AI and personalization tools further enables these systems to adapt to individual needs, making them more relevant and impactful.

Ultimately, successful gamification requires a careful balance between competition and collaboration, as well as an understanding of how cultural differences influence user preferences. Offering customizable game mechanics and ensuring alignment with user needs helps make these systems flexible and scalable across various contexts. Whether applied in the classroom, workplace, or healthcare setting, gamification remains a powerful tool when designed with thoughtful consideration and continuous feedback. By addressing the core challenges, professionals can leverage gamified systems to drive deeper engagement and lasting outcomes.

REFERENCES

Alsawaier, R. S. (2018). The effect of gamification on motivation and engagement. *International Journal of Information and Learning Technology*, 35(1), 56–79. DOI: 10.1108/IJILT-02-2017-0009

Arora, C., & Razavian, M. (2021). Ethics of Gamification in Health and Fitness-Tracking. *International Journal of Environmental Research and Public Health*, 18(21), 11052. DOI: 10.3390/ijerph182111052 PMID: 34769570

Bilgin, C. U., & Gul, A. (2019). Investigating the effectiveness of gamification on group cohesion, attitude, and academic achievement in collaborative learning environments. *TechTrends*, 64(1), 124–136. DOI: 10.1007/s11528-019-00442-x

Bitrián, P., Buil, I., & Catalán, S. (2021). Enhancing user engagement: The role of gamification in mobile apps. *Journal of Business Research*, 132, 170–185. DOI: 10.1016/j.jbusres.2021.04.028

Bojd, B., Song, X., Tan, Y., & Yan, X. (2018). Gamified challenges in online Weight-Loss communities. SSRN *Electronic Journal*. DOI: 10.2139/ssrn.3157331

Buckley, P., & Doyle, E. (2014). Gamification and student motivation. *Interactive Learning Environments*, 24(6), 1162–1175. DOI: 10.1080/10494820.2014.964263

Buckley, P., & Doyle, E. (2017). Individualising gamification: An investigation of the impact of learning styles and personality traits on the efficacy of gamification using a prediction market. *Computers & Education*, 106, 43–55. DOI: 10.1016/j.compedu.2016.11.009

Butler, N., & Spoelstra, S. (2023). "You just earned 10 points!": Gaming and grinding in academia. *Organization*, 135050842211455. Advance online publication. DOI: 10.1177/13505084221145589

Chans, G. M., & Castro, M. P. (2021). Gamification as a Strategy to Increase Motivation and Engagement in Higher Education Chemistry Students. *Computers*, 10(10), 132. DOI: 10.3390/computers10100132

Coelho, L., & Reis, S. (2020). Ethical Issues of Gamification in Healthcare. In *Advances in medical technologies and clinical practice book series* (pp. 1–19). DOI: 10.4018/978-1-7998-7472-0.ch001

Collie, R. J., & Martin, A. J. (2019). *Motivation and engagement in learning*. Oxford Research Encyclopedia of Education., DOI: 10.1093/acrefore/9780190264093.013.891

Dæhli, O., Kristoffersen, B., Lauvås, P.Jr, & Sandnes, T. (2021). Exploring Feedback and Gamification in a Data Modeling Learning Tool. *Electronic Journal of e-Learning*, 19(6), 559–574. DOI: 10.34190/ejel.19.6.2501

de Oliveira Durso, S., Reginato, L., & Cornacchione, E. (2019). GAMIFICATION IN ACCOUNTING AND STUDENTS' SKILLSET. *Advances in Scientific and Applied Accounting, 12*(3), 079-100. DOI: 10.14392/ASAA.2019120305

Deterding, S., Dixon, D., Khaled, R., & Nacke, L. (2011). From game design elements to gamefulness. In *MindTrek '11: Proceedings of the 15th International Academic MindTrek Conference: Envisioning Future Media Environments*. DOI: 10.1145/2181037.2181040

Edwards, S. H., & Li, Z. (2020). A Proposal to Use Gamification Systematically to Nudge Students Toward Productive Behaviors. In *Proceedings of the 20th Koli Calling International Conference on Computing Education Research*. DOI: 10.1145/3428029.3428057

Fan, M., Yu, L., Chen, S., Zhou, H., Luo, X., Li, S., Liu, Y., Liu, J., & Liu, T. (2020). An Empirical Evaluation of GDPR Compliance Violations in Android mHealth Apps. In *IEEE 31st International Symposium on Software Reliability Engineering (ISSRE)*. DOI: 10.1109/ISSRE5003.2020.00032

Fogg, B. (2009). A behavior model for persuasive design. In *Persuasive '09:Proceedings of the 4th International Conference on Persuasive Technology*. DOI: 10.1145/1541948.1541999

Gamification is Bullshit. (2011, August 8). Bogost.com. http://bogost.com/writing/blog/gamification_is_bullshit/

Gonzalez-Escribano, A., Lara-Mongil, V., Rodriguez-Gutiez, E., & Torres, Y. (2019). Toward improving collaborative behaviour during competitive programming assignments. In *IEEE/ACM Workshop on Education for High-Performance Computing (EduHPC)*. DOI: 10.1109/EduHPC49559.2019.00014

Hamari, J., Koivisto, J., & Sarsa, H. (2014). *Does Gamification Work? -- A Literature Review of Empirical Studies on Gamification*. DOI: 10.1109/HICSS.2014.377

Hammedi, W., Leclerq, T., & Van Riel, A. C. (2017). The use of gamification mechanics to increase employee and user engagement in participative healthcare services. *Journal of Service Management*, 28(4), 640–661. DOI: 10.1108/JOSM-04-2016-0116

Hassib, M., Schneegass, S., Eiglsperger, P., Henze, N., Schmidt, A., & Alt, F. (2017). *EngageMeter*. DOI: 10.1145/3025453.3025669

Hussain, S., Qazi, S., Ahmed, R., Streimikiene, D., & Vveinhardt, J. (2018). Employees Management: Evidence from Gamification Techniques. *MONTENEGRIN JOURNAL OF ECONOMICS*, 14(4), 97–107. DOI: 10.14254/1800-5845/2018.14-4.7

Hwang, J., & Choi, L. (2020). Having fun while receiving rewards?: Exploration of gamification in loyalty programs for consumer loyalty. *Journal of Business Research*, 106, 365–376. DOI: 10.1016/j.jbusres.2019.01.031

Indraganti, M. (2017). Enquiry-based learning workshop for deep learning in Middle Eastern classrooms – an action research approach. *Educational Action Research*, 26(4), 603–625. DOI: 10.1080/09650792.2017.1379423

Jacobides, M. G., Dalbert, M. M. A., Trantopoulos, K., & Vassalos, V. (2024). The Business Value of Gamification. *California Management Review*, 66(2), 91–107. DOI: 10.1177/00081256231218469

Johnson, D., Deterding, S., Kuhn, K., Staneva, A., Stoyanov, S., & Hides, L. (2016). Gamification for health and wellbeing: A systematic review of the literature. *Internet Interventions : the Application of Information Technology in Mental and Behavioural Health*, 6, 89–106. DOI: 10.1016/j.invent.2016.10.002 PMID: 30135818

Kaneen, C. K., & Petrakis, E. G. (2020). Towards evaluating GDPR compliance in IoT applications. *Procedia Computer Science*, 176, 2989–2998. DOI: 10.1016/j.procs.2020.09.204

Khoshkangini, R., Valetto, G., Marconi, A., & Pistore, M. (2020). Automatic generation and recommendation of personalized challenges for gamification. *User Modeling and User-Adapted Interaction*, 31(1), 1–34. DOI: 10.1007/s11257-019-09255-2

Koç, D., Seçkin, A. Ç., & Satı, Z. E. (2021). Evaluation of Participant Success in Gamified Drone Training Simulator Using Brain Signals and Key Logs. *Brain Sciences*, 11(8), 1024. DOI: 10.3390/brainsci11081024 PMID: 34439643

Landers, R. N., Bauer, K. N., & Callan, R. C. (2017). Gamification of task performance with leaderboards: A goal setting experiment. *Computers in Human Behavior*, 71, 508–515. DOI: 10.1016/j.chb.2015.08.008

Leite, R. M. C., Alves, L. R. G., Da Silva Paes Cardoso, L., & Neto, H. M. M. (2023). How Has Gamification in the Production Sector Been Developed in the Manufacturing and Construction Workplaces? *Buildings*, 13(10), 2614. DOI: 10.3390/buildings13102614

Lewis, Z. H., Swartz, M. C., & Lyons, E. J. (2016). What's the point?: A review of reward systems implemented in gamification interventions. *Games for Health Journal*, 5(2), 93–99. DOI: 10.1089/g4h.2015.0078 PMID: 26812253

Lister, C., West, J. H., Cannon, B., Sax, T., & Brodegard, D. (2014). Just a fad? Gamification in health and fitness apps. *JMIR Serious Games*, 2(2), e9. DOI: 10.2196/games.3413 PMID: 25654660

Magylaitė, K., Kapočius, K., Butleris, R., & Čeponienė, L. (2022). Towards High Usability in Gamified Systems: A Systematic Review of Key Concepts and Approaches. *Applied Sciences (Basel, Switzerland)*, 12(16), 8188. DOI: 10.3390/app12168188

Miller, A. S., Cafazzo, J. A., & Seto, E. (2014). A game plan: Gamification design principles in mHealth applications for chronic disease management. *Health Informatics Journal*, 22(2), 184–193. DOI: 10.1177/1460458214537511 PMID: 24986104

Mustafa, A. S., Ali, N., Dhillon, J. S., & Sedera, D. (2023). An Integrated Model for Evaluating the Sustainability of Gamified Mobile Health Apps: An Instrument Development and Validation. *Health Care*, 11(7), 1051. DOI: 10.3390/healthcare11071051 PMID: 37046978

Oke, A. E., Aliu, J., Tunji-Olayeni, P., & Abayomi, T. (2023). Application of gamification for sustainable construction: An evaluation of the challenges. *Construction Innovation*, 24(4), 1066–1084. DOI: 10.1108/CI-09-2022-0247

Ouariachi, T., Li, C., & Elving, W. J. L. (2020). Gamification Approaches for Education and Engagement on Pro-Environmental Behaviors: Searching for Best Practices. *Sustainability (Basel)*, 12(11), 4565. DOI: 10.3390/su12114565

Paiva, J. C., Leal, J. P., & Queirós, R. (2020). Fostering Programming Practice through Games. *Information (Basel)*, 11(11), 498. DOI: 10.3390/info11110498

Passalacqua, M., Sénécal, S., Frédette, M., Nacke, L. E., Pellerin, R., & Léger, P.-M. (2021). Should Gamification be Personalized? A Self- deterministic Approach. *AIS Transactions on Human-Computer Interaction*, •••, 265–286. DOI: 10.17705/1thci.00150

Patricio, R. (2017). A gamified approach for engaging teams in corporate innovation and entrepreneurship. *World Journal of Science Technology and Sustainable Development*, 14(2/3), 254–262. DOI: 10.1108/WJSTSD-10-2016-0057

Qi, X., Sun, G., & Yue, L. (2023). Applying Self-Optimised Feedback to a Learning Management System for Facilitating Personalised Learning Activities on Massive Open Online Courses. *Sustainability (Basel)*, 15(16), 12562. DOI: 10.3390/su151612562

Rabbi, M., Pfammatter, A., Zhang, M., Spring, B., & Choudhury, T. (2015). Automated Personalized Feedback for Physical Activity and Dietary Behavior Change With Mobile Phones: A Randomized Controlled Trial on Adults. *JMIR mHealth and uHealth*, 3(2), e42. DOI: 10.2196/mhealth.4160 PMID: 25977197

Ranjan, S., & Tyagi, M. (2022). Designing a gamification algorithm for language learning application. *2022 2nd International Conference on Innovative Practices in Technology and Management (ICIPTM), 7*, 496–502. DOI: 10.1109/ICIPTM54933.2022.9754177

Ren, W. (2023). Gamification in Test-Driven Development Practice. In *Proceedings of the 2nd International Workshop on Gamification in Software Development, Verification, and Validation* (pp. 38–46). DOI: 10.1145/3617553.3617889

Rodrigues, L., Palomino, P. T., Toda, A. M., Klock, A. C. T., Oliveira, W., Avila-Santos, A. P., Gasparini, I., & Isotani, S. (2021). Personalization improves gamification. In *Proceedings of the ACM on Human-Computer Interaction* (Vol. 5, Issue CHI PLAY, pp. 1–25). DOI: 10.1145/3474714

Ryan, R. M., & Deci, E. L. (2000). Self-determination theory and the facilitation of intrinsic motivation, social development, and well-being. *The American Psychologist*, 55(1), 68–78. DOI: 10.1037/0003-066X.55.1.68 PMID: 11392867

Sailer, M., Hense, J. U., Mayr, S. K., & Mandl, H. (2017). How gamification motivates: An experimental study of the effects of specific game design elements on psychological need satisfaction. *Computers in Human Behavior*, 69, 371–380. DOI: 10.1016/j.chb.2016.12.033

Sardi, L., Idri, A., & Fernández-Alemán, J. L. (2017). A systematic review of gamification in e-Health. *Journal of Biomedical Informatics*, 71, 31–48. DOI: 10.1016/j.jbi.2017.05.011 PMID: 28536062

Seaborn, K., & Fels, D. I. (2015). Gamification in theory and action: A survey. *International Journal of Human-Computer Studies*, 74, 14–31. DOI: 10.1016/j.ijhcs.2014.09.006

Shortt, M., Tilak, S., Kuznetcova, I., Martens, B., & Akinkuolie, B. (2021). Gamification in mobile-assisted language learning: A systematic review of Duolingo literature from public release of 2012 to early 2020. *Computer Assisted Language Learning*, 36(3), 517–554. DOI: 10.1080/09588221.2021.1933540

Tran, S., Smith, L., El-Den, S., & Carter, S. (2021). The use of gamification and incentives in mobile health apps to improve medication adherence: A scoping review (Preprint). *JMIR mHealth and uHealth*, 10(2), e30671. Advance online publication. DOI: 10.2196/30671 PMID: 35188475

Van Roy, R., & Zaman, B. (2019). Unravelling the ambivalent motivational power of gamification: A basic psychological needs perspective. *International Journal of Human-Computer Studies*, 127, 38–50. DOI: 10.1016/j.ijhcs.2018.04.009

Wang, Y., Hsu, Y., Fang, K., & Kuo, L. (2024). Gamification in medical education: Identifying and prioritizing key elements through Delphi method. *Medical Education Online*, 29(1), 2302231. Advance online publication. DOI: 10.1080/10872981.2024.2302231 PMID: 38194415

Wee, S., & Choong, W. (2019). Gamification: Predicting the effectiveness of variety game design elements to intrinsically motivate users' energy conservation behaviour. *Journal of Environmental Management*, 233, 97–106. DOI: 10.1016/j.jenvman.2018.11.127 PMID: 30572268

Westenhaver, Z. K., Africa, R. E., Zimmerer, R. E., & McKinnon, B. J. (2021). Gamification in otolaryngology: A narrative review. *Laryngoscope Investigative Otolaryngology*, 7(1), 291–298. DOI: 10.1002/lio2.707 PMID: 35155810

Woźniak, J. (2016). GAMIFICATION FOR SALES INCENTIVES. *Deleted Journal*, 22(3), 266–281. DOI: 10.58246/sjeconomics.v22i3.327

Zhang, C., Van Gorp, P., Derksen, M., Nuijten, R., IJsselsteijn, W. A., Zanutto, A., Melillo, F., & Pratola, R. (2021). Promoting Occupational Health through Gamification and E-Coaching: A 5-Month User Engagement Study. *International Journal of Environmental Research and Public Health*, 18(6), 2823. DOI: 10.3390/ijerph18062823 PMID: 33802082

Chapter 8
Gamifying the Classroom by Mediation of Technological Innovations in Enhancing Student Engagement and Learning in Ethiopia

Metasebia Adula
https://orcid.org/0000-0001-5732-2850
Bule Hora University, Ethiopia

Shashi Kant
https://orcid.org/0000-0003-4722-5736
Bule Hora University, Ethiopia

ABSTRACT

With an emphasis on the mediating function of technological advancements in Ethiopia, this study examines the impact of gamification in education on learning outcomes and student engagement. A survey was conducted with 400 participants, comprising educators, students, and professionals working in education technology. Confirmatory factor analysis (CFA) and exploratory factor analysis (EFA) were used to determine the underlying characteristics of gamification in education, technological advancements, and learning results as well as student engagement. The data's appropriateness for factor analysis was evaluated using Bartlett's test of sphericity and the Kaiser-Meyer-Olkin (KMO) measure of sampling adequacy. The mediating impact of technology advancements in the link among gamification in education

DOI: 10.4018/979-8-3693-8322-3.ch008

and student engagement and learning outcomes in Ethiopia was then investigated using structural equation modeling (SEM). The study's conclusions offer insightful information on how gamification in the classroom might raise student interest and boost academic performance.

INTRODUCTION

In the educational environment, gamification—the incorporation of aspects from games into non-gaming contexts—has emerged as a potential strategy to improve learning results and student engagement. This idea has drawn interest from all around the world because it has the ability to change the way that education is delivered and meet the changing demands of students in the twenty-first century. Ethiopia, an African nation that is expanding quickly, has realized the benefits of gamification in education and is actively looking for ways to use this strategy to raise student engagement and enhance learning results (Tsegaw et al., 2024). The idea of gamification first emerged in the latter half of the 20th century when academics and researchers started to realize how intrinsically motivating games can be and how they could be used in non-gaming contexts. The potential for gamification in education has increased as a result of the incorporation of cutting-edge technical solutions like virtual reality, mobile apps, and educational platforms (Asmolov & Ledentsov, 2023).

The beneficial effects of gamification on student engagement and learning outcomes have been shown by empirical research. Research carried out in several academic settings has demonstrated that integrating game-like components, such points, badges, leaderboards, and challenges, may boost student engagement, encourage proactive learning, and improve retention of knowledge. Furthermore, new paths for tailored and adaptable learning experiences that accommodate students' various requirements and learning preferences have been made possible by the convergence of gamification and technology advancements (Adaba, 2024). Nonetheless, there are a number of obstacles to overcome before gamification can be effectively implemented in Ethiopia's educational system. It's possible that teachers lack the tools and training needed to create and implement gamified learning experiences. Adoption of gamification may also be impeded by the availability and accessibility of IT infrastructure, especially in underdeveloped and distant places. Furthermore, it is imperative to tackle the sociological and cultural perspectives around the use of games in education, in addition to incorporating gamification into current curriculum and evaluation frameworks (Ahmed et al., 2024).

In order to close these gaps and overcome these obstacles, this chapter offers a thorough analysis of how gamification in the classroom might improve student engagement and learning results, with an emphasis on the mediating role that technology advancements play in the Ethiopian setting. The research will examine the theoretical underpinnings of gamification, investigate empirical data from local and global viewpoints, and assess the difficulties and practical applications encountered by educators and policymakers. This chapter will be a useful resource for upcoming researchers and policymakers, assisting them in the creation and application of successful gamified learning strategies in Ethiopia by filling in research gaps and providing insights into the harmonious fusion of gamification and technological innovations.

BACKGROUND OF THE STUDY

The notion of gamification has garnered noteworthy interest in the sphere of education due to its capacity to revolutionize the educational process and cater to the changing requirements of students in the twenty-first century. For the purpose of improving student engagement and learning outcomes, educational institutions all around the world, including Ethiopia, are adopting gamification—which is defined as the integration of game-like features and mechanisms into non-game environments (Mhlongo et al., 2023). The understanding of games' inherent motivating elements and their capacity to enthrall and engage players is the foundation for the application of gamification in education. By their very nature, games frequently include components like obstacles, prizes, feedback, and a sense of advancement, all of which can encourage players to actively engage in the learning process and develop intrinsic drive. Scholars and instructors have conjectured that by integrating these aspects of games into learning activities, students might become more interested, motivated, and invested in their own education (Liu et al., 2023).

The potential of gamification in education has been further enhanced by the advent of technological breakthroughs. The advent of virtual reality technology, smartphone applications, and digital platforms has made it possible to create immersive and interactive learning environments that easily incorporate gamified components. These technology solutions have the power to improve student engagement and academic success by personalizing the learning process, offering instant feedback, and accommodating each student's unique requirements and learning preferences (Adaba, 2024). Due to the government's emphasis on raising educational standards and developing students with 21st-century skills, gamification in Ethiopian classrooms has become more popular in recent years. The nation has realized the need of utilizing technology breakthroughs to develop cutting-edge educational opportunities and tackle the problems facing the educational system, such as uneven learning results, high dropout rates, and restricted access to educational resources. Although gamification in education is gaining popularity and has a lot of promise, there are a few obstacles that must be overcome before this method can be used in Ethiopia. It's possible that teachers lack the tools and training needed to create and implement gamified learning experiences, and the accessibility and availability of technology infrastructure—especially in rural and underprivileged areas—may prevent this strategy from being widely adopted. Furthermore, it is imperative to tackle the sociological and cultural perspectives around the use of games in education, in addition to incorporating gamification into current curriculum and evaluation frameworks (Tsegaw et al., 2024).

By offering a thorough analysis of the impact of gamification in education on improving student engagement and learning outcomes, and with a particular focus on the mediating role of technological innovations in the Ethiopian context, this study seeks to address these issues and close research gaps. The results of this study will add to the body of information already in existence and provide insightful guidance to academics, educators, and policymakers on how to successfully integrate gamification and technology advancements to raise the standard of education in Ethiopia.

STATEMENT OF THE PROBLEM

A highly motivated, thoroughly engaged student population that actively participates in the learning process would be the ideal condition of the Ethiopian educational system, producing better learning outcomes and the development of 21st-century skills (Nyoach et all., 2024). Nonetheless, the nation's contemporary educational landscape paints a paradoxical image, with many pupils exhibiting subpar learning outcomes and finding it difficult to stay engaged (Menberu, 2024). The challenges faced by the Ethiopian education system have been empirically demonstrated by a number of studies. These challenges include low levels of student engagement, high dropout rates, especially in secondary and tertiary education, and disparities in learning outcomes among different regions and socioeconomic backgrounds (Asefa et al., 2023). These problems negatively affect the nation's attempts to develop an educated and competent labor force, which is essential for its sustained economic and social progress (Islam et al., 2024). Although the incorporation of technological innovations—such as mobile applications, educational software, and digital learning platforms—has demonstrated potential in some contexts for improving student engagement and learning outcomes, the actual application of these solutions in Ethiopia has yielded conflicting results. The extensive effectiveness of these initiatives has been hampered by the unequal distribution of technical infrastructure, inadequate training for teachers, and a lack of thorough integration with the current educational framework (Aljehani, 2024).

Gamification is a theoretical notion that has the potential to improve learning outcomes and student engagement by utilizing both the intrinsic drive of games and the power of technology breakthroughs. But most of the current models and theoretical frameworks have been established and evaluated in Western and more developed educational environments, which leaves a big understanding gap when it comes to the subtleties and efficacy of gamification in Ethiopia's distinct socio-cultural and economic context (Emezirinwune et al., 2024). However, there is a dearth of empirical research examining the particular difficulties, enablers, and results of gamification in Ethiopian education, contributing to the little body of information on the subject. The lack of understanding of the incorporation of gamification and technology advancements into Ethiopia's educational system makes it more difficult to create plans and policies that effectively address the urgent problems facing the nation (Liu et al., 2023). By offering a thorough analysis of how gamification in education might improve learning outcomes and student engagement, this study seeks to close these gaps. It focuses on the mediating function that technology advancements have in the Ethiopian setting. Through an exploration of the pragmatic obstacles, enabling variables, and situational subtleties, this study will add to the corpus of current information and provide insightful information for educators, decision-makers, and future investigators. The results of this study will direct the creation of successful gamified learning policies and techniques that may be adjusted to the particular requirements and limitations of the Ethiopian educational system. This will eventually help the nation's efforts to advance the socioeconomic status of the country as well as the education sector by promoting the development of 21st-century skills, improving learning outcomes, and increasing student engagement.

THEORETICAL FOUNDATION

This study's conceptual underpinnings are based on a number of ideas that offer a strong theoretical framework for comprehending the impact of gamification in education, with an emphasis on the mediating function of technology advancements. This research is primarily theoretically supported by Ryan and Deci's Self-Determination Theory (SDT) from 2000. According to SDT, people have three basic psychological requirements that must be met for them to feel motivated and engaged on an intrinsic level: relatedness, competence, and autonomy. Gamification may increase engagement in the learning process and promote intrinsic motivation by introducing game-like aspects that address these psychological demands. To meet the requirement for competence, for example, challenges, prizes, and feedback systems can be used; social contact and teamwork can also be included (Tsegaw et al., 2024). Csikszentmihalyi (1990) established the Flow Theory, which adds to our knowledge of how gamification affects student engagement. According to this hypothesis, people fall into a state of "flow" when they are doing something that tests their abilities, gives them feedback and specific goals, and gives them a sense of control. Because gamified learning environments may balance difficulty and skill levels, set clear goals, and provide instant feedback, they can foster an atmosphere that encourages the flow state, which raises engagement and promotes deeper learning (Liu et al., 2023).

Sweller (1988) developed the Cognitive Load Theory (CLT), which sheds light on how technology advancements affect how successful gamification is. According to CLT, learning happens best when the cognitive load is optimized since the human cognitive system has a certain amount of capacity. Virtual reality apps and adaptive learning platforms are two examples of technological solutions that can assist control cognitive load by streamlining and personalizing information presentation, eliminating unnecessary cognitive demands, and improving the learning experience (Kaed et al., 2023). The relevance of the learning context and the incorporation of technology is further emphasized by Lave and Wenger's (1991) Situated Learning Theory (SLT). According to SLT, learning is a social and contextual process in which people actively participate in real-world, genuine activities to gain information and skills. Technology advancements that enable gamified learning environments can produce immersive and contextually relevant learning experiences that promote situated learning and enhance learning outcomes (Mashau & Farisani, 2023). A thorough framework for comprehending the intricate and nuanced interaction among gamification, technology advancements, student engagement, and learning outcomes in the Ethiopian educational system is provided by the combination of these ideas.

ORIGIN OF CONCEPTS

In order to improve user engagement, motivation, and overall experience, "gamification" is the process of incorporating game-like aspects, mechanics, and design concepts into non-gaming environments, such educational settings. The domains of game design, behavioral economics, and human-computer interaction are where the idea of gamification first emerged. British computer programmer and game designer Nick Pelling originally used the word in 2002. Pelling saw that adding elements of gaming to non-gaming applications may increase user involvement and engagement (Panigrahi et al., 2023). However, as academics and practitioners investigated the advantages of utilizing game-like aspects to promote desirable behaviors and outcomes, gamification began to gain traction in a number of areas, including education, in the late 2000s and early 2010s (Monteiro & Sousa, 2024).

The deliberate addition of game-like features, such as points, badges, leaderboards, challenges, and feedback systems, to educational activities, materials, and settings is known as "gamification" in the context of education. By utilizing games' intrinsic motivating properties and people's innate need for challenge, accomplishment, and social connection, gamification in education aims to improve student engagement, motivation, and learning outcomes. The understanding that traditional learning methods, which frequently rely on extrinsic motivators like grades and incentives, may not be in line with the evolving preferences and learning styles of contemporary students, is the foundation for the implementation of gamification in education. Contrarily, gamification seeks to promote intrinsic motivation by addressing students' fundamental needs for relatedness, competence, and autonomy, as indicated by the Self-Determination Theory (Gambo et al., 2024). The use of digital tools, platforms, and applications to improve learning and make gamification easier to use is referred to as technological advancements in education. Digital learning management systems, instructional software, mobile apps, augmented and virtual reality (AR) technologies and adaptive learning platforms are just a few of these developments.

EMPIRICAL LITERATURE REVIEW

Gamification and Student Engagement and Learning Outcomes

Numerous research works have proven the beneficial effects of gamification on student involvement. For example, a systematic review looked at the effects of gamification in a variety of educational domains and discovered that adding elements of a game, like leaderboards, badges, and points, can boost student motivation, engagement, and enjoyment of learning assignments. Comparatively to conventional teaching techniques, gamified course activities increased student happiness and engagement, according to a study conducted in a Turkish university by Monteiro & Sousa (2024). The literature has also examined how gamification affects learning objectives. Onjewu et al. (2024) meta-analysis compiled the results of 46 researches and found that gamification had a somewhat good impact on learning performance, with information acquisition and skill development showing the biggest gains. at a similar vein another study at a primary school revealed that students' academic success and memory of course material increased when a gamified learning platform was implemented (Al Shuraiaan et al., 2024).

Not all research, meanwhile, has had resoundingly excellent outcomes. Researchers have issued a warning, stating that individual characteristics and environmental circumstances may affect how successful gamification is. For example, a study conducted in a university context discovered that the influence of gamification on learning outcomes was mediated by variables including the kind of game components employed, the user's perception of the gamified system's utility, and their past gaming experiences (Mandujano et al., 2023). Furthermore, issues have been brought up about the possibility that gamification would undermine intrinsic drive and promote extrinsic incentive, both of which are critical for long-term learning and skill development. According to a research in an academic context, the usage of gamification components like leaderboards and badges eventually caused intrinsic motivation and course engagement to drop (Monteiro & Sousa, 2024). These contradictory results emphasize the need for a more thorough comprehension of the intricate and situation-specific ways that gamification affects learning outcomes and student engagement. The success of this strategy may depend on a number of factors, including the planning and execution of gamified learning environments, adherence to academic objectives, and consideration of individual and cultural variations.

Gamification and Technological Innovations

The function of individualized instructional technology and adaptive learning platforms has been the subject of one field of study. Students utilizing a gamified adaptive learning system in a university computer science course showed higher levels of engagement, learning performance, and satisfaction than those in a traditional lecture-based format, which looked at the system's effects (Durga et al., 2024). In a similar vein, researcher found that using an adaptive, gamified e-learning platform boosted student engagement, learning, and perceived usefulness in a university context (Lynch et al., 2024). The fusion of augmented reality (AR) and virtual reality (VR) technologies has also been investigated in relation to gamification and learning. In comparison to their peers in a traditional classroom, students using the AR-based gamified learning environment demonstrated higher levels of motivation, engagement, and conceptual understanding of the course material, according to a study that examined the use of a gamified AR application in a secondary school science class (Gambo et al., 2024).

Furthermore, there is potential for improving the efficacy of gamification through the utilization of mobile technology and game-based learning apps. The integration of a mobile game-based learning platform led to improved learning outcomes and increased student engagement, according to a study conducted in a university setting.

This was especially true when the gamified activities closely matched the learning objectives and instructional design (Coletto, 2023). The empirical research does, however, also emphasize how crucial it is to take gamification into account when designing and implementing technology solutions. The necessity of a user-centered design approach—in which the incorporation of technological advancements is directed by a comprehensive understanding of student preferences, learning styles, and technical competencies—was highlighted in a research (Dereso et al., 2024). Moreover, a number of studies have issued a warning, stating that gamification in educational settings cannot be guaranteed to succeed just because technology improvements exist. According to a, gamification's success depended on how the technology platform was specifically built and implemented; gamified systems that were poorly planned or misaligned failed to achieve the intended results (Coletto, 2023).

These contradictory results highlight how intricate the connection is among gamification, technology advancements, and how they affect student engagement and learning. The infrastructure and resources needed to support gamified learning experiences may be found in technology solutions, but the success of these innovations depends much on how well they are designed, integrated, and aligned with learner characteristics and educational objectives.

Technological Innovations Effect on Student Engagement and Learning Outcomes

Research has looked at how educational software and digital learning platforms affect student involvement. Students that actively participated in the learning management system (LMS) reported better levels of satisfaction, perceived learning, and overall engagement with the course material, according to a research that looked at the usage of LMS in higher education. In a similar vein, research conducted in the European environment found that incorporating information and communication technology (ICT) into the classroom raised student engagement, motivation, and teamwork (Kant & Adula, 2024). In the literature, the impact of technology advancements on learning outcomes has also been extensively studied. In comparison to conventional, non-technological methods, the use of technology-based instructional approaches, such as computer-assisted instruction and multimedia learning, had a moderately positive effect on student achievement, according to a meta-analysis that reviewed over 1,000 studies. Furthermore, a study examined how educational technology affected students' achievement in reading and math, and their conclusions revealed that technology-based interventions can significantly and favorably affect students' learning, especially in these important subject areas (Adul et al., 2024).

The empirical data does, however, also emphasize how crucial it is to take into account the precise planning, execution, and integration of technology breakthroughs within the context of education. According to a research, the kind of technology utilized, the pedagogical strategy, and the degree of teacher support and training all have an impact on how effective technology-based teaching (Gambo et al., 2024). Moreover, a number of studies have issued a warning, stating that enhanced student engagement and learning outcomes are not a given just because technology is present in the classroom. The incorporation of technology does not necessarily result in appreciable improvements in teaching methods or student learning, according to a research in the K–12 context. This suggests that the successful adoption of technological advancements requires a comprehensive strategy that addresses pedagogical, organizational, and cultural factors (Jabo et al., 2024).

Gamification, Engagement and Learning Outcomes, Technological Innovations

Several scholarly investigations have examined the possibilities of gamification, supported by technology advancements, to augment student involvement and education. According to a review, adding game-like components to technology-based learning platforms—like points, badges, and leaderboards—can boost students' engagement, motivation, and pleasure of the material. Comparably, gamified course activities backed by digital technologies led to better levels of student engagement and satisfaction than traditional instructional approaches, according to a study conducted in a university (Gambo et al., 2024). It has also been investigated how this gamification-technology synergy affects learning results. A meta-analysis compiled the results of 46 researches and found that gamification, when supported by technology, has a somewhat good impact on learning outcomes, especially in the areas of information acquisition and skill development. At a similar vein, study at a primary school revealed that students' academic success and memory of course material increased when a gamified learning platform was implemented (Coletto, 2023).

The research does, however, also emphasize how crucial it is to take into account the gamification of the learning environment when designing, integrating, and aligning technological advancements. According to a research, integrating technology solutions should be done with a complete awareness of students' preferences, learning styles, and technological capabilities. This is known as a user-centered design approach. The study hows that even in the presence of technical improvements, poorly designed or misaligned gamified systems may fail to generate the desired effects (Gambo et al., 2024). Moreover, some academics have issued a warning, stating that gamification—even with technological assistance—may have unforeseen repercussions. One such result is the detriment to intrinsic motivation, which is essential for long-term learning and skill development. According to a research in an academic context, the usage of gamification components like leaderboards and badges eventually caused intrinsic motivation and course engagement to drop (Guyo et al., 2024).

CONCEPTUAL FRAMEWORK

Figure 1. Conceptual Framework

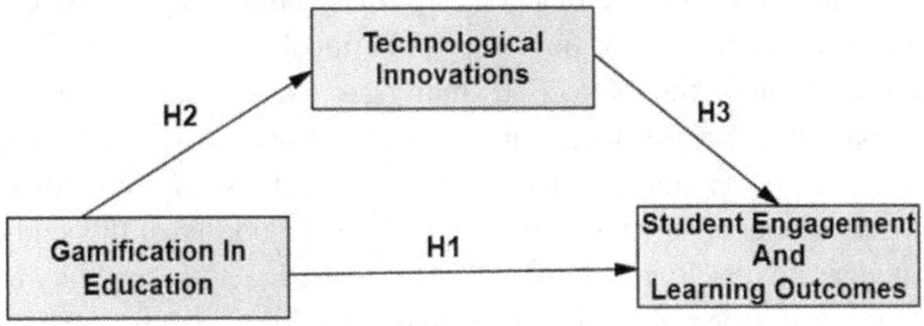

RESEARCH METHODOLOGY

A quantitative research methodology was used in this study to examine the relationship. Data were gathered from a sample of 390 individuals using a cross-sectional survey approach as part of the study design. A thorough analysis of the pertinent literature served as a roadmap for the scale development process and helped to operationalize the main concepts. The scale items for Gamification in Education were modified from earlier research that looked at how game-based components, such leaderboards, challenges, prizes, and feedback, are used in educational contexts. The literature on the integration of cutting-edge learning technologies, such as interactive platforms, virtual and augmented reality apps, and adaptive learning systems, served as the foundation for the development of the Technological Innovations scale. The idea that engagement is a multifaceted entity with behavioral, cognitive, and emotional components served as the basis for the development of the Student Engagement scale. Lastly, the Learning Outcomes scale was created to measure both the development of wider competences and academic accomplishment.

The target group, which comprised students enrolled in various educational programs, was given a standardized questionnaire as part of the data gathering procedure. A 5-point Likert scale, ranging from "Strongly Disagree" to "Strongly

Agree," was used to rate the questionnaire items. Using the AMOS program, a thorough statistical analysis was performed on the gathered data. The dataset was first checked for outliers, missing values, and violations of normalcy assumptions. Next, using Exploratory Factor Analysis (EFA) and Confirmatory Factor Analysis (CFA), the construct validity of the measurement scales was evaluated. While the CFA results demonstrated the scales' discriminant and convergent validity, the EFA results validated the underlying factor structures of the components.

Structural Equation Modeling (SEM) was utilized to investigate the proposed correlations among the components, enabling the investigation of both direct and indirect effects. The results of the SEM analysis showed that there are strong positive correlations among technological innovations, gamification in education, and student engagement and learning outcomes. Additionally, technological innovations play a mediating role in the interaction among gamification and the outcome variables. The extensive sample size, strong statistical procedures, and the application of established measurement scales are only a few of the stringent methodological strategies that enhance the general caliber and dependability of the study results. The thorough scale development procedure, which is based on the body of current literature, guarantees the conceptual and operational validity of the major components and lays the groundwork for further study and real-world applications.

DATA ANALYSIS

Factor analysis was performed on the data obtained for this study, according to Table 1's results. According to Kaiser's (1974) recommendations, a result of 0.844 is regarded "meritorious" for the Kaiser-Meyer-Olkin (KMO) Measure of Sampling Adequacy. This implies that there are enough significant partial correlations among the variables to move further with the factor analysis.

Table 1. KMO and Bartlett's Test

Kaiser-Meyer-Olkin Measure of Sampling Adequacy.		**.844**
Bartlett's Test of Sphericity	Approx. Chi-Square	1420.741
	df	102
	Sig.	.001

Source: Authors

Additionally, a statistically significant result (χ^2 = 1420.741, df = 102, p < 0.001) is shown by the Bartlett's Test of Sphericity. This result suggests that there exist meaningful interactions among the variables, which is a prerequisite for factor analysis, and that the correlation matrix is not an identity matrix. Factor analysis may be performed on the data because of the considerable Bartlett's Test of Sphericity and high KMO value. The KMO value indicates that the variables have sufficient common variance to support factor analysis and that the sample size is sufficient. The fact that the variables are associated and that the factor model fits the data is further supported by the significant Bartlett's Test.

Table 2. Total Variance Explained

Component	Initial Eigenvalues			Extraction Sums of Squared Loadings			Rotation Sums of Squared Loadings		
	Total	% of Variance	Cumulative %	Total	% of Variance	Cumulative %	Total	% of Variance	Cumulative %
1	4.51	32.23	32.235	4.5	32.23	32.235	3.0	21.45	21.451
2	1.37	9.787	42.022	1.3	9.787	42.022	2.1	15.49	36.942
3	1.27	9.087	51.110	1.2	9.087	51.110	1.9	14.16	51.110

Extraction Method: Principal Component Analysis.
Source: Authors

The Principal Component Analysis (PCA) results shown in Table 2 provide light on the data's component structure. For the extracted factors, the table displays the rotation sums of squared loadings, the extraction sums of squared loadings, and the starting eigenvalues. Three components have eigenvalues larger than 1.0, which is a frequently used PCA factor retention requirement, according to the first eigenvalues column. With an eigenvalue of 4.51, the first component accounts for 32.23% of the variance in total. With eigenvalues of 1.37 and 1.27, respectively, the second and third components account for 9.787% and 9.087% of the overall variance. Since no factors were eliminated at this point, the extraction sums of squared loadings column displays the same data as the original eigenvalues column. A satisfactory degree of explained variation for social science research is defined as the three maintained components explaining a cumulative 51.11% of the total variance in the data (Hair et al., 2010). The variation explained by the factors after rotation is shown in the column for rotation sums of squared loadings. In factor analysis, rotation is a frequent technique to enhance the components' interpretability. All things considered, the PCA results lend credence to the presence of a multidimensional factor structure in the data, which may be more thoroughly investigated and understood in the study that follows. The elements that have been found might reflect different but related facets of the phenomena that is being studied.

HYPOTHESES TESTING

Using a kind of statistics called confirmatory principle component analysis, the principle component arrangement of a collection of directed proxies is confirmed. By using CFA, investigators can assess hypotheses based on the underlying frame job and correlatives among observable proxies. Table 3 of the inquiry used CFA to assess the premise that there is a relationship among the proxies being guided and the latent notions that support them.

Table 3. Covariances

Covariance			Approximation	S.E.	C.R.	P	Hy.
Technological Innovations	<-->	Gamification in Education	.239	.19	8.364	***	H2
Technological Innovations	<-->	Student Engagement and Learning Outcomes	.299	.045	7.786	***	**H3**
Gamification in Education	<-->	Student Engagement and Learning Outcomes	.268	.32	7.218	***	**H1**

Source: Authors

The covariance table in Table 3 sheds light on the correlations among the study's major components that are postulated. Gamification in education is positively correlated with student engagement and learning outcomes, according to hypothesis 1 (H1). Student engagement and learning outcomes and gamification in education have a 0.268 covariance, a 7.218 critical ratio (C.R.), and a p-value less than 0.001. This suggests that these two constructs have a positive, statistically significant link, which supports Hypothesis 1. The positive correlation indicates that learning outcomes and student engagement are expected to improve along with an increase in gamification in education. The second hypothesis (H2) said that gamification in education is favorably correlated with technological innovations. With a p-value of less than 0.001 and a coefficient of determination of 8.364, the correlation among technological innovations and gamification in education is 0.239. These findings demonstrate a statistically significant beneficial link among technological innovations and gamification in education, which lends strong support to Hypothesis 2. This shows that the use of gamification in educational settings is likely to be made easier and more effective by technological innovations.

The third hypothesis (H3) held that technological innovations had a beneficial relationship with learning outcomes and student engagement. With a p-value of less than 0.001 and a coefficient of determination of 7.786, the correlation among technological innovations and student engagement and learning outcomes is 0.299. These results provide statistical evidence in favor of Hypothesis 3, showing a favorable statistical association among technological innovations and learning outcomes and student engagement. This suggests that incorporating technological innovations into educational settings might enhance student engagement and learning outcomes.

Table 4. Validity Concern

	CR	AVE	MSV	MaxR(H)	GIE	TI	SELO
GIE	0.746	0.643	0.219	0.852	**0.663**		
TI	0.762	0.657	0.132	0.763	0.171	**0.675**	
SELO	0.788	0.603	0.274	0.797	0.383	0.193	**0.679**

Note: GIE= Gamification in Education; TI= Technological Innovations; SELO= Student Engagement and Learning Outcomes

Source: Authors

An evaluation of the validity issues is given in Table 4, with a special emphasis on the discriminant validity of the study's constructs. The indicators of student engagement and learning outcomes (0.788), technological innovations (0.762), and gamification in education (0.746) all have Composite dependability (CR) values that are higher than the suggested cutoff point of 0.70, suggesting strong internal consistency and dependability. The constructs' Average Variance Extracted (AVE) values vary from 0.603 to 0.657, which is higher than the suggested threshold of 0.50. This implies that a significant portion of the variation in each of the latent constructs' corresponding observable indicators may be explained.

The constructs' Maximum Shared Variance (MSV) values are fewer than the corresponding AVE values, which suggested that the constructs explain less variance among themselves than they do among one another. This offers preliminary evidence in favor of discriminant validity. The measures' reliability is further confirmed by the fact that all of the highest Reliability (MaxR(H)) values, which indicate the constructions' highest reliability, are larger than the corresponding CR values. It is possible that the constructs share more variance with their own indicators than with the other constructs since all of the diagonal components in the correlation matrix (represented as the square root of the AVE values) are bigger than the off-diagonal elements. This demonstrates discriminant validity. Based on the data shown in Table 4 and the covariance table (Table 3), the following conclusions can be drawn. Overall results are consistent with the proposed links among the constructs, as shown by statistically significant covariances shown in Table 3. The study's findings are more credible and comprehensible due to the established measuring approach and the shown discriminant validity.

MEDIATING ROLE EXAMINATION

Figure 2. Structural Equation Model

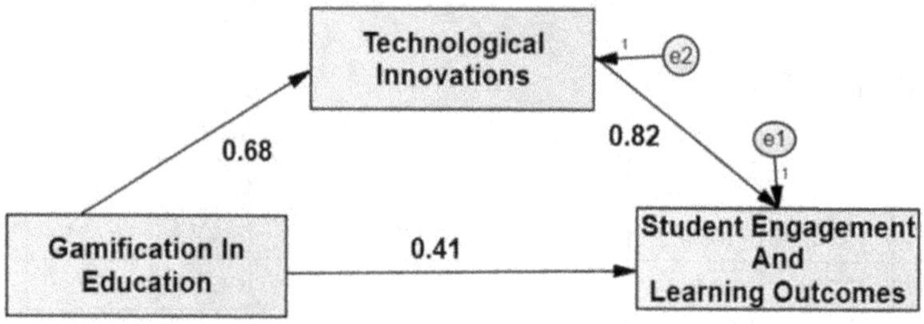

Model fit indices

Table 5. indices for Model Fit

Sig.	Chi-Sq	RMR	Fitness Goodness	Fitness Confirmatory	TLI	RMSEA
0.000	1.909	.027	0.922	0.919	0.906	.036

Source: Authors

The study model's model fit indices, which evaluate the overall goodness of fit among the proposed model and the observed data, are shown in Table 5. The chi-square statistic's significance level (Sig.) is 0.000, meaning that the null hypothesis of a perfect model fit is not supported. Even in cases when the model fit is deemed satisfactory, a significant p-value may frequently be observed for high sample sizes due to the sensitivity of the chi-square statistic to sample size. The observed data and the model appear to have a good fit, as shown by the Root Mean Square Residual (RMR) value of 0.027, which is less than the suggested criterion of 0.08. The values of the Adjusted Goodness of Fit Index (AGFI) and the Goodness of Fit Index (GFI) are 0.919 and 0.922, respectively. These two indices are higher than the suggested cutoff point of 0.90, which suggests that the model fits the data well. The model's strong fit is further supported by the Tucker-Lewis Index (TLI) result of 0.906, which is higher than the suggested cut-off of 0.90. The population covariance matrix and the model appear to be closely fitted, as shown by the Root

Mean Square Error of Approximation (RMSEA) value of 0.036, which is less than the suggested criterion of 0.08.

All things considered, the model fit indices shown in Table 5 show that the proposed research model does a good job of fitting the observed data. A successful model fit is indicated by the RMR, GFI, AGFI, TLI, and RMSEA values, all of which either reach or surpass the suggested standards. These findings give rise to confidence on the validity and reliability of the structural linkages among the concepts of student engagement and learning outcomes, technological innovations, and gamification in education. The model fit indices imply that the empirical data provide strong support for the suggested theoretical framework, which raises the validity and generalizability of the study's conclusions. Overall, the model fit study verifies that the research model accurately depicts the connections among the major constructs, and the proposed connections may be regarded as trustworthy and significant in the context of this study.

Table 6. Regression Examination

Relative			Approx.	S.E.	C.R.	P	Ass.
Technological Innovations	<---	Gamification in Education	.874	.152	7.438	***	H2
Student Engagement and Learning Outcomes	<---	Technological Innovations	.337	.143	2.702	***	H3
Student Engagement and Learning Outcomes	<---	Gamification in Education	.804	.205	7.183	***	H1

Source: Authors

The findings of the regression analysis, which looks at the potential correlations among the constructs in the study model, are shown in Table 6. Initial Hypothesis (H1): Learning outcomes and student engagement are positively and significantly impacted by gamification in the classroom. The critical ratio (C.R.) of 7.183, the p-value of less than 0.001, and the regression coefficient for the path from gamification in education to student engagement and learning outcomes are 0.804 and 7.193, respectively. These findings suggest a favorable and statistically significant association among gamification in education and learning outcomes as well as student engagement. As a result, the evidence supports Hypothesis 1.

The second hypothesis (H2) said that gamification in education has been positively and significantly impacted by technological innovations. The path from technological innovations to gamification in education has a regression coefficient of 0.874, a p-value of less than 0.001, and a critical ratio (C.R.) of 7.438. These results imply that gamification in education is positively and statistically significantly impacted by technological innovations. The empirical evidence thus supports

Hypothesis 2. Technological innovations have a positive and substantial effect on student engagement and learning outcomes, according to Hypothesis 3 (H3).The relationship among technological innovations and learning outcomes is represented by a regression coefficient of 0.337, a critical ratio (C.R.) of 2.702, and a p-value of less than 0.001. These findings suggest that student engagement and learning outcomes are positively and statistically significantly impacted by technological innovations. As a result, the evidence also supports Hypothesis 3. There are significant theoretical and practical ramifications to these discoveries. The investigation confirms the suggested conceptual framework and shows how the important concepts are interrelated from a theoretical standpoint. Empirically, the findings demonstrate how important gamification is in education and how technological innovations may raise student engagement levels.

Table 7. Mediating role Effect

	Influence	**worth**	**Path Influence**
Gamification in Education → Student Engagement and Learning Outcomes	Direct Influence	.41	Direct influence stated
Gamification in Education → Technological Innovations → Student Engagement and Learning Outcomes	Indirect Influence	.68*.82=.55	Indirect Influence Ensued
	Whole influence	.96	Partial mediation

Source: Authors

The data in Table 7 looks at how technological innovations mediate the link among gamification in education and learning outcomes and student engagement. Gamification's direct impact on learning outcomes and student engagement in the classroom is estimated to be 0.41. This suggests that gamification in education directly improves learning outcomes and student engagement. Through the mediating variable of technological innovations, the indirect impact of gamification in education on student engagement and learning outcomes is estimated as follows: $0.68 * 0.82 = 0.55$. This implies that the link among gamification in education and student engagement and learning outcomes is partially mediated by technological innovations. The combined effect of the direct and indirect effects is referred to as the "whole" influence, and its stated value is 0.96. This number shows how gamification in education has affected learning outcomes and student engagement overall, taking into account both direct and indirect effects from technological innovations. A case of partial mediation is shown when there is a considerable indirect effect in addition to the direct effect. This indicates that while gamification in education has a direct impact on the outcome variable, technological innovations also play a significant role in translating the effects of gamification in education to student engagement and learning outcomes.

There are significant theoretical and practical ramifications for the results displayed in Table 7. The findings highlight the significance of taking into account the mediating processes through which gamification in education affects student engagement and learning outcomes from a theoretical standpoint. Though Gamification in Education also has a direct effect on the outcome variables, the partial mediation effect indicates that technological innovations are an important channel. From a practical standpoint, these results emphasize how important it is for educational establishments and instructional designers to take into account all the factors that influence student engagement and learning outcomes, technological innovations, and gamification in education. In order to improve student engagement and learning results, strategies that make use of both gamification and technical improvements are probably more successful. When implementing gamification and technology-based initiatives in educational settings, it is crucial to take into account both the indirect pathways and the direct effects. This is highlighted by the analysis of the mediating role effect shown in Table 7, which offers insightful information about the intricate relationships among the key constructs.

DISCUSSION

The study's conclusions offer insightful information on how technological innovations and gamification in education might improve student engagement and learning outcomes. The findings show the strong positive correlations among these crucial concepts, underscoring the significance of taking into account both direct and indirect impacts when figuring out the mechanisms underlying enhanced learning and engagement among students. Regression analysis shows a positive and statistically significant relationship among Gamification in Education and Learning Outcomes and Student Engagement. This relationship lends support to the idea that gamification strategies can improve learning outcomes and increase student engagement when implemented in educational settings. This is consistent with the increasing amount of studies highlighting the cognitive and motivational advantages of gamification, which can stimulate heightened student interest.

The study also demonstrates how important technological innovations are in moderating the link among student engagement, learning outcomes, and gamification in education. According to the partial mediation effect, gamification techniques can have a significant impact on student engagement and learning through technological innovations. This research emphasizes how crucial it is to include cutting-edge technology into gamified learning settings, such as interactive learning platforms, virtual and augmented reality, and adaptive learning systems. The importance of utilizing technology innovations in educational settings is further highlighted by the direct positive impact of these innovations on student engagement and learning outcomes. By enabling real-time feedback, data-driven decision-making, adaptive content distribution, and immersive, individualized learning experiences, emerging technologies can improve student engagement. The overall result, which reflects the combined influence of technological innovations and gamification in education, emphasizes the synergistic potential of these two elements in promoting better learning outcomes and student engagement. In order to create dynamic, productive, and transforming learning environments, educational institutions and instructional designers should work to build integrated techniques that smoothly mix gamification concepts with technology developments.

CONCLUSION

To sum up, our study has produced strong evidence about how technological innovations and gamification in education may improve student engagement and learning outcomes. The results show a strong positive correlation among these dimensions, underscoring the significance of taking into account both direct and indirect impacts when analyzing the elements that lead to better learning and engagement among students. Gamification in Education has a favorable and statistically significant association with Student Engagement and Learning Outcomes, which highlights the cognitive and motivational advantages of using gamification techniques in educational settings. This is consistent with the increasing amount of studies highlighting the potential of gamification to promote higher levels of student engagement, curiosity, and retention of information. The study also shows how technological innovations play a crucial mediating role in the link among gamification in education, student engagement, and learning outcomes. According to the partial mediation effect, one of the most important ways that gamification tactics may affect student engagement and learning results is through the incorporation of cutting-edge technology like virtual/augmented reality, interactive learning platforms, and adaptive learning systems. The importance of utilizing technology innovations in educational settings is further highlighted by the direct positive impact of these innovations on student engagement and learning outcomes. By enabling real-time feedback, data-driven decision-making, adaptive content distribution, and immersive, individualized learning experiences, emerging technologies can improve student engagement. The overall result, which reflects the combined influence of technological innovations and gamification in education, emphasizes the synergistic potential of these two elements in promoting better learning outcomes and student engagement. In order to create dynamic, productive, and transforming learning environments, educational institutions and instructional designers should work to build integrated techniques that smoothly mix gamification concepts with technology developments.

MANAGERIAL IMPLICATIONS

The study's conclusions have important ramifications for instructional designers, educational managers, and legislators who want to improve learning outcomes and student engagement by carefully combining gamification and technology advancements. First off, it's critical to integrate gamification concepts into the planning and execution of educational programs, as evidenced by the favorable association found among gamification in education and student engagement and learning outcomes. The creation of gamified learning experiences that make use of components like challenge, reward, competition, and feedback should be given top priority by managers and instructional designers in order to boost student motivation, engagement, and retention of information. Teachers may build more immersive and engaging learning environments that attract students and encourage a deeper knowledge of the material by incorporating gamification tactics into the curriculum. Second, the necessity for educational institutions to invest in and incorporate cutting-edge technology into their gamified learning efforts is highlighted by the crucial mediating function of technological innovations. In order to increase the efficacy of gamification tactics, managers should actively seek out and adopt cutting-edge technical solutions, such as adaptive learning systems, virtual/augmented reality, and interactive learning platforms. Educational institutions may provide a synergistic environment where the benefits of gamification and technology breakthroughs are enhanced, resulting in better student engagement and learning outcomes, by smoothly integrating these technologies.

Thirdly, the significance of technology literacy and competency among educators is shown by the direct positive impact of technological innovations on student engagement and learning outcomes. It is important for managers to place a high priority on the professional development of their faculty members, making sure they possess the skills and knowledge needed to properly utilize technology and incorporate it into their teaching methods. Educational institutions may foster a culture of innovation and digital fluency that will improve student engagement and learning by enabling teachers to embrace and incorporate technology. Fourthly, the necessity for a comprehensive, well-thought-out strategy to educational change is highlighted by the combined effect of technological innovations and gamification in education. It is recommended that managers and policymakers create all-encompassing frameworks and rules that promote the collaborative integration of technology breakthroughs and gamification at every level of the educational system. With the help of this integrated approach, educational institutions will be able to design dynamic, flexible, and student-centered learning environments that meet the many requirements and preferences of learners in the twenty-first century.

PRACTICAL IMPLICATIONS

In order to improve student engagement and learning outcomes through the thoughtful integration of gamification and technological innovations, educators, instructional designers, and educational technology professionals can benefit from the practical implications of the study's findings. First and foremost, educators should aggressively integrate gamification components into their instructional design and delivery, as evidenced by the beneficial association among gamification in education and student engagement and learning outcomes. To do this, it may be necessary to employ game-based learning tools like leaderboards, digital badges, and immersive simulations to make the learning environment for students more interesting and inspiring. Through the alignment of gamification tactics with certain learning objectives and outcomes, educators may cultivate heightened student engagement, interest, and memory recall. The necessity for educational institutions to invest in and incorporate cutting-edge technology solutions into their gamified learning efforts is further highlighted by the crucial mediating function of technological innovations. To increase the efficacy of gamification tactics, educational technology specialists and instructional designers want to investigate a variety of interactive learning platforms, virtual and augmented reality apps, and adaptive learning systems. Through the smooth integration of these technologies, teachers may give students a more individualized and dynamic learning environment, which will increase their engagement and enhance their learning results.

The advancement of digital literacy and technical competency in educators and students must be given top priority by educational professionals in order to fully capitalize on the synergies among gamification and technology advancements. It should be the goal of professional development programs to provide teachers the abilities and know-how they need to create, administer, and manage gamified and technologically enhanced learning environments. In order for students to actively participate with and profit from these advances, they need also be given opportunity to enhance their digital skills and knowledge with the technical tools utilized in their educational settings. The institutional and policy levels are also affected practically. It is recommended that educational leaders and legislators create all-encompassing frameworks and rules that promote the deliberate and well-coordinated integration of technology advancements and gamification throughout all educational levels and disciplines. By taking a comprehensive strategy, educational institutions will be able to foster a culture of innovation and digital fluency, allowing for the full realization of the synergistic benefits of these two elements to improve learning outcomes and student engagement.

THEORETICAL IMPLICATIONS

Practical effects also extend to the levels of institutions and policies. Legislators and educational leaders should develop comprehensive frameworks and guidelines that encourage the thoughtful and well-coordinated integration of gamification and technological improvements across all grade levels and subject areas. Educational institutions may fully realize the synergistic benefits of digital fluency and innovation to improve learning outcomes and student engagement by implementing a comprehensive plan that fosters a culture of innovation. The study's conclusions also add to the expanding corpus of research on how technological innovations affect educational achievement. According to the partial mediation effect of technological innovations, gamification tactics can significantly impact student engagement and learning results when they use cutting-edge technology. This research complements and adds to the theoretical frameworks—such as the Unified Theory of Acceptance and Use of Technology and the Technology Acceptance Model—that emphasize the transformational potential of technology-enabled learning settings.

The theoretical foundations of the Cognitive Theory of Multimedia Learning and the Cognitive Load Theory are further supported by the immediate positive impact of technological innovations on student engagement and learning outcomes. According to these ideas, learning outcomes may be improved by the efficient integration of adaptive technology and multimedia, which can also lessen cognitive load and improve information processing. The study's conclusions, which emphasize the vital role that technology advancements play in promoting student engagement and learning, provide empirical support for these theoretical theories. A more thorough theoretical framework for comprehending the intricate interactions among these constructs is developed as a result of the synergistic influence of technological innovations and gamification in education on student engagement and learning outcomes. The theoretical underpinnings of educational technology, which highlight the significance of taking into account the dynamic and interrelated nature of technical, pedagogical, and social aspects in influencing educational results, are aligned with and expanded upon by this integrated approach.

RECOMMENDATIONS

Several important recommendations can be made to direct educational practitioners, instructional designers, and policymakers in their efforts to improve student engagement and learning outcomes through the thoughtful integration of gamification and technological innovations, based on the study's findings and implications. First and foremost, it is advised that academic institutions and instructional designers give top priority to gamification principles while developing their curricula and course designs. Teachers may build more stimulating and inspiring learning environments that promote higher student involvement, information retention, and overall learning outcomes by utilizing game-based components including challenges, awards, leaderboards, and feedback mechanisms. To guarantee that gamification techniques are effective in improving the learning process, they should be tightly matched with certain learning objectives and results. Second, in order to fully implement gamified learning efforts, educational institutions must invest in and masterfully integrate cutting-edge technology solutions. To maximize the advantages of gamification tactics, managers and instructional designers should investigate a variety of interactive learning platforms, virtual/augmented reality applications, and adaptive learning systems. A synergistic environment where students enjoy more immersive, customized, and data-driven learning experiences may be created by the purposeful integration of various technology breakthroughs, improving learning outcomes and student engagement.

Thirdly, it is advised that policymakers and educational institutions provide top priority to teachers and students developing their technology competence and digital literacy. In order to provide educators with the skills and knowledge they need to effectively create, administer, and oversee gamified and technologically enhanced learning environments, comprehensive professional development programs should be put in place. In order for students to actively participate with and profit from these advances, they need also be given opportunity to enhance their digital skills and knowledge with the technical tools utilized in their educational settings. Fourthly, it is advised that legislators and leaders in education create thorough frameworks and rules that promote the thoughtful and well-coordinated integration of gamification and technology advancements into all subject areas and educational levels. By taking a comprehensive strategy, educational institutions will be able to foster a culture of innovation and digital fluency, allowing for the full realization of the synergistic benefits of these two elements to improve learning outcomes and student engagement.

By putting these suggestions into practice, educators, instructional designers, and legislators may harness the potential of gamification and technology advancements to revolutionize the educational process and better equip students for the needs of the workforce of the twenty-first century. In addition to helping individual students, this all-encompassing approach to educational innovation will also progress the educational system as a whole and create a population of better-informed, capable global citizens.

FUTURE DIRECTIONS

Further investigation into the precise gamification mechanisms and design components that most successfully enhance student engagement and learning outcomes is an important avenue for future study. Scholars may choose to look at the distinct effects of different gamification strategies, such leaderboards, points, badges, and narrative-driven experiences, in order to obtain a more sophisticated knowledge of how these components might be best utilized for distinct student groups and learning environments. Research along these lines may result in the creation of more effective gamification techniques that are suited to the particular requirements and preferences of a wide range of learners. Future research could also investigate how individual differences and contextual factors moderate the relationships among gamification, technological innovations, and educational outcomes. Certain factors, like subject domains, learning styles, student demographics, and institutional cultures, may have an impact on how effective these interventions are. By analyzing these moderating effects, researchers can offer more context-specific advice to practitioners on how to adapt and implement gamification and technological innovations for highest impact.

Examining the long-term consequences of gamification and technology advancements on student engagement and learning is another productive subject for future study. The long-term, sustained effects of these therapies as well as the possibility of cumulative or compounding benefits over time may be clarified by longitudinal research. Policymakers and decision-makers in the field of education would find this information to be extremely helpful in developing and putting into practice comprehensive plans that encourage ongoing progress in student outcomes. Subsequent studies may also look at the possible obstacles and difficulties in integrating gamification and technology advancements successfully in educational environments. Comprehending the pragmatic and administrative challenges encountered by instructors, instructional designers, and institutional heads would facilitate the creation of stronger frameworks for implementation and support systems to surmount these impediments. Finally, it would be beneficial for future research to investigate how cutting-edge technology like sophisticated data analytics, machine learning, and artificial intelligence might be used to personalize learning and increase the efficacy of gamification techniques. By combining these cutting-edge technologies, learning environments that are gamified and maximize student engagement may become even more customized, flexible, and data-driven.

REFERENCES

Adaba, H. W. (2024). Efl Teachers' Implementations of Strategies of Contemporary Theories of Language Teaching and Its Challenges: The Case of Grade 12 English Teacher in Selected Secondary Schools in Ambo. *Journal of Indigenous Knowledge and Development Studies*, 6(1), 1–19.

Adula, M., Birbirsa, Z. A., & Kant, S. (2023). The effect of interpersonal, problem solving and technical training skills on performance of Ethiopia textile industry: Continuance, normative and affective commitment as mediators. *Cogent Business & Management*, 10(3), 2286672. Advance online publication. DOI: 10.1080/23311975.2023.2286672

Ahmed, U., Ismail, A. I., Fati, M., & Akour, M. A. (2024). E-learning during COVID-19: Understanding the nexus among instructional innovation, E-psychological capital, and online behavioural engagement. *Management in Education*, 38(3), 107–119. DOI: 10.1177/08920206211053101

Al Shuraiaan, A., Al Bloushi, B., & Al Bloushi, L. (2024). The double-edged sword: Analyzing the influence of technology on English language learning in Kuwait higher education institutions (HEIs). *International Journal of Middle Eastern Research*, 3(1), 15–23. DOI: 10.32996/ijmer.2024.3.1.3

Aljehani, S. B. (2024). Enhancing Student Learning Outcomes: The Interplay of Technology Integration, Pedagogical Approaches, Learner Engagement, and Leadership Support. *Educational Administration: Theory and Practice*, 30(4), 418–437.

Asefa, K., Kant, D. S., & Debela, K. L. (2023, November). Effect of Transformational Leadership on Organizational Performance: The Mediating Role of Employee Commitment and Expert Systems (AI) Inclusion in Ethiopia. In *2023 International Conference on Communication, Security and Artificial Intelligence (ICCSAI)* (pp. 305-310). IEEE.

Asmolov, A., & Ledentsov, A. (2023). Impact on educational effectiveness using digital gamification. [SABDA Journal]. *Startupreneur Business Digital*, 2(1), 98–105. DOI: 10.33050/sabda.v2i1.252

Coletto, S. (2023). *The Perceived Gameful Experience of Undergraduate Nursing Students Engaged in a Virtual Interactive Puzzle Escape Room Focusing on a Complex Clinical Intervention* (Doctoral dissertation, Université d'Ottawa/University of Ottawa).

Dereso, C. W., Kant, S., Muthuraman, M., & Tufa, G. (2023). Effect of Point of Service on Health Department Student's Creativity in Comprehensive Universities of Ethiopia: Moderating Role of Public-Private Partnership and Mediating Role of Work Place Learning. In: Jain, S., Groppe, S., Mihindukulasooriya, N. (eds) Proceedings of the International Health Informatics Conference. Lecture Notes in Electrical Engineering, vol 990. Springer, Singapore. https://doi.org/DOI: 10.1007/978-981-19-9090-8_13

Durga, P., Godavarthi, D., Kant, S., & Basa, S. S. (2024). Aspect-based drug review classification through a hybrid model with ant colony optimization using deep learning. *Discov Computing*, 27(1), 19. DOI: 10.1007/s10791-024-09441-w

Emezirinwune, M., Babatunde, D., Emezirinwune, D., & Denwigwe, I. (2024). The role of information and communication technologies in university education: taxonomies, perspectives, and challenges. *Reading Time, 2024*, 04-10.

Gambo, N., Musonda, I., & Zadawa, A. N. (2023). Effects of social media learning environments on AEC learning process among university students in Nigeria. *International Journal of Construction Education and Research*, 19(1), 99–127. DOI: 10.1080/15578771.2021.1974986

Guyo, D. M., Kant, S., & Kero, C. A. (2023, November). Mediation of Marketing Intermediaries and AI Adoption Between Livestock Products Marketing and Economic Status of Pastoralist in Ethiopia. In *2023 International Conference on Communication, Security and Artificial Intelligence (ICCSAI)* (pp. 311-316). IEEE.

Islam, Q., & Khan, S. M. F. A. (2024). Sustainability-infused learning environments: Investigating the role of digital technology and motivation for sustainability in achieving quality education. *International Journal of Learning. Teaching and Educational Research*, 23(1), 519–548.

Jabo, D., Borji, B., & Kant, S. (2024, February). Impact of Technical CRM on Ethiopia Bank Human-Computer Interface and Competitive Advantage as Mediators of Performance. In *2024 IEEE International Conference on Computing, Power and Communication Technologies (IC2PCT)* (Vol. 5, pp. 679-682). IEEE.

Kaed, E., Saany, S. I. A., Alhazmi, A. K., & Saif, G. (2023). A Model of Student Engagement in Online Learning. *Journal of Science and Technology*, 28(1), 38–52. DOI: 10.20428/jst.v28i1.2149

Kant, S., & Adula, M. (2024). Human-Machine Interaction in the Metaverse in the Context of Ethiopia. In *Impact and Potential of Machine Learning in the Metaverse* (pp. 196–212). IGI Global., DOI: 10.4018/979-8-3693-5762-0.ch008

Liu, T., Oubibi, M., Zhou, Y., & Fute, A. (2023). Research on online teachers' training based on the gamification design: A survey analysis of primary and secondary school teachers. *Heliyon*, 9(4), e15053. DOI: 10.1016/j.heliyon.2023.e15053 PMID: 37082639

Lynch, P., Singal, N., & Francis, G. A. (2024). Educational technology for learners with disabilities in primary school settings in low-and middle-income countries: A systematic literature review. *Educational Review*, 76(2), 405–431. DOI: 10.1080/00131911.2022.2035685

Mandujano, G. G., Riar, M., Morschheuser, B., & Hamari, J. (2023). Gamification as a Catalyst to the Circular Economy. In *The Routledge Handbook of Catalysts for a Sustainable Circular Economy* (pp. 312–336). Routledge. DOI: 10.4324/9781003267492-18

Mashau, P., & Farisani, T. R. (Eds.). (2023). *Accessibility of Digital Higher Education in the Global South*. IGI Global. DOI: 10.4018/978-1-6684-9179-9

Menberu, A. W. (2024). Technology-mediated financial education in developing countries: A systematic literature review. *Cogent Business & Management*, 11(1), 2294879. DOI: 10.1080/23311975.2023.2294879

Mhlongo, S., Mbatha, K., Ramatsetse, B., & Dlamini, R. (2023). Challenges, opportunities, and prospects of adopting and using smart digital technologies in learning environments: An iterative review. *Heliyon*, 9(6), e16348. DOI: 10.1016/j.heliyon.2023.e16348 PMID: 37274691

Monteiro, F., & Sousa, A. (2024). Pedagogical innovation to captivate students to ethics education in engineering. *Journal of Applied Research in Higher Education*, 16(4), 1029–1041. DOI: 10.1108/JARHE-02-2023-0056

Nyoach, T. D., Lemi, K., Debela, T., & Kant, S. (2024). Does Organizational Commitment Mediate the Relationship among Employee Relationship Management and Bank Performance? The Case of Banks in Ethiopia. *International Journal of Organizational Leadership*, 13(2), 355–376. DOI: 10.33844/ijol.2024.60419

Onjewu, A. K. E., Godwin, E. S., Azizsafaei, F., & Appiah, D. (2024). The influence of technology use on learning skills among generation Z: A gender and cross-country analysis. *Industry and Higher Education*, •••, 09504222241263227. DOI: 10.1177/09504222241263227

Panigrahi, A., Pati, A., Sahu, B., Das, M. N., Nayak, D. S. K., Sahoo, G., & Kant, S. (2023). En-MinWhale: An ensemble approach based on MRMR and Whale optimization for Cancer diagnosis. *IEEE Access : Practical Innovations, Open Solutions*, 11, 113526–113542. DOI: 10.1109/ACCESS.2023.3318261

Tsegaw, S. A., Filate, A. Y., & Kahsay, M. T. (2024). Effects of tool mediation on tertiary level EFL students' reading comprehension and vocabulary learning skills: A case for a cloud computing environment. *Cogent Education*, 11(1), 2330251. DOI: 10.1080/2331186X.2024.2330251

KEY TERMS WITH DEFINITIONS

Cognitive Load Theory: This theory emphasizes how a person's working memory is limited and how the way instructional materials are designed can have an influence on cognitive load, which in turn affects learning and performance.

Cognitive Theory of Multimedia Learning: This theory describes how people learn best when they combine verbal and visual information, and how well-integrated multimedia can improve learning outcomes and information processing.

Gamification in Education: Using game-based components in educational settings to improve student motivation, engagement, and learning results. Examples of these features include challenges, rewards, feedback, and competition.

Learning Outcomes: The quantifiable competences, knowledge, and skills that students gain throughout their educational experiences and which act as markers of their development and success in the classroom.

Self-Determination Theory: This motivational theory, which is applicable to gamification and education, highlights the role that intrinsic motivation, autonomy, and competence have in influencing human behavior and engagement.

Student Engagement: The degree to which students actively participate in, show interest in, and devote themselves to their educational experiences and activities, all of which can have an impact on their learning results.

Technological Innovations: Adaptive learning systems, virtual/augmented reality apps, and interactive learning platforms are a few examples of cutting-edge technology that are being incorporated into educational settings to promote and improve learning.

[illegible] A. [illegible] Das, M. [illegible] S. K. [illegible] (2023). [illegible] approach based on MRI [illegible] and [illegible] Computer [illegible]. [illegible]

[illegible]

KEY TERMS AND DEFINITIONS

[illegible]

Gamification in Education: [illegible]

Learning Analytics: [illegible]

Self-Determination Theory: [illegible]

Student Engagement: [illegible]

Technological Innovation: [illegible]

Chapter 9 Rethinking History Teaching: A New Multiplayer Digital Games Platform to Overcome the Challenges of Engagement

João Paulo Sousa
https://orcid.org/0000-0002-9005-084X
CeDRI, SusTEC, Instituto Politécnico de Bragança, Portugal

Julio César Leal de Faria
CeDRI, SusTEC, Instituto Politécnico de Bragança, Portugal

Rogério Tavares
CeDRI, SusTEC, Instituto Politécnico de Bragança, Portugal

Rui Pedro Lopes
CeDRI, SusTEC, Instituto Politécnico de Bragança, Portugal

ABSTRACT

This work introduces a new multiplayer digital game called TimeCraX, which aims to improve history education by making it more interactive, engaging, and fun. It highlights the challenges of traditional learning and how digital games can overcome them by utilizing gamification and game-based learning. The TimeCraX game platform is designed to be cooperative, allowing students to work together to complete a challenge based on a historical timeline. The goal is to promote learning through practical experience, encouraging critical thinking, and developing collaboration and teamwork skills. The article discusses the multiplayer platform architecture ofTimeCraX, which includes authentication modules, team and student

DOI: 10.4018/979-8-3693-8322-3.ch009

rankings, matchmaking, and reporting tools, all aimed at providing teachers with the tools to monitor student progress and create balanced student groups based on specific criteria. The article concludes with a discussion of the next steps for the game's development, including a play session with students to evaluate the platform's effectiveness.

INTRODUCTION

Nowadays, we have access to a wide range of innovations and digital tools. However, as previously highlighted, the discourse on innovation in education often exceeds actual implementation. Despite frequent discussions about the need for change, it is crucial to assess whether these changes take place in the classroom. In alignment with the perspective of some scholars, it is essential to emphasize that genuine innovation only occurs when real changes transpire. This is because transformations in teaching approaches and methods tend to evolve more slowly than technology itself.

Nevertheless, throughout the history of education, we can observe significant evolution (Fogarty et al., 2011). These educational changes have occurred in various ways, including some that were imposed and formalized by institutions, while others emerged more informally but consistently (Duarte, 2013). Digital games used in education can enhance cognitive skills, such as repetitive actions to improve performance, analysis of situations, strategic planning, information retention, and decision-making (Blumberg & Fisch, 2013; Boyle et al., 2011; Mayer, 2016, 2019). Furthermore, introducing technological resources and games in the classroom can make the learning process more playful and motivating for children, allowing pedagogical guidance on their appropriate use and raising awareness of potential issues associated with excessive and unsupervised usage (Ramos & Segundo, 2018). The next section will review the main concepts and technologies and how they can contribute to creating multiplayer games, motivating them to participate in learning activities, and improving their understanding of content. A description of the specifications for the new version of TimeCraX will follow this. The article closes with final considerations on the work presented and future work.

BACKGROUND

Using games in teaching has proved to be an important tool in the learning process (Barba-Martín et al., 2020; Mendieta et al., 2023). Students are more engaged and motivated when learning through didactic games, as they create a collaborative and motivating environment. In addition, games allow students to apply the knowledge they have acquired nearly, developing skills such as logical reasoning, problem-solving, and teamwork (Hinterplattner et al., 2019). As a result of this playful approach, information is retained more effectively, improving teaching effectiveness. Thus, games are a pedagogical strategy that promotes active participation of students and enhances their learning. This experience of integrating digital games into teaching is described by Bianchessi and Mendes (Bianchessi & Mendes, 2019), in which the authors use Kahoot! in history teaching to demonstrate improvements in learning when new concepts are connected to the student's existing relevant knowledge within their cognitive framework. Also, Nunes (Nunes, 2022) underscores the significance of choices and critical thinking in human life and relates them to the gaming experience. It accentuates how digital games can be effective educational tools, especially for Generation Z students.

Gamification

Gamification uses game principles, mechanics, and design elements in non-gaming contexts, often implemented through digital platforms (Luo, 2022). Its purpose is to solve problems, stimulate engagement, and motivate people to achieve specific goals. This methodology provides an interactive and playful experience, reinforcing participants' feelings of autonomy, competence, and interaction. With origins in various fields such as education, business, marketing, and services, gamification is a versatile tool that can enhance the user experience and create value in various contexts (Antal-Berbecaru et al., 2023). Its significant impact in various sectors has reshaped traditional engagement approaches, especially in education (Christopoulos & Mystakidis, 2023). Games and gamification-based evaluation and intervention hold significance due to various factors. Gamification can enhance the appeal and enjoyment of tasks, facilitating behavior modification and increasing adherence to interventions. It also effectively engages individuals who may be introverted or easily distracted, leading to greater engagement and improved communication (Saud et al., 2023). The strategic use of gamification can make learning more enjoyable, elevate engagement levels, and ultimately yield improved student outcomes (Rincón-Flores et al., 2019). When applied in human resource management, gamification can enhance job satisfaction, increase engagement, and boost overall performance (Sanmugam et al., 2015). In the context of assessment, gamification can significantly increase engagement and participation (Yıldırım, 2023).

Game-Based Learning

Digital Game-based Learning (DGBL) represents an innovative concept highlighting the effective utilization of video games in the classroom to enhance the learning experience for students (Zheng et al., 2024). Video games have the potential to facilitate learning due to their enjoyable, engaging nature and interactive user interfaces (Dondio, 2024). The Greek educational system delivers post-gymnasium vocational education and training at level three through Vocational Training Schools and Vocational Apprenticeship Schools under the Manpower Employment Organization. These schools aim to address issues such as school dropout, enhance fundamental skills for compulsory education graduates or their equivalents, and integrate them into the labor market (Triantafyllou, 2022). Developing interactive and entertaining games, primarily designed for educational purposes, is a significant step in implementing game-based learning (GBL). Serious games, designed to challenge players and test their skills, effectively facilitate learning by stimulating creativity, sparking interest, fostering discussion, and cultivating a competitive spirit for exploration in various fields (Dondio, 2024). Game-based learning has gained extensive acknowledgment as a proficient educational and training instrument (Zheng et al., 2024). In the last ten years, academia and edutainment domains have experienced a notable upswing in attention towards serious games, GBL, e-learning, and gamification (Allan et al., 2024). These concepts exhibit significant intersections and frequently incorporate common elements. In practical terms, discerning between games and "artifacts with game elements" can be challenging, emphasizing the complex interconnections among these educational methodologies (Shaheen et al., 2023).

Multiplayer Turn-Based Game

Turn-based games typically involve a structured sequence of actions each player takes in a turn-based manner, as in a traditional game of chess, where one player must wait for the other to finish their turn before playing their own. So, the gameplay of a digital turn-based game can be summarized as follows:

- Turn Structure: In a turn-based game, players take turns to make their moves or perform their actions. This could involve moving characters, attacking enemies, using items, or casting spells. In a digital game like Honkai Star Rail (MiHoYo, 2023), the player controls four characters who attack one or more enemies, after which the enemies fight back in a structured order.
- Action Selection: Players select from a set of available actions during their turns. These actions can vary depending on the game but commonly include movement, combat, defense, item usage, or special abilities. In Total War, the

player advances with his troops, chooses weapons, and monitors senate votes, among other actions.

- Planning and Strategy: Turn-based games often require strategic planning as players need to anticipate their opponent's moves and plan their actions accordingly. In Honkai Star Rail (MiHoYo, 2023) the player needs to study the enemies, and choose the best team with the best healers or damage dealers, to complete the missions. This strategic element is a key part of the gameplay experience.
- Resource Management: Many turn-based games involve managing resources such as health points, magic points, ammunition, or other consumable items. Players must decide how to allocate and use these resources effectively. In Sid Meyer´s Pirates! (Firaxis Games, 2004), players choose how to invest the money to improve their pirate ships; in Rome's Total War, (Creative Assembly, 2004) they decide if they will increase or decrease taxes so that the population can have more children and thus provide more soldiers or more money to pay the government bills.
- Turn Order: The turn order can be determined by various factors, such as character speed, player input, or a predefined sequence. Some games may allow for simultaneous turns or have variations in turn order based on specific game mechanics. Sometimes, it is a good idea to provide more speed for some characters so that they can make more moves, but this can break up the team's structured order, so the player must improvise to solve the lack of life or energy that the change in order may have caused. In Honkai Star Rail (MiHoYo, 2023) single-target damage characters usually get more speed so that they can attack more often, but this can change the team order, so they don't get the amount of energy they need to stay alive.
- Feedback and Resolution: After each player completes their turn, the game provides feedback on the actions' outcomes. This could involve displaying damage dealt, effects applied, or other consequences of the player's choices. The SimCity franchise (Arts, 1989) took this feedback from an investment and city growth spreadsheet. It was common for some players to print out these spreadsheets and display them on the notice board to show how well they performed as mayors of their digital cities.
- Win Conditions: The game typically has specific win conditions that players aim to achieve, such as defeating all opponents, reaching a particular objective, or fulfilling certain criteria. For example, players must complete the mission in less than ten turns with all the characters alive and with more than 20,000 points to get all the rewards.
- Strategic Depth: Since the resources are limited, turn-based games often offer a high degree of strategic depth, requiring players to consider their moves

carefully and plan several turns ahead. Some characters are better at long missions, and others are better at missions with fewer enemies.

- Adaptability and Decision-Making: Players must adapt to changing circumstances, make effective decisions, and react to their opponent's actions during the game. In the most difficult missions, players of Star Trek Timelines (Disruptor Beam, 2016) need to balance the team by choosing even the characters who won't be able to fulfill their part but will allow the others to progress to the end.
- Variety of Game Types: Turn-based it's not a genre by itself but a kind of gameplay that can be found in various genres, including role-playing games (RPGs), strategy games, tactical games, and more, each with its own set of mechanics and rules.

As we can see from the examples above, turn-based games exploit strategic thinking, while real-time games exploit quick decision-making and motor coordination approaches.

Multiplayer Architectures

Network models for multiplayer games delineate the architecture and design facilitating communication between information sources and destinations, whether between a client and server or among peers. In this context, a server, the entity determining the current state of the world, receives information from clients, entities sharing their version of the game or world state (Ali et al., 2009). The challenge addressed by multiplayer network models involves implementing net code solutions to deliver a consistent experience to all connected players across various devices. Two prevalent models are the client-server and peer-to-peer models. The client-server architecture involves a server hosting game logic and providing information to clients, who, in turn, can send data such as inputs and actions (Torreao, 2013). Within this model, any provider of information or services is labeled a server, while service requesters and receivers are referred to as clients. The server is typically a dedicated game server, focusing on simulating the game state and relaying information. Players may assume a server (or host) role in a peer-to-peer topology. The peer-to-peer model connects players directly without a central server. Unlike client-server models, which designate a server holding the authoritative state, each player's device in a peer-to-peer model is responsible for executing game logic and negotiating with others (Yahyavi & Kemme, 2013).

Turn-based multiplayer games can be a powerful tool for fostering student collaboration, critical thinking, and strategic decision-making (Gunter et al., 2008). By integrating these games into the educational environment, students can apply the knowledge they have acquired in a practical way while developing teamwork and communication skills (Hinterplattner et al., 2019). Furthermore, turn-based multiplayer games' interactive and competitive nature can stimulate student engagement, encouraging them to participate in learning activities actively. In summary, the gameplay of a turn-based game revolves around strategic decision-making, structured turn order, resource management, and achieving specific win conditions. This type of gameplay provides a different experience than real-time action games, emphasizing tactical planning and critical thinking.

TIMECRAX GAME DESIGN

Game design can be defined as the formal methods utilized in the specification and planning of a game's content and features (Gunter et al., 2008). Game designers produce game specifications that demonstrate the initial look and feel of the game interface and identify system behaviors for rules of interaction and procedures for gameplay and game controls that users will navigate in the virtual world (Rankin et al., 2008).

Storytelling

TimeCraX is a time-travel machine stumbled upon by four friends while playing explorers in the woods (Lopes et al., 2015). These Four Inseparables, as they dubbed themselves within their secret circle, often sneaked into the woods to embark on endless adventures, assuming various roles across different historical eras. They became crusaders journeying to the Holy Land, overseas explorers, nobles defending their territories from invaders, members of militias overthrowing governments, and devoted monks evangelizing and educating. One day, as the four soldiers advanced through the forest, they found themselves in an unfamiliar location. The thick and densely packed trees made navigation challenging, but they carefully pushed forward through the tangled branches. One of the soldiers, weary from their long trek, tripped and fell into the undergrowth. The others, unaware of their companion's difficulties, pressed ahead, distracted by the obstacles they encountered and vigilant for the unsettling sounds of their surroundings. Still recovering from his fall, the last soldier sought a stable footing to regain his balance. While surveying the area, he realized that what had tripped him was not a branch but a peculiar machine's lever. As he freed his foot, the machine suddenly roared to life, spinning gears and interlocking in a mesmerizing dance. Alone and bewildered, he cried out for his friends just as the world around him transformed. The trees vanished, replaced by the flow of a river leading to a castle that had not existed just moments before. The machine abruptly halted, leaving the four soldiers stranded in the same spot but at different historical points. One of held a broken lever while the other three called out for their missing companion, examining the fractured gear now resting in their hands.

Mechanics

TimeCraX Machine is a cooperative turn-based tabletop card game in which each player takes sequential actions before passing the turn to the next player (Figure 1).

Figure 1. TimeCraX game screen.

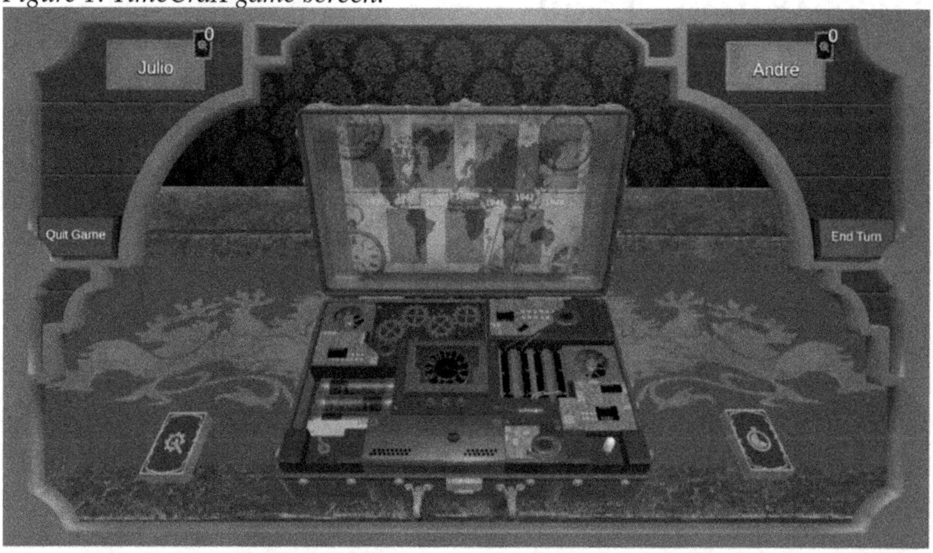

Based on the story of TimeCraX and the game mechanics, the main objective for players is to work together to complete the challenge imposed by the Timeline. They must correctly position historical events in the timeline slots before the time machine's integrity deteriorates. The machine, which is shared by all, is fragile and, as time progresses, it begins to collapse. If they fail to solve the puzzle within the given time, the players will be trapped forever in different moments of history.

Cooperation is essential for success, as each player must use their historical knowledge to minimize errors and save time. Every mistake compromises the machine's structure, making it harder to proceed. Therefore, uniting efforts and maintaining clear communication among players is key to winning the game, restoring the timeline, and escaping the eras to return to the present.

The TimeCraX Machine is divided into two main components: the Timeline and the Time Machine. The Timeline (Figure 2) is a panel featuring seven slots, each representing a specific historical year. The game's objective is for players to fill these slots with the correct event cards, thus completing the historical timeline so they can travel through time. A player's historical knowledge reduces the likelihood of timeline placement errors and earns rewards for accuracy. Misplaced events return to the deck, offering another opportunity for correct placement and promoting learning.

Figure 2. Timeline Panel.

The time machine is composed of 15 distinct components, and the conclusion of each round or an incorrect association of an event with the timeline will lead to the random malfunction of one of the time machine's components. If a component already experiencing malfunction is chosen to malfunction once more, it results in the catastrophic collapse of the time machine, signifying defeat for the players. During their respective turns, each player is limited to selecting and executing only one of four possible actions:

- Buy a repair card;
- Buy an Event Card and place it on the timeline;
- Give one of their Repair Cards to another player;
- Repair a malfunctioning component of the time machine.

Repair Cards are used to fix a malfunctioning component of the time machine. You need several Repair Cards equal to the number of players to repair each component. In other words, if there are 3 players in the game, then a total of 3 Repair Cards is necessary to restore a single component of the time machine. When possessing at least one repair card, players can provide a repair card to another player. Each player is allowed to keep a maximum of 5 repair cards. When this number is reached, the next repair card must either be used to repair the time machine or given to another player. This means that the difficulty can increase in games with more players, requiring a greater collaborative effort to gather the necessary repair cards.

Each Event Card features the name and an illustration of a world-historical event, and the player must examine the timeline and correctly associate the Event Card with its proper place. If the player is correct, the Event Card remains on the timeline. If the player is incorrect, the Event Card returns to the Event Deck, and one of the time machine's components malfunctions. The Event Deck consists of 7 historical Event Cards and is shuffled every time an Event Card returns to the deck.

Figure 3. Time Machine.

As the game progresses, the difficulty increases. With each new malfunction in the time machine, the likelihood of that faulty component being selected again rises, elevating the risk of a total breakdown. This is a multiplayer game where players work together against the machine, and each one must make strategic decisions. Their collective efforts must balance managing these growing risks with accurately placing historical events on the timeline. If any one player succeeds, they all win and return to the present. However, if just one player fails, they will all be trapped in time forever. Following the initial playtesting scenarios, the platform could incorporate other difficulty mechanisms to enhance the challenge. One option is introducing a timer for each round or the entire game, which would increase pressure on players, forcing them to make faster and more strategic decisions. Another enhancement could involve stricter penalties for errors, such as deducting more time from the timer or disabling additional time machine components, raising the stakes and difficulty. Additionally, random events could be implemented, such as sudden malfunctions in the time machine or changes in the order of historical events, adding unexpected challenges and testing players' adaptability.

ACTUAL GAME DESIGN

The entire game was built in a single scene but is visually structured in three parts: Menu (Fig. 4),

Lobby Screen, and Game Screen.

Figure 4. Game Menu.

Upon starting the game, the player is presented with the Menu, which includes a selection of 5 options:

- Enter your name: A text field for entering the player's name.
- Tutorial: Shows how to play the game.
- Select the number of players: You can choose between 1 and 4 players.
- Exit the game: Exits the program.
- Start game: Takes you to the lobby screen.

The lobby screen (Fig. 5) is where you can wait until all players are ready to start the game. In the lobby screen, you can see how many players are in the room, their names, and a log that shows who has entered and left the room. When the room is full, the room creator (the first to enter) can start the game by clicking the "Start" button, which will take all players to the game screen.

Figure 5. Lobby Screen

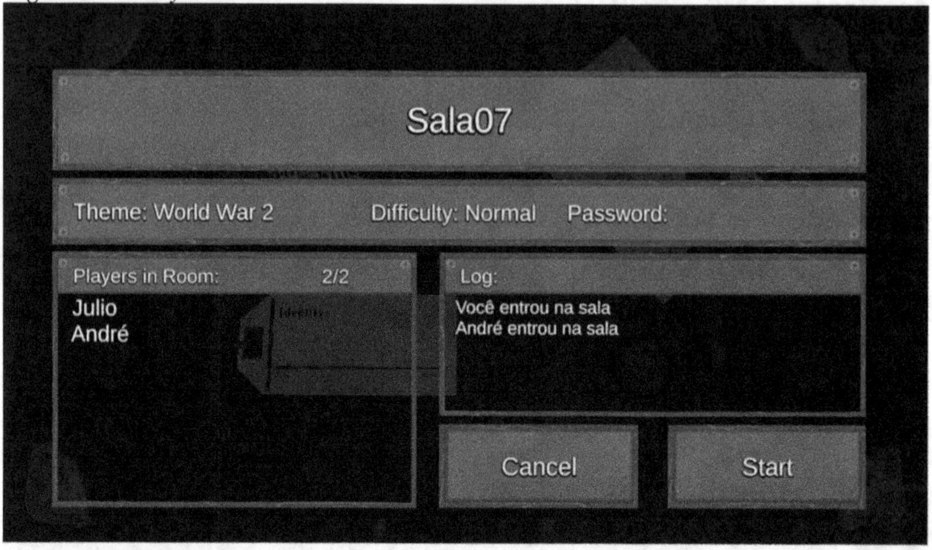

On the Game Screen (Fig. 6), players can see all the game elements: the Repair Card Deck, the Event Card Deck, the Timeline, the Time Machine, and the HUD. The HUD consists of the Exit Game button, the End Turn button, and various identification plates for each of the players. On each identification plate, players can also see an icon for the Repair Card and a corresponding number indicating the amount of Repair Cards the player has.

Figure 6. Game Screen and Round Information

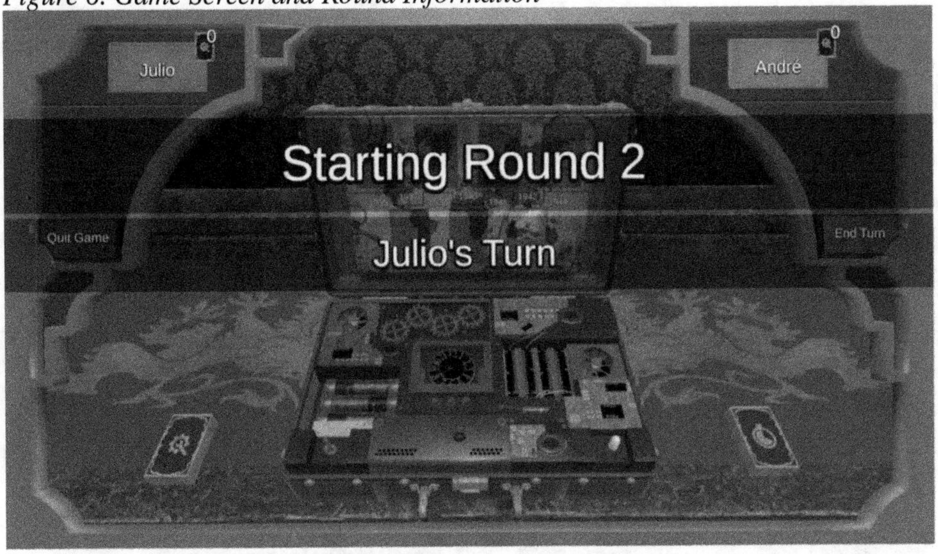

Players can see a notification in the middle of the screen indicating the round number whenever a new round starts. The same happens with each turn; when a player's turn starts, a text appears in the mid of the screen indicating the name of the player who is taking their turn. When a faulty component is drawn again, causing the time machine to collapse, a "Lost in time!" message indicates that the players have failed and that the game has ended. When the last historical Event Card is correctly placed on the Timeline, a message saying, "You're back!" indicates that the players successfully completed the game.

DIGITAL TIMECRAX MULTIPLAYER SPECIFICATION

The main goal of this platform is to develop a framework that enables the creation of multiplayer games for students as a tool for engagement and learning, integrating with TimeCraX, which is currently under development and presented in the previous section. The platform will be used in History classrooms, adapted for cooperative activities and problem-solving, where students must work together to solve challenges. Additionally, it will offer teachers tools to closely monitor students' progress throughout the activities.

The fundamental requirements of the platform are that it should support the creation of groups of students who will be thrown into individual game rooms that allow for a multiplayer game session. Based on these requirements, the proposed platform is organized into two main blocks (Figure 2): the Core and the Game Instances. The Core comprises five modules that interact with each other: Authentication, Team Leaderboards, Students, Matchmaking, and Reports.

Figure 7. TimeCraX Multiplayer platform architecture.

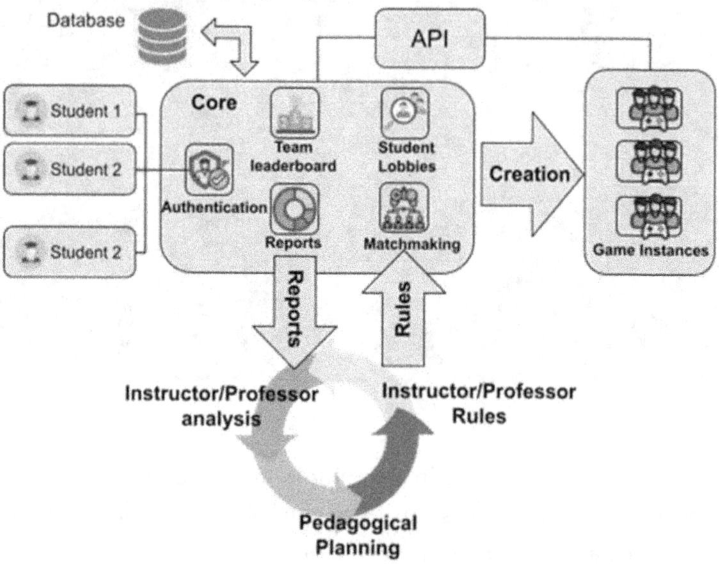

Matchmaking

The Matchmaking module's function is to create cohesive and balanced groups of students, thus promoting an environment conducive to collaboration and teamwork. The matchmaking system uses the rules set by the teacher to form groups that have an ideal combination of talents, skills, and group dynamics. Some examples to be considered in the matchmaking algorithm:

- Score-Based Grouping (Skill-Based Matchmaking): This algorithm groups players with similar skills, using a score that represents their level of performance in the game. This score can be calculated based on match history, such as wins, losses, and individual scores (Zook, 2019). The Elo system, used in games such as chess and League of Legends (Véron et al., 2018), is an example of a scoring system that could be adapted for TimeCraX.

- By ability: Grouping students based on their individual skills in certain subjects, allowing them to play together to support each other and develop their competencies.
- By interests: Form groups based on students' interests, making it easier to play games on topics that motivate them and get them more involved in learning.
- By performance: Group students according to their academic performance to support those struggling and more advanced challenges to those who excel during the game.
- More examples (Joshi et al., 2012; Oakes & Guiton, 1995; Olugbara et al., 2015; Störmann et al., 2010) can be used directly or adapted in the matchmaking module.

Adaptation to the scoring system:

- Defining Relevant Metrics: metrics for evaluating performance include:
  - Number of historical events correctly positioned.
  - Time taken to complete the timeline challenge.
  - Number of time machine failures.
  - Level of collaboration between players (e.g., number of repair cards shared).
- Assigning Weight to the Metrics: Determining the relative importance of each metric in calculating the overall score. For example, correctly positioning historical events might be more important than the time taken to complete the challenge.
- Teacher Interface: Allowing teachers to view student scores and, potentially, adjust the scoring system to align with their educational objectives.

Other considerations can be considered when developing the matchmaking module to ensure a balanced and enjoyable player experience. The system must account for the learning curve of new players, allowing them time to grasp the game's rules and mechanics. Additionally, it should be carefully balanced to maintain motivation for all participants, particularly those with lower scores, to prevent discouragement. Finally, the module should balance rewarding teamwork and recognizing individual performance, fostering collaborative play and personal skill development. By addressing these considerations, the matchmaking system can create fair, engaging matches that cater to players of all skill levels and play styles.

Team Leaderboard

The Team Leaderboard module offers a method to monitor and compare the performance of participants or teams over time, typically in games or competitions. In this context, the benefits of a Team Leaderboard include:

- Motivation and Competition: It fosters healthy competition among teams, encouraging them to enhance their performance and collaboration.
- Feedback and Learning: It provides clear feedback on team strengths and weaknesses, enabling them to identify areas for improvement.
- Continuous Engagement: The ability to track progress and compare performance with other teams increases student interest and involvement in the game.

Reports

The main objective of the Reports module is to provide teachers with information about student progress, both individually and as a team, so they can guide the learning process and adjust the matchmaking rules. Information to Include in Reports:

- Individual Performance:
    - Overall game score: Allows tracking the student's progress over time.
    - Number of historical events correctly positioned: Indicates the student's historical knowledge level and ability to apply that knowledge in the game.
    - Average time per round: Reveals the student's reasoning speed and ability to make strategic decisions under pressure.
    - Types of mistakes made: Help identify areas where the student needs more support, such as specific historical periods or critical concepts.
    - Repair cards used and received: Demonstrates the student's ability to collaborate and manage resources effectively.
- Team Performance:
    - Overall team score in games: Allows comparison of different groups' performance and identifies teams needing additional support.
    - Total number of events correctly positioned: Indicates the team's overall effectiveness in solving the challenge.
    - Total game time: Shows how quickly and efficiently the team works together.

- Communication and collaboration: A more advanced feature is to create a mechanism to evaluate the quality of communication and cooperation among team members.

Student Lobbies

The Student Lobbies module brings students together after matchmaking and before starting matches or between matches. Just like in the Lobby of a game, students/players can configure game options before the start of the match (e.g., team name, avatar, etc.).

Bringing it all together

The platform's operation can be described in three main phases: setup, where teachers customize the game, and students register; game cycle, featuring intelligent matchmaking and virtual lobbies; and monitoring, with detailed reports for pedagogical decisions and feedback.

Initial setup:

- Teacher Registration: The teacher registers by filling out their profile and creating virtual classrooms.
- Player Profile Creation: The teacher invites students to register on the platform, during which each student creates a player profile that will be stored persistently in a database.

Loop game:

- Login and Presence Status: Upon logging in, the student's presence status changes to "online," indicating that they can participate in games.
- Matchmaking Rules Definition: Based on performance reports, affinities, and individual preferences, the teacher establishes a set of personalized rules to guide the matchmaking process.
- Matchmaking Authorization: The teacher determines whether matchmaking will occur automatically or require authorization for each new game.
- Group Formation and Lobbies: Using the defined rules, the matchmaking module forms groups of students who are then directed to lobbies where they wait for the game to begin.
- Game Instance Creation: Once the group is formed and ready, the platform creates an instance of the TimeCraX game, adding the players to that game instance.
- Game Loop: Students play TimeCraX collaboratively in the created instance while the platform monitors individual and team performance.

- Leaderboard Updates: At the end of each game, the Team Leaderboard is updated with each team's overall performance, while the Player Leaderboard reflects the individual performance of each player. All scores are stored persistently in a database.

Monitoring and individual feedback:

- Detailed Reports: The teacher accesses detailed reports on students' performance, both individually and as a team.
- Adjustments and Interventions: Based on the reports, the teacher can adjust the matchmaking rules, adapt their teaching strategies, provide personalized feedback to students, and intervene in situations that require attention.

FINAL REMARKS

Multiplayer games can play a significant role in teaching, as they can provide a playful and interactive environment that stimulates learning more effectively. In addition, multiplayer games can provide opportunities for students to develop skills such as collaboration and teamwork, problem-solving and critical thinking, encouraging communication, and making the learning process more engaging and motivating.

This paper showed how we approached the design and implementation of a platform that supports the creation of multiplayer games based on rules derived from a pedagogical analysis based on the history of individual or team performance of students/players in these games. We are currently finalizing a prototype that uses the architecture presented in section 4.2, the TimeCraX Machine; this vertical slice is a 3D online multiplayer digital game in the style of a board game with up to 4 players that aims to convey and encourage general historical knowledge to players while providing fun and entertainment. Future work will involve finalizing the implementation details of the game, conducting a session with a group of students, and evaluating their learning experiences to assess the platform's effectiveness. Although the platform was initially designed for teaching history, which may restrict its applicability to other disciplines, efforts will be made to extend its use to a broader range of subjects.

REFERENCES

Ali, A., Ismail, A., & Bade, A. (2009). *An Overview of Networking Infrastructure for Massively Multiplayer Online Games*. https://www.semanticscholar.org/paper/An-Overview-of-Networking-Infrastructure-for-Online-Ali-Ismail/887b374b1010ca23a01bb89b71e40fd31e34ce92

Allan, R., McCann, L., Johnson, L., Dyson, M., & Ford, J. (2024). A systematic review of 'equity-focused' game-based learning in the teaching of health staff. *Public Health in Practice, 7.Public Health in Practice (Oxford, England)*, 7, 100462. Advance online publication. DOI: 10.1016/j.puhip.2023.100462 PMID: 38283754

Antal-Berbecaru, A., Larchen Costuchen, A., & Dev, S. (2023). Survey Gamification: Engaging Generation Z. *Computers in the Schools.Computers in the Schools*, 1–25. Advance online publication. DOI: 10.1080/07380569.2023.2271486

Arts, E. (1989). *Jogos SimCity™—Site Oficial da EA*. Electronic Arts Inc. https://www.ea.com/pt-br/games/simcity

Barba-Martín, R. A., Bores-García, D., Hortigüela-Alcalá, D., & González-Calvo, G. (2020). The application of the teaching games for understanding in physical education. Systematic review of the last six years. *International Journal of Environmental Research and Public Health, 17*(9). *International Journal of Environmental Research and Public Health*, 17(9), 3330. Advance online publication. DOI: 10.3390/ijerph17093330 PMID: 32403272

Bianchessi, C., & Mendes, A. (2019). Ensino de história por meio de jogos digitais: Relato de aprendizagem significativa com games. *Revista Tempos e Espaços em Educação*, 12(29), 13. DOI: 10.20952/revtee.v12i29.9660

Blumberg, F. C., & Fisch, S. M. (2013). Introduction: Digital Games as a Context for Cognitive Development, Learning, and Developmental Research. *New Directions for Child and Adolescent Development*, 2013(139), 1–9. DOI: 10.1002/cad.20026 PMID: 23483688

Boyle, E., Connolly, T. M., & Hainey, T. (2011). The role of psychology in understanding the impact of computer games. *Entertainment Computing*, 2(2), 69–74. DOI: 10.1016/j.entcom.2010.12.002

Christopoulos, A., & Mystakidis, S. (2023). Gamification in Education. *Encyclopedia*, 3(4), 4. Advance online publication. DOI: 10.3390/encyclopedia3040089

Creative Assembly. (2004). *Total War: Rome*. Total War. https://www.totalwar.com/

Disruptor Beam. (2016). *STAR TREK TIMELINES*. STAR TREK TIMELINES. http://www.startrektimelines.com/

Dondio, P. (2024). Does Playing Video Games Give a Child an Advantage in Digital Game-Based Learning? *Lecture Notes in Computer Science (Including Subseries Lecture Notes in Artificial Intelligence and Lecture Notes in Bioinformatics), 14475 LNCS*, 223–233. *Lecture Notes in Computer Science*, 14475, 223–233. Advance online publication. DOI: 10.1007/978-3-031-49065-1_22

Duarte, A. S. de C. (2013). *A utilização das TIC no ensino e aprendizagem da história* [masterThesis]. https://repositorio.ul.pt/handle/10451/10334

Firaxis Games. (2004). *Sid Meier's Pirates! [PC]*. Sid Meier's Pirates! [PC]. https://firaxis.com/

Fogarty, L., Strimling, P., & Laland, K. N. (2011). The Evolution of teaching. *Evolution; International Journal of Organic Evolution*, 65(10), 2760–2770. DOI: 10.1111/j.1558-5646.2011.01370.x PMID: 21967419

Gunter, G. A., Kenny, R. F., & Vick, E. H. (2008). Taking educational games seriously: Using the RETAIN model to design endogenous fantasy into standalone educational games. *Educational Technology Research and Development*, 56(5), 511–537. DOI: 10.1007/s11423-007-9073-2

Hinterplattner, S., Skogø, J., & Sabitzer, B. (2019). *Beyond the game: Exploring winning strategies with gifted students. 2019-October*, 325–331. *Scopus.*, 40. Advance online publication. DOI: 10.34190/GBL.19.116

Joshi, M., Manoj, L., Oludayo, O. O., Modiba, M. M., & Virendrakumar, C. B. (2012). Automated matchmaking of student skills and academic course requisites. *Proceedings of the CUBE International Information Technology Conference*, 514–519. DOI: 10.1145/2381716.2381814

Lopes, R., Tavares, R., & Mesquita, C. (2015, November 13). TimeCraX: Time-travelling to learn history. *Conference: SBGames 2015 - XIV Simpósio Brasileiro de Jogos e Entretenimento Digital*. SBGames 2015.

Luo, Z. (2022). Gamification for educational purposes: What are the factors contributing to varied effectiveness? *Education and Information Technologies*, 27(1), 891–915. DOI: 10.1007/s10639-021-10642-9

Mayer, R. E. (2016). What Should Be the Role of Computer Games in Education? *Policy Insights from the Behavioral and Brain Sciences*, 3(1), 20–26. DOI: 10.1177/2372732215621311

Mayer, R. E. (2019). Computer Games in Education. *Annual Review of Psychology, 70*(1), 531–549. DOI: 10.1146/annurev-psych-010418-102744 PMID: 30231003

Mendieta, C. H. A., Jara, J. P. C., Taco, C. E. C., Sánchez, R. P. S., & Pumagualle, M. L.-R. V. (2023). Innovative Educational Technology: The Impact of an Interactive Video Game on History Teaching for Basic Education Students and its Link to Cultural Identity in Migration Contexts. [Scopus.]. *Migration Letters : An International Journal of Migration Studies*, 20, 475–490.

MiHoYo. (2023). *Honkai Star Rail [PC, PlayStation 4, PlayStation 5]*. Honkai Star Rail [PC, PlayStation 4, PlayStation 5]. https://hsr.hoyoverse.com/pt-pt/

Nunes, V. A. (2022). *Descobrindo o passado: O uso do rpg digital como artefato para mobilizar o conceito de empatia histórica*. Universidade do estado do Rio de Janeiro 2022.

Oakes, J., & Guiton, G. (1995). Matchmaking: The Dynamics of High School Tracking Decisions. *American Educational Research Journal*, 32(1), 3–33. DOI: 10.3102/00028312032001003

Olugbara, O. O., Joshi, M., Modiba, M. M., & Bhavsar, V. C. (2015). *Automated Matchmaking to Improve Accuracy of Applicant Selection for University Education System* (arXiv:1507.02439). arXiv. https://doi.org//arXiv.1507.02439DOI: 10.48550

Ramos, D. K., & Segundo, F. R. (2018). Jogos Digitais na Escola: Aprimorando a atenção e a flexibilidade cognitiva. *Educação & Realidade*. https://doi.org/DOI: 10.1590/2175-623665738

Rankin, Y. A., McNeal, M., Shute, M. W., & Gooch, B. (2008). User centered game design: Evaluating massive multiplayer online role playing games for second language acquisition. *Proceedings of the 2008 ACM SIGGRAPH Symposium on Video Games*, 43–49. DOI: 10.1145/1401843.1401851

Rincón-Flores, E. G., Montoya, M. S. R., & Mena, J. (2019). *Engaging MOOC through gamification: Systematic mapping review*. 600–606. *Scopus.*, 600–606. Advance online publication. DOI: 10.1145/3362789.3362831

Sanmugam, M., Zaid, N. M., Mohamed, H., Abdullah, Z., Aris, B., & Suhadi, S. M. (2015). Gamification as an educational technology tool in engaging and motivating students; An analyses review. *Advanced Science Letters, 21*(10), 3337–3341. *Scopus.* Advance online publication. DOI: 10.1166/asl.2015.6489

Saud, S., Aeni, N., & Azizah, L. (2023). *Engaging the EFL Students in Online Class Through Gamification. 2736*(1). *Scopus.*, 090007. Advance online publication. DOI: 10.1063/5.0170648

Shaheen, A., Ali, S., & Fotaris, P. (2023). Assessing the Efficacy of Reflective Game Design: A Design-Based Study in Digital Game-Based Learning. *Education Sciences*, 13(12), 1204. DOI: 10.3390/educsci13121204

Störmann, S., Von Der Borch, P., & Dimitriadis, K. (2010). Online matchmaking enables large-scale individual mentoring. *Medical Education*, 44(5), 492–493. DOI: 10.1111/j.1365-2923.2010.03663.x PMID: 20374458

Torreao, V. de A. (2013). *Comparison between client-server, peer-to-peer and hybrid architectures for MMOGs.* https://www.semanticscholar.org/paper/Comparison-between-client-server-%2C-peer-to-peer-and-Torreao/3fb797609e219abdd9723d41aea37c19179afcf9

Triantafyllou, S. (2022). *Game-Based Learning and Interactive Educational Games for Learners – An Educational Paradigm from Greece*. DOI: 10.33422/6th.icmrss.2022.10.20

Véron, M., Marin, O., & Monnet, S. (2018). Matchmaking in multi-player on-line games: Studying user traces to improve the user experience. *Proceedings of Network and Operating System Support on Digital Audio and Video Workshop*, 7–12. DOI: 10.1145/2578260.2578265

Yahyavi, A., & Kemme, B. (2013). Peer-to-Peer Architectures for Massively Multiplayer Online Games: A Survey. *ACM Computing Surveys*, 46(1), 1–51. Advance online publication. DOI: 10.1145/2522968.2522977

Yıldırım, Ö. (2023). Assessment Based Games and Gamification. In *Digital Games and Gamification in Education* (pp. 143–153).

Zheng, Y., Zhang, J., Li, Y., Wu, X., Ding, R., Luo, X., Liu, P., & Huang, J. (2024). Effects of digital game-based learning on students' digital etiquette literacy, learning motivations, and engagement. *Heliyon, 10*(1). *Heliyon*, 10(1), e23490. Advance online publication. DOI: 10.1016/j.heliyon.2023.e23490 PMID: 38187224

Zook, A. (2019). Building Matchmaking Systems. In *Data Analytics Applications in Gaming and Entertainment*. Auerbach Publications. DOI: 10.1201/9780429286490-3

Chapter 10
Systemic Barriers and Support Mechanisms for Black Male Educators:
A Review of Recent Evidence and Policy Implications

S. Baranidharan
https://orcid.org/0000-0002-7780-4045
Christ University, India

G. Chandrakala
Dayananda Sagar University, India

ABSTRACT

This study investigates the challenges faced by Black male educators in K-12 education, focusing on recruitment, retention, and career advancement strategies. It reveals that Black male teachers experience systemic racism, lack of institutional support, and social isolation. To address these challenges, the study suggests targeted recruitment, better support systems, and community engagement. Additionally, it emphasizes the positive impact of Black male educators on student outcomes and calls for policies promoting equity and inclusion. Using a qualitative review of studies published between 2018 and 2024, thematic analysis identifies key issues and provides actionable insights for policymakers and educators.

DOI: 10.4018/979-8-3693-8322-3.ch010

INTRODUCTION

The representation and experiences of Black male educators have garnered increasing attention in recent years, reflecting a growing awareness of the critical role these individuals play in shaping educational environments and student outcomes. Despite their significant impact, Black male educators face a range of systemic challenges and barriers that affect their professional trajectories and effectiveness. Black male educators are often driven by a deep-seated commitment to their communities and a desire to serve as positive role models for students, particularly those from similar backgrounds. Studies have consistently shown that Black male teachers can significantly influence student outcomes by serving as mentors and providing culturally relevant instruction (Dovico, 2023; Bryant, 2023). Their presence in schools is linked to improved academic performance and social development among Black and Latino students (Carey, 2023; Salas, Lewis, & Siefert, 2021). This influence is especially critical in urban and underserved school districts where such role models are scarce. Despite their contributions, Black male educators face considerable challenges that hinder their effectiveness and career longevity. Systemic racism, inadequate institutional support, and a lack of mentorship are pervasive issues that impact their professional experiences (Wallace, 2023; Williams, 2023). These barriers not only affect job satisfaction but also contribute to high turnover rates, with many Black male educators leaving the profession prematurely (Royston, McKinney de, & Madkins, 2021; Marks, 2022). The persistence of these challenges highlights a critical need for systemic change within educational institutions to better support Black male educators. Black male educators often employ culturally responsive teaching strategies that address the diverse needs of their students. These strategies include implementing pedagogical approaches that are inclusive and reflective of students' cultural backgrounds (Jackson, 2019; Jett, Savage, & Ortiz, 2021). Such practices are essential for engaging students and creating an equitable learning environment. However, the underrepresentation of Black male educators limits the widespread application of these effective practices, thereby reducing their potential impact on student achievement (Bristol, 2023; Ohito, 2021). Efforts to address the challenges faced by Black male educators have led to the development of various support systems and policies aimed at improving recruitment, retention, and professional development. Programs such as the Black Educator Teacher Residency Program and targeted mentoring initiatives have been implemented to support these educators (Anderson, 2021; Mathwasa & Sibanda, 2021). Despite these efforts, existing policies often fall short of addressing the underlying systemic issues, such as biases in hiring practices and inadequate support structures, that continue to impede the effectiveness and career longevity of Black male educators (Nelson, 2020; Underwood, Taylor, Smith, & Johnson-Lutz, 2020).

LITERATURE REVIEW

Jackson and Dicks (2024) conducted a mixed methods study exploring the experiences of beginning Black male educators in teacher preparation programs. Their research highlighted the unique challenges and opportunities faced by these educators, emphasizing the need for targeted support within these programs to better prepare them for the realities of the classroom. The study contributed valuable insights into how these educators navigated their training and the structural issues that influenced their preparedness for teaching. Witherspoon (2024) carried out a phenomenological study examining student responsiveness towards Black male educators in K-12 urban school settings. This research provided a nuanced understanding of how Black male educators were perceived by their students and the impact of these perceptions on educational outcomes. The findings underscored the importance of understanding student perspectives in fostering more effective educational environments and supporting Black male educators. Lee (2024) focused on Black male early career educators in secondary science classrooms, aiming to rewrite narratives surrounding successful teaching in this context. Lee's study documented the strategies and practices that contributed to the success of these educators, challenging prevailing stereotypes and offering a more complex picture of their professional experiences. This work was instrumental in redefining success for Black male educators in science education. Young and Young (2023) conducted a 10-year content analysis of empirical research on Black male teachers, presented in their book chapter within "Men Educators of Color in US Public Schools." Their analysis revealed significant trends and gaps in the existing literature, providing a comprehensive overview of the evolving narratives and research on Black male educators over the past decade. This chapter served as a critical resource for understanding long-term trends and developments in the field. Hocutt Sr (2023) addressed the disparity of Black male educators by exploring strategies to build capacity for mentoring Black male youth. The study highlighted systemic challenges and proposed intervention strategies aimed at increasing the representation of Black male educators and enhancing their role in mentoring students. Hocutt's research contributed to the discourse on improving educator diversity and support systems. Woodson, Jones, and Gowder (2023) explored the intersection of Blackness, masculinities, and leadership through the experiences of Black male teachers. The featured in "Men Educators of Color in US Public Schools," examined how these educators navigated their identities and leadership roles within schools. The study offered insights into how personal and professional identities intersected and influenced their effectiveness as educators.

Thompson (2023) conducted a phenomenological study of the lived experiences of Black male educators, focusing on the personal and professional challenges they faced. Thompson's research provided an in-depth look at the difficulties encountered by these educators and the resilience they demonstrated. The study was a significant contribution to understanding the complexities of their experiences in the educational field. Jones Jr (2023) carried out a counter-narrative study examining the experiences of Black male educators. This research aimed to challenge dominant narratives by presenting alternative perspectives on the realities faced by these educators. Jones Jr's study offered a critical analysis of how these narratives shaped the experiences and perceptions of Black male educators in the field. Bryant (2023) investigated the Black male educator shortage in the Mississippi public school system, analyzing its impact, challenges, and potential intervention strategies. Bryant's study addressed the critical issues surrounding educator shortages and proposed solutions to mitigate the effects of this shortage on the educational system. Nelson (2023) explored the lived experiences of African American male educators, both as students and as professionals. Nelson's research provided a comprehensive look at how these educators' past experiences influenced their current roles and practices, offering valuable insights into the broader implications of their experiences for the education system. Dovico (2023) investigated the motivations driving Black males to pursue careers as elementary school educators. The study, available through ProQuest Dissertations & Theses, explored various factors influencing this career choice, including personal experiences, community impact, and aspirations to serve as role models. Dovico's research highlighted the intrinsic and extrinsic motivators that attract Black males to the field and emphasized the need for supportive policies to retain them in education. Bryant (2023) examined the practices of Black male educators within Georgia public school classrooms. The study focused on the teaching strategies, classroom management techniques, and pedagogical approaches employed by Black male teachers. Bryant's study provided insights into how these educators adapted their practices to meet the needs of their students and addressed challenges specific to their roles.

Cummings-Lewis (2023) explored the underrepresentation of Black men in early childhood education, specifically examining their career choices, retention, long-term sustainability, and influence on Black children. Identified barriers to entry and retention in the field and discussed the significant impact that Black male early childhood educators can have on their students. Carey (2023) presented a chapter in "Men Educators of Color in US Public Schools" that uncovered the pedagogies and positionalities of male teachers of color, focusing on their interactions with Black and Latino adolescent boys. Carey's research provided a critical analysis of how these educators navigated their roles and engaged with their students, highlighting the pedagogical strategies and positionalities that impacted student outcomes. Williams (2023) conducted a qualitative phenomenological study on the challenges affecting the careers of Black male teachers in the K-12 system in South Carolina. The research, available through Liberty University, delved into the personal and professional obstacles faced by these educators and offered recommendations for addressing these challenges to improve their career satisfaction and effectiveness. Warren (2023) explored race-gender oppression and the interactions between Black male teachers and Black boys. Warren's study provided a genre analysis of these interactions, revealing the complex dynamics of race and gender within educational settings and offering insights into how these interactions influenced teaching and learning.

Wallace (2023) critically examined the negotiations of leadership and learning by Black male teachers in London state schools. Wallace discussed the ways in which these educators navigated their roles and responsibilities amidst the challenges of diversity and inclusion, highlighting the complexities of their leadership and educational practices. Bristol (2023) proposed a theory of social isolation in organizations, focusing on Black men teaching addressed the social and professional isolation experienced by Black male educators and discussed how this isolation impacted their roles and interactions within educational institutions. Jeter and Melendez (2022) highlighted the issue of the insufficient number of Black male educators. The implications of this shortage and proposed strategies to address the disparity, emphasizing the importance of increasing the representation of Black male educators to improve educational outcomes. Wallace, Bol, and Hall (2022) addressed the significance of Black male educators in K-12 settings, explored the modeling and expectations associated with Black male teachers and demonstrated the positive impact they have on students, advocating for policies to support and increase their presence in schools.

Cormier, Scott, and Powell (2022) analyzed the experiences of Black male special education teachers. Black Male Special Education Teachers Socialized as Everything but Educators," explored the socialization and identity challenges faced by these teachers. The research highlighted how these educators were often marginalized and perceived through stereotypes, rather than being recognized for their professional roles and contributions. Cunningham (2022) presented a dissertation on the journey of a Black educator supporting Black males in an urban school district. Cunningham's work provided insights into the personal and professional struggles encountered while striving to make a positive impact on Black male students. Mayfield (2022) analyzed the motivating factors for Black men pursuing careers in education within a Southern urban school setting. The study explored the personal and contextual reasons driving Black men to become educators and how these factors influenced their professional journeys. Sims (2022) conducted a dissertation focused on the underrepresentation of Black male educators in New Mexico. The research provided a detailed analysis of the factors contributing to this underrepresentation and its effects on the education system. Sims' study highlighted the need for targeted strategies to increase the presence of Black male educators and address the disparities in educational settings.

Kimbrough-Scott (2022) explored the experiences of Black male educators in school leadership roles in their phenomenological study. The dissertation examined how these educators navigated their leadership positions and the unique challenges they faced. Kimbrough-Scott's research shed light on the complexities of leading as a Black male educator and the systemic issues impacting their leadership effectiveness. Felton (2022) conducted a qualitative narrative research study on the lack of diversity among educators, focusing on the educational experiences of Black males. The study investigated the barriers and challenges faced by Black male educators and the impact of their experiences on their professional development and retention in the field. Anderson and Gordon (2022) explored Black male educators' perceptions of their responsibility towards equitable representation in K-12 education. Their study perceptions about and Responsibility to Equitable Representation in K–12 Education, examined how these educators navigated their roles in the context of historical and ongoing challenges related to racial integration and representation. Sims Jr (2022) analyzed the effects of underrepresentation on Black male educators in New Mexico. This study provided a comprehensive overview of how the lack of representation impacted both the educators and the students they served, offering recommendations for addressing these issues and improving diversity in the education system. Williams (2022) examined educator perceptions of African American male recruitment in advanced placement courses. The study focused on the recruitment and representation of Black male students in advanced placement settings, highlighting the perceptions and challenges faced by educators in promoting diversity within these programs. Beachum, Khabbaz, and colleagues (2022) investigated the experiences of retired Black educators. The study explored the legacy and contributions of retired Black educators, emphasizing their impact on education and the challenges they faced throughout their careers. Ransaw (2022) provided a comprehensive guide for educators on mindful teaching practices aimed at enhancing Black male achievement, discussing various strategies and practices that educators can adopt to better support Black male students. Ransaw emphasized the importance of creating an inclusive and supportive learning environment tailored to the needs of these students.

Marks (2022) examined systems of support for Black educators through the Black Educator Teacher Residency Program in Multicultural Education. The study explored how this program facilitated the professional development and retention of Black educators. Marks highlighted the program's role in providing necessary support structures and resources to help Black educators succeed and advance in their careers. Watkins and Mensah (2022) provided insights into the persistence of Black men in science education and discussed strategies that multicultural science educators can employ to support and retain these students. The chapter underscored the importance of targeted support to improve their academic experiences and outcomes. Ohito (2021) explored the role of antiracist pedagogical approaches in teacher education in the United States Ohito proposed strategies for teacher educators to challenge systemic racism and foster a more inclusive educational environment. The study provided a framework for integrating antiracist principles into teaching practices. Reich-Shapiro, Cole, and Plaisir (2021) investigated how male educators conceptualize their impact on early childhood classrooms. The study revealed how male educators viewed their roles and contributions in early childhood settings, highlighting their unique impact on classroom dynamics and student development.

Gobert (2021) examined the experiences of African American male educators in primary grade levels. The research provided insights into the challenges and experiences of these educators, focusing on their interactions with students and the educational environment. Jett, Savage, Ortiz, and colleagues (2021) reflected on a symposium with Black male mathematics educators. These educators shared their experiences and perspectives, highlighting common themes and challenges faced in the field of mathematics education. Okeke and Nyanhoto (2021) addressed the recruitment and retention of male educators in preschools. The study discussed the implications for teacher education policy and practices, emphasizing the need for targeted strategies to attract and retain male educators in early childhood education. Salas, Lewis, and Siefert (2021) explored the experiences of Black males in new Latino South classrooms in The New Educator. Their article discussed the challenges and opportunities faced by Black male educators in diverse educational settings, focusing on their adaptation to new cultural contexts. Samuels, Wilkerson, and Dacres (2021) reflected on the struggles faced by Black women educators and the challenges Black women educators encounter and offered recommendations for improving their retention and support within the education system.

Royston, McKinney de Madkins, and Madkins (2021) explored the protective roles of Black educators for Black children The article examined how Black educators use their positionality to safeguard and support Black students within educational settings, emphasizing the deep, personal commitment to student well-being and success. Mathwasa and Sibanda (2021) addressed the recruitment of male educators in early childhood centers, discussed the implications of recruiting male educators for early childhood education, focusing on how teacher education programs can adapt to better support and integrate male educators into these roles. Anderson (2021) investigated the representation of African American/Black male educators in K-12 public schools. The research assessed the impacts of representation on recruitment, retention, and educators' responsibilities, providing valuable insights into the systemic challenges faced by Black male educators and proposing strategies for improvement. Scott, Brown, Wallace, Cormier, and colleagues (2021) conducted a qualitative study on Black special educators' persistence and examined the factors contributing to the persistence of Black special educators, highlighting their dedication and the unique challenges they face in their roles. Underwood, Taylor, Smith, and others (2020) explored the career trajectories of Black male educators in the study and provided insights into the professional experiences and pathways of Black male educators in P-12 education, emphasizing the importance of understanding these trajectories for improving support and retention. Reid (2020) examined White female educators' perceptions about adolescent Black boys. The study investigated how these perceptions influence educational practices and interactions with Black male students, providing insights into potential biases and areas for improvement in teacher training. Grant (2020) conducted an exploratory study on Black male educators' implementation of culturally relevant practices in a dissertation available. The research focused on personal and environmental factors affecting the adoption of culturally relevant practices, aiming to identify strategies for enhancing their effectiveness in diverse educational settings. Nelson (2020) researched the recruitment and retention of Black male math educators in middle and high schools in the United States. The study highlighted challenges and proposed strategies for improving the presence of Black male educators in mathematics education. Smith, Johnson-Lutz, Taylor, and others (2019) analyzed the career trajectories of Black male educators in P-12 education in a report from the National Network of State Teachers of the Year, available on ERIC. Their research provided a detailed look at the professional journeys of Black male educators and the factors influencing their career development.

Bristol and Goings (2019) explored the boundary-heightening experiences of Black male teachers. Their article discussed the unique challenges faced by Black male teachers and the lessons for teacher education programs to better support them. Jackson (2019) provided strategies, mindsets, and beliefs for supporting Black and Latino male students in Becoming the Educator They Need. Offered practical insights into effective support practices for educators working with Black and Latino male students, focusing on creating positive educational experiences. Mathews (2019) investigated the everyday struggles and stereotypes of Black male educators. The study explored the challenges faced by Black male educators and the impact of societal stereotypes on their professional lives. Gipson (2019) discussed resilience in Black male educators in Personal Narratives of Black Educational Leaders. Highlighted how Black male educators have overcome challenges and demonstrated resilience in their careers. Knight-Manuel, Marciano, Wilson, and others (2019) examined urban educators' perspectives on creating a culturally relevant, schoolwide, college-going culture for Black and Latino male students in *Urban Education*. Their study provided insights into effective strategies for fostering a supportive educational environment for these students. Msibi (2018) explored the hidden sexualities of South African teachers, focusing on Black male educators and same-sex desire. The intersection of sexuality and teaching, highlighting the complexities faced by Black male educators in South Africa. Bristol and Mentor (2018) analyzed the positioning of Black male teachers within the broader carceral system in The Urban Review. Their article "Positioning of Black Male Teachers as Agents in the Universal Carceral Apparatus," explored the dual roles of Black male teachers and their experiences of surveillance and control in educational settings.

STATEMENT OF THE PROBLEM

Despite increasing recognition of the critical role Black male educators play in shaping educational outcomes, there remains a persistent underrepresentation of Black males in the teaching profession, particularly within K-12 education. This underrepresentation is compounded by systemic barriers, including racial and gender biases, inadequate support structures, and institutional challenges. Additionally, existing literature highlights a range of issues related to recruitment, retention, and professional development that hinder the effectiveness and sustainability of Black male educators in educational settings. The problem this study addresses is the complex interplay of factors contributing to the underrepresentation and challenges faced by Black male educators. These factors include the systemic barriers and institutional practices that deter Black males from entering and remaining in the teaching profession. The adequacy of support structures and career advancement opportunities available to Black male educators. The extent to which Black male educators influence educational outcomes for their students and how their experiences and perspectives are understood and addressed within the educational system. This study seeks to identify the underlying causes of these issues, evaluate the effectiveness of current support mechanisms, and propose actionable recommendations to enhance the recruitment, retention, and effectiveness of Black male educators. This investigation aims to provide valuable insights into the systemic improvements needed to support Black male educators and to promote a more inclusive and equitable educational environment.

RESEARCH METHODOLOGY

This comprehensive review employs a qualitative research methodology to analyze the existing literature on Black male educators. The study focuses on synthesizing qualitative findings from various sources to gain an in-depth understanding of the experiences, motivations, and challenges faced by Black male educators in the educational system. This approach allows for a nuanced exploration of themes and patterns across a diverse range of studies. The review encompasses studies published from 2018 to 2024. This period was selected to ensure that the review reflects the most recent research trends and findings in the field. The chosen time frame allows for the inclusion of contemporary issues and developments related to Black male educators, providing a current perspective on the topic. The review utilized a comprehensive review study design, systematically gathering and analyzing qualitative research articles. This design involved a structured process to identify, evaluate, and synthesize relevant studies. The review was guided by the following steps. A thorough search of academic databases and repositories was conducted to identify studies relevant to Black male educators. Key databases included ProQuest Dissertations & Theses, ERIC, Google Scholar, and SpringerLink.

Articles were selected based on predefined criteria to ensure relevance and quality. The criteria included Studies must focus on Black male educators' experiences, challenges, and motivations within the education system. Only qualitative research articles were included to capture in-depth, descriptive data. Studies published between 2018 and 2024 were considered to ensure the review includes the latest research findings. Preference was given to peer-reviewed journals and reputable academic sources to ensure the credibility of the studies. Relevant data from selected articles were extracted, including study objectives, methodologies, findings, and conclusions. This process involved coding and categorizing data to identify recurring themes and patterns. The extracted data were synthesized to provide a comprehensive overview of the major findings across studies. This involved thematic analysis to group similar findings and draw overarching conclusions about the experiences of Black male educators.

THEMATIC LITERATURE REVIEW

Table 1.

Theme	Key Findings	Authors (Year)
Motivations and Career Choices	Black male educators are often driven by a sense of purpose and commitment to their communities. However, barriers such as systemic racism and lack of support impact their career decisions and sustainability.	Dovico (2023), Bryant (2023), Cummings-Lewis (2023), Cunningham (2022), Mayfield (2022)
Challenges and Barriers	Black male educators face numerous challenges, including underrepresentation, lack of mentorship, and systemic biases within the educational system. These challenges affect their career satisfaction and longevity.	Wallace (2023), Williams (2023), Royston et al. (2021), Scott et al. (2021), Reid (2020)
Pedagogical Practices	Effective pedagogical practices employed by Black male educators often involve culturally responsive teaching and mentorship. These practices positively impact student outcomes, particularly for Black and Latino students.	Carey (2023), Jett et al. (2021), Jackson (2019)
Impact on Students	Black male educators serve as role models and mentors for Black and Latino students, significantly influencing their academic and personal development. However, the lack of Black male educators limits these benefits.	Anderson & Gordon (2022), Salas et al. (2021), Knight-Manuel et al. (2019)
Retention and Support Systems	Retention of Black male educators is improved through targeted support systems, such as mentoring programs and professional development opportunities. These systems address the unique needs and challenges faced by these educators.	Marks (2022), Underwood et al. (2020), Mathwasa & Sibanda (2021)
Cultural and Social Identity	The intersection of race and gender plays a critical role in shaping the experiences of Black male educators. Their social identity affects their interactions with students and colleagues, as well as their overall job satisfaction.	Bristol (2023), Felton (2022), Gipson (2019)
Educational Policies and Practices	Policies aimed at increasing diversity among educators are essential but often insufficient. Effective policies must address systemic issues and provide tangible support for Black male educators.	Ohito (2021), Anderson (2021), Nelson (2020)

DISCUSSION

Addressing Underrepresentation

The study highlights the critical issue of the underrepresentation of Black male educators, which is crucial for understanding educational disparities and addressing diversity gaps. It provides valuable insights into how the presence of Black male educators can influence student outcomes, particularly for Black and Latino students. This research can guide policies aimed at increasing diversity in the teaching profession.

Diverse Perspectives

The study incorporates a range of perspectives from Black male educators in different roles and educational levels, including special education, leadership positions, and K-12 settings. By exploring various aspects such as pedagogical practices, challenges, and career trajectories, the study presents a comprehensive view of the experiences of Black male educators.

Highlighting Systemic Issues

The study examines systemic barriers and organizational issues that affect Black male educators, such as social isolation and lack of support. This helps in understanding the broader context of their experiences. It offers practical recommendations for improving support systems, retention strategies, and professional development for Black male educators.

QUALITATIVE AND QUANTITATIVE APPROACHES

The study employs both qualitative and quantitative methods to gather data, which enhances the robustness of the findings and provides a well-rounded analysis.

Limited Longitudinal Analysis - The study might lack a longitudinal perspective, which is important for understanding how experiences and challenges evolve over time for Black male educators. It may not adequately assess the long-term impact of various interventions or support systems on the retention and career progression of Black male educators.

Inadequate Focus on Policy Implications - While the study identifies issues and challenges, it may not sufficiently address how these findings can be translated into concrete policy changes or practical solutions.The study might lack detailed strategies for implementing recommended practices or interventions in educational settings.

SUGGESTIONS FOR IMPROVEMENT

Expand Sample Diversity - Include a more diverse sample of Black male educators from various regions, educational levels, and types of schools to enhance the generalizability of the findings. Engage with educators from different backgrounds and experiences to provide a more comprehensive view of the challenges and successes faced by Black male educators.

Longitudinal Studies - Conduct longitudinal studies to track the career trajectories of Black male educators over time, assessing changes in their experiences and the effectiveness of interventions. Examine the long-term impact of support systems and policies on the retention and professional development of Black male educators.

Address Biases and Improve Methodology - Use multiple researchers and peer review processes to reduce bias in qualitative data analysis. Employ triangulation methods to validate findings. Incorporate a mix of self-reported data with objective measures and observations to provide a more accurate representation of experiences.

Focus on Policy and Practical Solutions - Develop detailed recommendations for policy changes based on the study's findings, addressing specific issues such as recruitment, retention, and support. Provide actionable strategies for implementing recommended practices in educational settings, including guidelines for schools and policymakers.

Integrate Comparative Analysis - Compare the experiences of Black male educators across different countries or educational systems to identify common challenges and effective solutions. Use benchmarking against best practices in other sectors to enhance the strategies for supporting Black male educators.

MAJOR FINDINGS FROM THE STUDY OF BLACK MALE EDUCATORS

The body of research on Black male educators reveals several key findings regarding their motivations, experiences, and challenges within the education system. One major finding is the significant underrepresentation of Black male educators in K-12 education, which has been consistently highlighted across various studies. This underrepresentation is seen as a critical issue due to its implications for student outcomes, particularly for Black and Latino students who benefit from having role models that reflect their own racial and cultural backgrounds. Many studies emphasize the unique motivations driving Black males to enter the teaching profession. These motivations often include a desire to make a difference in their communities, address educational disparities, and serve as positive role models for young Black students. However, these educators frequently encounter systemic barriers, such as social isolation, lack of institutional support, and discriminatory practices, which can impact their job satisfaction and career longevity.

The research also highlights the diverse pedagogical approaches and practices employed by Black male educators. These educators often adopt culturally relevant teaching methods and strive to create supportive and nurturing environments for their students. Despite their efforts, they face challenges related to their roles being undervalued and their contributions frequently overlooked by the education system. Another prominent finding is the impact of systemic issues on Black male educators' career trajectories. Many studies point out that these educators experience barriers to career advancement and leadership roles due to institutional biases and a lack of mentorship opportunities. This results in lower retention rates and can discourage potential Black male educators from entering or remaining in the profession. Additionally, the studies underscore the need for targeted interventions to improve recruitment, retention, and support for Black male educators. Recommendations include implementing mentorship programs, creating supportive professional networks, and developing policies that address the specific challenges faced by Black male educators. The findings from the research point to the need for a multifaceted approach to addressing the disparities faced by Black male educators. This includes improving institutional support, fostering inclusive environments, and implementing policies that promote diversity and equity within the education system.

PRACTICAL IMPLICATIONS

1. The study's findings underscore the need for robust support systems for Black male educators. Schools and educational institutions should implement mentorship programs, professional development workshops, and counseling services tailored to address the unique challenges faced by Black male teachers. Practical support can include peer networking opportunities, mental health resources, and career guidance specifically designed to enhance job satisfaction and career progression.
2. Policymakers can use the insights from this study to formulate policies that address the barriers to entry and retention for Black male educators. This may include revising recruitment practices, ensuring equitable pay, and creating pathways for career advancement. By addressing systemic barriers and implementing supportive policies, educational institutions can foster a more inclusive environment that encourages and sustains the participation of Black male educators.

3. Practical strategies should involve engaging with communities to promote teaching as a viable and valued career path for Black males. Outreach programs, collaborations with community organizations, and increased visibility of Black male educators can inspire and attract future educators. Community engagement initiatives can also address stereotypes and enhance the perceived value of teaching professions among Black males.

RESEARCH IMPLICATIONS

1. The study highlights a gap in longitudinal research that tracks the career trajectories of Black male educators over time. Future research should focus on long-term studies to better understand how experiences and challenges evolve and how various support mechanisms impact career satisfaction and effectiveness. Further research should delve into the intersectionality of race, gender, and socio-economic status in shaping the experiences of Black male educators. Understanding how these factors interact can provide a more nuanced perspective on the specific needs and challenges faced by different subgroups within the Black male educator population.
2. Researchers should explore the impact of Black male educators on student outcomes in greater detail. Investigating how Black male teachers influence academic performance, student behavior, and engagement can provide valuable insights into the broader effects of teacher diversity on educational equity and effectiveness.

MANAGERIAL IMPLICATIONS

1. Managers and educational leaders should develop strategic plans for recruiting and retaining Black male educators. This includes creating targeted recruitment campaigns, offering competitive salaries and benefits, and ensuring a supportive work environment. Managers can also implement retention strategies such as career development opportunities and recognition programs to retain Black male educators.
2. Educational managers should invest in ongoing training and development programs that address the specific needs of Black male educators. This includes leadership training, diversity and inclusion workshops, and professional growth opportunities. By equipping Black male educators with the necessary skills and knowledge, managers can enhance their effectiveness and job satisfaction.

3. Creating an inclusive organizational culture that values diversity and equity is crucial. Managers should foster an environment where Black male educators feel respected, supported, and empowered. This involves promoting diversity in hiring practices, addressing biases, and ensuring that all educators have equal access to resources and opportunities for advancement.

CONCLUSION

The examination of literature from 2018 to 2024 reveals a compelling yet complex narrative regarding Black male educators. These educators play a crucial role in shaping the educational experiences and outcomes of their students, particularly within underrepresented and underserved communities. Their presence in schools is associated with positive impacts on student achievement and personal development, largely due to their ability to serve as role models and deliver culturally relevant instruction. The evidence indicates that Black male educators contribute significantly to the academic and social success of their students, particularly those from similar backgrounds (Dovico, 2023; Bryant, 2023; Carey, 2023). However, the persistent challenges faced by Black male educators cannot be overlooked. Systemic issues, including racial biases, inadequate institutional support, and lack of mentorship, are significant barriers that impede their professional growth and effectiveness (Wallace, 2023; Williams, 2023). These barriers contribute to high turnover rates and a reduction in the overall impact of Black male educators on the education system. The literature consistently highlights the need for systemic reforms to address these challenges and provide a more supportive and equitable working environment for Black male educators. Pedagogical practices employed by Black male educators often include culturally responsive teaching methods, which are crucial for engaging and supporting students from diverse backgrounds (Jackson, 2019; Jett, Savage, & Ortiz, 2021). Despite their effectiveness, these practices are underutilized due to the insufficient number of Black male educators in the field. The underrepresentation of Black male educators limits the broader application of these beneficial practices, thereby impacting their potential to effect widespread positive change in educational settings (Bristol, 2023; Ohito, 2021). Efforts to address these challenges have led to the development of various support systems and policies, such as targeted recruitment programs and mentoring initiatives (Anderson, 2021; Mathwasa & Sibanda, 2021). While these programs are steps in the right direction, they often fail to tackle the root causes of the issues faced by Black male educators. To create a more supportive and effective educational environment, it is essential to enact comprehensive policies that address systemic biases, enhance support structures, and provide equitable opportunities for professional development. The literature underscores the critical role that Black male educators play in enhancing educational outcomes for minority students. Their unique contributions and effective pedagogical practices highlight the need for a more inclusive and supportive educational system. Addressing the systemic challenges faced by Black male educators through targeted reforms and comprehensive support initiatives is essential for improving their professional experiences and ensuring that their impact on students is maximized. Continued research and policy development are crucial in creating an educational environment where Black male educators can thrive and continue to make significant contributions to student success.

REFERENCES

Anderson, T. K. G. (2021). *Representation of African American/Black men educators in K-12 public schools Impact on recruitment, retention, and responsibilities to education*. ProQuest Dissertations & Theses. https//search.proquest.com/openview/b1454fa6a960e355ae05d65fc4043053/1?pq-origsite=gscholar&cbl=18750&diss=y

Anderson, T. K. T. K., & Gordon, S. R. (2022). Resilience despite "integration" Black men educators' perceptions about and responsibility to equitable representation in K–12 education. *Journal of Critical Thought and Praxis*, 11(1), 22–35. https//www.iastatedigitalpress.com/jctp/article/id/12952/

Beachum, F. D., Khabbaz, T., & Hylton-Fraser, K. (2022). Life, learning, and legacy Retired Black educators and the quest for education. *Multicultural Learning and Teaching*, 18(2), 45–60. DOI: 10.1515/mlt-2022-0017

Bristol, T. J. (2023). Black men teaching Toward a theory of social isolation in organizations. In *Men educators of color in US public schools and* (pp. 31–45). Routledge., DOI: 10.4324/9781003392538-2

Bristol, T. J., & Goings, R. B. (2019). Exploring the boundary-heightening experiences of Black male teachers Lessons for teacher education programs. *Journal of Teacher Education*, 70(1), 48–61. DOI: 10.1177/0022487118789367

Bristol, T. J., & Mentor, M. (2018). Policing and teaching The positioning of Black male teachers as agents in the universal carceral apparatus. *The Urban Review*, 50(1), 56–70. DOI: 10.1007/s11256-018-0447-z

Bryant, J. (2023). *Black male educator shortage in the Mississippi public school system Impact, challenges, and intervention strategies*. University of Mississippi. https//egrove.olemiss.edu/hon_thesis/3017/

Bryant, J. (2023). *The practices of Black male educators in Georgia public school classrooms*. ProQuest Dissertations & Theses. https//search.proquest.com/openview/3900da2752c6b90b89fcccb1a065dd6e/1?pq-origsite=gscholar&cbl=18750&diss=y

Carey, R. L. (2023). Missing misters Uncovering the pedagogies and positionalities of male teachers of color in the school lives of Black and Latino adolescent boys. In *Men educators of color in US public schools* (pp. 99–118). Routledge., DOI: 10.4324/9781003392538-7

Cormier, C. J., Scott, L. R. A., Powell, C., & Hall, K. (2022). Locked in glass classrooms Black male special education teachers socialized as everything but educators. *Teacher Education and Special Education*, 45(1), 59–73. DOI: 10.1177/08884064211061038

Cummings-Lewis, E. N. (2023). *On the underrepresentation of Black men as early childhood educators—Exploring their career choice, retention, long-term sustainability, and influence on Black children*. ProQuest Dissertations & Theses. https//search.proquest.com/openview/c70b88a422d92fa8d8af3732126d4ed3/1?pq-origsite=gscholar&cbl=18750&diss=y

Cunningham, C. (2022). *Working for justice A Black educator's journey of supporting Black males in an urban school district*. ProQuest Dissertations & Theses. https//search.proquest.com/openview/0a83b842451051402e0bea42ee2894af/1?pq-origsite=gscholar&cbl=18750&diss=y

Dovico, A. (2023). *Examining motivations of Black males to become elementary school educators*. ProQuest Dissertations & Theses. https//search.proquest.com/openview/bbbe36d2438d52dca0c17fe98775f7ad/1?pq-origsite=gscholar&cbl=18750&diss=y

Felton, A. M. (2022). *Investigation of the lack of diversity amongst educators focusing on the educational experiences of Black males A qualitative narrative research study*. ProQuest Dissertations & Theses. https//search.proquest.com/openview/fcec41d5dec2c97bb5906f9e4c6541c1/1?pq-origsite=gscholar&cbl=18750&diss=y

Gipson, C. T. (2019). Delayed but not denied How a Black male educator mastered the power of resilience. In *Personal Narratives of Black Educational Leaders* (pp. 79–90). Taylor & Francis., DOI: 10.4324/9781315099743-9

Gobert, J. W. (2021). *The experiences of African American male educators in primary grade levels*. ProQuest Dissertations & Theses. https//search.proquest.com/openview/b5aaf74c9e872a51737dbe33f5a8feff/1?pq-origsite=gscholar&cbl=18750&diss=y

Grant, O. B. (2020). *An exploratory study on Black male educators' implementation of culturally relevant practices based on personal and environmental factors*. ProQuest Dissertations & Theses. https//search.proquest.com/openview/0f4633d08ee8b8bbb54fe35172f6ab60/1?pq-origsite=gscholar&cbl=18750&diss=y

Hocutt, T. D., Sr. (2023). *Addressing the disparity of Black male educators Building capacity to mentor Black male youth*. ProQuest Dissertations & Theses. https//search.proquest.com/openview/091d9187fbeb1dc0b962e0049a8e0546/1?pq-origsite=gscholar&cbl=18750&diss=y

Jackson, L., & Dicks, T. (2024). A call to action Black male educators! It is your time A mixed methods study on beginning Black male educators' experiences in teacher preparation programs. *Research Square*. https//www.researchsquare.com/article/rs-4384546/latest

Jackson, R. (2019). *Becoming the educator they need Strategies, mindsets, and beliefs for supporting male Black and Latino students*. Google Books. https//books.google.com/books?hl=en&lr=&id=2tGlDwAAQBAJ&oi=fnd&pg=PP1&dq=black+male+educators&ots=SIR9wPgdI6&sig=yuTRwlxd5YE7DMiKUmITQ92dNVI

Jeter, F., & Melendez, J. (2022). Too few Black male educators. *Impacting Education Journal on Transforming Education*, 7(2), 134-145. https//eric.ed.gov/?id=EJ1345690

Jett, C., Savage, K., Ortiz, N., ... (2021). Black male mathematics educators speak Reflections from a symposium. *Journal of African American Males in Education*. https//jaamejournal.scholasticahq.com/article/29843.pdf

Jones, D. C., Jr. (2023). *Through their eyes Counter-narrative study of Black male educators*. ProQuest Dissertations & Theses. https//search.proquest.com/openview/74b7e1830d8c6cd5b0b725a04077820f/1?pq-origsite=gscholar&cbl=18750&diss=y

Kimbrough-Scott, J. (2022). *Hiding in plain sight A phenomenological exploration of Black male educators in school leadership*. ProQuest Dissertations & Theses. https//search.proquest.com/openview/48003ef94e74f2dff62f85af2cb0f4ef/1?pq-origsite=gscholar&cbl=18750&diss=y

Knight-Manuel, M. G., Marciano, J. E., Wilson, M., Jackson, I., Vernikoff, L., Zuckerman, K. G., & Watson, V. W. M. (2019). "It's all possible" Urban educators' perspectives on creating a culturally relevant, schoolwide, college-going culture for Black and Latino male students. *Urban Education*, 54(1), 3–27. DOI: 10.1177/0042085916651320

Lee, D. (2024). *Black male early career educators in secondary science classrooms Rewriting narratives of successful teaching*. Georgia State University. https//scholarworks.gsu.edu/mse_diss/164/

Marks, S. (2022). Creating systems of support for Black educators through the Black Educator Teacher Residency Program. *Multicultural Education*, 29(3), 20–29. https//search.proquest.com/openview/f0929f8e1dd0ac0ddcd997c42632bdd1/1?pq-origsite=gscholar&cbl=33246

Mathews, J. D. W. (2019). *I don't wanna teach no more Everyday struggles and stereotypes of the Black male educator misunderstood*. ProQuest Dissertations & Theses. https//search.proquest.com/openview/566ffe40531b12c684c97db4a6d128ca/1?pq-origsite=gscholar&cbl=18750&diss=y

Mathwasa, J., & Sibanda, L. (2021). Male educator recruitment in early childhood centres Implications for teacher education. In *Teacher Education-New Perspectives* (pp. 103–116). Google Books., https//books.google.com/books?hl=en&lr=&id=_bdFEAAAQBAJ&oi=fnd&pg=PA103&dq=black+male+educators&ots=_qW4Z1NYWV&sig=8nhMKXIOoEMMiZH6A-w9Z0YK4T8 DOI: 10.5772/intechopen.97085

Mayfield, F. M. (2022). Black men in a Southern urban school of education An analysis of motivating factors for Black men as aspirant educators. *The Journal of Equity in Behavioral Health Therapy*, 5(1), 35–49. https//journals.auctr.edu/index.php/jebht/article/view/443

. Msibi, T. (2018). Hidden sexualities of South African teachers Black male educators and same-sex desire. *Routledge*, 129-143. DOI: 10.4324/9781315718293

Nelson, D. D. (2023). *African American male educators' lived experiences as students and educators The measure of a man*. ProQuest Dissertations & Theses. https//search.proquest.com/openview/6834a754400bf885d57c683faa874501/1?pq-origsite=gscholar&cbl=18750&diss=y

Nelson, V. T. F. (2020). *Recruiting and retaining Black male math educators in middle and high schools in the United States*. ProQuest Dissertations & Theses. https//search.proquest.com/openview/f0777df6361a40c31eeede296aca43f0/1?pq-origsite=gscholar&cbl=44156

Ohito, E. O. (2021). How to be an antiracist teacher educator in the United States A sketch of a Black male pedagogic provocateur. *Teaching and Teacher Education*, 105, 103448. https//www.sciencedirect.com/science/article/pii/S0742051X20314268. DOI: 10.1016/j.tate.2020.103235

Okeke, C. I., & Nyanhoto, E. (2021). Recruitment and retention of male educators in preschools Implications for teacher education policy and practices. *South African Journal of Education*, 41(3), 1–11. https//www.ajol.info/index.php/saje/article/view/209358. DOI: 10.15700/saje.v41n2a1910

Ransaw, T. S. (2022). *Mindful teaching practices for Black male achievement A student-focused guide for educators*. Google Books. https//books.google.com/books?hl=en&lr=&id=0CmgEAAAQBAJ&oi=fnd&pg=PP1&dq=black+male+educators&ots=-HesxdpR5s&sig=NZq5SEWdrQulagHXPv6WJBptIsY

Reich-Shapiro, M., Cole, K., & Plaisir, J. Y. (2021). "I am the teacher" How male educators conceptualize their impact on the early childhood classroom. *Journal of Early Childhood Teacher Education*, 42(1), 3–17. DOI: 10.1080/10901027.2020.1754310

Reid, T. M. (2020). *White female educators' perceptions about adolescent Black boys*. ProQuest Dissertations & Theses. https//search.proquest.com/openview/e78877503780f15b0ba3d9426dcf932a/1?pq-origsite=gscholar&cbl=51922&diss=y

Royston, M. (2021). "I'm a teacher, I'm gonna always protect you" Understanding Black educators' protection of Black children. *American Educational Research Journal*, 58(5), 915–946. DOI: 10.3102/0002831220921119 PMID: 39221111

Salas, S., Lewis, C. W., & Siefert, B. (2021). "You teach what?" Black males, new Latino South classrooms, and wanderlust. *New Educator*, 17(2), 160–176. DOI: 10.1080/1547688X.2021.1873475

Samuels, S. S., Wilkerson, A., & Dacres, S. S. (2021). Why they struggle to stay Black women educators reflect on the state of teachers. *The Clearing House: A Journal of Educational Strategies, Issues and Ideas*, 94(3), 140–149. DOI: 10.1080/00098655.2021.1907145

Scott, L. R. A., Brown, A., Wallace, W., Cormier, C. J., & Powell, C. (2021). If we're not doing it, then who? A qualitative study of Black special educators' persistence. *Exceptionality*, 15(2), 111–128. DOI: 10.1080/09362835.2020.1850453

Sims, R., Jr. (2022). *Analysis of New Mexico Black male educators' effects of underrepresentation in education*. ProQuest Dissertations & Theses. https//search.proquest.com/openview/6f8957e841755edf38db9e62f81cc94c/1?pq-origsite=gscholar&cbl=18750&diss=y

Sims, R. C. (2022). *Analysis of the issue of New Mexico Black male educators' underrepresentation in education within New Mexico*. ProQuest Dissertations & Theses. https//search.proquest.com/openview/579640b1ddc045a38b7b2e6857e67c3f/1?pq-origsite=gscholar&cbl=18750&diss=y

Thompson, B. J. (2023). *The endangered species A phenomenological study of the lived experiences of Black male educators*. ProQuest Dissertations & Theses. https//search.proquest.com/openview/eb2c481ccc217a0b365d3bd104abd3fa/1?pq-origsite=gscholar&cbl=18750&diss=y

Underwood, K., Smith, D., Johnson-Lutz, H., Taylor, J., ... (2019). Having our say Examining the career trajectories of Black male educators in P-12 education. *National Network of State Teachers of the Year*, ERIC. https//eric.ed.gov/?id=ED601059

Underwood, K., Taylor, J., Smith, D., & Roberts, J. M. (2020). Exploring the career trajectories of Black male educators in P-12 education. *Journal for Multicultural Education*, 14(1), 2–16. DOI: 10.1108/JME-02-2020-0012

Wallace, D. (2023). The diversity trap? Critical explorations of Black male teachers' negotiations of leadership and learning in London state schools. In *Men educators of color in US public schools and* (pp. 67–83). Routledge., DOI: 10.4324/9781003392538-5

Wallace, D., Bol, L., & Hall, K. (2022). Black male educators matter Modeling and expectations in K-12 settings. *Journal of African American Studies*, 26(4), 375–392. https//digitalcommons.odu.edu/efl_fac_pubs/105/. DOI: 10.1007/s12111-022-09594-2

Warren, C. A. (2023). Meeting myself Race-gender oppression and a genre study of Black men teachers' interactions with Black boys. In *Men educators of color in US public schools and* (pp. 84–98). Routledge., DOI: 10.4324/9781003392538-6

Watkins, S. E., & Mensah, F. M. (2022). Black men in US undergraduate and graduate science programs and their persistence Insights for multicultural science educators. In *Handbook of Research on Multicultural Science Education* (pp. 789–802). Springer., DOI: 10.1007/978-3-030-83122-6_49

Williams, C. (2022). *Educator perceptions of African American male recruitment in advanced placement courses*. ProQuest Dissertations & Theses. https//search.proquest.com/openview/3b68f07b6fbdfa7b11c4723bf8a61e43/1?pq-origsite=gscholar&cbl=18750&diss=y

Williams, D. J. (2023). *Challenges affecting educator careers of Black male teachers in K-12 system in South Carolina A qualitative phenomenological study*. Liberty University. https//digitalcommons.liberty.edu/doctoral/4976/

Witherspoon, Q. D. R. (2024). *Student responsiveness towards Black male educators in the K-12 urban school setting A phenomenological study*. ProQuest Dissertations & Theses. https//search.proquest.com/openview/86350f04bd88cf48418518b1f1de3864/1?pq-origsite=gscholar&cbl=18750&diss=y

Woodson, A. N., Jones, J., & Gowder, S. (2023). 'The world they've been born into' Black male teachers on Blackness, masculinities, and leadership. In *Men educators of color in US public schools* (pp. 23–30). Routledge., DOI: 10.4324/9781003392538-3

Young, J., & Young, J. (2023). The Black male teacher A 10-year content analysis of empirical research. In *Men educators of color in US public schools* (pp. 46–66). Routledge., DOI: 10.4324/9781003392538-4

KEY TERMS AND DEFINITIONS

Community Engagement: Involvement of educators with the local community to foster relationships, support networks, and mutual understanding between schools and families.

Equity and Inclusion: Principles aimed at ensuring fair treatment, access, and opportunities for all individuals, while promoting diversity and addressing disparities in educational settings.

Institutional Support: Resources and assistance provided by educational institutions to help educators succeed, including mentoring, professional development, and administrative backing.

Social Isolation: A condition where individuals feel disconnected or excluded from their peers or community, which can negatively impact their professional experience and mental well-being.

Systemic Racism: A form of racism that is embedded in the policies and practices of institutions, leading to discrimination against specific racial groups.

Targeted Recruitment: Strategies aimed at attracting specific groups of individuals, particularly underrepresented populations, to increase diversity within the workforce.

Thematic Analysis: A qualitative research method that involves identifying, analyzing, and reporting patterns (themes) within qualitative data.

Compilation of References

Ab Rahman, R., Ahmad, S., & Hashim, U. R. (2019). A study on gamification for higher education students' engagement towards education 4.0. In *Intelligent and Interactive Computing: Proceedings of IIC 2018* (pp. 491-502). Springer Singapore.

Abramovich, S., Schunn, C., & Higashi, R. M. (2013). Are badges useful in education?: It depends upon the type of badge and expertise of learner. *Educational Technology Research and Development*, 61(2), 217–232. DOI: 10.1007/s11423-013-9289-2

AbuShihab, K., Obaideen, K., Alameddine, M., Alkurd, R. A. F., Khraiwesh, H. M., Mohammad, Y., & Faris, M. E. (2023). Reflection on Ramadan fasting research related to sustainable development goal 3 (Good Health and Well-Being): A bibliometric analysis. [HTML]. *Journal of Religion and Health*, •••, 1–31. PMID: 38110843

Achten, H. H. (2003). New design methods for computer aided architectural design methodology teaching. *International Journal of Architectural Computing*, 1(1), 72–91. DOI: 10.1260/147807703322467441

Adaba, H. W. (2024). Efl Teachers' Implementations of Strategies of Contemporary Theories of Language Teaching and Its Challenges: The Case of Grade 12 English Teacher in Selected Secondary Schools in Ambo. *Journal of Indigenous Knowledge and Development Studies*, 6(1), 1–19.

Aderibigbe, S. A. (2020). Online discussions as an intervention for strengthening students' engagement in general education. *Journal of Open Innovation*, 6(4), 98. DOI: 10.3390/joitmc6040098

Adula, M., Birbirsa, Z. A., & Kant, S. (2023). The effect of interpersonal, problem solving and technical training skills on performance of Ethiopia textile industry: Continuance, normative and affective commitment as mediators. *Cogent Business & Management*, 10(3), 2286672. Advance online publication. DOI: 10.1080/23311975.2023.2286672

Afirando, R., Santoso, H., Junus, K., Putra, P., & Lawanto, O. (2023). Motivation to use gamification elements in e-learning for formal and non-formal education. *Indonesian Journal of Computer Science*, 12(1). Advance online publication. DOI: 10.33022/ijcs.v12i1.3151

Ahmed, U., Ismail, A. I., Fati, M., & Akour, M. A. (2024). E-learning during COVID-19: Understanding the nexus among instructional innovation, E-psychological capital, and online behavioural engagement. *Management in Education*, 38(3), 107–119. DOI: 10.1177/08920206211053101

Al Shuraiaan, A., Al Bloushi, B., & Al Bloushi, L. (2024). The double-edged sword: Analyzing the influence of technology on English language learning in Kuwait higher education institutions (HEIs). *International Journal of Middle Eastern Research*, 3(1), 15–23. DOI: 10.32996/ijmer.2024.3.1.3

Alam, M. I., Malone, L., Nadolny, L., Brown, M., & Cervato, C. (2023). Investigating the impact of a gamified learning analytics dashboard: Student experiences and academic achievement. [wiley.com]. *Journal of Computer Assisted Learning*, 39(5), 1436–1449. DOI: 10.1111/jcal.12853

Al-Hafdi, F. S., & Alhalafawy, W. S. (2024). Ten Years of Gamification-Based Learning: A Bibliometric Analysis and Systematic Review. *International Journal of Interactive Mobile Technologies*, 18(7), 188–212. DOI: 10.3991/ijim.v18i07.45335

Alhammad, M., & Moreno, A. (2018). Gamification in software engineering education: A systematic mapping. *Journal of Systems and Software*, 141, 131–150. DOI: 10.1016/j.jss.2018.03.065

Ali, A., Ismail, A., & Bade, A. (2009). *An Overview of Networking Infrastructure for Massively Multiplayer Online Games*. https://www.semanticscholar.org/paper/An-Overview-of-Networking-Infrastructure-for-Online-Ali-Ismail/887b374b10 10ca23a01bb89b71e40fd31e34ce92

Ali, W. (2023). Enhancing children's learning experience as a sustainable approach through gamified application design. *E3s Web of Conferences*, 426, 02115. https://doi.org/DOI: 10.1051/e3sconf/202342602115

Alija, M., López, M., Cao, M., Fernández-Castro, M., Garcia, S., Frutos, M., & Jiménez, J. (2019). Impact of educational games on academic outcomes of students in the degree in nursing. *PLoS One*, 14(7), e0220388. DOI: 10.1371/journal.pone.0220388 PMID: 31356621

Aljehani, S. B. (2024). Enhancing Student Learning Outcomes: The Interplay of Technology Integration, Pedagogical Approaches, Learner Engagement, and Leadership Support. *Educational Administration: Theory and Practice*, 30(4), 418–437.

Allan, R., McCann, L., Johnson, L., Dyson, M., & Ford, J. (2024). A systematic review of 'equity-focused' game-based learning in the teaching of health staff. *Public Health in Practice, 7.Public Health in Practice (Oxford, England)*, 7, 100462. Advance online publication. DOI: 10.1016/j.puhip.2023.100462 PMID: 38283754

Al-Nawafleh, A., Musleh, S., & Nawafleh, N. (2024). The patient safety curriculum: An interventional study on the effectiveness of patient safety education for Jordanian nursing students. *PLoS One*, 19(5), e0292713. DOI: 10.1371/journal.pone.0292713 PMID: 38722975

Aloisi, A. (2022). Platform work in Europe: Lessons learned, legal developments and challenges ahead. European Labour Law Journal. sagepub.com

Alrashidi, O., Phan, H. P., & Ngu, B. H. (2016). Academic engagement: An overview of its definitions, dimensions, and significant conceptualizations. *International Education Studies*, 9(12), 41–52. DOI: 10.5539/ies.v9n12p41

Alsawaier, R. S. (2018). The effect of gamification on motivation and engagement. *The International Journal of Information and Learning Technology*, 35(1), 56–79. DOI: 10.1108/IJILT-02-2017-0009

Alzahrani, F. K., & Alhalafawy, W. S. (2023). Gamification for learning sustainability in the blackboard system: Motivators and obstacles from faculty members' perspectives. *Sustainability (Basel)*, 15(5), 4613. DOI: 10.3390/su15054613

Amerstorfer, C. M., & Freiin von Münster-Kistner, C. (2021). Student perceptions of academic engagement and student-teacher relationships in problem-based learning. *Frontiers in Psychology*, 12, 713057. DOI: 10.3389/fpsyg.2021.713057 PMID: 34777094

Amugongo, L. M., Kriebitz, A., Boch, A., & Lütge, C. (2023). Operationalising AI ethics through the agile software development lifecycle: a case study of AI-enabled mobile health applications. AI and Ethics. springer.com

Anderson, T. K. G. (2021). *Representation of African American/Black men educators in K-12 public schools Impact on recruitment, retention, and responsibilities to education*. ProQuest Dissertations & Theses. https//search.proquest.com/openview/b1454fa6a960e355ae05d65fc4043053/1?pq-origsite=gscholar&cbl=18750&diss=y

Anderson, T. K. T. K., & Gordon, S. R. (2022). Resilience despite "integration" Black men educators' perceptions about and responsibility to equitable representation in K–12 education. *Journal of Critical Thought and Praxis*, 11(1), 22–35. https// www.iastatedigitalpress.com/jctp/article/id/12952/

Andia, A. (2002). Reconstructing the effects of computers on practice and education during the past three decades. *Journal of Architectural Education*, 56(2), 7–13. DOI: 10.1162/10464880260472512

Antal-Berbecaru, A., Larchen Costuchen, A., & Dev, S. (2023). Survey Gamification: Engaging Generation Z. *Computers in the Schools.Computers in the Schools*, 1–25. Advance online publication. DOI: 10.1080/07380569.2023.2271486

Arboleda-Tinay, M. (2021). Perception of university of Tripoli, faculty of nursing students on the bachelor of science in nursing (BSN) curriculum. *International Journal of Current Science Research and Review*, 04(08). Advance online publication. DOI: 10.47191/ijcsrr/V4-i8-11

Arora, C., & Razavian, M. (2021). Ethics of Gamification in Health and Fitness-Tracking. *International Journal of Environmental Research and Public Health*, 18(21), 11052. DOI: 10.3390/ijerph182111052 PMID: 34769570

Arts, E. (1989). *Jogos SimCity™—Site Oficial da EA*. Electronic Arts Inc. https:// www.ea.com/pt-br/games/simcity

Asefa, K., Kant, D. S., & Debela, K. L. (2023, November). Effect of Transformational Leadership on Organizational Performance: The Mediating Role of Employee Commitment and Expert Systems (AI) Inclusion in Ethiopia. In *2023 International Conference on Communication, Security and Artificial Intelligence (ICCSAI)* (pp. 305-310). IEEE.

Askew, R., & Ritter, A. (2023). When self-direction meets conformity: Surfacing Schwartz's 10 basic human values in drug policy dialogue with lived/living experience participants. [HTML]. *The International Journal on Drug Policy*, 122, 104257. DOI: 10.1016/j.drugpo.2023.104257 PMID: 37935077

Asmolov, A., & Ledentsov, A. (2023). Impact on educational effectiveness using digital gamification. [SABDA Journal]. *Startupreneur Business Digital*, 2(1), 98–105. DOI: 10.33050/sabda.v2i1.252

Attali, Y., & Arieli-Attali, M. (2015). Gamification in assessment: Do points affect test performance? *Computers & Education*, 83, 57–63. DOI: 10.1016/j.compedu.2014.12.012

Ayyash, M. M., & Herzallah, F. (2022, September). Understanding the Efficiency of Gamification on the Engagement Intention of the Customers with Mobile Payment Systems. In *International Conference on Emerging Technologies and Intelligent Systems* (pp. 294-310). Cham: Springer International Publishing. [HTML]

Babu, S. S., & Moorthy, A. D. (2023). Application of artificial intelligence in adaptation of gamification in education: A literature review. *Computer Applications in Engineering Education*. Advance online publication. DOI: 10.1002/cae.22683

Baghdadi, N., Sankarapandian, C., Arulappan, J., Taani, M. H., Snethen, J., & Andargeery, S. Y. (2023). The association between nursing students' happiness, emotional intelligence, and perceived caring behavior in Riyadh city, Saudi Arabia. *Health Care*, 12(1), 67. DOI: 10.3390/healthcare12010067 PMID: 38200973

Bahrami, M., Purfarzad, Z., Keshvari, M., & Rafiei, M. (2019). The components of nursing competence in caring for older people in Iranian hospitals: A qualitative study. *Iranian Journal of Nursing and Midwifery Research*, 24(2), 124. DOI: 10.4103/ijnmr.IJNMR_83_18 PMID: 30820224

Bailenson, J. N., Yee, N., Merget, D., & Schroeder, R. (2006). The effect of behavioral realism and form realism of real-time avatar faces on verbal disclosure, nonverbal disclosure, emotion recognition, and copresence in dyadic interaction. *Presence (Cambridge, Mass.)*, 15(4), 359–372. DOI: 10.1162/pres.15.4.359

Bai, S., Hew, K. F., & Huang, B. (2020). Does gamification improve student learning outcomes? Evidence from a meta-analysis and synthesis of qualitative data in educational contexts. *Educational Research Review*, 30, 100322. DOI: 10.1016/j.edurev.2020.100322

Balaji, S., Rajaram, V., & Sethu, S. (2023, April). Gamification of Learning using 3D Spaces in the Metaverse. In *2023 International Conference on Networking and Communications (ICNWC)* (pp. 1-5). IEEE. DOI: 10.1109/ICNWC57852.2023.10127461

Barba-Martín, R. A., Bores-García, D., Hortigüela-Alcalá, D., & González-Calvo, G. (2020). The application of the teaching games for understanding in physical education. Systematic review of the last six years. *International Journal of Environmental Research and Public Health, 17*(9). *International Journal of Environmental Research and Public Health*, 17(9), 3330. Advance online publication. DOI: 10.3390/ijerph17093330 PMID: 32403272

Barna, B., & Fodor, S. (2018). An empirical study on the use of gamification on IT courses at higher education. Teaching and Learning in a Digital World: Proceedings of the 20th International Conference on Interactive Collaborative Learning–Volume 1, Boss, S. (2009). Avatars teach teens about self-image. In: Edutopia. DOI: 10.1007/978-3-319-73210-7_80

Barney, J. (1991). Competitive Advantage. *Journal of Management*, 17(1), 99–120. DOI: 10.1177/014920639101700108

Basaraba, N. (2022). Transmedia Narratives for Cultural Heritage: Remixing History. [HTML]

Batlle Rodríguez, J., & Vicenta González Argüello, M. (2023). Gamification and learning Spanish as a modern language: Student perceptions in the university context. *Language Learning in Higher Education*, 13(1), 89–103. DOI: 10.1515/cercles-2023-2016

Beachum, F. D., Khabbaz, T., & Hylton-Fraser, K. (2022). Life, learning, and legacy Retired Black educators and the quest for education. *Multicultural Learning and Teaching*, 18(2), 45–60. DOI: 10.1515/mlt-2022-0017

Becker, S., Johnson, D., & Britton, P. (2019). Mapping the Challenges in Making the Transition to Taught Postgraduate Study in Psychology. *Psychology Teaching Review*, 25(1), 12–21. DOI: 10.53841/bpsptr.2019.25.1.12

Belland, B. R., Kim, C., & Hannafin, M. J. (2013). A framework for designing scaffolds that improve motivation and cognition. *Educational Psychologist*, 48(4), 243–270. DOI: 10.1080/00461520.2013.838920 PMID: 24273351

Bennani, S., Maalel, A., & Ghezala, H. (2021). Adaptive gamification in e-learning: A literature review and future challenges. *Computer Applications in Engineering Education*, 30(2), 628–642. DOI: 10.1002/cae.22477

Bhatia, M., Manani, P., Garg, A., Bhatia, S., & Adlakha, R. (2023). Mapping mindset about gamification: Teaching learning perspective in UAE education system and Indian education system. *Revue d'Intelligence Artificielle*, 37(1), 47–52. DOI: 10.18280/ria.370107

Bianchessi, C., & Mendes, A. (2019). Ensino de história por meio de jogos digitais: Relato de aprendizagem significativa com games. *Revista Tempos e Espaços em Educação*, 12(29), 13. DOI: 10.20952/revtee.v12i29.9660

Bigdeli, S., Hosseinzadeh, Z., Dehnad, A., Sohrabi, Z., Aalaa, M., Haghani, F., & Atlasi, R. (2023). Underpinning learning theories of medical educational games: A scoping review. *Medical Journal of the Islamic Republic of Iran*. Advance online publication. DOI: 10.47176/mjiri.37.26 PMID: 37180860

Bilgin, C. U., & Gul, A. (2019). Investigating the effectiveness of gamification on group cohesion, attitude, and academic achievement in collaborative learning environments. *TechTrends*, 64(1), 124–136. DOI: 10.1007/s11528-019-00442-x

Biryukov, A., Brikoshina, I., Mikhalevich, N., Sycheva, S., & Халимон, E. (2021). Gamification in education: threats or new opportunities. *SHS Web of Conferences*, 103, 02001. https://doi.org/DOI: 10.1051/shsconf/202110302001

Bitrián, P., Buil, I., & Catalán, S. (2021). Enhancing user engagement: The role of gamification in mobile apps. Journal of Business Research. sciencedirect.com

Bitrián, P., Buil, I., & Catalán, S. (2021). Enhancing user engagement: The role of gamification in mobile apps. *Journal of Business Research*, 132, 170–185. DOI: 10.1016/j.jbusres.2021.04.028

Blebil, A., Dujaili, J., Mohammed, A., Thiruchelvam, K., Lee, S., Elkalmi, R., Soh, Y. C., Yong, A., & Roien, R. (2022). Knowledge and attitude of pharmacy students regarding geriatric care: Questionnaire-based analysis in Malaysia. *Advances in Medical Education and Practice*, 13, 95–102. DOI: 10.2147/AMEP.S344872 PMID: 35082550

Blumberg, F. C., & Fisch, S. M. (2013). Introduction: Digital Games as a Context for Cognitive Development, Learning, and Developmental Research. *New Directions for Child and Adolescent Development*, 2013(139), 1–9. DOI: 10.1002/cad.20026 PMID: 23483688

Bojd, B., Song, X., Tan, Y., & Yan, X. (2018). Gamified challenges in online Weight-Loss communities. SSRN *Electronic Journal*. DOI: 10.2139/ssrn.3157331

Bonn, J., Mulkey, D., & Goers, J. (2022). Using gamification to engage clinical nurses in quality improvement. *Journal for Nurses in Professional Development*, 39(5), E148–E153. DOI: 10.1097/NND.0000000000000898 PMID: 37683219

Booth, R., Sinclair, B., McMurray, J., Strudwick, G., Watson, G., Ladak, H., Zwarenstein, M., McBride, S., Chan, R., & Brennan, L. (2018). Evaluating a serious gaming electronic medication administration record system among nursing students: Protocol for a pragmatic randomized controlled trial. *JMIR Research Protocols*, 7(5), e138. DOI: 10.2196/resprot.9601 PMID: 29807885

Boyle, E., Connolly, T. M., & Hainey, T. (2011). The role of psychology in understanding the impact of computer games. *Entertainment Computing*, 2(2), 69–74. DOI: 10.1016/j.entcom.2010.12.002

Breen, J. (2004). Changing Roles for (Multi) Media Tools in Design. *Architecture in the Network Society*, 529.

Breuer, H., & Ivanov, K. (2020). Gamification to address cultural challenges and to facilitate values-based innovation. *ISPIM Conference Proceedings*. [HTML]

Bristol, T. J. (2023). Black men teaching Toward a theory of social isolation in organizations. In *Men educators of color in US public schools and* (pp. 31–45). Routledge., DOI: 10.4324/9781003392538-2

Bristol, T. J., & Goings, R. B. (2019). Exploring the boundary-heightening experiences of Black male teachers Lessons for teacher education programs. *Journal of Teacher Education*, 70(1), 48–61. DOI: 10.1177/0022487118789367

Bristol, T. J., & Mentor, M. (2018). Policing and teaching The positioning of Black male teachers as agents in the universal carceral apparatus. *The Urban Review*, 50(1), 56–70. DOI: 10.1007/s11256-018-0447-z

Brown, K. G. (2005). An examination of the structure and nomological network of trainee reactions: A closer look at" smile sheets. *The Journal of Applied Psychology*, 90(5), 991–1001. DOI: 10.1037/0021-9010.90.5.991 PMID: 16162071

Brown, L. (2007). A consideration of the challenges involved in supervising international masters students. *Journal of Further and Higher Education*, 31(3), 239–248. DOI: 10.1080/03098770701424967

Bryant, J. (2023). *Black male educator shortage in the Mississippi public school system Impact, challenges, and intervention strategies*. University of Mississippi. https//egrove.olemiss.edu/hon_thesis/3017/

Bryant, J. (2023). *The practices of Black male educators in Georgia public school classrooms*. ProQuest Dissertations & Theses. https//search.proquest.com/openview/3900da2752c6b90b89fcccb1a065dd6e/1?pq-origsite=gscholar&cbl=18750&diss=y

Buckley, P., & Doyle, E. (2014). Gamification and student motivation. *Interactive Learning Environments*, 24(6), 1162–1175. DOI: 10.1080/10494820.2014.964263

Buckley, P., & Doyle, E. (2017). Individualising gamification: An investigation of the impact of learning styles and personality traits on the efficacy of gamification using a prediction market. *Computers & Education*, 106, 43–55. DOI: 10.1016/j.compedu.2016.11.009

Budhwar, P. S., & Boyne, G. (2004). Human resource management in the Indian public and private sectors: An empirical comparison. *International Journal of Human Resource Management*, 15(2), 346–370. DOI: 10.1080/0958519032000158554

Bugeja, M., & Grech, E. M. (2020). Using technology and gamification as a means of enhancing users' experience at cultural heritage sites. Rediscovering Heritage Through Technology: A Collection of Innovative Research Case Studies That Are Reworking The Way We Experience Heritage, 69-89. [HTML]

Burhenn, P., Ferrell, B., Johnson, S., & Hurria, A. (2016). Improving nurses' knowledge about older adults with cancer. *Oncology Nursing Forum*, 43(4), 497–504. DOI: 10.1188/16.ONF.497-504 PMID: 27314192

Burlacu, M., Coman, C., & Bularca, M. C. (2023). Blogged into the System: A Systematic Review of the Gamification in e-Learning before and during the COVID-19 Pandemic. *Sustainability (Basel)*, 15(8), 6476. DOI: 10.3390/su15086476

Buthelezi, N., & Shopo, K. D. (2023). Challenges experienced by nurse educators developing postgraduate nursing diploma curriculum programmes, Gauteng. *Curationis*, 46(1). Advance online publication. DOI: 10.4102/curationis.v46i1.2447 PMID: 37782237

Butler, N., & Spoelstra, S. (2023). "You just earned 10 points!": Gaming and grinding in academia. *Organization*, 135050842211455. Advance online publication. DOI: 10.1177/13505084221145589

Çağlar, S., & Okuyan, C. B. (2023). The impact of distance learning on the attitudes of nursing students: An online survey study. *Acta Scientiarum Health Sciences*, 46(1), e63213. DOI: 10.4025/actascihealthsci.v46i1.63213

Cai, Y., Li, X., & Shi, W. (2024). Does gamification affect knowledge-sharing behavior? The mediating role of intrinsic satisfaction needs. [HTML]. *Online Information Review*, 48(2), 354–373. DOI: 10.1108/OIR-05-2021-0288

Campanile, L., Iacono, M., Marulli, F., & Mastroianni, M. (2021). Designing a GDPR compliant blockchain-based IoV distributed information tracking system. [HTML]. *Information Processing & Management*, 58(3), 102511. DOI: 10.1016/j.ipm.2021.102511

Caponetto, I., Earp, J., & Ott, M. (2014, October). Gamification and education: A literature review. In *European conference on games based learning* (Vol. 1, p. 50). Academic Conferences International Limited.

Carey, R. L. (2023). Missing misters Uncovering the pedagogies and positionalities of male teachers of color in the school lives of Black and Latino adolescent boys. In *Men educators of color in US public schools* (pp. 99–118). Routledge., DOI: 10.4324/9781003392538-7

Carneiro, A., e Sousa, H. F. P., Dinis, M. A. P., & Leite, Â (2021). Human values and religion: Evidence from the european social survey. Social Sciences. mdpi.com

Castillo-Parra, B., Hidalgo-Cajo, B. G., Vásconez-Barrera, M., & Oleas-López, J. (2022). Gamification in Higher Education: A Review of the Literature. *World Journal on Educational Technology: Current Issues*, 14(3), 797–816. DOI: 10.18844/wjet.v14i3.7341

Castro, T., & Gonçalves, L. (2018). The use of gamification to teach in the nursing field. *Revista Brasileira de Enfermagem*, 71(3), 1038–1045. DOI: 10.1590/0034-7167-2017-0023 PMID: 29924165

Cavusoglu, H., Li, Z., & Kim, S. H. (2021). How do virtual badges incentivize voluntary contributions to online communities? [HTML]. *Information & Management*, 58(5), 103483. DOI: 10.1016/j.im.2021.103483

Cejka, P., & Mohelska, H. (2020). National Culture Influence on Organisational Trauma: A Conceptual Framework Review. In Occupational Stress: Breakthroughs in Research and Practice (pp. 238-262). IGI Global. [HTML] DOI: 10.4018/978-1-7998-0954-8.ch012

Chang, W. L., & Yeh, Y. C. (2021). A blended design of game-based learning for motivation, knowledge sharing and critical thinking enhancement. *Technology, Pedagogy and Education*, 30(2), 271–285.

Chans, G. M., & Castro, M. P. (2021). Gamification as a Strategy to Increase Motivation and Engagement in Higher Education Chemistry Students. *Computers*, 10(10), 132. DOI: 10.3390/computers10100132

Chen, K. C., Wu, C. J., & Chen, G. D. (2011, July). A digital board game-based learning system for authentic learning. In *2011 IEEE 11th International Conference on Advanced Learning Technologies* (pp. 25-29). IEEE. DOI: 10.1109/ICALT.2011.16

Chen, C. M., Ming-Chaun, L., & Kuo, C. P. (2023). A game-based learning system based on octalysis gamification framework to promote employees' Japanese learning. *Computers & Education*, 205, 104899. DOI: 10.1016/j.compedu.2023.104899

Cheng, V. W. S. (2020). Recommendations for implementing gamification for mental health and wellbeing. Frontiers in psychology. frontiersin.org

Cheng, Y. P., Lai, C. F., Chen, Y. T., Wang, W. S., Huang, Y. M., & Wu, T. T. (2023). Enhancing student's computational thinking skills with student-generated questions strategy in a game-based learning platform. *Computers & Education*, 200, 104794. DOI: 10.1016/j.compedu.2023.104794

Chickering, A. W., & Gamson, Z. F. (1987). Seven principles for good practice in undergraduate education. *AAHE Bulletin*, 3, 7.

Chotiratanapinun, T., & Suppipat, S. (2022). Games and gamification in sustainability learning: a peer-based approach for Thai design education. In *Handbook of Research on the Influence and Effectiveness of Gamification in Education* (pp. 241–270). IGI Global. [HTML] DOI: 10.4018/978-1-6684-4287-6.ch013

Chou, Y. K. (2019). *Actionable gamification: Beyond points, badges, and leaderboards*. Packt Publishing Ltd.

Christopoulos, A. & Mystakidis, S. (2023). Gamification in education. Encyclopedia. mdpi.com

Christopoulos, A., & Mystakidis, S. (2023). Gamification in Education. *Encyclopedia*, 3(4), 4. Advance online publication. DOI: 10.3390/encyclopedia3040089

Chung, C. H., Shen, C., & Qiu, Y. Z. (2019). Students' acceptance of gamification in higher education. *International Journal of Game-Based Learning*, 9(2), 1–19. DOI: 10.4018/IJGBL.2019040101

Chung, D. J., & Koo, K. R. (2023). The role of cultural diversity in creating value: A case study of South Korea's pop band BTS. [HTML]. *Asia Pacific Business Review*, 29(5), 1275–1299. DOI: 10.1080/13602381.2023.2243242

Ciuchita, R., Heller, J., Köcher, S., Köcher, S., Leclercq, T., Sidaoui, K., & Stead, S. (2023). It is really not a game: An integrative review of gamification for service research. [sagepub.com]. *Journal of Service Research*, 26(1), 3–20. DOI: 10.1177/10946705221076272

Coelho, L., & Reis, S. (2020). Ethical Issues of Gamification in Healthcare. In *Advances in medical technologies and clinical practice book series* (pp. 1–19). DOI: 10.4018/978-1-7998-7472-0.ch001

Coletto, S. (2023). *The Perceived Gameful Experience of Undergraduate Nursing Students Engaged in a Virtual Interactive Puzzle Escape Room Focusing on a Complex Clinical Intervention* (Doctoral dissertation, Université d'Ottawa/University of Ottawa).

Collie, R. J., & Martin, A. J. (2019). *Motivation and engagement in learning*. Oxford Research Encyclopedia of Education., DOI: 10.1093/acrefore/9780190264093.013.891

Connolly, T. M., Boyle, E. A., MacArthur, E., Hainey, T., & Boyle, J. M. (2012). A systematic literature review of empirical evidence on computer games and serious games. *Computers & Education*, 59(2), 661–686. DOI: 10.1016/j.compedu.2012.03.004

Cormier, C. J., Scott, L. R. A., Powell, C., & Hall, K. (2022). Locked in glass classrooms Black male special education teachers socialized as everything but educators. *Teacher Education and Special Education*, 45(1), 59–73. DOI: 10.1177/08884064211061038

Costa, F. A., Viana, J., & Raleiras, M. (2020, June). What do higher education students have to say about gamification? In *International Conference in Methodologies and intelligent Systems for Techhnology Enhanced Learning* (pp. 56-65). Cham: Springer International Publishing. [HTML]

Costa, F. A., Viana, J., & Raleiras, M. (2020, June). What do higher education students have to say about gamification? In *International Conference in Methodologies and Intelligent Systems for Technology Enhanced Learning* (pp. 56-65). Cham: Springer International Publishing.

Coughlin, V., Ho, M. R., & Alvarez, G. (2023). Escape the room! utilizing gamification in a preceptor training workshop. *Journal for Nurses in Professional Development*. Advance online publication. DOI: 10.1097/NND.0000000000000977 PMID: 37812131

Cowley, S. A., Tzouvara, V., & Horta Reis da Silva, T. (2023). Public Health: healthy ageing and well-being. *In Redfern's Nursing Older People*. Fifth edition. Editors: Ross, Harris, Fitzpatrick and Abley. Elsevier.

Craig, S., Stark, P., Wilson, C., Carter, G., Clarke, S., & Mitchell, G. (2023). Evaluation of a dementia awareness game for undergraduate nursing students in Northern Ireland: A pre-/post-test study. *BMC Nursing*, 22(1), 177. Advance online publication. DOI: 10.1186/s12912-023-01345-2 PMID: 37217937

Creative Assembly. (2004). *Total War: Rome*. Total War. https://www.totalwar.com/

Crouch, S., Fillmore, L., Fly, L., & Ukot, E. (2015). Impact of inter-professional education on nursing student outcomes in the online environment. [AJHS]. *American Journal of Health Sciences*, 6(2), 101–110. DOI: 10.19030/ajhs.v6i2.9499

Csikszentmihalyi, M. (2008). *Flow: The psychology of optimal experience*. Harper & Row New York.

Cummings-Lewis, E. N. (2023). *On the underrepresentation of Black men as early childhood educators—Exploring their career choice, retention, long-term sustainability, and influence on Black children*. ProQuest Dissertations & Theses. https// search.proquest.com/openview/c70b88a422d92fa8d8af3732126d4ed3/1?pq-origsite =gscholar&cbl=18750&diss=y

Cunningham, C. (2022). *Working for justice A Black educator's journey of supporting Black males in an urban school district*. ProQuest Dissertations & Theses. https//search.proquest.com/openview/0a83b842451051402e0bea42ee2894af/1?pq -origsite=gscholar&cbl=18750&diss=y

da Silva, T. H. R. (2022). Emotional awareness and emotional intelligence. *British Journal of Community Nursing*, 27(12), 573–574. DOI: 10.12968/bjcn.2022.27.12.573 PMID: 36519463

da Silva, T. H. R., & Rodrigues, E. C. P. (2023). Body Image Related Discrimination. In Leal Filho, W., Azul, A. M., Brandli, L., Lange Salvia, A., Özuyar, P. G., & Wall, T. (Eds.), *Reduced Inequalities. Encyclopedia of the UN Sustainable Development Goals*. Springer., DOI: 10.1007/978-3-319-71060-0_61-1

Dæhli, O., Kristoffersen, B., Lauvås, P.Jr, & Sandnes, T. (2021). Exploring Feedback and Gamification in a Data Modeling Learning Tool. *Electronic Journal of e-Learning*, 19(6), 559–574. DOI: 10.34190/ejel.19.6.2501

Dahalan, F., Alias, N., & Shaharom, M. (2023). Gamification and game based learning for vocational education and training: A systematic literature review. *Education and Information Technologies*, 29(2), 1279–1317. DOI: 10.1007/s10639-022-11548-w PMID: 36688221

Daniel, B. (2022). Common Challenges Postgraduate Students and Early-Career Academics face when Engaging with Scholarly Literature. *Electronic Journal of Business Research Methods*, 20(3), 142–152. DOI: 10.34190/ejbrm.20.3.2503

De Bruyckere, P., & Kirschner, P. A. (2017). Measuring teacher authenticity: Criteria students use in their perception of teacher authenticity. *Cogent Education*, 4(1), 1354573. DOI: 10.1080/2331186X.2017.1354573 de Oliveira Durso, S., Reginato, L., & Cornacchione, E. (2019). GAMIFICATION IN ACCOUNTING AND STUDENTS' SKILLSET. *Advances in Scientific and Applied Accounting, 12*(3), 079-100. DOI: 10.14392/ASAA.2019120305

de Sousa Borges, S., Durelli, V. H., Reis, H. M., & Isotani, S. (2014). A systematic mapping on gamification applied to education. Proceedings of the 29th annual ACM symposium on applied computing, Deterding, S., Dixon, D., Khaled, R., & Nacke, L. (2011). From game design elements to gamefulness: defining" gamification". Proceedings of the 15th international academic MindTrek conference: Envisioning future media environments, Devedžić, V., & Jovanović, J. (2015). Developing open badges: A comprehensive approach. *Educational Technology Research and Development*, 63, 603–620.

Dečman, N., Rep, A., & Titgemeyer, M. (2022). Who is more eager to use gamification in economic disciplines? comparison of students and educators. *Business Systems Research Journal*, 13(2), 96–116. DOI: 10.2478/bsrj-2022-0017

Dehghanzadeh, H., Farrokhnia, M., Dehghanzadeh, H., Taghipour, K., & Noroozi, O. (2024). Using gamification to support learning in K-12 education: A systematic literature review. *British Journal of Educational Technology*, 55(1), 34–70. DOI: 10.1111/bjet.13335

Deloitte. (2019). Deloitte Global Human Capital Trends. Retrieved 2 July 2020, from https://www2.deloitte.com/content/dam/insights/us/articles/5136_HC-Trends-2019/DI_HC-Trends-2019.pdf

Dereso, C. W., Kant, S., Muthuraman, M., & Tufa, G. (2023). Effect of Point of Service on Health Department Student's Creativity in Comprehensive Universities of Ethiopia: Moderating Role of Public-Private Partnership and Mediating Role of Work Place Learning. In: Jain, S., Groppe, S., Mihindukulasooriya, N. (eds) Proceedings of the International Health Informatics Conference. Lecture Notes in Electrical Engineering, vol 990. Springer, Singapore. https://doi.org/DOI: 10.1007/978-981-19-9090-8_13

Deterding, S., Dixon, D., Khaled, R., & Nacke, L. (2011). From game design elements to gamefulness: defining "Gamification". MindTrek '11, Proceedings from the 15th International Academic MindTrek Conference: Envisioning Future Media Environments, (pp. 9-15). DOI: 10.1145/2181037.2181040

Deterding, S., Dixon, D., Khaled, R., & Nacke, L. (2011). From game design elements to gratefulness: defining "gamification." In: *Proceedings of the 15th International Academic MindTrek Conference: Envisioning Future Media Environments*. Tampere, Finland, 28-30 September 2011. New York: ACM, pp. 9-15.

Di Raddo, E. (2020). From the artwork to the museum: Gamification as an instrument of art. In *Digital Transformation in the Cultural and Creative Industries* (pp. 32–50). Routledge. [HTML] DOI: 10.4324/9780429329852-4

Dicheva, D., & Dichev, C. (2015). Gamification in education: Where are we in 2015? E-learn: World conference on E-learning in corporate, government, healthcare, and higher education, Fernandez-Antolin, M. M., del Río, J. M., & Gonzalez-Lezcano, R. A. (2021). The use of gamification in higher technical education: perception of university students on innovative teaching materials. *International Journal of Technology and Design Education*, 31(5), 1019–1038. DOI: 10.1007/s10798-020-09583-0

Dichev, C., & Dicheva, D. (2017). Gamifying education is a critical review of what is known, what is believed, and what remains uncertain. *International Journal of Educational Technology in Higher Education*, 14(1), 9. DOI: 10.1186/s41239-017-0042-5

Dietrich, T., & Balli, S. J. (2014). Digital Natives: Fifth-Grade Students' Authentic and Ritualistic Engagement with Technology. *International Journal of Instruction*, 7(2), 21–34.

Disruptor Beam. (2016). *STAR TREK TIMELINES*. STAR TREK TIMELINES. http://www.startrektimelines.com/

Doležalová, J., Tóthová, V., & Neugebauer, J. (2022). Selected aspects of nursing practice related to the usage of evaluation tools for population aged over 60 years. *Kontakt*, 24(2), 131–136. DOI: 10.32725/kont.2021.044

Dolmans, D. H., De Grave, W., Wolfhagen, I. H., & Van Der Vleuten, C. P. (2005). Problem-based learning: Future challenges for educational practice and research. *Medical Education*, 39(7), 732–741. DOI: 10.1111/j.1365-2929.2005.02205.x PMID: 15960794

Domínguez, A., Saenz-de-Navarrete, J., de-Marcos, L., Fernández-Sanz, L., Pagés, C., & Martínez-Herráiz, J. J. (2013). Gamifying learning experiences: Practical implications and outcomes. *Computers & Education*, 63, 380–392. DOI: 10.1016/j.compedu.2012.12.020

Dondio, P. (2024). Does Playing Video Games Give a Child an Advantage in Digital Game-Based Learning? *Lecture Notes in Computer Science (Including Subseries Lecture Notes in Artificial Intelligence and Lecture Notes in Bioinformatics), 14475 LNCS*, 223–233. *Lecture Notes in Computer Science*, 14475, 223–233. Advance online publication. DOI: 10.1007/978-3-031-49065-1_22

Doroudi, F., Ashourizadeh, H., Moosapour, S., Ganjizadeh, A., Ranjbar Shourabi, A., Parnia, A., Kazemipour, F., Mohraz, M., & Bayat Jozani, Z. (2023). Gamified educational learning path on HIV/aids stigma and discrimination (redxir): Design, development and pilot study. *Medical Journal of the Islamic Republic of Iran*. Advance online publication. DOI: 10.47176/mjiri.37.136 PMID: 38318411

Dovico, A. (2023). *Examining motivations of Black males to become elementary school educators*. ProQuest Dissertations & Theses. https//search.proquest.com/openview/bbbe36d2438d52dca0c17fe98775f7ad/1?pq-origsite=gscholar&cbl=18750&diss=y

Drissi, S., Chefrour, A., Boussaha, K., & Zarzour, H. (2024). Exploring the effects of personalized recommendations on student's motivation and learning achievement in gamified mobile learning framework. *Education and Information Technologies*, •••, 1–38. DOI: 10.1007/s10639-024-12477-6

Duarte, A. S. de C. (2013). *A utilização das TIC no ensino e aprendizagem da história* [masterThesis]. https://repositorio.ul.pt/handle/10451/10334

Durga, P., Godavarthi, D., Kant, S., & Basa, S. S. (2024). Aspect-based drug review classification through a hybrid model with ant colony optimization using deep learning. *Discov Computing*, 27(1), 19. DOI: 10.1007/s10791-024-09441-w

Dutta, R., Mantri, A., & Singh, G. (2022). Evaluating system usability of mobile augmented reality application for teaching Karnaugh-Maps. Smart Learning Environments. springer.com

Ebel, P., Orlovska, J., Hünemeyer, S., Wickman, C., Vogelsang, A., & Söderberg, R. (2021). Automotive UX design and data-driven development: Narrowing the gap to support practitioners. [sciencedirect.com]. *Transportation Research Interdisciplinary Perspectives*, 11, 100455. DOI: 10.1016/j.trip.2021.100455

Edwards, S. H., & Li, Z. (2020). A Proposal to Use Gamification Systematically to Nudge Students Toward Productive Behaviors. In *Proceedings of the 20th Koli Calling International Conference on Computing Education Research*. DOI: 10.1145/3428029.3428057

Elattar, N., Osman, F., & Mahmoud, H. (2023). Effect of emotional intelligence based training program on burnout, psychological capital and job performance among psychiatric nurses. *Menoufia Nursing Journal*, 8(1), 259–276. DOI: 10.21608/menj.2023.303432

Emezirinwune, M., Babatunde, D., Emezirinwune, D., & Denwigwe, I. (2024). The role of information and communication technologies in university education: taxonomies, perspectives, and challenges. *Reading Time, 2024*, 04-10.

Erdoğan, Ç., & Turan, T. (2022). Evaluation of the effectiveness of digital game-based learning given to nursing students for the developmental care of infants in neonatal intensive care unit. *Computers, Informatics, Nursing*, 41(5), 300–308. DOI: 10.1097/CIN.0000000000000920 PMID: 37145853

Eseryel, D., Law, V., Ifenthaler, D., Ge, X., & Miller, R. (2014). Investigating the interrelationships between motivation, engagement, and complex problem-solving in game-based learning. *Journal of Educational Technology & Society*, 17(1), 42–53.

Espinosa, J., Vaquero-Abellán, M., Perea-Moreno, A., Pedrós-Pérez, G., Martínez-Jiménez, P., & Aparicio-Martínez, P. (2022). Gamification as a promoting tool of motivation for creating sustainable higher education institutions. *International Journal of Environmental Research and Public Health*, 19(5), 2599. DOI: 10.3390/ijerph19052599 PMID: 35270291

Eybers, S., & Hattingh, M. (2018). Enhancing Student Engagement: One Game at a Time. In *Innovative Technologies and Learning: First International Conference, ICITL 2018, Portoroz, Slovenia, August 27–30, 2018* [Springer International Publishing.]. *Proceedings*, 1, 231–240.

Faiella, F., & Ricciardi, M. (2015). Gamification and learning: a review of issues and research. *Journal of e-learning and knowledge society, 11*(3).

Fallatah, A. I. (2023). The Effectiveness of a Platform based on Gamification in developing Creative thinking among Middle School Students. *JALHSS*, (93), 299-316. 93. https://doi.org/DOI: 10.33193/JALHSS.93.2023.864

Fan, M., Yu, L., Chen, S., Zhou, H., Luo, X., Li, S., Liu, Y., Liu, J., & Liu, T. (2020). An Empirical Evaluation of GDPR Compliance Violations in Android mHealth Apps. In *IEEE 31st International Symposium on Software Reliability Engineering (ISSRE)*. DOI: 10.1109/ISSRE5003.2020.00032

Farhana, A., Kouser, S., Ghani, M., Khatoon, T., & Asghar, R. (2023). Effect of emotional intelligence on job satisfaction among nurses: Descriptive study. *PJMHS*, 17(6), 127–129. DOI: 10.53350/pjmhs2023176127

Felton, A. M. (2022). *Investigation of the lack of diversity amongst educators focusing on the educational experiences of Black males A qualitative narrative research study*. ProQuest Dissertations & Theses. https//search.proquest.com/openview/fcec41d5dec2c97bb5906f9e4c6541c1/1?pq-origsite=gscholar&cbl=18750&diss=y

Fernandes, A., Melo, M., & Machado, C. F. (2022). The use of gamification in training and socialization processes in a multicultural context. In *Technological challenges: The human side of the digital age* (pp. 93–108). Springer International Publishing. [HTML] DOI: 10.1007/978-3-030-98040-5_4

Fijačko, N., Gosak, L., Debeljak, N., Skok, P., Štiglic, G., & Cilar, L. (2020). Gamification in nursing. *Slovenian Nursing Review*, 54(2), 133–152. DOI: 10.14528/snr.2020.54.2.2991

Firaxis Games. (2004). *Sid Meier's Pirates! [PC]*. Sid Meier's Pirates! [PC]. https://firaxis.com/

Fitzpatrick, J. M., Bianchi, L. A., Hayes, N., Da Silva, T., & Harris, R. (2023). Professional development and career planning for nurses working in care homes for older people: A scoping review. *International Journal of Older People Nursing*, 18(1), e12519. DOI: 10.1111/opn.12519 PMID: 36441621

Fiuza-Fernández, A., Portela, L., Soto-Carballo, J., & Juste, M. (2022). Study of the knowledge about gamification of degree in primary education students. *PLoS One*, 17(3), e0263107. DOI: 10.1371/journal.pone.0263107 PMID: 35349574

Fogarty, L., Strimling, P., & Laland, K. N. (2011). The Evolution of teaching. *Evolution; International Journal of Organic Evolution*, 65(10), 2760–2770. DOI: 10.1111/j.1558-5646.2011.01370.x PMID: 21967419

Fogg, B. (2009). A behavior model for persuasive design. In *Persuasive '09:Proceedings of the 4th International Conference on Persuasive Technology*. DOI: 10.1145/1541948.1541999

Fonseca, D., Villagrasa, S., Navarro, I., Redondo, E., Valls, F., & Sánchez, A. (2017, Apr 11-13). Urban Gamification in Architecture Education.*Advances in Intelligent Systems and Computing* [Recent advances in information systems and technologies, vol 3]. *World Conference on Information Systems and Technologies (WorldCIST)*, Madeira, Portugal.

Fornari, L., & Fonseca, R. (2023). Critical-emancipatory educational intervention through games to face gender violence. *Revista Brasileira De Enfermagem*, 76(suppl 2). https://doi.org/DOI: 10.1590/0034-7167-2022-0299

Fox, M., Butler, J., Persaud, M., Tregunno, D., Sidani, S., & McCague, H. (2015). A multi-method study of the geriatric learning needs of acute care hospital nurses in Ontario, Canada. *Research in Nursing & Health*, 39(1), 66–76. DOI: 10.1002/nur.21699 PMID: 26471253

Fredricks, J. A., Blumenfeld, P. C., & Paris, A. H. (2004). School engagement: Potential of the concept, state of the evidence. *Review of Educational Research*, 74(1), 59–109. DOI: 10.3102/00346543074001059

Frego, K. A. (2006). Authenticity and relationships with students. *New adult and continuing education directions, 2006*(111), 41-50.

Freiermuth, M. R. & Ito, M. (2022). Battling with books: The gamification of an EFL extensive reading class. Simulation & Gaming. sagepub.com

Furr, S., Lane, S., Serafica, R., & Hodge, M. (2015). Service-learning and inter-professional education in nursing. *Journal of Christian Nursing*, 32(3), 162–167. DOI: 10.1097/CNJ.0000000000000178 PMID: 26211302

Gagné, N. O. (2021). Reworking Japan: changing men at work and play under neoliberalism. [HTML]

Gagné, M., Parker, S. K., Griffin, M. A., Dunlop, P. D., Knight, C., Klonek, F. E., & Parent-Rocheleau, X. (2022). Understanding and shaping the future of work with self-determination theory. [nature.com]. *Nature Reviews Psychology*, 1(7), 378–392. DOI: 10.1038/s44159-022-00056-w PMID: 35574235

Gambo, N., Musonda, I., & Zadawa, A. N. (2023). Effects of social media learning environments on AEC learning process among university students in Nigeria. *International Journal of Construction Education and Research*, 19(1), 99–127. DOI: 10.1080/15578771.2021.1974986

Gamification is Bullshit. (2011, August 8). Bogost.com. http://bogost.com/writing/blog/gamification_is_bullshit/

Gao, X., & Chen, P. (2024). Establishment of a geriatric nursing curriculum with human caring by situational simulation. *Journal of Curriculum and Teaching*, 13(1), 71. DOI: 10.5430/jct.v13n1p71

Gao, Y., Zhang, P., Wen, S., & Chen, Y. (2017). Challenge, opportunity and development: Influencing factors and tendencies of curriculum innovation on undergraduate nursing education in the mainland of China. *Clinical Nursing Research*, 4(3), 113–116. DOI: 10.25164/SEP.2017040202

García, S. A., Jiménez, C. R., de la Cruz Campos, J. C., & Villalba, M. J. S. (2021). Applications of Gamification in the Context of Higher Education. A Theoretical Approach. International Conference in Methodologies and intelligent Systems for Techhnology Enhanced Learning, Gee, J. P. (2003). What video games have to teach us about learning and literacy. [CIE]. *Computers in Entertainment*, 1(1), 20–20.

Gentry, S., Gauthier, A., Ehrstrom, B., Wortley, D., Lilienthal, A., Car, L., & Car, J. (2019). Serious gaming and gamification education in health professions: Systematic review. *Journal of Medical Internet Research*, 21(3), e12994. DOI: 10.2196/12994 PMID: 30920375

Ghamgosar, A., Zarghani, M., & Nemati-Anaraki, L. (2021). Bibliometric analysis on geriatric nursing research in web of science (1900–2020). *BioMed Research International*, 2021, 1–11. DOI: 10.1155/2021/8758161 PMID: 34621898

Ghonim, M. (2017). Toward calibrating architectural education: An approach to promote students' design abilities. *The International Journal of Architectonic, Spatial, and Environmental Design*, 11(4), 37–62. DOI: 10.18848/2325-1662/CGP/v11i04/37-62

Ghonim, M., & Eweda, N. (2018). Investigating elective courses in architectural education. *Frontiers of Architectural Research*, 7(2), 235–256. DOI: 10.1016/j.foar.2018.03.006

Gipson, C. T. (2019). Delayed but not denied How a Black male educator mastered the power of resilience. In *Personal Narratives of Black Educational Leaders* (pp. 79–90). Taylor & Francis., DOI: 10.4324/9781315099743-9

Glazer, S. (2021). Organizational role ambiguity as a proxy for uncertainty avoidance. [HTML]. *International Journal of Intercultural Relations*, 85, 1–12. DOI: 10.1016/j.ijintrel.2021.08.011

Gligorea, I., Cioca, M., Oancea, R., Gorski, A. T., Gorski, H., & Tudorache, P. (2023). Adaptive learning using artificial intelligence in e-learning: A literature review. [mdpi.com]. *Education Sciences*, 13(12), 1216. DOI: 10.3390/educsci13121216

Gobert, J. W. (2021). *The experiences of African American male educators in primary grade levels*. ProQuest Dissertations & Theses. https//search.proquest.com/openview/b5aaf74c9e872a51737dbe33f5a8feff/1?pq-origsite=gscholar&cbl=18750&diss=y

Gonzalez-Escribano, A., Lara-Mongil, V., Rodriguez-Gutiez, E., & Torres, Y. (2019). Toward improving collaborative behaviour during competitive programming assignments. In *IEEE/ACM Workshop on Education for High-Performance Computing (EduHPC)*. DOI: 10.1109/EduHPC49559.2019.00014

González-González, C. S., Muñoz-Cruz, V., Toledo-Delgado, P. A., & Nacimiento-García, E. (2023). Personalized gamification for learning: A reactive chatbot architecture proposal. *Sensors (Basel)*, 23(1), 545. DOI: 10.3390/s23010545 PMID: 36617143

Grabinger, S., & Dunlap, J. C. (2002, October). Problem-based learning as an example of active learning and student engagement: Invited talk. In *International Conference on Advances in Information Systems* (pp. 375-384). Berlin, Heidelberg: Springer Berlin Heidelberg.

Graetz, D., Chen, Y., Devidas, M., Antillón-Klussmann, F., Fú, L., Quintero, K., Fuentes-Alabi, S. L., Gassant, P. Y., Kaye, E. C., Baker, J. N., Rodriguez Galindo, C., & Mack, J. (2023). Interdisciplinary care of pediatric oncology patients: A survey of clinicians in Central America and the Caribbean. *Pediatric Blood & Cancer*, 70(5), e30244. Advance online publication. DOI: 10.1002/pbc.30244 PMID: 36788461

Grant, O. B. (2020). *An exploratory study on Black male educators' implementation of culturally relevant practices based on personal and environmental factors*. ProQuest Dissertations & Theses. https//search.proquest.com/openview/0f4633d08ee8b8bbb54fe35172f6ab60/1?pq-origsite=gscholar&cbl=18750&diss=y

Grech, J., & Grech, J. (2021). Nursing students' evaluation of a gamified public health educational webinar: A comparative pilot study. *Nursing Open*, 8(4), 1812–1821. DOI: 10.1002/nop2.826 PMID: 33675289

Greipl, S., Moeller, K., & Ninaus, M. (2020). Potential and limits of game-based learning. *International Journal of Technology Enhanced Learning*, 12(4), 363–389. DOI: 10.1504/IJTEL.2020.110047

Grenni, S., Horlings, L. G., & Soini, K. (2020). Linking spatial planning and place branding strategies through cultural narratives in places. European Planning Studies. tandfonline.com

Gunter, G. A., Kenny, R. F., & Vick, E. H. (2008). Taking educational games seriously: Using the RETAIN model to design endogenous fantasy into standalone educational games. *Educational Technology Research and Development*, 56(5), 511–537. DOI: 10.1007/s11423-007-9073-2

Gupta, P., & Goyal, P. (2022). Is game-based pedagogy just a fad? A self-determination theory approach to gamification in higher education. [HTML]. *International Journal of Educational Management*, 36(3), 341–356. DOI: 10.1108/IJEM-04-2021-0126

Guyo, D. M., Kant, S., & Kero, C. A. (2023, November). Mediation of Marketing Intermediaries and AI Adoption Between Livestock Products Marketing and Economic Status of Pastoralist in Ethiopia. In *2023 International Conference on Communication, Security and Artificial Intelligence (ICCSAI)* (pp. 311-316). IEEE.

Hamari, J., Koivisto, J., & Sarsa, H. (2014). *Does Gamification Work? -- A Literature Review of Empirical Studies on Gamification*. DOI: 10.1109/HICSS.2014.377

Hamari, J., Koivisto, J., & Sarsa, H. (2014, January). Does gamification work?--a literature review of empirical studies on gamification. In 2014 47th Hawaii international conference on system sciences (pp. 3025-3034). Ieee.

Hamari, J., Koivisto, J., & Sarsa, H. 2014. Does gamification work? – A literature review of empirical studies on gamification. In: 2014 47th Hawaii International Conference on System Sciences. Waikoloa, HI, USA, 6-9 January 2014. IEEE, pp. 3025-3034.

Hamari, J., & Koivisto, J. (2013). Social Motivations To Use Gamification: An Empirical Study Of Gamifying Exercise. ECIS, Hanus, M. D., & Fox, J. (2015). Assessing the effects of gamification in the classroom: A longitudinal study on intrinsic motivation, social comparison, satisfaction, effort, and academic performance. *Computers & Education*, 80, 152–161.

Hammedi, W., Leclerq, T., & Van Riel, A. C. (2017). The use of gamification mechanics to increase employee and user engagement in participative healthcare services. *Journal of Service Management*, 28(4), 640–661. DOI: 10.1108/JOSM-04-2016-0116

Hamouda, G., & Nagshabandi, E. (2018). The perception of emotional intelligence self-assessment among nursing students. *American Journal of Nursing Science*, 7(5), 173. DOI: 10.11648/j.ajns.20180705.13

Han, H. (2021). Consumer behavior and environmental sustainability in tourism and hospitality: A review of theories, concepts, and latest research. Sustainable Consumer Behaviour and the Environment. tandfonline.com

Han, L., Cao, Q., Xie, T., Chen, X., Liu, Y., & Bai, J. (2021). Exploring the experience of nursing undergraduates in using gamification teaching mode based on the flow theory in nursing research: A qualitative study. [HTML]. *Nurse Education Today*, 107, 105158. DOI: 10.1016/j.nedt.2021.105158 PMID: 34607296

Harsaya, E. R. T., Permana, A. A., & Khaeruzaman, Y. A. M. A. N. (2023). Design Application Simple Learn Based on Mobile With Implementation Gamification for Learning Online. *Journal of Theoretical and Applied Information Technology*, 101(6), 2255–2262.

Haske-Palomino, M., Carlson, R., & Gatley, L. (2023). Elder veteran program: A description of a nurse practitioner–led inpatient geriatric consult model. *Journal of the American Association of Nurse Practitioners*, 35(4), 229–234. DOI: 10.1097/JXX.0000000000000844 PMID: 36857530

Hassib, M., Schneegass, S., Eiglsperger, P., Henze, N., Schmidt, A., & Alt, F. (2017). *EngageMeter*. DOI: 10.1145/3025453.3025669

Hayes, A. F. (2018). Partial, conditional, and moderated moderated mediation: Quantification, inference, and interpretation. *Communication Monographs*, 85(1), 4–40. DOI: 10.1080/03637751.2017.1352100

Hayes, S. C., Strosahl, K. D., & Wilson, K. G. (2009). *Acceptance and commitment therapy*. American Psychological Association.

Hellberg, A. (2023). The story of the hatter and the agile methods course: gamification and game thinking in education. *Journal of Pedagogical Research*. https://doi.org/DOI: 10.33902/JPR.202320130

Hellín, C. J., Calles-Esteban, F., Valledor, A., Gómez, J., Otón-Tortosa, S., & Tayebi, A. (2023). Enhancing student motivation and engagement through a gamified learning environment. [mdpi.com]. *Sustainability (Basel)*, 15(19), 14119. DOI: 10.3390/su151914119

Herkanaidu, R., Furnell, S. M., & Papadaki, M. (2021). Towards a cross-cultural education framework for online safety awareness. [HTML]. *Information and Computer Security*, 29(4), 664–679. DOI: 10.1108/ICS-11-2020-0183

Heyik, M. A., Erdoğan, M., & Tong, T. (2023). Ostrakinda: A Game-Based Learning Toolkit for Ancient Mediterranean Cities. *ICONARP International Journal of Architecture and Planning*, 11(2), 838–865. DOI: 10.15320/ICONARP.2023.266

Hill, M., Salmon, D., Chudleigh, J., & Aitken, L. (2020). Practice nurses' perceptions of their immunization role and strategies used to promote measles, mumps, and rubella vaccine uptake in 2014 – 2018: A qualitative study. *Journal of Advanced Nursing*, 77(2), 948–956. DOI: 10.1111/jan.14652 PMID: 33222235

Hinterplattner, S., Skogø, J., & Sabitzer, B. (2019). *Beyond the game: Exploring winning strategies with gifted students. 2019-October*, 325–331. *Scopus.*, 40. Advance online publication. DOI: 10.34190/GBL.19.116

Hmelo, C. E., & Ferrari, M. (1997). The problem-based learning tutorial: Cultivating higher order thinking skills. *Journal for the Education of the Gifted*, 20(4), 401–422. DOI: 10.1177/016235329702000405

Hmelo-Silver, C. E. (2004). Problem-based learning: What and how do students learn? *Educational Psychology Review*, 16(3), 235–266. DOI: 10.1023/B:EDPR.0000034022.16470.f3

Hocutt, T. D., Sr. (2023). *Addressing the disparity of Black male educators Building capacity to mentor Black male youth*. ProQuest Dissertations & Theses. https// search.proquest.com/openview/091d9187fbeb1dc0b962e0049a8e0546/1?pq-origsite =gscholar&cbl=18750&diss=y

Hodijah, A. (2022). Application of gamification in ethnic excellence-based character education programs. [Journal of Art Design Art Education and Culture Studies]. *JADECS*, 7(2), 103. DOI: 10.17977/um037v7i22022p103-114

Hökkä, M., Rajala, M., Kaakinen, P., Lehto, J., & Pesonen, H. (2022). The effect of teaching methods in palliative care education for undergraduate nursing and medical students: A systematic review. *International Journal of Palliative Nursing*, 28(6), 245–253. DOI: 10.12968/ijpn.2022.28.6.245 PMID: 35727833

Hong, Y., Saab, N., & Admiraal, W. (2024). Approaches and game elements used to tailor digital gamification for learning: A systematic literature review. *Computers & Education*, 212, 105000. DOI: 10.1016/j.compedu.2024.105000

Hooshyar, D., Pedaste, M., Yang, Y., Malva, L., Hwang, G. J., Wang, M., Lim, H., & Delev, D. (2021). From gaming to computational thinking: An adaptive educational computer game-based learning approach. [HTML]. *Journal of Educational Computing Research*, 59(3), 383–409. DOI: 10.1177/0735633120965919

Hope, D., Grant, G., Rogers, G., & King, M. (2022). Gamification in pharmacy education: A systematic quantitative literature review. *International Journal of Pharmacy Practice*, 31(1), 15–31. DOI: 10.1093/ijpp/riac099 PMID: 36472962

Hosseini, M. (2023). Crossover design in triage education: The effectiveness of simulated interactive vs. routine training on student nurses' performance in a disaster situation. *BMC Research Notes*, 16(1), 313. Advance online publication. DOI: 10.1186/s13104-023-06596-5 PMID: 37926836

Hou, H. T. (2023). Learning science through cloud gamification: A framework for remote gamified science learning activities integrating cloud tool sets and three-dimensional scaffolding. *Information (Basel)*, 14(3), 165. DOI: 10.3390/info14030165

Hrefish, Z. A., & Al-Hadrawi, H. H. (2020). Emotional intelligence and work-related stress among nurses working in psychiatric hospitals. *Indian Journal of Forensic Medicine Toxicology*, 14(1), 1–5. DOI: 10.37506/ijfmt.v14i1.227

Hu, F., Lee, H., & Li, Y. (2021). Exploration of geriatric care competencies in registered nurses in hospitals. *The Journal of Nursing Research*, 29(4), e159. DOI: 10.1097/JNR.0000000000000441 PMID: 34034305

Hung, D., Tan, S. C., & Koh, T. S. (2006). Engaged learning: Making learning an authentic experience. *Engaged learning with emerging technologies*, 29-48.

Hung, D., Tan, S. C., & Koh, T. S. (2006). From traditional to constructivist epistemologies: A proposed theoretical framework based on activity theory for learning communities. *Journal of Interactive Learning Research*, 17(1), 37–55.

Hunicke, R., LeBlanc, M., & Zubek, R. (2004). MDA: A formal approach to game design and game research. Proceedings of the AAAI Workshop on Challenges in Game AI, Kan, J. W., & Gero, J. S. (2017). *Quantitative methods for studying design protocols*. Springer.

Huseinović, L. (2024). The effects of gamification on student motivation and achievement in learning English as a foreign language in higher education. *MAP Education and Humanities*, 4(1), 10–36. DOI: 10.53880/2744-2373.2023.4.10

Hussain, S., Qazi, S., Ahmed, R., Streimikiene, D., & Vveinhardt, J. (2018). Employees Management: Evidence from Gamification Techniques. *MONTENEGRIN JOURNAL OF ECONOMICS*, 14(4), 97–107. DOI: 10.14254/1800-5845/2018.14-4.7

Hutson, J., & Hutson, P. (2024). Immersive technologies. In Inclusive Smart Museums: Engaging Neurodiverse Audiences and Enhancing Cultural Heritage (pp. 153-228). Cham: Springer Nature Switzerland. [HTML] DOI: 10.1007/978-3-031-43615-4_5

Hu, Y. Z., Wei, H. T., & Chignell, M. (2023). Impact of rewards on cognitive game performance: Competition with peers increases enjoyment in easy, but not difficult tasks. [HTML]. *Computers in Human Behavior*, 149, 107952. DOI: 10.1016/j.chb.2023.107952

Hwang, J., & Choi, L. (2020). Having fun while receiving rewards?: Exploration of gamification in loyalty programs for consumer loyalty. *Journal of Business Research*, 106, 365–376. DOI: 10.1016/j.jbusres.2019.01.031

Ianole-Călin, R., Francioni, B., Masili, G., Druică, E., & Goschin, Z. (2020). A cross-cultural analysis of how individualism and collectivism impact collaborative consumption. [HTML]. *Resources, Conservation and Recycling*, 157, 104762. DOI: 10.1016/j.resconrec.2020.104762

İnangil, D., Dinçer, B., & Kabuk, A. (2022). Effectiveness of the use of animation and gamification in online distance education during pandemic. *Computers, Informatics, Nursing*, 40(5), 335–340. DOI: 10.1097/CIN.0000000000000902 PMID: 35266898

Indraganti, M. (2017). Enquiry-based learning workshop for deep learning in Middle Eastern classrooms – an action research approach. *Educational Action Research*, 26(4), 603–625. DOI: 10.1080/09650792.2017.1379423

Isangula, K., Pallangyo, E., & Ndirangu-Mugo, E. (2023). Improving nursing education curriculum as a tool for strengthening the nurse–client relationships in maternal and child healthcare: Insights from a human-centered design study in rural Tanzania. *Frontiers in Public Health*, 11, 1072721. Advance online publication. DOI: 10.3389/fpubh.2023.1072721 PMID: 36817890

Islam, Q., & Khan, S. M. F. A. (2024). Sustainability-infused learning environments: Investigating the role of digital technology and motivation for sustainability in achieving quality education. *International Journal of Learning. Teaching and Educational Research*, 23(1), 519–548.

Jabo, D., Borji, B., & Kant, S. (2024, February). Impact of Technical CRM on Ethiopia Bank Human-Computer Interface and Competitive Advantage as Mediators of Performance. In *2024 IEEE International Conference on Computing, Power and Communication Technologies (IC2PCT)* (Vol. 5, pp. 679-682). IEEE.

Jackson, R. (2019). *Becoming the educator they need Strategies, mindsets, and beliefs for supporting male Black and Latino students*. Google Books. https//books.google.com/books?hl=en&lr=&id=2tGlDwAAQBAJ&oi=fnd&pg=PP1&dq=black+male+educators&ots=SIR9wPgdI6&sig=yuTRwlxd5YE7DMiKUmITQ92dNVI

Jackson, L., & Dicks, T. (2024). A call to action Black male educators! It is your time A mixed methods study on beginning Black male educators' experiences in teacher preparation programs. *Research Square*. https//www.researchsquare.com/article/rs-4384546/latest

Jacobides, M. G., Dalbert, M. M. A., Trantopoulos, K., & Vassalos, V. (2024). The Business Value of Gamification. *California Management Review*, 66(2), 91–107. DOI: 10.1177/00081256231218469

Jacobs-Wingo, J., Schlegelmilch, J., Berliner, M., Airall-Simon, G., & Lang, W. (2018). Emergency preparedness training for hospital nursing staff, New York City, 2012–2016. *Journal of Nursing Scholarship*, 51(1), 81–87. DOI: 10.1111/jnu.12425 PMID: 30296004

Jainurakhma, J., Martina, I., Sekarini, S., Fanani, Q., & Nuraini, I. (2022). Nursing education resilience: The effective strategies to address the challenges of stakeholders during the covid-19 pandemic. *JAMP Jurnal Administrasi Dan Manajemen Pendidikan*, 5(2), 105–114. DOI: 10.17977/um027v5i22022p105

Jaskari, M. M. & Syrjälä, H. (2023). A mixed-methods study of marketing students' game-playing motivations and gamification elements. Journal of Marketing Education. sagepub.com

Jawabreh, R., & Bicen, H. (2020). Content analysis of articles that related to the use of google classroom and gamification in education from 2016 to 2020. *Near East University Online. Journal of Education*, 3(2), 53–65. DOI: 10.32955/neuje.v3i2.247

Jehanzeb, K. (2022). How perception of training impacts organizational citizenship behavior: Power distance as moderator. [HTML]. *Personnel Review*, 51(3), 922–944. DOI: 10.1108/PR-07-2020-0566

Jeter, F., & Melendez, J. (2022). Too few Black male educators. *Impacting Education Journal on Transforming Education*, 7(2), 134-145. https//eric.ed.gov/?id=EJ1345690

Jett, C., Savage, K., Ortiz, N., ... (2021). Black male mathematics educators speak Reflections from a symposium. *Journal of African American Males in Education*. https//jaamejournal.scholasticahq.com/article/29843.pdf

Jin, H., Dong, G., Zou, L., Shen, X., & Li, D. (2020). History and status quo of higher public health education in China. Public Health Reviews. springer.com

Ji, Y., Lee, H., Lee, T., Choi, M., Lee, H., Kim, S., Do, H. K., Kim, S., Chu, S. H., Park, J., Kim, Y. M., & Park, T. (2021). Developing an integrated curriculum for patient safety in an undergraduate nursing program: A case study. *BMC Nursing*, 20(1), 172. Advance online publication. DOI: 10.1186/s12912-021-00694-0 PMID: 34535121

Johnson, D., Deterding, S., Kuhn, K., Staneva, A., Stoyanov, S., & Hides, L. (2016). Gamification for health and wellbeing: A systematic review of the literature. *Internet Interventions : the Application of Information Technology in Mental and Behavioural Health*, 6, 89–106. DOI: 10.1016/j.invent.2016.10.002 PMID: 30135818

Johnson, Z. D., & LaBelle, S. (2017). An examination of teacher authenticity in the college classroom. *Communication Education*, 66(4), 423–439. DOI: 10.1080/03634523.2017.1324167

Jones, D. C., Jr. (2023). *Through their eyes Counter-narrative study of Black male educators*. ProQuest Dissertations & Theses. https//search.proquest.com/openview/74b7e1830d8c6cd5b0b725a04077820f/1?pq-origsite=gscholar&cbl=18750&diss=y

Jones, H. (2017). Humanizing the Online Experience Through Effective Use and Analysis of Discussion Forums. In *Handbook of Research on Humanizing the Distance Learning Experience* (pp. 334–363). IGI Global. DOI: 10.4018/978-1-5225-0968-4.ch015

Joshi, M., Manoj, L., Oludayo, O. O., Modiba, M. M., & Virendrakumar, C. B. (2012). Automated matchmaking of student skills and academic course requisites. *Proceedings of the CUBE International Information Technology Conference*, 514–519. DOI: 10.1145/2381716.2381814

Kabilan, M. K., Annamalai, N., & Chuah, K. M. (2023). Practices, purposes and challenges in integrating gamification using technology: A mixed-methods study on university academics. *Education and Information Technologies*, 28(11), 14249–14281. DOI: 10.1007/s10639-023-11723-7 PMID: 37361777

Kaed, E., Saany, S. I. A., Alhazmi, A. K., & Saif, G. (2023). A Model of Student Engagement in Online Learning. *Journal of Science and Technology*, 28(1), 38–52. DOI: 10.20428/jst.v28i1.2149

Kalogiannakis, M., Papadakis, S., & Zourmpakis, A. I. (2021). Gamification in science education. A systematic review of the literature. Education sciences. mdpi.com

Kalpokas, I. (2021). The Malleable Self: Immersion, Self-optimisation and Gamification. In *Malleable, Digital, and Posthuman* (pp. 47-76). Emerald Publishing Limited.

Kaneen, C. K., & Petrakis, E. G. (2020). Towards evaluating GDPR compliance in IoT applications. *Procedia Computer Science*, 176, 2989–2998. DOI: 10.1016/j.procs.2020.09.204

Kang, Y., Yang, I., Lee, E., & Bang, C. (2022). Development of international nursing standard–based curriculum for north Korean nurses. *International Nursing Review*, 69(4), 503–513. DOI: 10.1111/inr.12761 PMID: 35775835

Kant, S., & Adula, M. (2024). Human-Machine Interaction in the Metaverse in the Context of Ethiopia. In *Impact and Potential of Machine Learning in the Metaverse* (pp. 196–212). IGI Global., DOI: 10.4018/979-8-3693-5762-0.ch008

Kapp, K. M. (2012). *The gamification of learning and instruction: game-based methods and strategies for training and education*. John Wiley & Sons.

Kapp, K. M. (2013). *The gamification of learning and instruction fieldbook: Ideas into practice*. John Wiley & Sons.

Kapp, K. M. (2016). Gamification designs for instruction. In *Instructional-Design Theories and Models* (Vol. IV, pp. 367–400). Routledge.

Karkoub, M., Yang, C.-L., Karkoub, W., & Raslan, M. (2020). Undergraduate Cross-Class Research Projects for Deep Learning in Engineering Education. *Advances in Engineering Education*, 8(2), n2. DOI: 10.18260/3-1-1114-36024

Kashive, N., & Mohite, S. (2023). Use of gamification to enhance e-learning experience. *Interactive Technology and Smart Education*, 20(4), 554–575. DOI: 10.1108/ITSE-05-2022-0058

Kaya, O. S., & Ercag, E. (2023). The impact of applying challenge-based gamification program on students' learning outcomes: Academic achievement, motivation and flow. *Education and Information Technologies*, 28(8), 10053–10078. DOI: 10.1007/s10639-023-11585-z PMID: 36691635

Kew, S. N., & Tasir, Z. (2021). Analysing Students' Cognitive Engagement in E-Learning Discussion Forums through Content Analysis. *Knowledge Management & E-Learning*, 13(1), 39–57.

Khaldi, A., Bouzidi, R., & Nader, F. (2023). Gamification of e-learning in higher education: A systematic literature review. *Smart Learning Environments*, 10(1), 10. DOI: 10.1186/s40561-023-00227-z

Kharvari, F., & Höhl, W. (2019). The role of serious gaming using virtual reality applications for 3D architectural visualization. 2019 11th International Conference on Virtual Worlds and Games for Serious Applications (VS-Games), Kiang, D. (2014). Using gaming principles to engage students. *Edutopia. Recuperado de:http:// www. edutopia. org/blog/using-gaming-principles-engage-students-douglas-kiang*

Khoshkangini, R., Valetto, G., Marconi, A., & Pistore, M. (2020). Automatic generation and recommendation of personalized challenges for gamification. *User Modeling and User-Adapted Interaction*, 31(1), 1–34. DOI: 10.1007/s11257-019-09255-2

Khoshnoodifar, M., Ashouri, A., & Taheri, M. (2023). Effectiveness of gamification in enhancing learning and attitudes: A study of statistics education for health school students. *Journal of Advances in Medical Education & Professionalism*, 11(4), 230. PMID: 37901759

Kickmeier-Rust, M. (2023). Effects of gamifying mathematics lessons at high school level. *European Conference on Games Based Learning*, 17(1), 319-326. https://doi.org/DOI: 10.34190/ecgbl.17.1.1593

Killam, L., Timmermans, K., & Shapiro, S. (2021). Motivation and engagement of nursing students in 2 gamified courses. *Nurse Educator*, 46(6), E173–E178. DOI: 10.1097/NNE.0000000000001065 PMID: 34359066

Kim, S., Song, K., Lockee, B., Burton, J., Kim, S., Song, K., Lockee, B., & Burton, J. (2018). Theories for gamification in learning and education. *Gamification in Learning and Education: Enjoy Learning Like Gaming*, 39-47.

Kim, B., Lee, M., & Jang, S. (2021). Hospital nurses' empathy and moral sensitivity toward elderly care: A cross-sectional study. *Journal of Nursing Management*, 30(7), 2138–2146. DOI: 10.1111/jonm.13442 PMID: 34350659

Kimbrough-Scott, J. (2022). *Hiding in plain sight A phenomenological exploration of Black male educators in school leadership*. ProQuest Dissertations & Theses. https//search.proquest.com/openview/48003ef94e74f2dff62f85af2cb0f4ef/1?pq-origsite=gscholar&cbl=18750&diss=y

Kim, H., & Kim, B. (2022). Effects of situation-based flipped learning and gamification as combined methodologies in psychiatric nursing education: A quasi-experimental study. *Health Care*, 10(4), 644. DOI: 10.3390/healthcare10040644 PMID: 35455822

Kim, H., Lee, J., & Lee, E. (2021). Virtual experience of perioperative patients: Walking in the patients' shoes using virtual reality and blended learning. *International Journal of Environmental Research and Public Health*, 18(12), 6457. DOI: 10.3390/ijerph18126457 PMID: 34203661

Kim, J. T., & Lee, W. H. (2015). Dynamical model for gamification of learning (DMGL). *Multimedia Tools and Applications*, 74(19), 8483–8493. DOI: 10.1007/s11042-013-1612-8

Kimura, R., Matsunaga, M., Barroga, E., & Hayashi, N. (2023). Asynchronous e-learning with technology-enabled and enhanced training for continuing education of nurses: A scoping review. *BMC Medical Education*, 23(1), 505. Advance online publication. DOI: 10.1186/s12909-023-04477-w PMID: 37442970

Kiryakova, G., Angelova, N., & Yordanova, L. (2014). Gamification in education. Proceedings of 9th international Balkan education and science conference, Koster, R. (2013). *Theory of fun for game design.* " O'Reilly Media, Inc.".

Kline, T. J. (2005). *Psychological testing: A practical approach to design and evaluation.* Sage Publications. DOI: 10.4135/9781483385693

Klipfel, K. M. (2014). Authentic engagement: Assessing the effects of authenticity on student engagement and information literacy in academic library instruction. *RSR. Reference Services Review*, 42(2), 229–245. DOI: 10.1108/RSR-08-2013-0043

Klock, A. C. T., Gasparini, I., Pimenta, M. S., & Hamari, J. (2020). Tailored gamification: A review of literature. [sciencedirect.com]. *International Journal of Human-Computer Studies*, 144, 102495. DOI: 10.1016/j.ijhcs.2020.102495

Knight-Manuel, M. G., Marciano, J. E., Wilson, M., Jackson, I., Vernikoff, L., Zuckerman, K. G., & Watson, V. W. M. (2019). “It’s all possible” Urban educators’ perspectives on creating a culturally relevant, schoolwide, college-going culture for Black and Latino male students. *Urban Education*, 54(1), 3–27. DOI: 10.1177/0042085916651320

Koç, D., Seçkin, A. Ç., & Satı, Z. E. (2021). Evaluation of Participant Success in Gamified Drone Training Simulator Using Brain Signals and Key Logs. *Brain Sciences*, 11(8), 1024. DOI: 10.3390/brainsci11081024 PMID: 34439643

Kostolányová, K., & Klubal, L. (2018). Gamification in LMS courses. *International Journal of Information and Communication Technology Education*, 7(2), 46–50. DOI: 10.1515/ijicte-2018-0009

Krath, J., Schürmann, L., & Von Korflesch, H. F. O. (2021). Revealing the theoretical basis of gamification: A systematic review and analysis of theory in research on gamification, serious games and game-based …. Computers in Human Behavior. sciencedirect.com

Krath, J., Schürmann, L., & Von Korflesch, H. F. (2021). Revealing the theoretical basis of gamification: A systematic review and analysis of theory in research on gamification, serious games and game-based learning. *Computers in Human Behavior*, 125, 106963. DOI: 10.1016/j.chb.2021.106963

Lampropoulos, G., Keramopoulos, E., Diamantaras, K., & Evangelidis, G. (2022). Augmented reality and gamification in education: A systematic literature review of research, applications, and empirical studies. applied sciences, 12(13), 6809. mdpi.com

Lampropoulos, G., & Kinshuk, . (2024). Virtual reality and gamification in education: A systematic review. *Educational Technology Research and Development*, 72(3), 1–95. DOI: 10.1007/s11423-024-10351-3

Landers, R. N., Bauer, K. N., Callan, R. C., & Armstrong, M. B. (2015). Psychological theory and the gamification of learning. *Gamification in education and business*, 165-186.

Landers, R. N. (2014). Developing a theory of gamified learning: Linking serious games and gamification of learning. *Simulation & Gaming*, 45(6), 752–768. DOI: 10.1177/1046878114563660

Landers, R. N. (2019). Gamification misunderstood: How badly executed and rhetorical gamification obscures its transformative potential. *Journal of Management Inquiry*, 28(2), 137–140. DOI: 10.1177/1056492618790913

Landers, R. N., & Armstrong, M. B. (2015). Enhancing instructional outcomes with gamification: An empirical test of the Technology-Enhanced Training Effectiveness Model. *Computers in Human Behavior*, 71, 499–507. DOI: 10.1016/j.chb.2015.07.031

Landers, R. N., Bauer, K. N., & Callan, R. C. (2017). Gamification of task performance with leaderboards: A goal setting experiment. *Computers in Human Behavior*, 71, 508–515. DOI: 10.1016/j.chb.2015.08.008

Landers, R. N., & Callan, R. C. (2011). Casual social games as serious games: The psychology of gamification in undergraduate education and employee training. In *Serious games and edutainment applications* (pp. 399–423). Springer. DOI: 10.1007/978-1-4471-2161-9_20

Landers, R. N., & Sanchez, D. R. (2022). Game-based, gamified, and gamefully designed assessments for employee selection: Definitions, distinctions, design, and validation. [wiley.com]. *International Journal of Selection and Assessment*, 30(1), 1–13. DOI: 10.1111/ijsa.12376

Lavoué, E., Monterrat, B., Desmarais, M., & George, S. (2018). Adaptive gamification for learning environments. *IEEE Transactions on Learning Technologies*, 12(1), 16–28. DOI: 10.1109/TLT.2018.2823710

Lawrie, S. I., Eom, K., Moza, D., Gavreliuc, A., & Kim, H. S. (2020). Cultural variability in the association between age and well-being: The role of uncertainty avoidance. [sagepub.com]. *Psychological Science*, 31(1), 51–64. DOI: 10.1177/0956797619887348 PMID: 31850828

Lee, D. (2024). *Black male early career educators in secondary science classrooms Rewriting narratives of successful teaching*. Georgia State University. https// scholarworks.gsu.edu/mse_diss/164/

Leite, R. M. C., Alves, L. R. G., Da Silva Paes Cardoso, L., & Neto, H. M. M. (2023). How Has Gamification in the Production Sector Been Developed in the Manufacturing and Construction Workplaces? *Buildings*, 13(10), 2614. DOI: 10.3390/buildings13102614

Lester, D., Skulmoski, G., Fisher, D., Mehrotra, V., Lim, I., Lang, A., & Keogh, J. (2023). Drivers and barriers to the utilisation of gamification and game-based learning in universities: A systematic review of educators' perspectives. *British Journal of Educational Technology*, 54(6), 1748–1770. DOI: 10.1111/bjet.13311

Lewis, R. K. (2013). *Architect?: a candid guide to the profession*. Mit Press.

Lewis, Z. H., Swartz, M. C., & Lyons, E. J. (2016). What's the point?: A review of reward systems implemented in gamification interventions. *Games for Health Journal*, 5(2), 93–99. DOI: 10.1089/g4h.2015.0078 PMID: 26812253

Li, W., Xiao, J. X., & Zhang, M. T. (2024, June). Optimizing Urban e-Commerce Experiences: A Cross-Cultural Interface Design Approach for Enhanced Connectivity and Consumer Engagement. In International Conference on Human-Computer Interaction (pp. 219-234). Cham: Springer Nature Switzerland. [HTML] DOI: 10.1007/978-3-031-60441-6_15

Lilia, R., & Elena, T. (2019). Gamification is a field landmark in educational research. *Journal of language and education, 5*(3 (19)), 4-10.

Li, M., Ma, S., & Shi, Y. (2023). Examining the effectiveness of gamification as a tool promoting teaching and learning in educational settings: A meta-analysis. *Frontiers in Psychology*, 14, 1253549. DOI: 10.3389/fpsyg.2023.1253549 PMID: 37876838

Li, M., Qin, G., & Li, Y. (2022). Mediating effects of emotional intelligence on the relationship between empathy and humanistic care ability in nursing students: A cross-sectional descriptive study. *Medicine*, 101(46), e31673. DOI: 10.1097/MD.0000000000031673 PMID: 36401377

Li, M., Wang, Y., Wu, Y., & Liu, H. (2021). Gamification narrative design as a predictor for mobile fitness app user persistent usage intentions: A goal priming perspective. [HTML]. *Enterprise Information Systems*, 15(10), 1501–1545. DOI: 10.1080/17517575.2021.1941272

Lindberg, S. (2019). Gamification for self-directed learning in higher education. In *EDULEARN19 Proceedings* (pp. 1764-1773). IATED. DOI: 10.21125/edulearn.2019.0507

Li, Q., Bu, Z., Xue, M., Huang, A., Tu, W., & Xu, G. (2022). Visual analysis of research hotspots in geriatric nursing education in China and abroad. *Journal of Healthcare Engineering*, 2022, 1–7. DOI: 10.1155/2022/7472188 PMID: 35480150

Lister, C., West, J. H., Cannon, B., Sax, T., & Brodegard, D. (2014). Just a fad? Gamification in health and fitness apps. *JMIR Serious Games*, 2(2), e9. DOI: 10.2196/games.3413 PMID: 25654660

Liu, L., Ross, H., & Ariyawardana, A. (2020). Community development through supply chain responsibility: A case study of rice supply chains and connected rural communities in Central China. Sustainability. mdpi.com

Liu, R. Z., Benitez, J., Zhang, L., Shao, Z., & Mi, J. N. (2024). Exploring the influence of gamification-enabled customer experience on continuance intention towards digital platforms for e-government: An empirical …. Information & Management. sciencedirect.com

Liu, G. Z., Fathi, J., & Rahimi, M. (2024). Using digital gamification to improve language achievement, foreign language enjoyment, and ideal L2 self: A case of English as a foreign language learners. *Journal of Computer Assisted Learning*, 40(4), 1347–1364. DOI: 10.1111/jcal.12954

Liu, T., Oubibi, M., Zhou, Y., & Fute, A. (2023). Research on online teachers' training based on the gamification design: A survey analysis of primary and secondary school teachers. *Heliyon*, 9(4), e15053. DOI: 10.1016/j.heliyon.2023.e15053 PMID: 37082639

Looyestyn, J., Kernot, J., Boshoff, K., Ryan, J., Edney, S., & Maher, C. (2017). Does gamification increase engagement with online programs? A systematic review. *PLoS One*, 12(3), e0173403. DOI: 10.1371/journal.pone.0173403 PMID: 28362821

Lopes, A. P., Soler, M., Caña, R., Cortés, L., Bentabol, M., Bentabol, A., Muñoz, M. M., Esteban, A., & Luna, M. J. (2019, Jul 01-03). Gamification In Education And Active Methodologies At Higher Education. *Edulearn Proceedings* [Edulearn19: 11th international conference on education and new learning technologies]. 11th International Conference on Education and New Learning Technologies (EDULEARN), Palma, SPAIN. DOI: 10.21125/edulearn.2019.0480

Lopes, R., Tavares, R., & Mesquita, C. (2015, November 13). TimeCraX: Time-travelling to learn history. *Conference: SBGames 2015 - XIV Simpósio Brasileiro de Jogos e Entretenimento Digital.* SBGames 2015.

Lowry, P. B., Petter, S., & Leimeister, J. M. (2020). Desperately seeking the artefacts and the foundations of native theory in gamification research: Why information systems researchers can play a legitimate role in this discourse and how they can better contribute. [tandfonline.com]. *European Journal of Information Systems*, 29(6), 609–620. DOI: 10.1080/0960085X.2020.1841574

Luarn, P., Chen, C. C., & Chiu, Y. P. (2023). Enhancing intrinsic learning motivation through gamification: A self-determination theory perspective. [HTML]. *The International Journal of Information and Learning Technology*, 40(5), 413–424. DOI: 10.1108/IJILT-07-2022-0145

Luokkamäki, S., Härkänen, M., Saano, S., Kokkonen, K., & Vehviläinen-Julkunen, K. (2023). Registered nurses' experiences of using a 3d game in the development of clinical competency: A qualitative study. *Journal of Medical Education*, 22(1). Advance online publication. DOI: 10.5812/jme-129060

Luo, Z. (2022). Gamification for educational purposes: What are the factors contributing to varied effectiveness? *Education and Information Technologies*, 27(1), 891–915. DOI: 10.1007/s10639-021-10642-9

Lu, Y., & Shorey, S. (2021). Nurses' perceptions of emotional intelligence in the clinical setting: A qualitative systematic review. *Journal of Nursing Management*, 29(8), 2453–2460. DOI: 10.1111/jonm.13406 PMID: 34216499

Lynch, P., Singal, N., & Francis, G. A. (2024). Educational technology for learners with disabilities in primary school settings in low-and middle-income countries: A systematic literature review. *Educational Review*, 76(2), 405–431. DOI: 10.1080/00131911.2022.2035685

Mace, K. (2005). Vygotsky's social development theory. Encyclopedia of Educational Technology.

MacKinnon, R. J., Stoeter, R., Doherty, C., Fullwood, C., Cheng, A., Nadkarni, V., Stenfors-Hayes, T., & Chang, T. P. (2015). Self-motivated learning with gamification improves infant CPR performance, a randomised controlled trial. *BMJ Simulation & Technology Enhanced Learning*, 1(3), 71–76. DOI: 10.1136/bmjstel-2015-000061 PMID: 35515202

Magylaitė, K., Kapočius, K., Butleris, R., & Čeponienė, L. (2022). Towards High Usability in Gamified Systems: A Systematic Review of Key Concepts and Approaches. Applied Sciences. mdpi.com

Magylaitė, K., Kapočius, K., Butleris, R., & Čeponienė, L. (2022). Towards High Usability in Gamified Systems: A Systematic Review of Key Concepts and Approaches. *Applied Sciences (Basel, Switzerland)*, 12(16), 8188. DOI: 10.3390/app12168188

Malik, G., McKenna, L., & Griffiths, D. (2015). An analysis of evidence-based practice curriculum integration in Australian undergraduate nursing programs. *GSTF Journal of Nursing and Health Care*, 3(1). Advance online publication. DOI: 10.5176/2345-718X_3.1.104

Malm, B. (2008). Authenticity in teachers' lives and work: Some philosophical and empirical considerations. *Scandinavian Journal of Educational Research*, 52(4), 373–386. DOI: 10.1080/00313830802184525

Mandujano, G. G., Riar, M., Morschheuser, B., & Hamari, J. (2023). Gamification as a Catalyst to the Circular Economy. In *The Routledge Handbook of Catalysts for a Sustainable Circular Economy* (pp. 312–336). Routledge. DOI: 10.4324/9781003267492-18

Mariati, L., Jakri, Y., & Djerubu, D. (2022). The effect of emotional intelligence on nurse's communication skill. [Journal of Ners and Midwifery]. *Jurnal Ners Dan Kebidanan*, 9(2), 218–226. DOI: 10.26699/jnk.v9i2.ART.p218-226

Marín, J. A. M., Soto, M. N. C., Navas-Parejo, M. R., & García, G. G. (2021). Gamification as a Motivational and Socio-educational Resource in Classrooms with Students at Risk of Social Exclusion. International Conference in Methodologies and intelligent Systems for Techhnology Enhanced Learning, Maslow, A. H. (1969). A theory of human motivation. *Classics of organization theory*, 167-178.

Marks, S. (2022). Creating systems of support for Black educators through the Black Educator Teacher Residency Program. *Multicultural Education*, 29(3), 20–29. https//search.proquest.com/openview/f0929f8e1dd0ac0ddcd997c42632bdd1/1?pq-origsite=gscholar&cbl=33246

Marques, C. G., Pedro, J. P., & Araújo, I. (2023). A systematic literature review of gamification in/for cultural heritage: Leveling up, going beyond. Heritage. mdpi.com

Mashau, P., & Farisani, T. R. (Eds.). (2023). *Accessibility of Digital Higher Education in the Global South*. IGI Global. DOI: 10.4018/978-1-6684-9179-9

Matallaoui, A., Hanner, N., & Zarnekow, R. (2017). Introduction to gamification: Foundation and underlying theories. *Gamification: Using game elements in serious contexts*, 3-18.

Mathew, J., & Nair, S. (2024). *Level up your learning: The power of gamification*. Nova Science Publishers. DOI: 10.52305/UIFH5384

Mathews, J. D. W. (2019). *I don't wanna teach no more Everyday struggles and stereotypes of the Black male educator misunderstood*. ProQuest Dissertations & Theses. https//search.proquest.com/openview/566ffe40531b12c684c97db4a6d128ca/1?pq-origsite=gscholar&cbl=18750&diss=y

Mathwasa, J., & Sibanda, L. (2021). Male educator recruitment in early childhood centres Implications for teacher education. In *Teacher Education-New Perspectives* (pp. 103–116). Google Books., https//books.google.com/books?hl=en&lr=&id=_bdFEAAAQBAJ&oi=fnd&pg=PA103&dq=black+male+educators&ots=_qW4Z1NYWV&sig=8nhMKXIOoEMMiZH6A-w9Z0YK4T8 DOI: 10.5772/intechopen.97085

Mayer, R. E. (2016). What Should Be the Role of Computer Games in Education? *Policy Insights from the Behavioral and Brain Sciences*, 3(1), 20–26. DOI: 10.1177/2372732215621311

Mayer, R. E. (2019). Computer Games in Education. *Annual Review of Psychology*, 70(1), 531–549. DOI: 10.1146/annurev-psych-010418-102744 PMID: 30231003

Mayfield, F. M. (2022). Black men in a Southern urban school of education An analysis of motivating factors for Black men as aspirant educators. *The Journal of Equity in Behavioral Health Therapy*, 5(1), 35–49. https//journals.auctr.edu/index.php/jebht/article/view/443

Mayo, M. J. (2009). Video games: A route to large-scale STEM education? *Science*, 323(5910), 79–82. DOI: 10.1126/science.1166900 PMID: 19119223

McClure, J. W. (2001). Developing language skills and learner autonomy in international postgraduates. *ELT Journal*, 55(2), 142–148. DOI: 10.1093/elt/55.2.142

McDermott, R., Zarb, M., Daniels, M., Nylén, A., Pears, A., Isomöttönen, V., & Caspersen, M. (2017, October). The authenticity of 'authentic ' assessment of some faculty perceptions. In *2017 IEEE Frontiers in Education Conference (FIE)* (pp. 1-9). IEEE.

McFarlane, A., Sparrowhawk, A., & Heald, Y. (2002). *Report on the educational use of games*. TEEM (Teachers evaluating educational multimedia), Cambridge.

McLaren, H., Patmisari, E., Hamiduzzaman, M., Jones, M., & Taylor, R. (2021). Respect for religiosity: Review of faith integration in health and wellbeing interventions with Muslim minorities. [mdpi.com]. *Religions*, 12(9), 692. DOI: 10.3390/rel12090692

Meaning, C. E. (2024). 176 I. Araújo Gamification Gamification was firstly defined as" the use of game design elements in non-game contexts"(Deterding, et al., 2011 p. 9). This definition is the basis for many others that have emerged, adapting their characteristics to each context. For education context we got the Karl Kapp definition:" gamification is using game-based mechanics. In International Conference on Lifelong Education and Leadership for All (ICLEL 2023) (Vol. 17, p. 175). Springer Nature. [HTML]

Mellado, R., & Cubillos, C. (2024). Gamification improves learning: Experience in a training activity of computer programming in higher education. *Journal of Computer Assisted Learning*, 40(4), 1959–1973. DOI: 10.1111/jcal.13000

Menberu, A. W. (2024). Technology-mediated financial education in developing countries: A systematic literature review. *Cogent Business & Management*, 11(1), 2294879. DOI: 10.1080/23311975.2023.2294879

Mendieta, C. H. A., Jara, J. P. C., Taco, C. E. C., Sánchez, R. P. S., & Pumagualle, M. L.-R. V. (2023). Innovative Educational Technology: The Impact of an Interactive Video Game on History Teaching for Basic Education Students and its Link to Cultural Identity in Migration Contexts. [Scopus.]. *Migration Letters : An International Journal of Migration Studies*, 20, 475–490.

Mersin, S., Kilic, H., & İbrahimoğlu, Ö. (2020). Learning outcomes of nursing curriculum in turkey: A cross-sectional study. *Frontiers of Nursing*, 7(2), 129–134. DOI: 10.2478/fon-2020-0011

Messner, W. (2021). Connections between cultures: Using empirical distributions for measuring cultural differences. [HTML]. *Journal of Cross-Cultural Psychology*, 52(2), 129–154. DOI: 10.1177/0022022120982370

Mhlongo, S., Mbatha, K., Ramatsetse, B., & Dlamini, R. (2023). Challenges, opportunities, and prospects of adopting and using smart digital technologies in learning environments: An iterative review. *Heliyon*, 9(6), e16348. DOI: 10.1016/j.heliyon.2023.e16348 PMID: 37274691

MiHoYo. (2023). *Honkai Star Rail [PC, PlayStation 4, PlayStation 5]*. Honkai Star Rail [PC, PlayStation 4, PlayStation 5]. https://hsr.hoyoverse.com/pt-pt/

Milenkova, V. & Lendzhova, V. (2021). Digital citizenship and digital literacy in the conditions of social crisis. Computers. mdpi.com

Miller, A. S., Cafazzo, J. A., & Seto, E. (2014). A game plan: Gamification design principles in mHealth applications for chronic disease management. *Health Informatics Journal*, 22(2), 184–193. DOI: 10.1177/1460458214537511 PMID: 24986104

Mokoena, S. (2013). Engagement with and participation in online discussion Forums. *Turkish Online Journal of Educational Technology-TOJET*, 12(2), 97–105.

Monteiro, F., & Sousa, A. (2024). Pedagogical innovation to captivate students to ethics education in engineering. *Journal of Applied Research in Higher Education*, 16(4), 1029–1041. DOI: 10.1108/JARHE-02-2023-0056

Moseikina, M., Toktamysov, S., & Danshina, S. (2022). Modern technologies and gamification in historical education. *Simulation & Gaming*, 53(2), 135–156. DOI: 10.1177/10468781221075965

Mousavi, S., Hassanvand, P., Mahmoudi, A., Hosseinigolafshani, S. Z., Rajabi, M., & Rashvand, F. (2023). The relationship between emotional intelligence and the moral performance of nurses. *Journal of Nursing and Midwifery Sciences*, 10(4). Advance online publication. DOI: 10.5812/jnms-141609

Mulcahy, R. F., McAndrew, R., Russell-Bennett, R., & Iacobucci, D. (2021). "Game on!" Pushing consumer buttons to change sustainable behavior: A gamification field study. [HTML]. *European Journal of Marketing*, 55(10), 2593–2619. DOI: 10.1108/EJM-05-2020-0341

Murray, J., & Summerlee, A. (2007). The Impact of Problem-Based Learning in an Interdisciplinary First-Year Program on Student Learning Behaviour. *Canadian Journal of Higher Education*, 37(3), 87–107.

Mustafa, A. S., Ali, N., Dhillon, J. S., & Sedera, D. (2023). An Integrated Model for Evaluating the Sustainability of Gamified Mobile Health Apps: An Instrument Development and Validation. *Health Care*, 11(7), 1051. DOI: 10.3390/healthcare11071051 PMID: 37046978

Nam, H. & Kannan, P. K. (2020). Digital environment in global markets: Cross-cultural implications for evolving customer journeys. Journal of International Marketing. sagepub.com

Nasirzadeh, E., & Fathian, M. (2020). Investigating the effect of gamification elements on bank customers to personalize gamified systems. [HTML]. *International Journal of Human-Computer Studies*, 143, 102469. DOI: 10.1016/j.ijhcs.2020.102469

Nelson, D. D. (2023). *African American male educators' lived experiences as students and educators The measure of a man*. ProQuest Dissertations & Theses. https//search.proquest.com/openview/6834a754400bf885d57c683faa874501/1?pq-origsite=gscholar&cbl=18750&diss=y

Nelson, V. T. F. (2020). *Recruiting and retaining Black male math educators in middle and high schools in the United States*. ProQuest Dissertations & Theses. https//search.proquest.com/openview/f0777df6361a40c31eeede296aca43f0/1?pq-origsite=gscholar&cbl=44156

Nevid, J. S. (2007). *Psychology: Concepts and applications*. Houghton, Mifflin and Company.

Nicholson, S. (2015). A recipe for meaningful gamification. *Gamification in education and business*, 1-20.

Noorbehbahani, F., & Salehi, F. (2021). A serious game to extract Hofstede's cultural dimensions at the individual level. [HTML]. *User Modeling and User-Adapted Interaction*, 31(2), 225–259. DOI: 10.1007/s11257-020-09280-6

Noran, O. (2016, February). On gamification in action learning. In *Proceedings of the Australasian Computer Science Week Multiconference* (pp. 1-9).

Nunes, V. A. (2022). *Descobrindo o passado: O uso do rpg digital como artefato para mobilizar o conceito de empatia histórica*. Universidade do estado do Rio de Janeiro 2022.

Nursing and Midwifery Council. (2023). Standards for pre-registration nursing programmes. Link: https://www.nmc.org.uk/globalassets/sitedocuments/standards/2024/standards-for-pre-registration-nursing-programmes.pdf

Nyoach, T. D., Lemi, K., Debela, T., & Kant, S. (2024). Does Organizational Commitment Mediate the Relationship among Employee Relationship Management and Bank Performance? The Case of Banks in Ethiopia. *International Journal of Organizational Leadership*, 13(2), 355–376. DOI: 10.33844/ijol.2024.60419

O'Connor, S., Jolliffe, S., Stanmore, E., Renwick, L., & Booth, R. (2018). Social media in nursing and midwifery education: A mixed study systematic review. *Journal of Advanced Nursing*, 74(10), 2273–2289. DOI: 10.1111/jan.13799 PMID: 30019486

Oakes, J., & Guiton, G. (1995). Matchmaking: The Dynamics of High School Tracking Decisions. *American Educational Research Journal*, 32(1), 3–33. DOI: 10.3102/00028312032001003

Oak, J. (2018). A systematic literature review on utilization of gamification in nursing. *International Journal of Advanced Nursing Education and Research*, 3(1), 43–48. DOI: 10.21742/IJANER.2018.3.1.08

O'Brien, H. L., Roll, I., Kampen, A., & Davoudi, N. (2022). Rethinking (Dis) engagement in human-computer interaction. Computers in human behavior. sciencedirect.com

Ohito, E. O. (2021). How to be an antiracist teacher educator in the United States A sketch of a Black male pedagogic provocateur. *Teaching and Teacher Education*, 105, 103448. https//www.sciencedirect.com/science/article/pii/S0742051X20314268. DOI: 10.1016/j.tate.2020.103235

Oke, A. E., Aliu, J., Tunji-Olayeni, P., & Abayomi, T. (2023). Application of gamification for sustainable construction: An evaluation of the challenges. *Construction Innovation*, 24(4), 1066–1084. DOI: 10.1108/CI-09-2022-0247

Okeke, C. I., & Nyanhoto, E. (2021). Recruitment and retention of male educators in preschools Implications for teacher education policy and practices. *South African Journal of Education*, 41(3), 1–11. https//www.ajol.info/index.php/saje/article/view/209358. DOI: 10.15700/saje.v41n2a1910

Oliveira, R. P., Souza, C. G., Reis, A. C., & Souza, W. M. (2021). Gamification in e-learning and sustainability: A theoretical framework. Sustainability. mdpi.com

Oliveira, W., Hamari, J., Joaquim, S., Toda, A. M., Palomino, P. T., Vassileva, J., & Isotani, S. (2022). The effects of personalized gamification on students' flow experience, motivation, and enjoyment. [springer.com]. *Smart Learning Environments*, 9(1), 16. DOI: 10.1186/s40561-022-00194-x

Oliveira, W., Hamari, J., Shi, L., Toda, A. M., Rodrigues, L., Palomino, P. T., & Isotani, S. (2023). Tailored gamification in education: A literature review and future agenda. [springer.com]. *Education and Information Technologies*, 28(1), 373–406. DOI: 10.1007/s10639-022-11122-4

Olugbara, O. O., Joshi, M., Modiba, M. M., & Bhavsar, V. C. (2015). *Automated Matchmaking to Improve Accuracy of Applicant Selection for University Education System* (arXiv:1507.02439). arXiv. https://doi.org//arXiv.1507.02439DOI: 10.48550

ONeill, K., Robb, M., Kennedy, R., Bhattacharya, A., Dominici, N. R., & Murphy, A. (2018). Mobile Technology, Just-in-Time Learning and Gamification: Innovative Strategies for a CAUTI Education Program. *On-Line Journal of Nursing Informatics*, 22(2).

Onjewu, A. K. E., Godwin, E. S., Azizsafaei, F., & Appiah, D. (2024). The influence of technology use on learning skills among generation Z: A gender and cross-country analysis. *Industry and Higher Education*, •••, 09504222241263227. DOI: 10.1177/09504222241263227

Oo, B. L., & Lim, B. T.-H. (2016). Game-based learning in construction management courses: A case of bidding game. *Engineering, Construction, and Architectural Management*, 23(1), 4–19. DOI: 10.1108/ECAM-02-2015-0029

Ouariachi, T., Li, C. Y., & Elving, W. J. L. (2020). Gamification approaches for education and engagement on pro-environmental behaviors: Searching for best practices. Sustainability. mdpi.com

Ouariachi, T., Li, C., & Elving, W. J. L. (2020). Gamification Approaches for Education and Engagement on Pro-Environmental Behaviors: Searching for Best Practices. *Sustainability (Basel)*, 12(11), 4565. DOI: 10.3390/su12114565

Ozdamli, F., & Milrich, F. (2023). Positive and negative impacts of gamification on the fitness industry. *European Journal of Investigation in Health, Psychology and Education*, 13(8), 1411–1422. DOI: 10.3390/ejihpe13080103 PMID: 37623300

Özdemir, İ., & Kadıoğlu, H. (2023). A curriculum development project for a school nursing certification program in turkey: A Delphi study. *Clinical and Experimental Health Sciences*, 13(1), 122–128. DOI: 10.33808/clinexphealthsci.1060107

Özhan, Ş. Ç., & Kocadere, S. A. (2020). The effects of flow, emotional engagement, and motivation on success in a gamified online learning environment. [HTML]. *Journal of Educational Computing Research*, 57(8), 2006–2031. DOI: 10.1177/0735633118823159

Özkar, M. (2007). Learning by doing in the age of design computation. Computer-Aided Architectural Design Futures (CAADFutures) 2007: Proceedings of the 12th International CAADFutures Conference, Palócz, K., & Katona, V. (2021). The Applicability Of Gamification In Architectural Design Education. *Symmetry-Culture and Science, 32*(4), 489-505. https://doi.org/DOI: 10.26830/symmetry_2021_4_489

Paiva, J. C., Leal, J. P., & Queirós, R. (2020). Fostering Programming Practice through Games. *Information (Basel)*, 11(11), 498. DOI: 10.3390/info11110498

Paliokas, I., Patenidis, A. T., Mitsopoulou, E. E., Tsita, C., Pehlivanides, G., Karyati, E., Tsafaras, S., Stathopoulos, E. A., Kokkalas, A., Diplaris, S., Meditskos, G., Vrochidis, S., Tasiopoulou, E., Riggas, C., Votis, K., Kompatsiaris, I., & Tzovaras, D. (2020). A gamified augmented reality application for digital heritage and tourism. [mdpi.com]. *Applied Sciences (Basel, Switzerland)*, 10(21), 7868. DOI: 10.3390/app10217868

Palmquist, A., Jedel, I., & Goethe, O. (2024). Design Implications and Processes for an Attainable Game Experience. In *Universal Design in Video Games: Active Participation Through Accessible Play* (pp. 67–97). Springer International Publishing. [HTML] DOI: 10.1007/978-3-031-30595-5_3

Panigrahi, A., Pati, A., Sahu, B., Das, M. N., Nayak, D. S. K., Sahoo, G., & Kant, S. (2023). En-MinWhale: An ensemble approach based on MRMR and Whale optimization for Cancer diagnosis. *IEEE Access : Practical Innovations, Open Solutions*, 11, 113526–113542. DOI: 10.1109/ACCESS.2023.3318261

Papastergiou, M. (2009). Digital game-based learning in high school computer science education impacts educational effectiveness and student motivation. *Computers & Education*, 52(1), 1–12. DOI: 10.1016/j.compedu.2008.06.004

Parkerson, R. (2023). Five key areas to consider before using gamification in learning and development. *Strategic HR Review*, 22(4), 115–120. DOI: 10.1108/SHR-01-2023-0005

Park, K., Cha, M., Kwak, H., & Chen, K.-T. (2017). Achievement and friends: Key factors of player retention vary across player levels in online multiplayer games. Proceedings of the 26th international conference on world wide web companion, Pedreira, O., García, F., Brisaboa, N., & Piattini, M. (2015). Gamification in software engineering–A systematic mapping. *Information and Software Technology*, 57, 157–168.

Park, S., & Kim, S. (2021). Is sustainable online learning possible with gamification?—The effect of gamified online learning on student learning. *Sustainability (Basel)*, 13(8), 4267. DOI: 10.3390/su13084267

Passalacqua, M., Sénécal, S., Frédette, M., Nacke, L. E., Pellerin, R., & Léger, P.-M. (2021). Should Gamification be Personalized? A Self- deterministic Approach. *AIS Transactions on Human-Computer Interaction*, •••, 265–286. DOI: 10.17705/1thci.00150

Patricio, R. (2017). A gamified approach for engaging teams in corporate innovation and entrepreneurship. *World Journal of Science Technology and Sustainable Development*, 14(2/3), 254–262. DOI: 10.1108/WJSTSD-10-2016-0057

Paul, J., Akbari, M., Mondal, S., & Das, S. (2024). Knowledge sharing leads to engagement during Covid-19 for online gamers. [HTML]. *Information & Management*, 61(4), 103948. DOI: 10.1016/j.im.2024.103948

Paulsen, K. (2021). Integrated storytelling by design: Concepts, principles and methods for new narrative dimensions. [HTML]

Perez-Aranda, J., Medina-Claros, S., & Urrestarazu-Capellán, R. (2024). Effects of a collaborative and gamified online learning methodology on class and test emotions. *Education and Information Technologies*, 29(2), 1823–1855. DOI: 10.1007/s10639-023-11879-2 PMID: 37361848

Perrenet, J. C., Bouhuijs, P. A., & Smits, J. G. (2000). The suitability of problem-based learning for engineering education: Theory and practice. *Teaching in Higher Education*, 5(3), 345–358. DOI: 10.1080/713699144

Phuong, T. T. K., & Tran, T. V. (2020). Job Satisfaction, Employee Loyalty and Job Performance in the Hospitality Industry: A Moderated Model. *Asian Economic and Financial Review*, 10(6), 698–713. DOI: 10.18488/journal.aefr.2020.106.698.713

Piaget, J. (1954). *The Construction of Reality in the Child.* Basic Books. DOI: 10.1037/11168-000

Pinto, R. D., Peixoto, B., Melo, M., Cabral, L., & Bessa, M. (2021). Foreign language learning gamification using virtual reality—a systematic review of empirical research. Education Sciences. mdpi.com

Pinto, R., Filgueiras, E., & Moutinho, K. (2020). Emotional design and gamification in educational processes: predictor model to increase video game efficiency. In Design, User Experience, and Usability. Case Studies in Public and Personal Interactive Systems: 9th International Conference, DUXU 2020, Held as Part of the 22nd HCI International Conference, HCII 2020, Copenhagen, Denmark, July 19–24, 2020 [Springer International Publishing.]. *Proceedings*, 22(Part III), 506–517.

Pishchanska, V., Altukhova, A., Prusak, Y., Kovmir, N., & Goncharov, A. (2022). Gamification of education: Innovative forms of teaching and education in culture and art. *Eduweb*, 16(2), 119–133. DOI: 10.46502/issn.1856-7576/2022.16.02.8

Polat, E. (2023). Gamification implementation for educational purposes: A scoping review (2013-2018). *Educational Technology Quarterly*, 2023(3), 367–400. DOI: 10.55056/etq.589

Prensky, M. (2005). Computer games and learning: Digital game-based learning. *Handbook of computer game studies, 18*(2005), 97-122.

Prensky, M. (2003). Digital game-based learning. [CIE]. *Computers in Entertainment*, 1(1), 21–21. DOI: 10.1145/950566.950596

Puni, A. & Hilton, S. K. (2020). Power distance culture and whistleblowing intentions: the moderating effect of gender. International Journal of Ethics and Systems. [HTML]

Puspitasari, I., & Arifin, S. (2023). Implementation of gamification on learning motivation: A meta-analysis study. *International Journal of Progressive Sciences and Technologies*, 40(1), 356. DOI: 10.52155/ijpsat.v40.1.5596

Qian, M., & Clark, K. R. (2016). Game-based Learning and 21st century skills: A review of recent research. *Computers in Human Behavior*, 63, 50–58. DOI: 10.1016/j.chb.2016.05.023

Qi, X., Sun, G., & Yue, L. (2023). Applying Self-Optimised Feedback to a Learning Management System for Facilitating Personalised Learning Activities on Massive Open Online Courses. *Sustainability (Basel)*, 15(16), 12562. DOI: 10.3390/su151612562

Qureshi, H. (2019). Collaborative architectural design studio environment: An experiment in the studio of Architectural Design-I. *Archnet-IJAR: International Journal of Architectural Research*, 14(2), 303–324. DOI: 10.1108/ARCH-12-2018-0049

Rabah, J., Cassidy, R., & Beauchemin, R. (2018). Gamification in education: Real benefits or edutainment. 17th European Conference on e-Learning, Athens, Greece, Reinhart, C. F., Dogan, T., Ibarra, D., & Samuelson, H. W. (2012). Learning by playing–teaching energy simulation as a game. *Journal of Building Performance Simulation*, 5(6), 359–368.

Rabbi, M., Pfammatter, A., Zhang, M., Spring, B., & Choudhury, T. (2015). Automated Personalized Feedback for Physical Activity and Dietary Behavior Change With Mobile Phones: A Randomized Controlled Trial on Adults. *JMIR mHealth and uHealth*, 3(2), e42. DOI: 10.2196/mhealth.4160 PMID: 25977197

Ramos, D. K., & Segundo, F. R. (2018). Jogos Digitais na Escola: Aprimorando a atenção e a flexibilidade cognitiva. *Educação & Realidade*. https://doi.org/DOI: 10.1590/2175-623665738

Ranjan, S., & Tyagi, M. (2022). Designing a gamification algorithm for language learning application. *2022 2nd International Conference on Innovative Practices in Technology and Management (ICIPTM), 7*, 496–502. DOI: 10.1109/ICIPTM54933.2022.9754177

Rankin, Y. A., McNeal, M., Shute, M. W., & Gooch, B. (2008). User centered game design: Evaluating massive multiplayer online role playing games for second language acquisition. *Proceedings of the 2008 ACM SIGGRAPH Symposium on Video Games*, 43–49. DOI: 10.1145/1401843.1401851

Ransaw, T. S. (2022). *Mindful teaching practices for Black male achievement A student-focused guide for educators*. Google Books. https//books.google.com/books?hl=en&lr=&id=0CmgEAAAQBAJ&oi=fnd&pg=PP1&dq=black+male+educators&ots=-HesxdpR5s&sig=NZq5SEWdrQulagHXPv6WJBptIsY

Rau, P. L. P. (2020). Cross-Cultural Design. User Experience of Products, Services, and Intelligent Environments: 12th International Conference, CCD 2020, Held as Part of the.... [HTML]

Reich-Shapiro, M., Cole, K., & Plaisir, J. Y. (2021). "I am the teacher" How male educators conceptualize their impact on the early childhood classroom. *Journal of Early Childhood Teacher Education*, 42(1), 3–17. DOI: 10.1080/10901027.2020.1754310

Reid, T. M. (2020). *White female educators' perceptions about adolescent Black boys*. ProQuest Dissertations & Theses. https//search.proquest.com/openview/e78877503780f15b0ba3d9426dcf932a/1?pq-origsite=gscholar&cbl=51922&diss=y

Reis da Silva, T. (2024a). The Evolution of Nursing for Older Adult: A Historical Perspective. *Associative J Health Sci*. 3(3). AJHS. 000561. 2024. DOI: . Link: https://crimsonpublishers.com/ajhs/pdf/AJHS.000561.pdfDOI: 10.31031/AJHS.2024.03.000561

Reis da Silva, T. H. (2024f) The Value of Emotional Intelligence in Midwifery: Enhancing Care and Outcomes for Mothers and Infants through Sustainable Development Goals and Leadership. *Journal of Womens Healthcare & Midwifery Research*.https://www.onlinescientificresearch.com/articles/the-value-of-emotional-intelligence-in-midwifery-enhancing-care-and-outcomes-for-mothers-and-infants-through-sustainable-developme.pdfDOI: 10.47363/JWHMR/2024(3)119

Reis da Silva, T. H. (2024g). Chapter 6 – Navigating Healthcare Complexity: Integrating Business Fundamentals into Nursing Leadership. In Sedky, A. *Resiliency Strategies for Long-Term Business Success*. Pp. 145-168. IGI Global. DOI: 10.4018/979-8-3693-9168-6.ch006

Reis da Silva, T. H. (2024h). Chapter 11 - Integrating business essentials into Gerontological Nursing: Enhancing Care for Older Adults in Diverse Settings. In Sedky, A. *Resiliency Strategies for Long-Term Business Success*. Pp. 283-316. IGI Global. DOI: DOI: 10.4018/979-8-3693-9168-6.ch011

Reis da Silva, T. (2024e). Can supplementing vitamin B12 improve mental health outcomes?: A literature review. *British Journal of Community Nursing*, 29(3), 137–146. DOI: 10.12968/bjcn.2024.29.3.137 PMID: 38421889

Reis da Silva, T. H. (2023a). Falls assessment and prevention in the nursing home and community. *British Journal of Community Nursing*, 28(2), 68–72. DOI: 10.12968/bjcn.2023.28.2.68 PMID: 36735363

Reis da Silva, T. H. (2023b). Ageing in place: Ageing at home and in the community. *British Journal of Community Nursing*, 28(5), 213–214. DOI: 10.12968/bjcn.2023.28.5.213 PMID: 37130715

Reis da Silva, T. H. (2024b). Pharmacokinetics in older people: An overview of prescribing practice. *Journal of Prescribing Practice*, 6(9), 374–381. DOI: 10.12968/jprp.2024.6.9.374

Reis da Silva, T. H. (2024c). Falls prevention in older people and the role of nursing. *British Journal of Community Nursing*, 29(7), 335–339. DOI: 10.12968/bjcn.2024.0005 PMID: 38963269

Reis da Silva, T. H. (2024d). Understanding body fluid balance, dehydration and intravenous fluid therapy. *Emergency Nurse*. Advance online publication. DOI: 10.7748/en.2024.e2201 PMID: 38978385

Reis da Silva, T. H. (2024i). Emotional Intelligence in Higher Education: Humanising Technology for Holistic Student Development. In Tikadar, S. (Ed.), *Liu, H.; Bhattacharya, P.; Bhattacharya, S. Humanizing Technology With Emotional Intelligence*. IGI Global., DOI: 10.4018/979-8-3693-7011-7.ch007

Reis da Silva, T. H., & Mitchell, A. (2024). Integrating Digital Transformation in Nursing Education: Best Practices and Challenges in Curriculum Development. In Lytras, M., Serban, A. C., Alkhaldi, A., Malik, S., & Aldosemani, T. (Eds.), *Digital Transformation in Higher Education, Part B Cases, Examples and Good Practices*. Emerald Publishing Limited.

Reis da Silva, T. M., Hammett, R., & Low, G. (2024). Emotional Intelligence in Business: Enhancing Leadership, Collaboration, and Performance. In Sedky, A. (Ed.), *Building Business Knowledge for Complex Modern Business Environments* (pp. 149–178). IGI Global., DOI: 10.4018/979-8-3693-6447-5.ch006

Ren, W. (2023). Gamification in Test-Driven Development Practice. In *Proceedings of the 2nd International Workshop on Gamification in Software Development, Verification, and Validation* (pp. 38–46). DOI: 10.1145/3617553.3617889

Riar, M., Hamari, J., & Zarnekow, R. (2021). The Gamification of Enterprise Cooperation: A Cross-Comparison of Case Studies. Organizational gamification. [HTML]

Riar, M., Morschheuser, B., Zarnekow, R., & Hamari, J. (2022). Gamification of cooperation: A framework, literature review and future research agenda. [sciencedirect.com]. *International Journal of Information Management*, 67, 102549. DOI: 10.1016/j.ijinfomgt.2022.102549

Richter, G., Raban, D. R., & Rafaeli, S. (2015). *Studying gamification: The effect of rewards and incentives on motivation*. Springer.

Rincón-Flores, E. G., Montoya, M. S. R., & Mena, J. (2019). *Engaging MOOC through gamification: Systematic mapping review*. 600–606. *Scopus.*, 600–606. Advance online publication. DOI: 10.1145/3362789.3362831

Rivera, E. S. & Garden, C. L. P. (2021). Gamification for student engagement: a framework. Journal of further and higher education. tandfonline.com

Rodrigues, L., Palomino, P. T., Toda, A. M., Klock, A. C. T., Oliveira, W., Avila-Santos, A. P., Gasparini, I., & Isotani, S. (2021). Personalization improves gamification. In *Proceedings of the ACM on Human-Computer Interaction* (Vol. 5, Issue CHI PLAY, pp. 1–25). DOI: 10.1145/3474714

Royston, M. (2021). “I’m a teacher, I’m gonna always protect you” Understanding Black educators’ protection of Black children. *American Educational Research Journal*, 58(5), 915–946. DOI: 10.3102/0002831220921119 PMID: 39221111

Ryan, R. M., & Deci, E. L. (2000). Self-determination theory and the facilitation of intrinsic motivation, social development, and well-being. *The American Psychologist*, 55(1), 68–78. DOI: 10.1037/0003-066X.55.1.68 PMID: 11392867

Şahbaz, E. (2018). A Proposal for an Interactive Computre Gagme to Teach Curtain Wall Systems.

Şahbaz, E., & Özköse, A. (2018). Experiencing historical buildings through digital computer games. *International Journal of Architectural Computing*, 16(1), 22–33. DOI: 10.1177/1478077117749960

Sailer, M., Hense, J. U., Mayr, S. K., & Mandl, H. (2017). How gamification motivates: An experimental study of the effects of specific game design elements on psychological need satisfaction. *Computers in Human Behavior*, 69, 371–380. DOI: 10.1016/j.chb.2016.12.033

Sailer, M., Hense, J., Mandl, H., & Klevers, M. (2017). *Fostering development of work competencies and motivation via gamification*. Springer. DOI: 10.1007/978-3-319-41713-4_37

Sailer, M., & Homner, L. (2020). The gamification of learning: A meta-analysis. *Educational Psychology Review*, 32(1), 77–112. DOI: 10.1007/s10648-019-09498-w

Salas, S., Lewis, C. W., & Siefert, B. (2021). “You teach what?” Black males, new Latino South classrooms, and wanderlust. *New Educator*, 17(2), 160–176. DOI: 10.1080/1547688X.2021.1873475

Salimon, M. G., Aliyu, O. A., Yusr, M. M., & Perumal, S. (2021). Smartphone banking usage in Nigeria: Gamification, technology acceptance and cultural factors empirical perspectives. [wiley.com]. *The Electronic Journal on Information Systems in Developing Countries*, 87(4), e12174. DOI: 10.1002/isd2.12174

Salter, N. P., & Conneely, M. R. (2015). Structured and unstructured discussion forums as tools for student engagement. *Computers in Human Behavior*, 46, 18–25. DOI: 10.1016/j.chb.2014.12.037

Samuels, S. S., Wilkerson, A., & Dacres, S. S. (2021). Why they struggle to stay Black women educators reflect on the state of teachers. *The Clearing House: A Journal of Educational Strategies, Issues and Ideas*, 94(3), 140–149. DOI: 10.1080/00098655.2021.1907145

Sanmugam, M., Zaid, N. M., Mohamed, H., Abdullah, Z., Aris, B., & Suhadi, S. M. (2015). Gamification as an educational technology tool in engaging and motivating students; An analyses review. *Advanced Science Letters, 21*(10), 3337–3341. *Scopus*. Advance online publication. DOI: 10.1166/asl.2015.6489

Santórum, M., Carrión-Toro, M., Morales-Martínez, D., Maldonado-Garcés, V., Araujo, E., & Acosta-Vargas, P. (2023). An accessible serious game-based platform for process learning of people with intellectual disabilities. [mdpi.com]. *Applied Sciences (Basel, Switzerland)*, 13(13), 7748. DOI: 10.3390/app13137748

Santosa, M. H., Harismayanti, I., & Putra, I. N. A. J. (2022). Technology in Action: Developing Gamification Handbook in English Teaching and Learning for the 21st Century Learners. *Tesl-Ej*, 26(1), n1. DOI: 10.55593/ej.26101a2

Santos, W., Toda, A., Isotani, S., & Bittencourt, I. (2018). Does gamified educational systems change students' learning behaviors? a case study with postgraduate students. *Renote*, 16(2). Advance online publication. DOI: 10.22456/1679-1916.89253

Sapuarachchi, D. B. (2021). Cultural distance and inter-organizational knowledge transfer: A case study of a multinational company. [HTML]. *Journal of Knowledge Management*, 25(9), 2316–2333. DOI: 10.1108/JKM-06-2020-0439

Sardi, L., Idri, A., & Fernández-Alemán, J. L. (2017). A systematic review of gamification in e-Health. *Journal of Biomedical Informatics*, 71, 31–48. DOI: 10.1016/j.jbi.2017.05.011 PMID: 28536062

Sargent, R. (2017). Gamifying Self-Assessments in Online Corporate Training: Points and Levels (Doctoral dissertation, Northcentral University).

Sarı, İ., Ekici, S., Soyer, F., & Eskiler, E. (2015). Does self-confidence link to motivation? A study in field hockey athletes. *Journal of Human Sport and Exercise*, 10(1), 24–35. DOI: 10.14198/jhse.2015.101.03

Saud, S., Aeni, N., & Azizah, L. (2023). *Engaging the EFL Students in Online Class Through Gamification. 2736*(1). *Scopus.*, 090007. Advance online publication. DOI: 10.1063/5.0170648

Scaffidi, M., Khan, R., Walsh, C., Pearl, M., Winger, K., Kalaichandran, R., Lin, P., & Grover, S. (2019). Protocol for a randomised trial evaluating the effect of applying gamification to simulation-based endoscopy training. *BMJ Open*, 9(2), e024134. DOI: 10.1136/bmjopen-2018-024134 PMID: 30804029

Schöbel, S. M., Janson, A., & Söllner, M. (2020). Capturing the complexity of gamification elements: A holistic approach for analysing existing and deriving novel gamification designs. [tandfonline.com]. *European Journal of Information Systems*, 29(6), 641–668. DOI: 10.1080/0960085X.2020.1796531

Schoenenberger, H. (2024). Connected Learning: Origins, Opportunities, and Perspectives of Contemporary Educational Design: A Machine-Generated Literature Overview. [HTML]

Schumacher, C., Eggers, F., Verhoef, P. C., & Maas, P. (2023). The effects of cultural differences on consumers' willingness to share personal information. [sagepub.com]. *Journal of Interactive Marketing*, 58(1), 72–89. DOI: 10.1177/10949968221136555

Scott, L. R. A., Brown, A., Wallace, W., Cormier, C. J., & Powell, C. (2021). If we're not doing it, then who? A qualitative study of Black special educators' persistence. *Exceptionality*, 15(2), 111–128. DOI: 10.1080/09362835.2020.1850453

Scurati, G. W., Bertoni, M., Graziosi, S., & Ferrise, F. (2021). Exploring the use of virtual reality to support environmentally sustainable behavior: A framework to design experiences. Sustainability. mdpi.com

Seaborn, K., & Fels, D. I. (2015). Gamification in theory and action: A survey. *International Journal of Human-Computer Studies*, 74, 14–31. DOI: 10.1016/j.ijhcs.2014.09.006

Seligman, M. E., & Csikszentmihalyi, M. (2000). *Positive psychology: An introduction* (Vol. 55). American Psychological Association.

Senge, P. M., Carstedt, G., & Porter, P. L. (2001). Next industrial revolution. *MIT Sloan Management Review*, 42(2), 24–38.

Seo, K., Fels, S., Kang, M., Jung, C., & Ryu, H. (2021). Goldilocks conditions for workplace gamification: How narrative persuasion helps manufacturing workers create self-directed behaviors. [tandfonline.com]. *Human-Computer Interaction*, 36(5-6), 473–510. DOI: 10.1080/07370024.2020.1744145

Serrano, M. (2023). Gamification and the history of art in secondary education: A didactic intervention. *Education Sciences*, 13(4), 389. DOI: 10.3390/educsci13040389

Settembre-Blundo, D., González-Sánchez, R., Medina-Salgado, S., & García-Muiña, F. E. (2021). Flexibility and resilience in corporate decision making: A new sustainability-based risk management system in uncertain times. [springer.com]. *Global Journal of Flexible Systems Managment*, 22(S2, Suppl 2), 107–132. DOI: 10.1007/s40171-021-00277-7

Shaban, A., Pearson, E., & Chang, V. (2021). Evaluation of user experience, cognitive load, and training performance of a gamified cognitive training application for children with learning disabilities. Frontiers in Computer Science. frontiersin.org

Shaheen, A., Ali, S., & Fotaris, P. (2023). Assessing the Efficacy of Reflective Game Design: A Design-Based Study in Digital Game-Based Learning. *Education Sciences*, 13(12), 1204. DOI: 10.3390/educsci13121204

Shareef, S. S., & Rauf, H. L. (2022). Learning technical courses in architectural education through gamification. *Computer Applications in Engineering Education*, 30(6), 1872–1884. DOI: 10.1002/cae.22562

Sheldon, L. (2020). *The multiplayer classroom: Designing coursework as a game*. CRC Press. DOI: 10.1201/9780429285035

Shin, H., & Rim, D. (2023). Development and assessment of a curriculum model for virtual simulation in nursing: Curriculum development and pilot-evaluation. *BMC Medical Education*, 23(1), 284. Advance online publication. DOI: 10.1186/s12909-023-04283-4 PMID: 37101191

Shonfeld, M., Cotnam-Kappel, M., Judge, M., Ng, C. Y., Ntebutse, J. G., Williamson-Leadley, S., & Yildiz, M. N. (2021). Learning in digital environments: A model for cross-cultural alignment. [springer.com]. *Educational Technology Research and Development*, 69(4), 1–20. DOI: 10.1007/s11423-021-09967-6 PMID: 33654347

Shortt, M., Tilak, S., Kuznetcova, I., Martens, B., & Akinkuolie, B. (2021). Gamification in mobile-assisted language learning: A systematic review of Duolingo literature from public release of 2012 to early 2020. *Computer Assisted Language Learning*, 36(3), 517–554. DOI: 10.1080/09588221.2021.1933540

Silva-Jurado, R. J., & Silva-Jurado, M. D. (2024). Educational Innovation in the 21st Century: Gamification, Artificial Intelligence and Art as Transformative Tools. *YUYAY: Estrategias. Metodologías & Didácticas Educativas*, 3(1), 35–52. DOI: 10.59343/yuyay.v3i1.60

Sims, R. C. (2022). *Analysis of the issue of New Mexico Black male educators' underrepresentation in education within New Mexico*. ProQuest Dissertations & Theses. https//search.proquest.com/openview/579640b1ddc045a38b7b2e6857e67c3f/1?pq-origsite=gscholar&cbl=18750&diss=y

Sims, R., Jr. (2022). *Analysis of New Mexico Black male educators' effects of underrepresentation in education*. ProQuest Dissertations & Theses. https//search.proquest.com/openview/6f8957e841755edf38db9e62f81cc94c/1?pq-origsite=gscholar&cbl=18750&diss=y

Singh, S. (2024). Gamify with caution–a three-pronged model to alleviate the dark side of gamification in learning and development. *Development and Learning in Organizations*. Advance online publication. DOI: 10.1108/DLO-12-2023-0264

Smith, J., Sawhney, M., Duhn, L., & Woo, K. (2021). The association between new nurses' gerontological education, personal attitudes toward older adults, and intentions to work in gerontological care settings in Ontario, Canada. *Canadian Journal of Nursing Research*, 54(2), 190–198. DOI: 10.1177/08445621211063702 PMID: 34964357

Snape, P., & Fox-Turnbull, W. (2013). Perspectives of authenticity: Implementation in technology education. *International Journal of Technology and Design Education*, 23(1), 51–68. DOI: 10.1007/s10798-011-9168-2

Soliman, S., Taha, D., & El Sayad, Z. (2019). Architectural education in the digital age Computer applications: Between academia and practice. *Alexandria Engineering Journal*, 58(2), 809–818. DOI: 10.1016/j.aej.2019.05.016

Squire, K. (2005). Changing the game: What happens when video games enter the classroom? *Innovate: Journal of online education, 1*(6).

Störmann, S., Von Der Borch, P., & Dimitriadis, K. (2010). Online matchmaking enables large-scale individual mentoring. *Medical Education*, 44(5), 492–493. DOI: 10.1111/j.1365-2923.2010.03663.x PMID: 20374458

Su, J., Zhong, Y., & Ng, D. T. K. (2022). A meta-review of literature on educational approaches for teaching AI at the K-12 levels in the Asia-Pacific region. Computers and Education: Artificial Intelligence. sciencedirect.com

Subiyantoro, S., & Musa, M. Z. (2023). Exploring Teachers' and Students' Perspectives on Gamification in Learning Management Systems. *Jurnal Komunikasi Pendidikan*, 7(2), 52–60. DOI: 10.32585/jurnalkomdik.v7i2.4613

Suh, A., & Wagner, C. (2017). How gamification of an enterprise collaboration system increases knowledge contribution: An affordance approach. *Journal of Knowledge Management*, 21(2), 416–431. DOI: 10.1108/JKM-10-2016-0429

Sushra, T., Iyengar, N., Shah, M., & Kshirsagar, A. (2022). Judging a book by its cover: Significance of UX design in gamification and computing systems. [HTML]. *Iran Journal of Computer Science*, 5(2), 117–126. DOI: 10.1007/s42044-021-00096-0

Sutcliffe, A. (2022). Designing for user engagment: Aesthetic and attractive user interfaces. [HTML]

Tang, K. (2023). Gamification to improve participation in an environmental science course: An educator's reflection. *Acta Pedagogia Asiana*, 2(2), 54–63. DOI: 10.53623/apga.v2i2.192

Tanouri, A., Kennedy, A. M., & Veer, E. (2022). A conceptual framework for transformative gamification services. *Journal of Services Marketing*, 36(2), 185–200. DOI: 10.1108/JSM-12-2020-0527

Taşçı, B. G. (2016). Theoretical framework for using digital games in architecture education. *Architecture Research*, 6(3), 51–56.

Tavsan, C., Tavsan, F., & Sonmez, E. (2014, Nov 28-29). Biomimicry in Architectural Design Education.*Procedia Social and Behavioral Sciences* [4th world conference on educational technology researches (wcetr-2014)]. 4th World Conference on Educational Technology Researches (WCETR), Univ Barcelona, Barcelona, Spain.

Tejedor, S., Cervi, L., Pérez-Escoda, A., & Jumbo, F. T. (2020). Digital literacy and higher education during COVID-19 lockdown: Spain, Italy, and Ecuador. Publications. mdpi.com

Teófilo, T., Veras, R., Silva, V., Cunha, N., Oliveira, J., & Vasconcelos, S. (2018). Empathy in the nurse–patient relationship in geriatric care: An integrative review. *Nursing Ethics*, 26(6), 1585–1600. DOI: 10.1177/0969733018787228 PMID: 30071772

Teo, J., Ramachandran, H., Jiang, Y., Seah, A., Lim, S., Nguyen, H., & Wang, W. (2023). The characteristics and acceptance of technology-enabled diabetes prevention programs (T-DPP) amongst individuals with prediabetes: A scoping review. *Journal of Clinical Nursing*, 32(17-18), 5562–5578. DOI: 10.1111/jocn.16649 PMID: 36775886

Thompson, B. J. (2023). *The endangered species A phenomenological study of the lived experiences of Black male educators*. ProQuest Dissertations & Theses. https// search.proquest.com/openview/eb2c481ccc217a0b365d3bd104abd3fa/1?pq-origsite =gscholar&cbl=18750&diss=y

Thompson, M. B. (2015). Authenticity in education: From narcissism and freedom to the messy interplay of self-exploration and acceptable tension. *Studies in Philosophy and Education*, 34(6), 603–618. DOI: 10.1007/s11217-015-9459-2

Toda, A. M., Valle, P. H. D., & Isotani, S. (2017, Mar 20-24). The Dark Side of Gamification: An Overview of Negative Effects of Gamification in Education. *Communications in Computer and Information Science* [Higher education for all: From challenges to novel technology-enhanced solutions]. *1st International Workshop on Social, Semantic, Adaptive and Gamification Techniques and Technologies for Distance Learning (HEFA)*, Maceio, Brazil.

Torreao, V. de A. (2013). *Comparison between client-server, peer-to-peer and hybrid architectures for MMOGs*. https://www.semanticscholar.org/paper/ Comparison-between-client-server-%2C-peer-to-peer-and-Torreao/3fb797609e 219abdd9723d41aea37c19179afcf9

Tran, S., Smith, L., El-Den, S., & Carter, S. (2021). The use of gamification and incentives in mobile health apps to improve medication adherence: A scoping review (Preprint). *JMIR mHealth and uHealth*, 10(2), e30671. Advance online publication. DOI: 10.2196/30671 PMID: 35188475

Triantafyllou, S. (2022). *Game-Based Learning and Interactive Educational Games for Learners – An Educational Paradigm from Greece*. DOI: 10.33422/6th. icmrss.2022.10.20

Trimblett, S. M. (2016). Gamification in nursing jurisprudence (Doctoral dissertation, Royal Roads University (Canada).

Tsegaw, S. A., Filate, A. Y., & Kahsay, M. T. (2024). Effects of tool mediation on tertiary level EFL students' reading comprehension and vocabulary learning skills: A case for a cloud computing environment. *Cogent Education*, 11(1), 2330251. DOI: 10.1080/2331186X.2024.2330251

Turjuman, F., & Alilyyani, B. (2023). Emotional intelligence among nurses and its relationship with their performance and work engagement: A cross-sectional study. *Journal of Nursing Management*, 2023, 1–8. DOI: 10.1155/2023/5543299

Uaidullakyzy, E., Rizakhojayeva, G., Sartayeva, K., Zeinep, B., Turmanov, R., & Rysbayeva, G. (2022). Creating integration situations of students' computer lesson and learning with gamification. [IJET]. *International Journal of Emerging Technologies in Learning*, 17(19), 207–223. DOI: 10.3991/ijet.v17i19.32177

Uluoğlu, B. (1990). Mimari tasarım eğitimi tasarım bilgisi bağlamında stüdyo eleştirileri.

Underwood, K., Smith, D., Johnson-Lutz, H., Taylor, J., ... (2019). Having our say Examining the career trajectories of Black male educators in P-12 education. *National Network of State Teachers of the Year*, ERIC. https//eric.ed.gov/?id=ED601059

Underwood, K., Taylor, J., Smith, D., & Roberts, J. M. (2020). Exploring the career trajectories of Black male educators in P-12 education. *Journal for Multicultural Education*, 14(1), 2–16. DOI: 10.1108/JME-02-2020-0012

Unternährer, C., Termine, F., & De Santo, A. (2024). Enhancing Knowledge Transmission: The Perspective of Gamification User Profiles. Procedia Computer Science. sciencedirect.com

Valls, F., Redondo, E., Sánchez, A., Fonseca, D., Villagrasa, S., & Navarro, I. (2017, Apr 11-13). Simulated Environments in Architecture Education. Improving the Student Motivation.*Advances in Intelligent Systems and Computing* [Recent advances in information systems and technologies, vol 3]. World Conference on Information Systems and Technologies (WorldCIST), Madeira, PORTUGAL.

Van der Heijden, B. I. J. M., Burgers, M. J., Kaan, A. M., Lamberts, B. F., Migchelbrink, K., Van den Ouweland, R. C. P. M., & Meijer, T. (2020). Gamification in dutch businesses: An explorative case study. [sagepub.com]. *SAGE Open*, 10(4), 2158244020972371. DOI: 10.1177/2158244020972371

Van Eck, R. (2006). Digital game-based learning: It's not just the digital natives who are restless. *EDUCAUSE Review*, 41(2), 16.

Van Roy, R., & Zaman, B. (2019). Unravelling the ambivalent motivational power of gamification: A basic psychological needs perspective. *International Journal of Human-Computer Studies*, 127, 38–50. DOI: 10.1016/j.ijhcs.2018.04.009

Véron, M., Marin, O., & Monnet, S. (2018). Matchmaking in multi-player on-line games: Studying user traces to improve the user experience. *Proceedings of Network and Operating System Support on Digital Audio and Video Workshop*, 7–12. DOI: 10.1145/2578260.2578265

Vlachogianni, P., & Tselios, N. (2022). Perceived usability evaluation of educational technology using the System Usability Scale (SUS): A systematic review. [HTML]. *Journal of Research on Technology in Education*, 54(3), 392–409. DOI: 10.1080/15391523.2020.1867938

Volberda, H. W., Khanagha, S., Baden-Fuller, C., Mihalache, O. R., & Birkinshaw, J. (2021). Strategizing in a digital world: Overcoming cognitive barriers, reconfiguring routines and introducing new organizational forms. *Long Range Planning*, 54(5), 102110. DOI: 10.1016/j.lrp.2021.102110

Vrontissi, M. (2015). The physical model in structural studies within architecture education: paradigms of an analytic rationale? Proceedings of IASS annual symposia, Waggoner, Z. (2009). *My avatar, my self: Identity in video role-playing games*. McFarland.

Waheed, N. (2017, July). Effects of an online discussion forum on student engagement and learning in a first-year undergraduate nursing unit: An action research study. In *Worldwide Nursing Conference* (pp. 18-25). GSTF Digital Library. DOI: 10.5176/2315-4330_WNC17.35

Walker, A., & Leary, H. (2009). A problem-based learning meta-analysis: Differences across problem types, implementation types, disciplines, and assessment levels. *The Interdisciplinary Journal of Problem-Based Learning*, 3(1), 12–43. DOI: 10.7771/1541-5015.1061

Wallace, D., Bol, L., & Hall, K. (2022). Black male educators matter Modeling and expectations in K-12 settings. *Journal of African American Studies*, 26(4), 375–392. https//digitalcommons.odu.edu/efl_fac_pubs/105/. DOI: 10.1007/s12111-022-09594-2

Waluyo, B., Phanrangsee, S., & Whanchit, W. (2023). Gamified grammar learning in online English courses in Thai higher education. *Online Journal of Communication and Media Technologies*, 13(4), e202354. DOI: 10.30935/ojcmt/13752

Wang, Y. F., Hsu, Y. F., & Fang, K. (2022). The key elements of gamification in corporate training–The Delphi method. Entertainment Computing. sciencedirect.com

Wang, J., Bu, L., Li, Y., Song, J., & Li, N. (2021). The mediating effect of academic engagement between psychological capital and academic burnout among nursing students during the covid-19 pandemic: A cross-sectional study. *Nurse Education Today*, 102, 104938. DOI: 10.1016/j.nedt.2021.104938 PMID: 33934039

Wang, Y. H. (2023). Can gamification assist learning? A study to design and explore the uses of educational music games for adults and young learners. *Journal of Educational Computing Research*, 60(8), 2015–2035. DOI: 10.1177/07356331221098148

Wang, Y., Hsu, Y., Fang, K., & Kuo, L. (2024). Gamification in medical education: Identifying and prioritizing key elements through Delphi method. *Medical Education Online*, 29(1), 2302231. Advance online publication. DOI: 10.1080/10872981.2024.2302231 PMID: 38194415

Watkins, S. E., & Mensah, F. M. (2022). Black men in US undergraduate and graduate science programs and their persistence Insights for multicultural science educators. In *Handbook of Research on Multicultural Science Education* (pp. 789–802). Springer., DOI: 10.1007/978-3-030-83122-6_49

Weaver, M., Jenkins, R., Wichman, C., Robinson, J., Potthoff, M., Menicucci, T., & Vail, C. (2019). Sowing across a state: Development and delivery of a grassroots pediatric palliative care nursing curriculum. *Journal of Palliative Care*, 36(1), 22–28. DOI: 10.1177/0825859719889700 PMID: 31771423

Wee, S., & Choong, W. (2019). Gamification: Predicting the effectiveness of variety game design elements to intrinsically motivate users' energy conservation behaviour. *Journal of Environmental Management*, 233, 97–106. DOI: 10.1016/j.jenvman.2018.11.127 PMID: 30572268

Westenhaver, Z. K., Africa, R. E., Zimmerer, R. E., & McKinnon, B. J. (2021). Gamification in otolaryngology: A narrative review. *Laryngoscope Investigative Otolaryngology*, 7(1), 291–298. DOI: 10.1002/lio2.707 PMID: 35155810

Whitton, N., & Moseley, A. (2012). *Using games to enhance learning and teaching*. Taylor & Francis New York. DOI: 10.4324/9780203123775

Wiggins, B. (2016). An overview and study on the use of games, simulations, and gamification in higher education. *International Journal of Game-Based Learning*, 6(1), 18–29. DOI: 10.4018/IJGBL.2016010102

Williams, C. (2022). *Educator perceptions of African American male recruitment in advanced placement courses*. ProQuest Dissertations & Theses. https//search.proquest.com/openview/3b68f07b6fbdfa7b11c4723bf8a61e43/1?pq-origsite=gscholar&cbl=18750&diss=y

Williams, D. J. (2023). *Challenges affecting educator careers of Black male teachers in K-12 system in South Carolina A qualitative phenomenological study*. Liberty University. https//digitalcommons.liberty.edu/doctoral/4976/

Williams, L., & Lahman, M. (2011). Online discussion, student engagement, and critical thinking. *Journal of Political Science Education*, 7(2), 143–162. DOI: 10.1080/15512169.2011.564919

Wilson, L. (2003). Interactivity or interpassivity: A question of agency in digital play. Fine Art Forum, Yildirim, T., & Yavuz, A. O. (2012, May 01-04). Comparison of traditional and digital visualization technologies in architectural design education. *Procedia Social and Behavioral Sciences* [World conference on design, arts and education (dae-2012)]. World Conference on Design, Arts and Education (DAE), Antalya, TURKEY.

Witherspoon, Q. D. R. (2024). *Student responsiveness towards Black male educators in the K-12 urban school setting A phenomenological study*. ProQuest Dissertations & Theses. https//search.proquest.com/openview/86350f04bd88cf48418518b1f1de3864/1?pq-origsite=gscholar&cbl=18750&diss=y

Witoszek-Kubicka, A. (2020). Implementation of Gamification in Polish Companies—Stages, Elements, Ethics. Information. mdpi.com

Woods, O. (2021). Feminist geographies of online gaming. Digital Geography and Society. sciencedirect.com

Woźniak, J. (2016). GAMIFICATION FOR SALES INCENTIVES. *Deleted Journal*, 22(3), 266–281. DOI: 10.58246/sjeconomics.v22i3.327

Xi, N. & Hamari, J. (2020). Does gamification affect brand engagement and equity? A study in online brand communities. Journal of Business Research. sciencedirect.com

Xiao, R., Wu, Z., & Hamari, J. (2022). Internet-of-gamification: A review of literature on IoT-enabled gamification for user engagement. [tandfonline.com]. *International Journal of Human-Computer Interaction*, 38(12), 1113–1137. DOI: 10.1080/10447318.2021.1990517

Xiao, Y., & Hew, K. F. T. (2024). Intangible rewards versus tangible rewards in gamified online learning: Which promotes student intrinsic motivation, behavioural engagement, cognitive engagement and learning performance? *British Journal of Educational Technology*, 55(1), 297–317. DOI: 10.1111/bjet.13361

Xie, L., Li, D., & Keh, H. T. (2020). Customer participation and well-being: The roles of service experience, customer empowerment and social support. [HTML]. *Journal of Service Theory and Practice*, 30(6), 557–584. DOI: 10.1108/JSTP-11-2019-0228

Yahyavi, A., & Kemme, B. (2013). Peer-to-Peer Architectures for Massively Multiplayer Online Games: A Survey. *ACM Computing Surveys*, 46(1), 1–51. Advance online publication. DOI: 10.1145/2522968.2522977

Yang, Y. T. C., & Chang, C. H. (2013). Empowering students through digital game authorship: Enhancing concentration, critical thinking, and academic achievement. *Computers & Education*, 68, 334–344. DOI: 10.1016/j.compedu.2013.05.023

Yaşar, H., Kıyıcı, M., & Karatas, A. (2020). The views and adoption levels of primary school teachers on gamification, problems and possible solutions. *Participatory Educational Research*, 7(3), 265–279. DOI: 10.17275/per.20.46.7.3

Yazici, S. (2024). *In memory of Geert Hofstede: A pioneer in comparative cross-cultural management research and practice*. Hofstede Matters. [HTML] DOI: 10.4324/9781003410348-3

Yıldırım, Ö. (2023). Assessment Based Games and Gamification. In *Digital Games and Gamification in Education* (pp. 143–153).

Young, S., & Tullo, E. (2020). From criminology to gerontology: Case studies of experiential authenticity in higher education. *Journal of Perspectives in Applied Academic Practice*, 8(1), 127–134. DOI: 10.14297/jpaap.v8i1.408

Yu, C., Liu, Z. Q., Zhao, M., Liu, Y., Zhang, Y., Lin, A., Sang, X., & Wan, H. (2023). The mediating role of emotion management, self-efficacy and emotional intelligence in clinical nurses related to negative psychology and burnout. *Psychology Research and Behavior Management*, 16, 3333–3345. DOI: 10.2147/PRBM.S417729 PMID: 37650114

Yu, Q., Yu, K., & Li, B. (2024). Can gamification enhance online learning? Evidence from a meta-analysis. *Education and Information Technologies*, 29(4), 4055–4083. DOI: 10.1007/s10639-023-11977-1

Yürekli, İ. (2003). *Mimari tasarım eğitiminde oyun*. Fen Bilimleri Enstitüsü.

Zain, S. (2021). Digital transformation trends in education. In *Future directions in digital information* (pp. 223–234). Chandos Publishing. DOI: 10.1016/B978-0-12-822144-0.00036-7

Zainuddin, Z., Chu, S. K. W., Shujahat, M., & Perera, C. J. (2020). The impact of gamification on learning and instruction: A systematic review of empirical evidence. *Educational Research Review*, 30, 100326. DOI: 10.1016/j.edurev.2020.100326

Zakrzewski, P. (2022). Extended reality experience design: The multimodal rhetorical framework for creating persuasive immersion. In Designing, X. R. (Ed.), *A Rhetorical Design Perspective for the Ecology of Human+ Computer Systems* (pp. 183–213). Emerald Publishing Limited. [HTML] DOI: 10.1108/978-1-80262-365-920221005

Zaniboni, S., Fraccaroli, F., Truxillo, D. M., Bertolino, M., & Bauer, T. N. (2011). Training valence, instrumentality, and expectancy scale (T-VIES-it). *Journal of Workplace Learning*, 23(2), 133–151. DOI: 10.1108/13665621111108792

Zeybek, N., & Saygı, E. (2024). Gamification in education: Why, where, when, and how?—A systematic review. *Games and Culture*, 19(2), 237–264. DOI: 10.1177/15554120231158625

Zhakupova, A., Yerkebayeva, S., Zhumasheva, T., Myshbayeva, G., Zhandildina, R., & Mukhanbetzhanova, A. (2022). Improvement of soft skills in preschool teachers through gamification. *Cypriot Journal of Educational Sciences*, 17(9), 3556–3567. DOI: 10.18844/cjes.v17i9.8128

Zhang, H., Cui, Y., Shan, H., Qu, Z., Zhang, W., Tu, L., & Wang, Y. (2020, June). Hotspots and trends of virtual reality, augmented reality and mixed reality in education field. In 2020 6th international conference of the Immersive Learning Research Network (iLRN) (pp. 215-219). IEEE. [HTML] DOI: 10.23919/iLRN47897.2020.9155170

Zhang, C., Van Gorp, P., Derksen, M., Nuijten, R., IJsselsteijn, W. A., Zanutto, A., Melillo, F., & Pratola, R. (2021). Promoting Occupational Health through Gamification and E-Coaching: A 5-Month User Engagement Study. *International Journal of Environmental Research and Public Health*, 18(6), 2823. DOI: 10.3390/ijerph18062823 PMID: 33802082

Zhao, F. (2024). Gamification Design. In User Experience Methods and Tools in Human-Computer Interaction (pp. 373-441). CRC Press. [HTML] DOI: 10.1201/9781003495161-16

Zheng, Y., Zhang, J., Li, Y., Wu, X., Ding, R., Luo, X., Liu, P., & Huang, J. (2024). Effects of digital game-based learning on students' digital etiquette literacy, learning motivations, and engagement. *Heliyon, 10*(1). *Heliyon*, 10(1), e23490. Advance online publication. DOI: 10.1016/j.heliyon.2023.e23490 PMID: 38187224

Zichermann, G., & Cunningham, C. (2011). *Gamification by design: Implementing game mechanics in web and mobile apps*. O'Reilly Media, Inc.

Zook, A. (2019). Building Matchmaking Systems. In *Data Analytics Applications in Gaming and Entertainment*. Auerbach Publications. DOI: 10.1201/9780429286490-3

Zourmpakis, A., Kalogiannakis, M., & Papadakis, S. (2023). Adaptive gamification in science education: An analysis of the impact of implementation and adapted game elements on students' motivation. *Computers*, 12(7), 143. DOI: 10.3390/computers12070143

Zou, T. X., & Ko, E. I. (2012). Teamwork development across the curriculum for chemical engineering students in Hong Kong: Processes, outcomes and lessons learned. *Education for Chemical Engineers*, 7(3), e105–e117. DOI: 10.1016/j.ece.2012.04.003

About the Contributors

Ricardo Marcão, PhD, MBA, PMP, is a globally recognized expert in Project Management, Finance, and Strategy, currently serving as a Senior International Project Manager at SIBS, a leader in the Payments and Banking industry. With deep experience across sectors like Pharma and MedTech, IT, and Professional Services, Ricardo's unique expertise spans Grand Strategy, Democracy, and International Relations, positioning him as a thought leader in driving innovation, governance, and strategic transformation on a global scale. As the coordinator of several advanced programs at ISLA Santarém, including the Masters in Business Administration and Post-Graduations in Project Management, Quality Management, and Diplomacy and Financial-Economic Management, Ricardo shapes the next generation of business leaders through a strategic lens that integrates organizational management with international relations and democratic governance. A distinguished international speaker and academic, Ricardo plays a key role in fostering transatlantic relations between the US and Europe, contributing to global discourse on strategy, leadership, and governance. His active involvement with SCIP Portugal, APMP in NYC, PMI Portugal, and PMI South Florida underscores his commitment to strategic intelligence, project management excellence, and international cooperation.

Vasco Santos holds a PhD in Business Sciences with specialization in Marketing (Fernando Pessoa University, Portugal), a PhD in Tourism (Seville University, Spain), a Post-Doc in Innovation Management applied to Sustainable Luxury Tourism (Aveiro University, Portugal), an Habilitation in Management (European University, Portugal), an MSc in Marketing and Tourism Promotion, and a BA in Hospitality Management (Higher School of Tourism and Maritime Technology, Polytechnic of Leiria). Lecturer at the Polytechnic University of Tomar. Lecturer at the Higher Institute of Management and Administration of Santarém. Full researcher in GOVCOPP (Competitiveness, Innovation and Sustainability Research Group), University of Aveiro. Effective and founding member of PNT - National Tourism

Platform. Author of several scientific papers and book chapters. Research areas: tourism, marketing, employer branding and management.

* * *

Andi Asrifan, S.Pd, M.Pd, a distinguished figure in the realm of education, particularly in English Language Education, has made significant contributions through his extensive research, teaching, and leadership roles. As the Head of the Institute for Cooperation and International Affairs at Universitas Muhammadiyah Sidenreng Rappang, Dr. Asrifan's academic journey is marked by a rich tapestry of achievements, including a Doctor of Education in English Language Education. His work spans various facets of education, language, and technology, reflecting the diverse topics covered in his publications and research endeavors. These include, but are not limited to, the impact of the COVID-19 pandemic on educational practices, methodologies in English as a Foreign Language (EFL) classrooms, and the integration of technology in teaching and learning processes. Dr. Asrifan's commitment to advancing educational standards and practices is further evidenced by his active participation in international conferences, webinars, and workshops across countries like India, the Philippines, and Pakistan. These events, organized by various institutions and associations, underscore his role as a global educator and thought leader. His dedication to professional development is also highlighted through his involvement in numerous courses and certifications in personal branding, public speaking, and literacy teaching. Moreover, Dr. Asrifan's leadership extends beyond academia into organizational and educational development, where he has served in various capacities, including as an external examiner for Ph.D. dissertations and a reviewer for scientific journals. His accolades, memberships in professional organizations, and roles as an ambassador for international associations speak volumes of his influence and commitment to fostering educational excellence and sustainable development goals globally.

Júlio Faria is Brazilian and has been living in Bragança, Portugal, since 2022. He began his academic journey in the Digital Games program at the Pontifical Catholic University of Minas Gerais in 2012 but did not complete the course. Between 2015 and 2016, he studied Sculpture Modeling at the Ômega School of Arts in Curitiba. In 2017, he was accepted into the Software Engineering program at the Federal University of Technology – Paraná. He worked as a Back-End Developer at Codengage from 2020 to 2022. In 2021, he was selected for the Master's in Computer Science at the Polytechnic Institute of Bragança, Portugal, through the Dual Degree program. During his master's, he developed TimeCrax Machine, a 3D online multiplayer game designed to teach History in a fun, challenging, and engaging way. Currently, Júlio continues to work on improving the TimeCrax Machine project, focusing on implementing new mechanics and features that bring the game closer to fulfilling its purpose.

Azmil Hashim is Professor at Faculty of Human Sciences, Universiti Pendidikan Sultan Idris, Malaysia.

Miftachul Huda is a researcher at Faculty of Human Sciences, Universiti Pendidikan Sultan Idris Malaysia. His research interest includes the field of educational studies: moral, Islamic and multicultural education, learning theory, adaptive teaching and learning technology. He has been experienced in working on research for more than five years. Contributing several works, he is currently the member of the advisory editorial board in some international journals. Traveling in some countries with scholarly intent makes him extensive experience on his research expertise in international trend and issues. Thus, he commits to contributing his knowledge to the benefit of society through professional and social activities.

Baso Jabu is a professor of EFL at Universitas Negeri Makassar. He completed his undergraduate studies in 1987, majoring in Teaching English as a Foreign Language (TEFL) at Ujung Pandang Institute of Teacher Training and Education (currently Universitas Negeri Makassar), Indonesia. He completed his Master's and doctoral degrees in the field of applied linguistics at Hasanuddin University in Makassar, Indonesia, in 1995 and 2007, respectively. He was awarded a Specialist Certificate in Language Testing at the Regional Language Centre Singapore in 1996. Professor Jabu has been teaching EFL and the related education subjects at Universitas Negeri Makassar for over 30 years. Prof. Jabu is a member of AsiaTEFL, TEFLIN (Teaching English as a Foreign Language in Indonesia), and MLI (Indonesia Linguistic Society). His research interests are TEFL and language assessment.

Mohammad Jailani is a lecturer of Universitas Ahmad Dahlan, Yogyakarta, Indonesia.

Zidan Kachhi is a dedicated Counselling Psychologist, Assistant Professor, Researcher, Author, and Trainer with over five years of experience in psychology and more than two years in teaching and training. His work prioritizes individual contexts, intersectionality, and inclusivity in counselling, organizational settings, and academia. As a Queer Affirmative practitioner, fostering an inclusive therapeutic environment is paramount to his practice. He utilizes an integrative approach and is trained in Couple and Family Therapy as well as Transactional Analysis. He contributes to enhancing individual and collective well-being through research, education and practice. His diverse research interests span Gender and Sexuality Studies, Marginalization and Intersectionality, Applications and Implications of Technological Advancement, Organizational and Consumer Behaviour, Behavioral Finance, Marketing, and Sustainability. He has established a robust research profile, highlighted by numerous conference presentations and an array of publications, including books, internationally indexed book chapters, and peer-reviewed journal articles.

Badruddin Kaddas, S.Ag., M.Ag., Ph.D, is a highly respected academic and leader in Islamic education, with a career spanning over two decades. Born in Timurung, he pursued his undergraduate and master's degrees at Universitas Muslim Indonesia, focusing on Islamic Communication and Broadcasting. He later earned his Ph.D. in Islamic Communication from Universiti Utara Malaysia, further solidifying his expertise in the field. Throughout his career, Dr. Badruddin has held various significant academic and administrative roles at Universitas Islam Makassar, where he has been instrumental in shaping the institution's educational landscape. His roles have included serving as the Dean of the Faculty of Teacher Training and Education and currently as Vice Rector II. In these capacities, he has overseen numerous initiatives aimed at improving the quality of education, enhancing faculty capabilities, and integrating modern educational technologies. Beyond his institutional responsibilities, Dr. Badruddin is deeply involved in professional organizations, particularly within Nahdlatul Ulama, where he has served in leadership roles such as Vice Secretary and Vice Chairman at both regional and national levels. His involvement in these organizations reflects his commitment to community development and his dedication to promoting inclusive and accessible education. Dr. Badruddin's contributions extend to research and publication as well. He has been involved in various research projects focused on empowering Islamic institutions and has published works on the effectiveness of Islamic communication strategies. His research interests include the role of communication in Islamic education, the development of Islamic broadcasting, and the application of technology in educational settings. In recognition of his contributions, Dr. Badruddin has received several awards, including being named the Best Lecturer at Universitas Islam Makassar. His ongoing work continues to impact the field of Islamic education, making significant strides in fostering a more inclusive and innovative educational environment.

Rui Pedro Sanches de Castro Lopes received the MSc in Electronics and Telecommunications, and the PhD in Electrical Engineering from the University of Aveiro, Portugal. He is an associate professor at the Polytechnic Institute of Braganca. His main research interests focus on distributed systems, operating systems and network management. More recently, he has been learning, reflecting and researching on methodologies and approaches that can contribute to improve the way students learn and how to keep them motivated. In this context, he structured a curricular unit around gamification, including formative assessment, educational games, student grading and feedback. He also designed learning experiences that appeal to increasing the student autonomy and other horizontal competencies, such as communication skills, critical thinking, creativity and lifetime learning.

Mulyadi, an academic professional with a significant background in educational management, has cultivated an extensive career in teaching and research. Born on November 4, 1973, in Bone, he pursued his higher education at Universitas Muslim Indonesia (UMI), earning his bachelor's degree in Ushuluddin in 1997. He furthered his education by obtaining a master’s degree in Educational Management from PPS UNM in 2002 and a doctorate in Educational Science from the same institution in 2018. Over the years, Dr. Mulyadi has actively contributed to the academic community through teaching various subjects in educational foundations, evaluation, and counseling at Universitas Islam Makassar. His professional development includes participating in numerous workshops, seminars, and training sessions, both as a participant and a contributor, enhancing his expertise in educational methodologies and Islamic education. In addition to his academic duties, he has played a pivotal role in organizational activities, including serving as a secretary for the Nahdlatul Ulama in Makassar and contributing to educational development programs at various levels. His research interests are diverse, encompassing the evaluation of teacher performance post-certification, the development of educational models for marginalized communities, and the social-emotional development of early childhood education.

João Paulo Sousa is graduated in Electrical and Computer Engineering from UTAD University. After three years, he gets a Master's degree in Engineering Technology. He received his Ph.D. degree in Computer Science at UTAD University. He published dozens of publications in international journals and conferences. He served as Chair of Videojogos2020 - 12th International Conference on Videogame Sciences and Arts and is on several scientific committees of international journals and conferences. His research activities concern video games, serious games, gamification, and artificial intelligence. In recent years he has been: director of the degree in Computer Science and Communications; director of the degree in Game Design and is the current director of the Master's Degree in Digital Game Design and Development at the Polytechnic Institute of Bragança (IPB), and director of the ESACT Computer Resources Center. He is currently an Adjunct Professor at the Polytechnic Institute of Bragança (IPB) and an internal member of the Digitization and Intelligent Robotics Research Centre (CeDRI) at the Polytechnic Institute of Bragança.

Supriadi, S.Pd., M.Pd., is a dedicated academic and expert in the field of Indonesian language and literature education. Born in Barru on February 11, 1982, he has built an impressive career as a lecturer and educator, currently serving as a permanent faculty member at Universitas Islam Makassar. Dr. Supriadi completed his undergraduate, master's, and doctoral studies at Universitas Negeri Makassar, specializing in Indonesian language education. His academic journey reflects a deep commitment to enhancing the quality of language education in Indonesia. Dr. Supriadi has a wealth of experience in teaching various subjects, including Scientific Writing, Language Skills, and the Development of Indonesian Language Learning in Primary Schools. He has been actively involved in research, focusing on innovative teaching strategies, such as the effectiveness of the Synectic Model in poetry appreciation and the use of Mind Mapping to improve listening skills in elementary students. His research has contributed significantly to the advancement of teaching methodologies and the promotion of critical discourse in language education. In addition to his teaching and research, Dr. Supriadi has played a crucial role in community service, particularly in enhancing literacy and language skills in rural areas. His efforts include providing language training to village officials and promoting the use of correct Indonesian spelling in elementary schools. Dr. Supriadi's dedication to education is also evident in his involvement in national and international seminars, where he has contributed as both a participant and a presenter. Through his work, Dr. Supriadi continues to impact the field of education, striving to improve the quality of language instruction and fostering a greater appreciation for Indonesian literature among students and educators alike.

Roger Tavares holds a diverse and impressive academic background, having earned degrees in Industrial Design (FAAP), Education (Mackenzie Presbyterian University), Communication & Semiotics (PUCSP), and a post-doctoral degree from the University of Coimbra. His extensive knowledge spans multiple disciplines, including Arts, Technology and Design. He holds an adjunct professorship at IPB – the Polytechnic Institute of Bragança, where he is deeply involved in advising, evaluating, and delivering short courses. Dr. Tavares has a proven track record of professional engagement advisory boards and participation in numerous events, publications, and presentations. His work focuses on the interdisciplinary field of Humanities and its technological advancements, with particular emphasis on Arts, Technology, and Design. In communication, Dr. Tavares has specialized expertise in video games. He excels in 3D design, multimedia development, software engineering, and game design principles. His technical proficiencies include graphic software such as Blender 3D, Krita and music production tools like Reaper and Ableton Live. He is also adept at utilizing open-source software and conducts research on generative AI tools, including Stable Diffusion, and its applications. Dr. Tavares actively engages in collaborative research projects within the CeDRI (Research Centre in Digitalization and Intelligent Robotics) group at IPB and the CISUC (Centre for Informatics and Systems) at the University of Coimbra. His research interests, which include the intersection of Humanities with technological advancements, particularly in Arts, Technology, and Design, and the potential impact of generative AI tools, such as Stable Diffusion, on these fields, demonstrate his forward-thinking approach and potential for future contributions. Dr. Tavares is also a member of the Portuguese Society for Video Game Sciences Directory Board.

Index

Symbols

A

B

C

D

E

G

I

L

N

P

R

S

T

U

www.ingramcontent.com/pod-product-compliance
Lightning Source LLC
LaVergne TN
LVHW061547290926
849162LV00004B/938